Contemporary Chinese Art and Film

Also by Jason C. Kuo

Wang Yuanqi de shanshuihua yishu [Wang Yuanqi's Art of Landscape Painting]
Long tiandi yu xingnei [Trapping Heaven and Earth in the Cage of Form]
Innovation within Tradition: The Painting of Huang Pin-hung
The Austere Landscape: The Paintings of Hung-jen
Word as Image: The Art of Chinese Seal Engraving
Zhuang Zhe, 1991–92
Cuo wanwu yu biduan [Embodying Myriad of Things at the Tip of Brush]
Chen Qikuan
Yishushi yu yishu piping de tansuo [Rethinking Art History and Art Criticism]
Art and Cultural Politics in Postwar Taiwan
Yishushi yu yishu piping de shijian [Practicing Art History and Art Criticism]
Transforming Traditions in Modern Chinese Painting: Huang Pin-hung's Late Work
Chinese Ink Painting Now

As Editor

Meigan yu zaoxing [Sense of Beauty and Creation of Form]
Luo Qing huaji [The Paintings of Luo Qing]
Dangdai Taiwan huihua wenxuan, 1945-1990 [Essays on Contemporary Painting Taiwan, 1945-1990]
Born of Earth and Fire: Chinese Ceramics from the Scheinman Collection
Heirs to a Great Tradition: Modern Chinese Paintings from the Tsien-hsiang-chai Collection
The Helen D. Ling Collection of Chinese Ceramics
Taiwan shijue wenhua [Visual Culture in Taiwan]
Discovering Chinese Painting: Dialogues with American Art Historians Understanding Asian Art
Double Beauty: Qing Dynasty Couplets from the Lechangzai Xuan Collection (with Peter Sturman)
Discovering Chinese Painting: Dialogues with Art Historians
Visual Culture in Shanghai, 1850s–1930s
Perspectives on Connoisseurship of Chinese Painting
Stones from Other Mountains: Chinese Painting Studies in Postwar America

Contemporary Chinese Art and Film:

Theory Applied and Resisted

Edited with an Introduction by
Jason C. Kuo

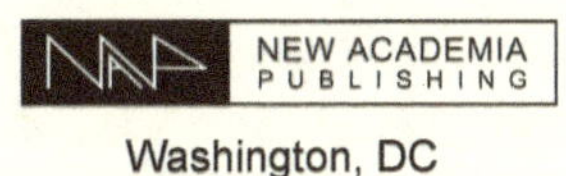

Washington, DC

New Academia Publishing 2013

Printed in the United States of America

Library of Congress Control Number: 2012954655
ISBN 978-0-9860216-6-4 paperback (alk. paper)

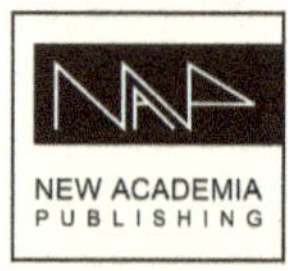

New Academia Publishing
PO Box 27420, Washington, DC 20038-7420
info@newacademia.com - www.newacademia.com

Rudolf Arnheim
in memoriam

Contents

Acknowledgments

This anthology has grown out of the presentations and discussions at "The Status of Theory in Contemporary Chinese Film and Visual Culture," a conference I organized in February 2009 at the University of Maryland. I wish to thank the following units for their support and contribution: Department of Art History and Archaeology, Confucius Institute, Center for East Asian Studies, Department of Women's Studies, Nathan and Jeanette Miller Center for Historical Studies, Wang Fangyu Endowment for Calligraphy Education, and the School of Languages, Literatures, and Cultures. The support of the University of Maryland Designated Research Initiative Fund (DRIF) was critical to the success of the project.

For their enthusiasm, patience, generosity, and cooperation, I am grateful to all the participants in the conference and contributors to the present volume, especially Yingjin Zhang, Sasha S. Welland, Ping Fu, Shu-chin Tsui, Megan Ferry, Stephen J. Goldberg, Tom Vick, Kevin Lee, Paul Gladston, Meiqin Wang, Yiyang Shao, Hajimei Nakatani, Po-shin Chiang, Joyce Chi-hui Liu, and Nick Kaldis. In addition, I am most grateful to Yingjin Zhang for his scholarly advice in the past few years. I am grateful to Paul Gladston for his generous editorial advice. I also would like to thank many colleagues at the University of Maryland, especially Sally Promey, Bill Pressly, Meredith Gill, Jianmei Liu, Minglang Zhou, and Robert Ramsey for their support and encouragement. The technical support of Lauree Sails and Quint Gregory of the Michelle Smith Collaboratory for Visual Culture is very much appreciated. Once again, Joel Kalvesmaki's editorial expertise has made my job much easier.

This book is dedicated to the memory of Rudolf Arnheim who taught me how to read art and film.

Jason C. Kuo

Note on Transcription

In general, the pinyin system of transcribing Chinese names and terms is used in this book. Exceptions include self-chosen names of modern Chinese scholars and artists (such as Eileen Chang and Stanley Kwan), names and terms in titles of publications using different systems of transcription (such as the Wade-Giles system), and a few names in Southern Chinese dialects. Japanese names and terms are transcribed according to the modified Hepburn system.

Introduction

Jason C. Kuo

In the past two decades, contemporary Chinese art and film have attracted a great deal of media and academic attention in the West, and scholars have adopted a variety of approaches to Chinese film and visual studies. As English scholarship in this area has continued to expand, it is time for us to assess progress, problems, and prospects in our research agendas and methodologies.[1] The present volume focuses, therefore, on the uses and status of theory originating in non-Chinese places in the creation, curating, narration, and criticism of contemporary Chinese visual culture (broadly defined to include traditional media in the visual arts as well as cinema, installation, video, etc.). One of the main themes of the book is the appropriateness (that is, the uses, abuses, appropriations, limits, etc.) of Western theory. Contributors reflect on the written and, even more interestingly, the unwritten assumptions of artists, critics, historians, and curators in applying or resisting these theories. They also reflect on the status of theory in our scholarship; by necessity, theory in this case is broadly conceived to include not only critical theory in the West but also basic concepts that enable us to engage in different modes of perception, articulation, negotiation, and interrogation. Theory is also linked to our disciplinary traditions and innovations, as scholars from art history, film studies, and Chinese studies investigate different aspects of Chinese art and film in our knowledge production.

The book begins with Paul Gladston's essay "Traces of Empire: Deconstructing Hou Hanru's 'Postcolonialist' Reading of Contemporary Chinese Art." "Contemporary Chinese Art" is the term widely used in an Anglophone context to refer to modern forms of Chinese art produced since the late 1970s that involve the active translation of attitudes and techniques historically associated with the western avant-gardes and post–avant-gardes in relation to the demands of an autochthonous Chinese art world (the corresponding term in Mandarin Chinese is *Zhongguo dangdai yishu*—which can be translated into English as "Chinese Contemporary Art"). As a result, contemporary Chinese art can be understood—from the point of view of contemporary Western poststructuralist theory—to have severely problematized ontological-essentialist notions of cultural identity, not only those historically associated with western Orientalism, but also those that inform recent calls among Chinese commentators for a reassertion of the essential "Chineseness" of contemporary Chinese art.

According to a number of commentators, including the Chinese curator and theorist Hou Hanru, the cultural hybridity of contemporary Chinese art has a strong affinity with the Chinese intellectual tradition's historical reliance on what might be described as a "nonrationalist" dialectics. By contrast with the Western philosophical tradition's durable belief in the negation of difference as part of some sort of transcendental unity or whole, vernacular Chinese thought and practice upholds the Daoist/Chan Buddhist notion that there is the possibility of reciprocal interaction between persistently differing states of being (viz. the dynamic interrelationship between *yin* and *yang* given visual expression by the well-known Chinese symbol of the *Ba Gua*). Such notions are, it is argued, closely allied to Western poststructuralist conceptions such as "différance" and "trace-structure."

In his essay, Gladston argues that the conjunction of Western poststructuralism and Chinese Daoism/Chan Buddhism is ultimately a problematic one that overlooks the continuing, and distinctly metaphysical, tendency of vernacular Chinese thought and practice to look toward nonrationalist dialectics as a basis for the (provisional) harmonization of persistently differing states of being. He also argues (with reference to a range of sources, including interviews conducted with contemporary Chinese artists) that this tendency finds significant expression through the formal construction of contemporary Chinese art, which—like traditional Chinese *literati* painting—can often be understood to engender an unfolding multiplicity of (aesthetic) feelings while also seeking to harmonize those feelings in an ultimately pleasurable way with respect to the presentation of distinctly "good" artistic forms—a process conventionally referred to in Chinese as *wanshang* ("play-appreciation"). On this basis, Gladston seeks to frame contemporary Chinese art not simply as an instance of critical cultural hybridity but also as an attempt to resist the assumed hegemony of Western artistic theory and practice—and in particular the now-pervasive notion of transcultural/national "Third-Space"—through an assimilation of western otherness to an insistently Chinese "empire" of aesthetic feeling.

From a sociopolitical and economic perspective, post-Deng China continues most of the legacies from Deng Xiaoping's market reform policy. What seems to be new, such as the legalization of the culture industry and the heavy leaning upon cultural nationalism and globalization, can be seen as rational developments as China moves ahead following the strategies that Deng conceived. In the art world, however, the cumulative effects of continuous market expansion and the increasing impact of globalization have greatly challenged the existing mechanism and power structure of the official art establishment.

The Chinese art world now operates in a different way and shows an unprecedented energy. A significant difference is that the Chinese Artists Association, the national organization of artists, art historians, and critics, seems to have stopped being the only officially sanctioned agency of the Chinese art world. This consequentially brings many changes to the official art world and fosters new social relationships among artists of different camps: official, unofficial, underground, independent, and international. The conflict between official art and avant-garde art of the 1980s, or underground art of the 1990s, is finally absorbed into the new ideology that combines the desires of being global, marketable, and nationalistic all at once.

Grounded upon the dynamic economic, political, and cultural developments of Chinese society since the mid-1990s, Meiqin Wang's essay, "The Art World of Post-Deng China: Market, Globalization, and Cultural Nationalism," explores the most influential forces in the transformation of the Chinese art world. It illuminates how marketization, globalization, and cultural nationalism have introduced contemporary media, formats, and issues, as well as Western modes of presenting art, thereby transforming the operating system of Chinese official art. It also examines how the interactive impacts of these forces have complicated the relationship between official art and unofficial art, shaken the supremacy of the Chinese Artists Association in presenting state-sanctioned art, and created room for new discourses from various artistic groups with different agendas. It argues that in the recent tide of transformation and reconstruction, previous boundaries and conflicts in the art world dissolve while new divisions and forces grow. Among these, exhibition of contemporary art stands out as a most attention-absorbing force, calling into question the old practice of the art-displaying-and-perceiving system. Un-unofficial or independent art emerges and steps onto the stage of the Chinese art world, to a large degree replacing unofficial art. At the same time, within the scope of official art, internal divisions emerge and expand, which have put the mainstream art in China on the track of disintegration and reformation.

In the 1990s, Chinese art was widely displayed in some privileged international art exhibitions. But one pertinent subject may need to be addressed: the unduly exaggerated influence that it had on collectors, curators, and museums based in the West in determining the representation of contemporary Chinese art in an international arena. This situation is the result of a specific historical and theoretical condition centered on the concepts of modernism and modernization—concepts that have framed and continue to determine prevailing perceptions about contemporary Chinese art. Focusing on the debates about the international identity of Chinese art, in particular the inside voice, Yiyang Shao's essay, "The International Identity of Chinese Art: Theoretical Debates on Chinese Contemporary Art in the 1990s," questions the legitimacy of Euro-American power in shaping and defining the arts of China by determining the theme and content of international exhibitions, and the intensity of the Chinese internal urge for integration into the international art world.

One of the best-known Chinese works of art since the Cultural Revolution ended in 1976 is perhaps *Father*, a painting completed in

1980 by Luo Zhongli (born 1948), an artist from Sichuan province. Stephen Goldberg's essay, "Oh Father, Where Art Thou? A Bakhtinian Reading of Luo Zhongli's *Father*" is an exploration of the possible relevance of the theories on language and literature of Mikhail Bakhtin (1895–1975), working in the aftermath of the Russian Revolution, to an artist working in the aftermath of the Chinese Cultural Revolution. Goldberg's exploration is motivated by the fact that each in their own ways was obliged to make accommodations with Marxist regimes. Tzvetan Todorov called Bakhtin the *fondateur moderne* of pragmatics.[2] While Ferdinand de Saussure's structural linguistics limited its field of inquiry to the language system as a separate entity, Bakhtin and his circle were concerned with the study of discourse, "with the socially-situated utterance and with the structuring of linguistic form and meaning by context." These, as Trevor Pateman observes, "relate much more obviously to the contemporary literature on pragmatics...."[3] Bakhtin's writings on literature as a polyphonic, heterogeneous discourse must also be seen in contradistinction to Russian Formalism, which attempted to distinguish the poetic use of language from ordinary, everyday usage.

Goldberg's essay undertakes an examination of Bakhtin's thought, with a specific focus on his dialogical theory of "double-voiced discourse" and "addressivity," through a reading of *Father*. Double-voicing (here redefined as the internal bifurcation of visual modes of address) is shown to be an implicit strategy in the artist's attempt to offer a countermemory of the events of the Cultural Revolution. Luo Zhongli's *Father* posed a challenge to the sovereignty of the Communist Party state by undermining, through a rhetorical strategy of parodic inversion, two of the principal discursive instruments by which the legitimacy of this sovereignty was inscribed and rationalized: Socialist Realist paintings and political propaganda posters. First exhibited in 1980, *Father* ignited a decade-long countercultural revolution in contemporary Chinese art, brought to an end by the tragic events of the Tiananmen Incident in 1989.

The appropriateness of Bakhtin's thought to Luo Zhongli's painting, of course, is based solely on one criterion: the relevancy of this theoretical approach to the issues raised by this work, issues, it should be noted, that are certainly contingent on the critical concerns of our own cultural location. If one were to admit a different set of concerns, this would necessitate a different methodological approach.

A landmark of contemporary Chinese art, Xu Bing's *Book from the Sky* is usually interpreted under the sign of skepticism. Like the numerous works by other Chinese artists that engage the script as central motif, Xu Bing's opus is taken to enact a radical critique of writing, a sustained deconstruction of the cultural and political authorities that language and the script serve to channel. While this may have been the professed intention of the artist, a careful reconsideration of the artwork can take us beyond such authorial intent, bringing us into a far more unsettling theoretical terrain in which the very terms *modern critiques* and *deconstructions* begin to lose their efficacy and self-evidence. Evacuated of meaning and thus divorced from language, Xu's presumably nonsensical pseudocharacters ironically come to assume the autonomy of a graphic system that is subject to no law but its own morphological rules and principles. In "Imperious Griffonage: Xu Bing and the Graphic Regime," Hajime Nakatani shows that the graphic vision of *A Book from the Sky* lends modern expression to the classical Chinese conception of the script, a graphic cosmology in which the world as such is seen as a form of writing whose implicit systematicity the script makes manifest. Nakatani argues that the aim of such a seemingly classicizing interpretation, however, is not to posit a monolithic "Chinese theory" of writing. It is, rather, to suggest how writing in China constituted—and continues to constitute—an irreducible problem, a traumatic kernel to which questions of order and meaning are repeatedly and obsessively referred back.

In his essay "The Discursive Formation of the Role of the Independent Curator in Taiwan during the 1990s," Po-shin Chiang analyzes how the subject position of Taiwan art has continually developed in the context of the international contemporary art exhibitions held in Taiwan since the 1996 Taipei Biennial. Organizing exhibitions used to be the job of museum professionals. Prior to the 1990s, there were a few instances of Taiwan art critics participating in exhibit curation. In the early 1990s, art critics became more actively involved in organizing Taiwan's contemporary art shows. And since 1996, independent curators who have put together contemporary art shows have begun to attract extensive attention and interest from both public and private institutes since 1996. Government-run art museums have even held large seminars and invited curators from across Taiwan and around the world to address topics in curatorship, which has since evolved into an independent field of knowledge and expertise. Hence, Chiang's essay focuses on international contemporary art exhibitions organized by independent curators since 1996.

By inviting six outside curators to organize the 1996 Biennial, the government-run Taipei Fine Arts Museum gave up the power of interpretation it had retained for many years and distributed it to the curators in a network of power. Taiwanese art then no longer became the predominant subject advocated by art museums. Rather, it was reduced to an object of information, hidden in a moral education apparatus called an international exhibition. Curators produced and copied their versions of Taiwanese art with an anonymous operating strategy. What kind of subject position has been created in the discursive formation process while curating these exhibitions—is it "Asian-Pacific" or "Asian" or "Chinese"? What kind of evolution has Taiwanese art experienced under multiple pressures from different international blocks?

In his essay, Chiang conducts a genealogical review of the curatorial discourses. He reveals the derivative and connective power relations between the spatialization of curatorial discourse and curatorial discourse per se. He also deals with the process of discursive formation in which Taiwanese art is produced and reproduced. First, after discussing the spatialization of curatorial discourse, he analyzes the origin of, and the backdrop for, Taiwanese curators organizing international contemporary art exhibitions in Taiwan since 1996. Second, by focusing on two international modern art exhibitions held in Taiwan in 1997, he examines and compares the international diagrams depicted in curatorial statements for those shows, and how the subject position of Taiwanese art was addressed. Finally, he explores how the identities of artists from different nations were interconnected by curators using the concept of a geographic sphere. Also, he discusses how Taiwanese artists were positioned in such social sites, and what impact a curatorial model might have on art creation.

Rural China serves as the barometer for Chinese political and historical weather. The notion of rural China, deeply rooted in the Chinese mentality, has navigated and shaped national policy-making and individuals' words and deeds over China's long history. In her essay "Encircling the City: Peasant Migration in Contemporary Chinese Media," Ping Fu traces the complex history of the ever-changing representation of the Chinese peasantry in Chinese cinema and media and examines the rural-urban embattlements and dialectics through a number of acclaimed Chinese films and other media work. She investigates Chinese farmers' once-privileged position, their disappearance, and their regained recognition, both on- and off-screen, against the major social, economic, and political changes and transformations in China throughout last six decades. She responds to inquiries of how Chinese socialist and postsocialist experiences impact the (re)presentation and imagination of the rural-urban dynamics in Chinese cinema, and exhibits how Chinese filmmakers understand and present changing operations and ideologies on the rural-urban paradox and the local-global paradigm depicted in the studied visual materials. She argues the political and historical dimensions have heavily circumscribed the cinematic configuration of both urban and rural spaces in films from 1950s to today. The popular and massive act of farmers encircling the city in China today has greatly enriched and enlarged the film genres of both Chinese urban cinema and rural cinema in terms of cinematic aesthetics and meaning production.

Along with increasing urbanization, globalization, and marketization of art, the complex issues of sexuality and gender have been taken up by many contemporary Chinese artists and filmmakers. In her essay, "Between Realism and Romanticism: Queering Gender Representation in Cui Zi'en's *Night Scene*," Megan Ferry undertakes to read filmmaker Cui Zi'en's *Night Scene* (*Yejing*, 2002), with its focus on male prostitution and homosexuality, as an intervention in the construction and bodily configuration of sexualized individuals in post-Maoist society. Cui's focus on the Chinese gay man upsets the power-invested heterosexual male figure prominent in contemporary Chinese media representation, and underscores the male body as caught within the intricate web of a libidinal economy where both men and women have become objects of consumption. Employing three formal elements of film (the documentary, feature narrative, and reenactments), Cui disrupts the narrative sequence common in feature and documentary films in order to draw attention to the correlation between sexuality and capitalist enterprise. The paper argues that he is less interested in metaphor than in calling our attention to how bodies and commerce intersect in contemporary China, thereby exposing new sexual economies. Subsequently, the paper explores how the film does not satisfy a need to know the lived experiences of gay male prostitutes as much as it questions the act of knowing itself.

Widely praised by international audiences and film critics, *Crouching Tiger, Hidden Dragon* (*CTHD*) is one of the most successful Chinese-language films ever made, having earned in excess of $208 million worldwide (as of 2001), and it stands as the highest-grossing foreign language film of all time in the United States. Much of the academic scholarship on the film explores its transnational co-production and other global dimensions. Yet although transnational in its production and reception, *CTHD* is thoroughly "Chinese" in its diegesis, taking place entirely within the (imagined) historical, geographical, and linguistic boundaries of Qing Dynasty China. This combination of localized content with global box office success and international film awards has led many Chinese viewers to praise the film for attracting a worldwide audience, depicting an edifying representation of Chinese people and culture, and establishing an influential Chinese presence in the global film market.

Though a variety of scholars, journalists, filmmakers, and others have focused on both the film's global and local features, what has yet to receive appropriate attention is the ubiquitous logic of racial binarism in the film. The essay "Couching Race in the Global Era: Intra-Asian Racism in *Crouching Tiger, Hidden Dragon*" by Nick Kaldis is a critical dialogue with the extant scholarship on *CTHD*. Simultaneously expanding upon and critically responding to the many insights and compelling arguments to be found in that scholarship, Kaldis argues that *CTHD*'s manipulation of familiar orientalist tropes for global audiences takes place within a novel representational scheme—an *intranational* racialized exaltation of Han ethnicity, its traditions and social mores. Han Chinese in this film are models of social conformity and propriety, upholding quasi-

Confucian *jianghu* (江湖 "knight-errant culture") codes; they are thoroughly conservative and hostile toward any type of illicit, uncivil, or antisocial behavior. The lead non-Han characters, on the other hand, are violators of the same social mores, laws, and values dear to the Han characters; they prioritize the carnal over the mental and spiritual, abandoning themselves to lust and impetuously acting on their emotional impulses.

Ang Lee's film is arguably the first globally successful Hollywood-style Chinese language film with a ubiquitous domestic racist logic as a key element of its narrative structure. Kaldis's essay carefully dissects the mechanisms by which *CTHD* reconfigures the representation of Chinese culture for a global audience, via its ubiquitous binary racial logic. Careful analysis of the content and cinematic grammar reveals this narrative fantasy in which race, ethnicity, and culture are successfully deployed to serve both global and local cultural nationalist identities and aspirations at once.

In "Filmic Transposition of the Roses: Stanley Kwan's Feminine Response to Eileen Chang's Women," Joyce Chi-hui Liu argues that Stanley Kwan's film *Red Rose/White Rose* of 1994 should be read as his "feminine" rereading of the "feminist" writer Eileen Chang's fiction of 1944, half a century before. Through Kwan's filmic rereading and transposition, the power of Eileen Chang's words, and the hidden male-dominated ideology behind her text, is literally and figuratively challenged and canceled. Liu points out that Kwan presents before the audience a feminine cinema that not only maneuvers the substratum of the filmic space as his commentary on Chang's reticence on the historical context, but also unveils the possibility of the fluidity of female desire and the growth of female subjectivity, which are both denied by Eileen Chang. Stanley Kwan thinks and speaks through the materiality of the film. Unlike western avant-garde countercinema, which rejects narrative all together, Kwan retains the storytelling tradition but shifts the focus by forcing the marginalized off-screen space upon the viewer's consciousness. Furthermore, Kwan pieces together the historical background of China during the modernization period in the 1930s and 1940s, which was never treated directly in Eileen Chang's fiction, and reveals his remarks on the center-margin dialectics. In doing so, Kwan, unlike Eileen Chang, not only charges against the phallogocentric collective morality of traditional Chinese culture but also proposes the possibility of the autonomy of women's subjectivity, and hence subverts Chang's prepossessed bias against the freedom and the growth of women's desire.

In his broad-ranging essay "Ethnicity, Nationality, Translocality: A Critical Reflection on the Question of Theory in Chinese Film Studies," Yingjin Zhang addresses the question, What is the current status of theory in Chinese film studies? This question itself begs questions because "theory" often refers to "Western theory" and, as such, it actually carries a plural designation to cover "theories" of semiotics, formalism, psychoanalysis, poststructuralism, postmodernism, postcolonialism, Marxism, feminism, and so on. The dominance of Western theory in film studies means that Chinese aesthetic concepts are rarely explored in contemporary film criticism, especially in English scholarship. On the other hand, Chinese-language discussions of Chinese aesthetics are often linked to cultural nationalism, according to which cinematic examples of "Chineseness" are enumerated to confirm certain essential elements of national culture. In this context, Chinese national cinema is seen to work for cultural self-preservation and self-invigoration. The irony, however, is that as a theory originated from the West, national cinema has been challenged or even discredited in the West, but it continues to gain favor from states and scholars in Asia.

Zhang emphasizes the horizontal tactics of translocality and argues that more often than not, film production, distribution, exhibition, and reception take place at the scale of the local or translocal rather than that of the national, especially in the market economy. Translocality thus prefers place-based imagination and reveals dynamic processes of the local/global (or glocal)—processes that involve not just the traffic of capital and people but also that of ideas, images, styles, and technologies across places in polylocality. Moreover, translocal traffic is never a one-way street, although it could be if one insists on imposing Western theory on Chinese cinema and pursue problematic readings. On the contrary, the polylocality of capital, people, ideas, images, styles, and technologies allows for the reconfiguration of different spaces and patterns of collaboration, competition, contestation, and contradiction. Filmmaking has always been a translocal practice, and Chinese film studies must rethink such translocality in filmmaking as well as in film scholarship.[4]

The essays in the present volume demonstrate clearly that Western theory can be useful in explicating Chinese art and film, as long as it is applied judiciously; the essays, taken as a whole, also suggest that cultural exchange is never a one-way street. Ideas from traditional Chinese aesthetics have also traveled to the West. It is a challenge to examine what travels and what does not, as well as what makes such travel possible or impossible. The present volume thus provides an opportunity to rethink how theories and texts travel across cultures, languages, disciplines, and media.

1

Traces of Empire: Deconstructing Hou Hanru's "Postcolonialist" Reading of Contemporary Chinese Art

Paul Gladston

Since the mid-1980s, the production of contemporary Chinese art has involved the active assimilation/translation of images, styles, and techniques historically associated with Western Modernism and Postmodernism in relation to an autochthonous modernizing Chinese desire for innovation and freedom of self-expression. Seen from the point of view of postcolonialist theory, contemporary Chinese art of the last quarter of a century can therefore be thought of as a problematic cultural hybrid that deconstructs the asymmetrical relations of power historically associated with Western Orientalism/cultural imperialism by performatively suspending ontological-essentialist conceptions of East-West cultural difference.

According to the Chinese curator and theorist Hou Hanru, there is a discernible affinity between contemporary Chinese art's performative suspension of cultural difference and the perceived outcome of traditional Chinese divinatory/geomantic practices associated with the *Yi Jing* (*The Book of Changes*) and *Fengshui*, which, as Hou has indicated, also seek to affect a blurring of conceptual limits—in the case of *Fengshui*, for example, that between the "constructed world" and "Nature." As Hou would have it, these traditional Chinese practices consequently have the potential to be used as "cultural strategies" against the continuation of Western Orientalism/cultural imperialism. In making this point, Hou effectively seeks to draw parallels between a traditional Chinese dependency upon the conceptual indeterminacy of "nonrationalist" (rationalist-irrationalist) dialectical thinking as a guide to individual and collective action (the striking of a "middle way") and the poststructuralist figuring of *différance*, whose performative enactment of a persistent deconstructive differing-deferring between linguistic signs has strongly informed postcolonialist theory and, in particular, Homi Bhabha's use of the terms *hybridity* and *Third Space*.

In this chapter, I shall argue that the conjunction of contemporary Chinese art and traditional Chinese divinatory/geomantic practices as mediated by postcolonialist theory is ultimately a problematic one that overlooks the tendency of traditional Chinese thought and practice to uphold conceptual indeterminacy as a basis for the interconnectedness and harmonization of otherwise differing states of being. I shall also argue that this tendency, which is symbolized in graphic form by the familiar *yin-yang* symbol, or *Bagua*, is inescapably "metaphysical" in its outlook and therefore at odds with the pervasively unsettling hybridity valorized by postcolonialist theory. Thus, a conclusion shall be drawn that Hou's citing of traditional Chinese practices associated with the *Yi Jing* and *Fengshui* as a strategic resistance to Western Orientalism/cultural imperialism is a fundamentally contradictory one whose implicit invocation of a nonrationalist Chinese dialectical metaphysics carries with it the persistent traces not only of a traditional Chinese belief in the superiority of an inherently "harmonious" Chinese culture (*wenhua*), but also, by extension, in the exclusivity of the Chinese empire/civilization as "everything under heaven" (*tianxia*). Moreover, it shall also be argued that the persistence of these traces is commensurate with historical attitudes toward modernism within mainland China since the early twentieth century, where there has been a constant and unresolved struggle to reconcile the disruptive assimilation of modernizing cultural influences from outside with a desire to uphold a distinctively Chinese sense of cultural identity for fear of what the historian of Chinese art David Clarke has referred to as some sort of "felt deracination."

Mapping the Perceived Limits of Contemporary Chinese Art

The term *contemporary Chinese art* is now widely used in an Anglophone context to denote various forms of avant-garde, experimental, and museum-based visual art produced as part of the liberalization of culture which has taken place in mainland China since the confirmation of Deng Xiaoping's program of economic and social reforms at the plenary session of XI Central Committee of the Chinese Communist Party (CCP) in December 1978. Its use extends not only to scholarly texts, but also to an ever-growing body of magazine and newspaper articles, exhibition catalogues, tourist guides, and market surveys aimed at popular audiences eager to learn more about contemporary Chinese culture. For writers in Mandarin Chinese (*putonghua*) the corresponding term is *Zhongguo dangdai yishu,* which is often translated literally into English within a Mandarin-speaking context as "Chinese contemporary art."[1]

While the use of the adjective *dangdai* in *Zhongguo dangdai yishu* signifies something that is "of the present time," in the general sense of the English word "contemporary," it also connotes meanings specific to a vernacular Chinese understanding of contemporary Chinese art. During the 1980s, avant-garde art in China was usually referred to not as "contemporary," but as "modern" (*xiandai*); hence, the Chinese title of the milestone China/Avant-Garde Exhibition of 1989, *Xiandai meishu dazhan* ("A Grand Exhibition of Modern Art"). The term *Zhongguo dangdai yishu,* which is now used to refer to all avant-garde, experimental, and museum-based forms of Chinese visual art produced since the late 1970s, first gained widespread currency during the early 1990s, when, as the curator and critic Wu Hung has indicated, there was a move away from the collective optimism associated with the "modern" Chinese art of the 1980s to more individualistic and less hopeful (oppositional) attitudes in the wake of the Tiananmen killings of June 4, 1989.[2] What is more, within mainland China *Zhongguo dangdai yishu* is widely used to signify *qianwei* or "avant-garde" forms of art which are seen as challenging established social, political, and cultural norms. Consequently, the term *Zhongguo dangdai yishu* also implies a degree of separation from Western avant-garde art insofar as the latter is now widely considered, in relation to postmodernist thinking, to be something of a spent force, while the former maintains a certain critical currency within a mainland Chinese context.[3]

Throughout the existing literature on the subject (both Chinese and non-Chinese in origin), there is a general agreement that contemporary Chinese art first emerged during the late 1970s in response to an idealizing humanistic (European Renaissance-Enlightenment influenced) desire for freedom of artistic self-expression[4] running contrary to the Chinese communist state's requirement that art should take the view of the masses and be entirely subservient to the political aims of the CCP (a requirement first promulgated by Mao Zedong in his Yan'an talks of 1942). There is also a widely held view that this breaking with established political convention first manifested itself in relation to the activities of the largely self-taught Beijing-based art group known as *Xingxing* (The Stars), who, in December 1979, mounted an unofficial exhibition of artworks attached somewhat provocatively to railings in a public park adjacent to the National Gallery in Beijing. Commentators have pointed to earlier instances of heterodox art-making during the revolutionary period in mainland China prior to 1979. However, these can be differentiated from the work of *Xingxing* on the grounds that they either took place squarely under the auspices of mainland China's state controlled system—for example, Fu Baoshi's highly selective pictorial response to a poem by Mao Zedong, *Heavy Rain Falls on Youyan* of 1961[5] and Luo Zhongli's seminal work of "Rural Realism," *Father* of 1979[6]—or that they were carried out in a more or less clandestine manner and without any obviously challenging political intent—most notably, the combined work of the *No Name Group*, which spanned the period from the early 1960s to the early 1980s.[7]

Throughout the existing literature on the subject (again both Chinese and non-Chinese in origin), there is also a general agreement that since the ending of the Anti-Spiritual Pollution Campaign of 1984 to 1985 (an attempt by conservative forces within the CCP to resist the Westernizing consequences of Deng Xiaoping's program of openness and economic reform) and the subsequent coming to prominence of the "avant-garde" art movement known as the '85 New Wave (whose activities spanned the period from the mid-1980s to the era defining China/Avant-Garde exhibition of 1989), contemporary Chinese artists have sought to challenge established norms both inside mainland China and elsewhere principally through the appropriation/translation of images, styles, and techniques associated with Western Modernism and Postmodernism,[8] and, in particular, the disjunctive collage-montage techniques habitually used by the Western avant-gardes and post avant-gardes. Moreover, this engagement with Western Modernism and Postmodernism is also understood to have been informed by an interest among contemporary Chinese artists in Western theoretical and art-historical writings, including those of the poststructuralists Michel Foucault and Jacques Derrida, which began to enter into China in translation during the early to mid-1980s. As a consequence, from the mid-1980s to the early 1990s it is possible to discern an increasingly marked shift within contemporary Chinese art away from the humanistic idealism which had dominated that art since the late 1970s toward self-consciously deconstructive ways of working[9]—a position also informed by the collective loss of optimism among contemporary Chinese artists which, as previously indicated, had taken hold in the wake of the post-Tiananmen crackdown. What is more, during the late 1980s and throughout the 1990s many contemporary Chinese artists sought to mesh the collage-montage techniques of the Western avant-gardes and post avant-gardes with a revisiting of the mass dissemination of texts—for example, the use of *dazi bao* (big character posters) and the seemingly endless reproduction of portraits of Mao Zedong—which had taken place during the Cultural Revolution of the 1960s and 1970s, thereby seeking to reveal the mass dissemination of texts during the Cultural Revolution as a means of inculcating communist party ideology.[10] Consider here, for example, the "Political Pop" paintings of Wang Guangyi and the "big character" installations of Wu Shanzhuan, both of which involve the recontextualization and critical remotivation of imagery culled more or less directly from the time of the Cultural Revolution.

At the same time, contemporary Chinese art can also be understood to have been strongly informed by a continuing desire among Chinese artists to combine modern Western influences with traditional modes of Chinese art making. As the art historian David Clarke has indicated, this desire—which has been a persistent aspect of Chinese modernism since the New Culture Movement of the early twentieth century[11]—can be seen as a reaction to the "seeming unavoidability of the inherited visual tradition in China, and the difficulty of simply denying or discarding it to achieve modernity without risking some kind of felt deracination," that is to say, a loss of vernacular cultural identity, "and yet the difficulty of simply continuing to produce the kind of art that had been made in quite different premodern cultural circumstances."[12] As a consequence, Clarke argues, it is necessary to mark the "Chinese experience of the modern" as different from that of early Western avant-garde artists whose "artistic modernity consisted quite straightforwardly in a disavowal of the past," an option which, Clarke goes on to aver, has "rarely seemed adequate in the Chinese context."[13] Prominent examples of this tendency in relation to contemporary Chinese art include the work of the artists Shu Qun and Wang Guangyi, who, from 1984 to 1989, during their time as leading members of the Harbin-based *Beifang yishu qunti* (Northern Art Group), produced paintings simultaneously influenced by both Western surrealism and the lofty aesthetics of Chinese Confucianism as a modernizing response to the ideological conformity of Chinese socialist-realism.[14]

It is therefore possible to differentiate contemporary Chinese art substantively from two other—sometimes overlapping—genres of "present day" Chinese art, both of which have continued to occupy the cultural mainstream in mainland China during the period of Deng's reforms: modern variations on traditional Chinese *shanshui* (literally, "mountain and water") ink and brush painting known as *Guohua* (National Painting); and institutionally acceptable forms of realism/abstraction sometimes referred to (somewhat confusingly) in English under the title of "Chinese Modern Art."[15] Both genres can trace their beginnings to the Chinese New Culture and May 4 movements of the early twentieth century. While both genres have been influenced by Western visual art, that influence has been limited almost entirely, in the case of *Guohua* and institutionally acceptable forms of abstraction, to a perceived affinity between the explicit brushwork of Western Expressionism/Abstract Expressionism and that of traditional Chinese painting, and, in the case of institutionally acceptable forms of realism, to the persistence within Chinese art schools of academic (socialist-realist) teaching methods imported from the Soviet Union during the 1950s. As a result, both can be seen to diverge from the deconstructive tendencies exhibited by contemporary Chinese art through their adherence to a rather less challenging formalism/aestheticism.

It is important to note here that since 1978 there has been a progressive, if somewhat intermittent, relaxation of government controls on artistic production in mainland China, to the extent where art is now no longer expected to reflect the view of the masses, nor simply to act as a tool of the CCP. Nevertheless, none of the visual arts in present-day mainland China could, as yet, be described as openly critical of the conduct and legitimacy of the CCP, which continues to assert itself as an unimpeachable source of political authority. One of the ways in which the CCP has asserted its authority is through the censoring or closure of exhibitions of visual art that might be viewed as unacceptably transgressive and, therefore, problematic with regard to the authoritative standing of the party as a guarantor of public order. Such exhibitions include China/Avant-Garde, which was staged in Beijing shortly before the Tiananmen protests in 1989, and Fuck Off—Uncooperative Stance (whose title in Mandarin Chinese, Buhezuo fangshi, can be translated into English as "Ways of Non-Cooperation"), which was staged alongside the Shanghai Biennale in 2000. While *Guohua* and institutionally acceptable forms of realism/abstraction maintain an obvious distance from public political critique by concentrating primarily on questions of form and aesthetics, contemporary Chinese art can be understood to have made full use of the uncertainties of meaning brought about by its appropriation of various forms of collage-montage as well as the linguistic detours associated with pictorial allegory to present images that are open to interpretation as critical by a knowing audience, but whose evident ambiguities also leave room for a simultaneous disavowal of critical intent; thus bringing about what Martina Köppel-Yang has described as a semiologically encoded "demystification and…overcoming of aesthetic and linguistic patterns, and of authoritative structures."[16] Exemplary here is the genre of contemporary Chinese art known as "Cynical Realism," which, since the late 1980s, has upheld—more often than not through the multiple depiction of generic human figures displaying fixed grimaces and hollow smiles—an understandably disingenuous critique of the ideological contradictions inherent in mainland China's current, centrally driven (socialist-capitalist) program of modernization.

Contemporary Chinese Art and Chinese National Cultural Identity

Another notable feature of the existing literature on the subject of contemporary Chinese art is a tendency to define that art as an object of historical/critical knowledge in strongly nationalistic terms. Here, there is a generally held assumption that the term contemporary Chinese art refers almost exclusively to work produced by artists of ethnic Chinese descent who were born in mainland China and whose careers were initially established there. This allows for the unequivocal inclusion of the work of artists of ethnic Chinese descent who continue to live and work within mainland China as well as a number of others who have chosen to live and work abroad (such as the artist Huang Yongping, who has been based in Paris since 1989). Excluded or heavily marginalized are artists of ethnic Chinese descent belonging to the extended Chinese diaspora (*haiwai huaren* or, "Overseas Chinese") who were either born outside mainland China or whose careers as artists were established away from there. Also excluded or heavily marginalized are artists of non-Chinese descent who live and work in China as well as artists of ethnic Chinese descent working in parts of China historically identified as Chinese but which currently lie outside the geopolitical control of the mainland (i.e., Taiwan), or that have a degree of autonomy from Beijing (i.e., Hong Kong–Macau). This assumption as to the meaning of the term contemporary Chinese art can be seen to run more or less intact through a wide range of scholarly and popular writings on the subject, including high-profile texts by both Chinese and non-Chinese writers, such as Gao Minglu's monumental art-historical survey *The Wall: Reshaping Contemporary Chinese Art*,[17] Wu Hung's collection of critical essays *Making History*, Karen Smith's biographical study *Nine Lives: The Birth of the Avant-Garde in China*[18] and Martina Köppel-Yang's semiotic analysis *Semiotic Warfare: The Chinese Avant-Garde, 1979–1989*. Indeed, even in the case of transcultural publications, such as the Canada-based journal *Yishu*, which have from time to time sought to encompass artworks outside the limits conventionally associated with the term contemporary Chinese art, there is still an abiding sense that *Chinese* here refers principally to mainland China. It is therefore possible to view the term contemporary Chinese art as a linguistic marker for the imposition of tight spatiotemporal limits that, despite the conceptually unsettling deconstructive tendencies of much of the art to which it refers, nevertheless seeks to restrict our view of contemporary Chinese artistic practice to a particular time—the period from 1979 to the present—and to a particular geographical space—the mainland of the People's Republic of China.

Alongside the imposition of these tight spatiotemporal limits, it is also possible to find numerous examples, particularly during the last decade, of Chinese writers and critics who have advocated decidedly ontological-essentialist ways of interpreting contemporary Chinese art. Strongly indicative of this standpoint is a statement by the art critic and historian Li Xu published in the catalogue accompanying the exhibition "Beyond Boundaries," which was held at the then newly opened Shanghai Gallery of Art in 2003. In this statement, Li contends that contemporary Chinese art has, after an initial two decade period of development, reached some sort of crossroads or boundary. According to Li, this situation has been arrived at as the result of contemporary Chinese art having achieved a position of equality with Western contemporary art on an international stage. As a result, he argues, contemporary Chinese art is now faced by questions of its own national cultural identity in relation to that of the West. As Li would have it, this is not simply a matter of the assimilation/translation of Western cultural influences in relation to the demands and concerns of an autochthonous Chinese art world (as many other commentators have argued), but, instead, of the capacity of contemporary Chinese art to exceed Westernization by rediscovering "the resources of our traditional national spirit"—often referred to elsewhere as "Chineseness." Li adds the (somewhat unsettling) assertion that "culture is to a nation...what the flowing blood is to our body."[19] Such thinking is strongly representative of persistent leanings toward nationalism within modern China, which have manifested themselves more or less consistently throughout China's republican (*xiandai*) and communist (*dangdai*) periods and most recently through the CCP's adoption of a pragmatic ideology of patriotic nationalism since the early 2000s as a means of maintaining social stability in the face of the precipitous changes brought about by Deng's reforms. It is also possible to link ontological-essentialist thinking of this sort to two related aspects of premodern Chinese culture: a traditional Chinese belief in the inherent superiority of Chinese culture (*wenhua*; literally, a process of "transformation through writing") over barbaric (incoherent) non-Chinese others;[20] and, as the Chinese cultural historian Kam Louie has indicated, the "remnants of imperial times when 'China'," *Zhongguo* (literally, "the middle kingdom"), "was not only the centre of the world, but also 'all under heaven' (*tianxia*), a term that indicated the traditional Chinese view of the world: that the Chinese civilization was all there was in the universe."[21] Any relationship between national cultural readings of contemporary Chinese art and these aspects of premodern Chinese culture is, of course, far from being historically immediate and may therefore appear to be somewhat tenuous. However, as a poststructuralist analysis of Western discourse shows, the traces of traditional thought and practice, while open to continual recontextualization and remotivation in the face of changing historical circumstances, may nevertheless persist as part of an extended genealogy of discursive transformations. There is little reason to believe why this persistence of the traces of traditional thought and practice should not also be the case within the context of Chinese discourse.

Postcolonialist Interpretations of Contemporary Chinese Art

For many other commentators, the national-cultural limits of contemporary Chinese art are far less clear. Since the late 1980s the production and reception of contemporary Chinese art has entered an international stage both through the inclusion of works of contemporary Chinese art in dedicated exhibitions and survey shows outside mainland China (including the now notorious Magiciens de la Terre at the Centre Pompidou in 1989 and the widely toured China's New Art, Post-1989) and through the emigration of numerous mainland Chinese artists in response to the renewed conservatism within mainland China following the Tiananmen killings of 1989. What is more, the sale of contemporary Chinese art can also be seen to be part of a general commoditization of Chinese culture by the international art market as part of globalization. The internationalization of contemporary Chinese art can thus be seen to have extended that art's "deconstructive" reach beyond the immediate geographical limits of mainland China to a far wider range of cultural, social, and economic contexts. Set against this background, there has been a tendency among many critics and scholars—and here I include Chinese artists and intellectuals such as Hou Hanru, Gao Minglu, Fei Dawei, Ai Weiwei, Feng Boyi, and Huang Yongping—to view contemporary Chinese art as a suitably indeterminate, culturally hybrid, focus for Western poststructuralist theory and in particular the critique of Western Orientalism/cultural imperialism associated with the terms *postcolonialism* and *Third Space*.

According to Edward Said, writing in his seminal text, *Orientalism*, historically the West has sought to construct a coherent sense of its own identity by casting the Orient as a subordinate "other"; one whose supposed characteristics stand in a negative relationship to those that the West imputes to itself and that the West has imposed on the Orient often violently through its colonialist and imperialist enterprises. As a result, the Orient can be understood to have become immersed in the logic of an asymmetrical cultural binarism so powerful that it has continued to be implicated in its own cultural subordination even after the withdrawal of Western countries from their former positions as imperial or colonial powers.[22] Against this background, the contemporary processes of globalization, which have seen the worldwide dissemination of what might be thought of as Western modernity, present themselves not only as a movement from a positive geographical position—the West—to a negative one—the East—but also as a belated reiteration of pre-existing cultural and social values. In his highly influential text *The Location of Culture,* Homi Bhabha contends that the West's historical structuration of its own identity and that of the non-Western "other" can be challenged on the grounds that both Western and non-Western identities have developed in actuality through various forms of cultural hybridization. This hybridization plays across, and deconstructs, the boundaries of the asymmetrical cultural binarism which—as Said indicates—can be understood to have been enforced by the West as part of the process of Orientalization. According to Bhabha, what is at stake here is an understanding of the self as something constructed through multiple discourses which often traverse neat conceptual divisions of race, gender, ethnicity, and sexuality and the asymmetrical power relations (relations of dominance) associated with those divisions, as well as the self's continual and problematic subordination to conventional notions of identity such as nationality (center and periphery), which, he argues, are imposed—often violently—by the prevailing logic of Western capitalism/modernity. For Bhabha, those with conspicuously hybrid identities—for example, the colonized, the marginalized, the displaced, the stateless, the multiracial, diasporas, sexual minorities, and women—provide an important critical foil to the repressive homogenizing tendencies of Western capitalism's/Modernism's "connective narrative." As Bhabha would have it, the unsettling potential of these hybridities lies in their capacity to create "imagined communities" beyond the limits of nationhood and its associated structuring of categorical identities—a notion now commonly associated with the term *Third Space*. According to poststructuralist theory, meaning is never made wholly present in any one place or at any one time. Instead it is strung out along an unfolding chain of linguistic signification (differing-deferring between signs) that continually leaves existing meanings open to reinterpretation. This suggests that the subject who speaks (the subject of enunciation) is, therefore, not a given presence reflected in language. Moreover, it also suggests that context—a present time and specific space—cannot be read mimetically from the content of a linguistic proposition; in other words, individual texts cannot be taken deductively as fragments of a greater contextual whole. Moreover, the *I* and the *You* (*I* and *other*) implicated in any linguistic proposition are no longer to be seen as fixed presences between which communication takes place. Instead they are to be viewed as being constantly mediated through language as an interstitial Third Space, always somewhere betwixt one and the other. By implication, this Third Space therefore renders all cultural meanings hybrid. As a result, cultural meaning can be understood as having no originary presence or essence (culture is not inherently original or pure) and as something that is continually open to linguistic recontextualization and re-motivation.[23]

One of the most prominent exponents of the use of such thinking in relation to the interpretation of contemporary Chinese art has been the internationally renowned curator and critic Hou Hanru, who, through numerous essays and conversations published in periodicals and exhibition catalogues, has consistently argued that while contemporary Chinese art involves an undeniable assimilation of Western cultural influences, that assimilation has taken place, of necessity, in relation to the particular (localized) circumstances of Chinese culture and society. As a consequence, Hou has averred, contemporary Chinese art can be understood to have replaced a concept of identity based on the traditional opposition between East and West with a deconstructive state of cultural "in-betweenness."[24]

As Hou would have it, as part of this deconstructive resistance to a dualistic conception of East-West identity some contemporary Chinese artists have developed "cultural strategies" that seek to make use of traditional Chinese practices whose perceived outcomes can be understood to have an affinity with those of cultural hybridity/Third Space, and which, therefore, serve to reinforce a deconstructive reorientation of "Western expectations of the oriental."[25] Among the practices cited by Hou in this regard are the ancient Chinese divinatory system associated with the *Yi Jing* (*The Book of Changes*), which, he indicates, "not only suggests a process of constant change in the universe, the duality and interconnectedness of necessity and chance, of the rational and irrational, culture and anticulture, but also a strategy to launch 'attacks' on the legitimacy of the West-centric monopoly in intellectual life,"[26] and the geomantic system associated with *Fengshui* (literally "Wind and Water"), whose emphasis on "the importance of respecting the world's natural state…is meant to help the constructed world harmonise with nature by indicating the correct locus for architectural and urban construction," thereby "presenting a liberating alternative to the dominant Western model of urbanization—as the voice of the Other in the current process of globalization."[27] It is therefore possible to interpret Hou's position as one that seeks to draw parallels between a traditional Chinese dependency upon the conceptual indeterminacy of "nonrationalist" (rationalist-irrationalist) dialectical thinking as a guide to individual and collective action (the striking of a "middle way") and the poststructuralist figuring of *différance,* whose performative enactment of a persistent deconstructive differing-deferring between linguistic signs has strongly informed postcolonialist theory and, in particular, Homi Bhabha's use of the terms "hybridity" and "Third Space."

Considered more comprehensively in relation to the deconstructive effects of cultural hybridity, contemporary Chinese art can thus be understood to resist a concept of identity based on the traditional opposition between East and West on three specific counts. First, as a cultural hybrid of Western and Chinese cultural influences, contemporary Chinese art can be viewed as an undecidable supplement both to Western Modernism/Postmodernism and China's vernacular artistic traditions, thereby problematizing the continued standing of both as supposedly discrete—spatially differentiated—cultural entities. Second, contemporary Chinese art's appropriation of Western Modernism and Postmodernism can be understood to involve a retroactive engagement with the traces of the Western avant-garde's own prior translations of traditional Chinese cultural thought and practice. Consider here, for example, Western Dada's assimilation of Buddhist thought and practice during the early years of the twentieth century as a critical response to the prevailing means-end rationality of modern life[28] as well as the inclusion of Daoist thinking within the curriculum of North American art schools throughout the twentieth century.[29] In light of both examples, it is possible to register a wider uncertainty about the sequential relationship between Western Modernism/Postmodernism and contemporary Chinese art that impinges on the standing of both as historically bounded—temporally distinct—phenomena; a point amply supplemented by Clarke's view that a straightforward (avant-garde) disavowal of the past has never been an adequate option in China's artistic modernity. Third, contemporary Chinese art's reworking of Western Modernism and Postmodernism is one that can be thought of as having significantly compounded existing Western postmodernist doubts over the existence of a categorical aesthetic. As the contemporary Chinese artist Huang Yongping has argued, the emergence of neo-Dadaist ("avant-garde") forms of anti-artistic practice in China since the mid-1980s can be viewed not just as an appropriation of the deconstructive practices of the Western avant-gardes, but in addition as a "modern renaissance" of Chinese Chan Buddhist techniques traditionally used to blur the conceptual boundary between art and nature.[30] Chinese contemporary avant-garde art is, Huang avers, thus open to interpretation as a historically cumulative, transcultural demonstration of the ontological uncertainty of art as an essential, culturally defined, category of being. The term "contemporary Chinese art" is thus revealed through this tripartite intervention to be something of a misnomer, representing as it does a phenomenon that is—to borrow a linguistic conceit from Fred Orton's reading of the work of Jasper Johns[31]—neither wholly "contemporary" nor "traditional," neither wholly "Chinese" nor "non-Chinese," and neither wholly "art" nor "non-art," but that is also simultaneously "contemporary" and "traditional," "Chinese" and "non-Chinese," and "art" and "non-art."

At the same time, postcolonialist thinking also draws our attention toward inconsistencies with regard to the imposition of conventional discursive limits confining our view of contemporary Chinese art to artists who were born and whose careers were first established within mainland China. Consider here, for example, the somewhat uncertain positioning of the artist Song Ling, who, even though he was a founding member of the Hangzhou-based avant-garde art group *Chi She* (The Pond Association) before moving to live and work in Australia at the end of the 1980s, is not widely considered to be a contemporary Chinese artist.[32] This is in sharp contrast to the standing of the internationally renowned artist Huang Yongping, who first established his career within mainland China as a leading member of the art group Xiamen Dada before moving to live and work in Paris, and whose accumulated work and writings are widely considered, not least because of the intervention of the influential Chinese curators and critics in exile Hou Hanru and Fei Dawei, to be one of the pillars of contemporary Chinese artistic practice.[33] There are, of course, issues here of the scale and quality of an individual's contribution. That said, the exclusion of the overall body of work produced by Song Ling from the category of contemporary Chinese art is in the main almost certainly due to the artist's long-term disengagement from the development of contemporary Chinese art since his emigration to Australia and, therefore, a resulting lack of *guanxi* (social connectedness) within the extended Chinese art world (including its highly influential manifestations in exile); crucially, Song was invited to participate in the

China/Avant-Garde exhibition of 1989 but was unable to do so, and since then has worked as a Chinese-Australian artist. In effect this has consigned Song's work as a member of *Chi She* to the footnotes of the accepted history of contemporary Chinese art. What is more, it has placed Song's work since leaving China somewhat arbitrarily beyond the perceived boundaries of that history.[34]

Inconsistencies of this sort are by no means limited to individuals. They can also be understood to extend to the standing of whole communities. Take here, for example, Taiwan, which has its own well-established contemporary avant-garde visual culture, whose inception predates that of mainland China but which is generally discussed in a highly qualified way as one of the sites of contemporary Chinese artistic production. The reasons for this qualification almost certainly grow out of Taiwan's position as a disputed geopolitical entity; a situation which not only detaches Taiwan from the prevailing socioeconomic and cultural conditions of mainland China, but which also renders any attempt to include Taiwanese contemporary art as part of the study of contemporary Chinese art an intensely political act on both sides of the Western-Chinese ideological divide. Also of note is the standing of contemporary artistic production among the wider Chinese diaspora. While these communities are themselves largely detached in practical terms from the material conditions prevailing in mainland China, they can nevertheless be understood to persist in upholding a distinctive sense of Chinese cultural identity and in some cases in asserting that identity as somehow more authentic than that of mainland China. Consequently it is possible to see the underlying violence of the limitations that currently inform the term contemporary Chinese art as foreclosing a wider consideration of the rather more complex relationship between Chinese cultural identity and international contemporary artistic practice.

Furthermore, it is important to consider here the pronounced diversity of regional approaches to contemporary Chinese art within the present borders of mainland China over the last quarter of a century. While mainland China maintains a notional identity as a unified republic under the governance of Beijing, and while that identity is strongly allied to the supposed homogeneity of a Han Chinese ethnic majority as well as the imposition since the 1950s of *putonghua* as a national *lingua franca,* China is nevertheless in actuality a patchwork of sometimes sharply divergent linguistic and cultural identities. What is more, during the last three decades there has been an unprecedented displacement of China's population as a result of Deng's economic reforms, which has seen the migration of countless numbers of people to major urban centers such as Beijing, Shanghai, Shenzhen, and Guangzhou in search of better economic prospects (an immense network of internal diasporas, if you will). As a result, mainland China's already complex state of cultural plurality has been significantly compounded by the comingling of previously remote communities. Arguably this increasingly complex (entropic) state of cultural plurality is something that has also been exhibited as part of the development of contemporary Chinese art since its inception during the late 1970s. Throughout the 1980s as part of the '85 New Wave there were numerous regional art groups that sought to make more or less explicit links between their work as artists and traditionally established cultural, social and geographical identities. Consider here, for example, the way in which the Harbin-based Northern Art Group sought to frame its conception of Rational Painting in terms of the coldness, openness, and vastness of China's northern landscapes as well as the historical influences within that locality of a traditionally lofty and detached Chinese Confucian aesthetic. Consider here also, by way of contrast, links made by members of Xiamen Dada and the Hangzhou-based group *Chi She* between their activities as artists in southeast China and China's southern school of Chan Buddhism. With the dispersal of many of the members of these groups through national and international travel as well as migration to more commercially/culturally attractive locations within China such as Shanghai and Beijing since the early 1990s, it is possible to see a mixing of cultural outlooks which parallels that found among mainland China's general population.

It is also important here to draw attention to the continuing and unjustifiable marginalization of women artists as part of the study of contemporary Chinese art. While there have been recent attempts to raise the profile of women artists in mainland China through group shows and public lectures both in Shanghai and Beijing,[35] there is nevertheless a continuing bias against the contribution of women artists that runs throughout the current discourse surrounding contemporary Chinese art. For evidence of this one need look no further than high-profile writings such as Karen Smith's *Nine Lives* and major retrospectives such as the recent '85 New-Wave exhibition at the Ullens Foundation in Beijing, which have significantly downplayed the contribution of women to the early development of contemporary art in mainland China. Consider here, by way of example, the work of Ka San, whose contribution to the work of the Northern Arts Group was conspicuous by its absence from the '85 New-Wave exhibition at the Ullens Foundation. Again, questions about the scale and quality of the contribution might be raised. However, as the art historian Linda Nochlin has pointed out, such questions can be understood to impose assumptions about the nature of "good" art to which women's art does not of necessity conform.[36] Consequently, it might be averred that the discursive limits currently imposed in relation to contemporary Chinese art serve not only to obscure the historical contribution of women artists but also to severely restrict our vision of their practice.

Finally, questions can also be raised about the perceived distinction between contemporary Chinese art and the parallel genres of *Guohua* and modern Chinese Art. It is important to note here that there are numerous artworks that can be seen to straddle the accepted division between contemporary Chinese art and *Guohua*/"Modern Chinese Art." Consider, for example, the contemporary Chinese artists Xu Bing, Song Dong, and Gu Wenda, who have all at one time or another used or made reference to traditional forms of Chinese calligraphy in their work. Consider also the respected academician Pan Gongkai, whose particular brand of *Guohua,* while ostensibly detached from any sort of critical engagement with modern life, nevertheless offers a highly ambitious reworking of the techniques and aesthetic concerns of traditional Chinese painting strongly reminiscent of large-scale abstract paintings made in the West.

Deconstructing Hou Hanru's "Postcolonialist" Reading of Contemporary Chinese Art

In light of all the above, it is, therefore, possible to discern two markedly differing positions in relation to the interpretation of contemporary Chinese art: one that seeks to make explicit links between contemporary Chinese art and Chinese national cultural identity as delimited by the present geographical boundaries of the People's Republic of China (which may stretch in principle, if not always in practice, to governmentally detached or semidetached territories such as Taiwan and Hong Kong–Macau); and another that seeks to look beyond these assumed geographical limitations toward a more complex—spatially extended—relationship between contemporary Chinese art and Chinese cultural identity. In the case of the former, the evident cultural hybridity of contemporary Chinese art can be seen to have been either significantly downplayed or overlooked altogether, while in the case of the latter it can be viewed as something of a *sine qua non*.

As the communications scholar Qing Cao has indicated in relation to Western representations of the Chinese "Other," it is possible to go further in this regard by interpreting these competing positions in relation to the Foucauldian concept of "discourse"; that is to say, in relation to discourse as that which "constructs the topic, defines and produces the object of knowledge, governs the way that a topic can be meaningfully reasoned about, defines an acceptable and intelligible way to talk or write about a topic, and restricts other ways of talking and writing about it."[37] According to this interpretative standpoint, representations of contemporary Chinese art can thus be understood to fall into two broad discursive categories: to one side, "reflectivist" views which interpret contemporary Chinese art as a mirroring or embodiment of definitive social and cultural truths; and to the other, "constructivist" views which conceive of contemporary Chinese art as complexly constructed in terms of its formative cultural influences and, therefore, as persistently open to renewed interpretation from differing spatiotemporal perspectives. In arriving at a manageable (culturally/politically agreeable) sense of the significance and/or function of contemporary Chinese art both of these positions (which are, of course, rather more variegated in their scope than the somewhat crude description offered here suggests) can thus be understood to have erected—to varying degrees—discursive boundaries that effectively repulse, exclude, negate, or marginalize the concerns of the other.

Seen from a specifically Chinese cultural point of view, this apparent divergence in interpretations of contemporary Chinese art is, however, not quite as clear-cut as it might first appear. As Clarke has indicated, since the early twentieth century China's engagement with outside cultural influences has continued to threaten an unacceptable loss of vernacular cultural identity. Consequently, while critics such as Hou Hanru have sought to embrace postcolonialism as a means of undermining Western cultural dominance, others within mainland China have openly resisted such thinking on the grounds that it involves an unquestioning assimilation of "Western(ized)" cultural values (even though, in practice, postcolonialism is far from being an exclusively Western preserve). Examples of this resistance within mainland China fall into two parts: first, nakedly essentialist arguments which see postcolonialist theory as an unacceptable attempt to undermine China's indigenous national cultural identity; and, second, less clearly defined points of view which seek to resist the orthodoxy of "Western(ized)" postcolonialism while seeking to arrive at some new, nonessentialist, form of cultural critique. Consider here, for example, in relation to the former a comment posted on the Internet by Professor Zhang Gan of Tsinghua University in Beijing which seeks to frame postcolonialist criticism of Chinese national cultural essentialism as an assertion of Western cultural imperialism;[38] and in relation to the latter the recent Guangzhou Triennial, Farewell to Post-Colonialism, whose multicultural curatorial team, Chang Tsong-sung (Hong Kong), Gao Shiming (Hangzhou), and Sarat Maharaj (London), explicitly set out to question the critical efficacy of postcolonialism as a way of framing contemporary art on the grounds that its once-heterodox critical attack on cultural homogeneity has now become an orthodoxy which demands new "Post-West" approaches to criticism.[39] It is therefore possible in relation to the second example, to discern the emergence of a third interpretative position that significantly problematizes the perceived distinction between "reflectivist" and "constructivist" views of contemporary Chinese art. Indeed, from a Chinese cultural point of view, with its continuing desire to uphold a distinctively Chinese sense of cultural identity in the face of modernity, it is difficult to imagine a situation in which one might choose a definitively "constructivist" view of contemporary Chinese art.

Arguably, this is the case even in relation to Hou's postcolonialist readings of contemporary Chinese art, which, despite their active espousal of deconstructive uncertainty, can, I would argue, be seen to have carried out an implicit reworking of postcolonialist theory along distinctly Chinese lines. Central to Hou's position is not only an apparent embracing of postcolonialist theory but, as previously indicated, the view that contemporary Chinese art's deconstructive resistance to Western Orientalism/cultural imperialism can be aligned successfully with the perceived outcome of traditional Chinese divinatory/geomantic practices associated with the *Yi Jing* and *Fengshui,* a position that, as previously indicated, effectively seeks to draw parallels between a traditional Chinese reliance upon "nonrationalist" (rationalist-irrationalist) dialectical thinking and the poststructuralist figuring of *differánce.* As a consequence, Hou's position can be understood to point toward Chinese cultural practices whose implications are consonant with, but historically "in advance" of, those related to a postcolonialist conception of cultural hybridity. Hou's alignment with postcolonialism is, therefore, far from being a straightforward eschewal of Chinese cultural tradition. Rather it is arguably a variation upon Paul Gilroy's notion of "anti-anti-essentialism";[40] that is to say, a doubly resistant combination of cultural hybridity as a refusal of Western Orientalism/cultural imperialism with a knowingly critical assertion of a localized, non-Western sense of cultural identity. Indeed, as Hou has argued, the reintroduction of *Fengshui* as cultural strategy should be viewed as "more of a political struggle than a simple nostalgic recovery of an Oriental tradition" and, therefore, as a "tentative fiction designed to deconstruct the dominance of the West."[41]

What should also be noted, however, is that Hou's alignment of contemporary Chinese art with traditional Chinese divinatory/geomantic practices associated with the *Yi Jing* and *Fengshui* is something of an intellectual conceit. On the face of it, Hou's line of argument is compelling, since contemporary Chinese art and traditional Chinese divinatory/geomantic practices associated with the *Yi Jing* and *Fengshui* can both be interpreted as bringing about a dynamic blurring of boundaries between supposedly different states of being: in the case of *Fengshui,* for example, the "constructed world" and "Nature." However, as Hou's writings also make clear, divinatory/geomantic practices associated with the *Yi Jing* and *Fengshui* have been conventionally understood within the context of traditional Chinese culture as pointing toward conceptual uncertainty as a basis for the "interconnectedness"[42] of differing states of being and, therefore, the possibility of a "harmonious relationship" between those differing states.[43] As such, traditional Chinese divinatory/geomantic practices associated with the *Yi Jing* and *Fengshui* can therefore be understood to enfold the notion of a persistent differing-deferring between differing states of being within a larger metaphysical schema explicitly resisted by the "Western(ized)" theory and practice of deconstruction.[44] Consequently, Hou's alignment of contemporary Chinese art and traditional Chinese divinatory/geomantic practices begins to look less like a straightforward affirmation of the critical value of conceptual uncertainty than an attempt to uphold that uncertainty as a potential source of stability in the face of encroaching disorder; a position consistent with historical attitudes toward modernism within mainland China since the early twentieth century, where there has been a constant, and unresolved, struggle to reconcile the disruptive assimilation of modernizing cultural influences from outside with a desire to uphold the supposed equilibrium of China's established cultural traditions. Indeed, As Hou himself has admitted, the seductive "glamour" of the present spectacle of modernity "can never hide the un-balance and fear of losing the self in front of a complicated and complex world."[45]

It is therefore possible to conclude that Hou's citing of traditional Chinese practices associated with the *Yi Jing* and *Fengshui* as a strategic resistance to Western Orientalism/cultural imperialism is a fundamentally contradictory one whose implicit, and somewhat paradoxical, recourse to the metaphysics of traditional Chinese thought inescapably brings into play notions of interaction and harmony running counter to conventional readings of postcolonialism as a critical foil to homogenizing conceptions of national cultural identity. Indeed, one might go further by arguing that Hou's implicit invocation of a nonrationalist Chinese dialectical metaphysics carries with it by historical association the persistent traces not only of a traditional Chinese belief in the superiority of an inherently "harmonious" Chinese culture (*wenhua*) over barbaric (incoherent) non-Chinese others, but also, in the exclusivity of the Chinese empire/civilization as "everything under heaven" (*tianxia*). A point reinforced by Hou's own assertion that while "real cultural hybridity is in our lives" the "East and West should remain an eternal pair of antagonists."[46]

At the beginning of his acclaimed work *Simulacra and Simulation,* the late Jean Baudrillard cites a fable of Jorge Luis Borges (*The Exactitude of Science*) about the ruination of a map coextensive with the actual territory of an empire to draw attention to what he would have us see as the precession of simulacra over reality; a precise, deconstructive inversion of the conceptual ordering of Borges' fable in which representation without any basis in reality (the "hyperreal") asserts itself in relation to the remains of classical, "reflectivist" mappings of the world.[47] In the case of Hou's "postcolonialist" reading of contemporary Chinese art, the order of Baudrillard's thinking would itself appear to have been thrown into a notional reverse. With Hou's "postcolonialist" reading of contemporary Chinese art, it is the traces of the metaphysical "reality" of empire which have begun to reassert themselves amid the deconstructive remappings of postcolonialism. This is not to negate outright Hou's "postcolonialist" readings of contemporary Chinese art as an intended resistance to Western Orientalism/cultural imperialism. Rather, it is to point out that this intended resistance involves inescapable slippages/reversals of meaning as part of an interpretative shift in the understanding of postcolonialist theory from one cultural context to another and, by extension, the persistence of cultural heterogeneity.

2

The Art World of Post-Deng China: Market, Globalization, and Cultural Nationalism

Meiqin Wang

A 2007 article in *The New York Times* on Chinese contemporary art by reporter David Barboza carries the intriguing title: "In China's New Revolution, Art Greets Capitalism."[1] This "New Revolution" is the precipitous increase in the price of works by a few contemporary Chinese artists in the international art market and the resulting "revolutionary" change in their economic status and lifestyle. In his article Barboza reports on a series of record-breaking auctions of Chinese contemporary art held by the world's biggest auction houses—Sotheby's and Christie's, in New York, London, and Hong Kong—over the preceding two years. As Barboza makes clear, accompanying the huge market success of their work, leading Chinese contemporary artists "have morphed into multi-millionaires who show up at exhibitions wearing Gucci and Ferragamo."[2]

The striking success of Chinese contemporary art in the international marketplace corresponds to the ever-booming scene of contemporary art in China. In recent years, new exhibitions, galleries, art spaces, and artists' studios have opened almost daily in big cities across China. So many things are going on at the same time within the Chinese contemporary art scene that visitors to one event often worry about missing other events of significance because of conflicting schedules.[3] In Beijing, famous art districts such as the 798 Factory and the Song Zhuang Artists Village are thriving. The 798 Factory is in northeast Beijing alongside the highway that connects the international airport to Beijing's city center. Located in the Dashanzi area (also known as Dashanzi Art District), the 798 Factory was designed by East German architects during the 1950s as a military ordnance factory for the Chinese government. Like many state-owned enterprises in China during the period of economic and social reform after 1978, the business of the factory declined and most of the warehouses and workshops were abandoned and opened up for alternative uses by whoever would pay the rent. Starting in 1995, artists attracted by the ample space and cheap rents began to set up studios in the 798 Factory. During the past seven years, the attraction of the 798 Factory has soared to an unprecedented level. By 2005, this refurbished concrete industrial complex housed around a hundred galleries, experimental and commercial, as well as studios used by artists from China, Germany, Britain, the U.S.A., Japan, and Singapore. The 798 Factory is now a mini-global art world, symptomatic of the accelerating speed of globalization.

Not all the excitement generated by the 798 district relates to the production and display of contemporary art. Beside artists' studios and galleries, there are graphic design companies, furniture stores, architecture companies, gift shops, bars, cafés, restaurants, and bookstores, most of which opened after 2002. The 798 Factory has become a business enclave for the newly established Chinese middle class to produce, seek out, and consume alternative, trendy urban culture. Drawn by the reputation of previous experimental spaces for contemporary art, an increasing number of commercial enterprises have been attracted to the 798 Factory. As consequence the 798 Factory now exhibits an overwhelming tendency toward commerciality. The development of the 798 Factory was driven initially by a small group of artists, who were the first to see the potential of the area and were among the first to leave as its commerciality grew.[4] The 798 Factory vividly illustrates the speed of commercialization in China—the main theme of Chinese society since the late 1970s—and its striking power to devour any avant-garde, experimental, or alternative art in China.

Regardless of the encroachment of commercial forces in

Beijing and elsewhere, most artists in China remain positive and forward looking, with a strongly held belief that they are living at the greatest moment ever in Chinese art history.[5] This attitude can be understood to have emerged as a consequence of the mixing of commercial and liberal approaches toward artistic production that the Chinese government has embraced since the mid-1980s. Chinese artists talk feverishly about the rapidly increasing purchasing power of rising domestic entrepreneurs with an interest in contemporary art. They are also excited about the recent emergence of official government support for contemporary art, evident in government-sponsored projects, domestic exhibitions, and international shows. "Globalization" and "internationalization" are now everyday words that emerge spontaneously in conversations about Chinese contemporary art. Newly established curators of contemporary art are often involved simultaneously in several exhibitions and fly about China for openings in different cities. Likewise, contemporary artists are racing to and from exhibitions in other parts of the country and across the world. One cannot help but think that they may be spending more time on travel, openings, festivals, and seminars than on making art.

The exuberant atmosphere that pervades art districts in China is comparable to that surrounding the soaring auction prices of Chinese contemporary art in the global marketplace. The landscape of the Chinese art world is undergoing rapid, extensive, and intensive transformation. But what are the underlying forces that have shaped the unparalleled development of contemporary art in China in recent years and that have brought to the surface all the excitement and anticipation now shared by Chinese contemporary artists? What is behind the breakdown of the relatively uniform art world constructed under Marxist-Maoist ideology within China from the late 1940s to the late 1970s and the subsequent emergence of a reformed art world informed by Deng Xiaoping's "Socialism with Chinese characteristics" in the 1980s and early 1990s?[6] Out of many disparate and interrelated factors, it is possible to pinpoint three primary forces. First of all, the internal marketization and commercialization of Chinese society has brought about a new wave of reform and transformation in the cultural world of China. The emergence and legitimization of the culture industry in China at the end of the twentieth century symbolized a new drive toward a commercial society, which is fundamentally changing the way art is made, viewed, and circulated in China. Second, globalization as a compelling force has reinforced the above-mentioned processes and at the same time has brought new complexity as well as opportunity, together with new information, new concepts, new media, and new materials into the Chinese art world. Third, as a way of responding to the encroachment of global culture and, importantly, as a strategy of maintaining and reinforcing authority over the entire society, the Chinese Communist Party has launched a broad movement of cultural nationalism, which also sees its immediate resonance in the Chinese art world.

Marketization, Culture Industry, and Art

Following the Reform and Opening Policy launched by Deng Xiaoping in 1978 and ever since the 1990s, the Chinese Communist Party has sought to construct China's national market economy ever more rapidly and extensively. The Party's eagerness and determination to create a wealthy, affluent society has been accompanied inevitably by social and cultural liberalization. The administrative strategy of China's government under the leadership of Deng Xiaoping was pragmatic. Its main concern was with practical rather than ideological matters, with great emphasis being placed on the economy. Deng's famous phrase "it does not matter if it is a black cat or white cat as long as it catches mice" vividly illustrates his pragmatic approach.[7] Under Deng's economic reform policy, the Chinese central government systematically gave autonomy to previously subordinate economic sectors, thus submitting them to market rule (i.e., the laws of supply and demand). People from every walk of life were encouraged to explore their imagination for creating marketable goods. Deng's famous "Southern Tour" and the ensuing official announcement of the market economy as a goal for further economic reform in 1992 gave additional impetus to the already growing economy and profoundly changed the social and cultural life of the Chinese people.[8]

The essential impact of Deng's economic reforms on the Chinese art world has been the emergence of market/private patronage of the arts, which has, in turn, functioned as a rival to established state patronage of artists and their artworks. During the Maoist period, artists were labeled as cultural workers and they worked for the Chinese Communist Party and the people. The state, the representative of the people, was their only patron. Because of the legislative denial of private property and trading, the practice of private art galleries, art dealers, and collectors was not allowed. Only state-owned museums and galleries were in operation, and they promoted art not for the personal aggrandizement of artists or the sale of their works, but to promulgate state ideology.[9] Individual artists did not sell their work. Actually there were no formal mechanisms for pricing and selling artwork. Artistic creativity was channeled exclusively in the service of the people, of public education, and for the construction of socialist China.

These conditions gradually changed after the implementation of Deng's Reform and Opening Policy, which relaxed firm centralized control over the economic sector within China and which led to the building up of diplomatic relationships with Western capitalist nations. In the early years of Deng's reforms, art dealers, primarily from Hong Kong, Taiwan, and parts of South and East Asia, came to China searching for paintings, mainly traditional ink-and-brush and realistic oil paintings.[10] Then, starting in the late 1980s, private art galleries emerged, scattered across a handful of big cities within mainland China. After 1992, many more private art galleries emerged and soon flourished across the country. Initially, most of these galleries were invested in by art dealers coming from Hong Kong and Western countries. With the growth of the market economy in China, many domestic entrepreneurs and businessmen also started to invest in art through the funding of private museums and galleries or by building up personal and corporate collections. Art fairs and auctions also appeared in major cities. Some of these private institutions dealt with or collected artworks that had not been accepted by official institutions, thereby opening up opportunities for young artists who did not want to follow the official path toward career growth and success.

New conflicts have inevitably emerged as China, steered by the force of the market economy, has moved rapidly to catch up with developed Western countries. In the cultural field, traditional ways were not readily abandoned, however. Traditional culture during the Maoist period was established according to the demands of the planned economy and was under a centralized administration. Within this system, culture was seen as a tool for ideological shaping and moral education. Other possible functions such as the critique of the state, trading, and consumption were denied, as were culture's role in contributing to the development of the economy in market terms. In order to counteract the influence of market in the cultural sphere, the authorities constantly issued official documents to regulate the increasingly diversified cultural production. In this way, the state attempted to keep hold of the initiative in producing culture. During the 1980s and early 1990s, many literary and cinematic artworks produced by individuals and organizations funded by the state criticized the corrupting power of the market. They warned of the consequences of a self-indulgent pursuit of material gain. Within the Chinese art world, the desire to keep a pure land free from "market contamination" was equally apparent, particularly in art criticism published in official media.[11] Official art institutions, including the Chinese Artists Association (CCA), worked hard to support art that corresponded to the government's ideological point of view. During the 1990s, the evaluation systems established under the guidelines of a centralized administration were still applied to test the merits of artists and their art.

This established way of controlling culture and art was transformed as a result of the extensive social and economic reforms that took place in post-Deng China. In particular, an awareness of international competition in the contemporary world motivated state administrators into seeking new potentials for Chinese culture. In a speech given on the occasion of the Seventh National Congress of The China Federation of Literary and Art Circles (CFLAC) in December 18, 2001, President Jiang Zemin gave a brief summary of the prevailing situation:

> The drastic competition of comprehensive national strength in today's world includes not only economic, scientific, and national defense strength, but also culture.... In general, the majority of developing countries are faced not only with severe challenges in their economic development but also cultural development. It is very important for developing

> countries to preserve and develop the excellent traditions of their native national cultures, largely promote national spirit, actively absorb the fine cultural fruits from other nations, and push the update of native culture. All these are crucial for the future and fate of the developing countries.[12]

Jiang then went on to reinforce his emphasis on the importance of developing Chinese culture:

> Striving to construct an advanced culture so it would exert a strong appeal to both Chinese people and people around the world is as important a strategic task for us to realize socialist modernization as endeavoring to develop an advanced productivity so China would join the list of developed countries. Only when we construct an advanced socialist culture that is national, scientific, and popular and that is oriented toward modernization, the whole world, and the future, can we meet our people's increasing demand in spiritual and cultural life; continue to improve people's ideological, moral, scientific, and cultural qualities; and provide right direction and powerful intelligent support for the development of the economy and advanced productivity.[13]

Before his speech at CFLAC's National Congress in 2001, Jiang had already delivered similar remarks on various occasions and had repeatedly emphasized the strategic significance of culture as part of contemporary world competition. Official intellectuals published theoretical analyses on this issue even earlier.[14] Under the guidelines set out by Jiang's remarks, Chinese cultural administrators began to seek ways to activate and encourage the development of Chinese culture. Following huge successes in the economic sphere after the formal launch of the market economy, China began to consider full-scale collaboration between market and culture. In 1998, the Ministry of Culture established a new public body, the Culture Industry Bureau, which was made responsible for investigating, researching, organizing, planning, and making policies for the cultural market. In October 2000, a state proposal was passed by the Fifth Plenum of the 15th Communist Party Central Committee that repeated the term "culture industry" at least six times in describing the state's policy for reforming cultural production and administration in China.[15] It proposed that the government should "perfect policies of culture industry, strengthen the construction and administration of the cultural market, and drive the development of the culture industry."[16] In addition, the official report of the Chinese Communist Party's 16th National Congress in 2002, clearly states that "In the current market economy, developing the culture industry is a very important way to achieve socialist cultural prosperity and to meet the spiritual and cultural needs of the people."[17]

Thus, "culture industry," a term that had already been circulated by Chinese state media, finally entered into the Chinese government's strategic and legal documents. Researches funded by the state on cultural industries in other countries confirmed the necessity and urgency to develop cultural industries in China. It was reported that in developed Western countries, such as the United States, Britain, and Canada, the production value created by the culture industry made up a significant portion of GDP and contributed greatly to an individual country's comprehensive national power. One report states:

> Through a developed culture industry, developed countries not only exert a subtle and extensive influence on consumers but also make a big profit out of it, and subsequently increase and strengthen the discrepancy of national power between them and the developing countries. Therefore, developing countries, including China, should see the development of culture industry as a significant strategy for strengthening comprehensive national power in contemporary time.... The culture industry is a mainstay of the economy in the twenty-first century.[18]

Another author discusses the political significance of the development of cultural industries in China:

> Along with the entry of China into the WTO, there is an influx of foreign capital and cultural products into our country, a higher level of international cultural exchanges

> and cooperation, and a more drastic scale of infiltration and conflict between different cultures. Provided with strong economic power and an advanced cultural dissemination system, Western developed countries have exported a large amount of spiritual and cultural products, political thoughts, and social values with the intention to occupy the cultural market in China. We should be aware of [the negative impact of] this process. In order to maintain the sovereignty and independence of Chinese culture, to defend against the negative influence of foreign culture, and especially to eliminate the [spiritual] contamination from [Western] decadent cultures, we should vigorously develop our own culture industry, enhance the market-competitive power of our cultural products, and increase the occupation ratio in the cultural market.[19]

Here, the development of cultural industries is heightened to an imperative and essential status; one directly related to national survival and independence. In recognizing the significant contribution that cultural industries could make to China's national economy and strength, the government turned that contribution into an integral part of the overall economic plan for China.

While it is possible to see the emergence of cultural industries taking place in China as early as 1979,[20] it is at the beginning of the twenty-first century that the state began its official promulgation of commercializing cultural production. This has also prompted the beginning of reform in current cultural systems.

At the present time, experts are still struggling with the definition, boundary, and evaluation of the cultural industries sector in China. However, it is abundantly clear that culture is now expected to perform an important role in the overall development of the national economy. As a result, the idea that culture is a kind of spiritual or mental commodity comparable to other market commodities has finally entered into the public mentality of Chinese society. Even though culture in China is still divided into "cultural undertakings" (meaning cultural products/activities produced by nonprofit institutions/organizations for performing public services) and "cultural industries" (meaning cultural products/activities produced by institutions/organizations for making profit), it is nevertheless possible to see that culture in China is no longer a domain reserved exclusively for political ideology, but one open to the ideology of the market, in other words, the rule of supply and demand.

In promoting the cultural industries sector, the Chinese central government has encouraged its subsidiary cultural institutions to handle their own financial responsibilities and to respond to the demands of the market directly. This tendency is seen at every level of government, prompting the continuing transformation of the cultural administrative system from a centralized and fixed system to a multiform and flexible one. Zhang Xinjian, the director of the Culture Industry Bureau at the Ministry of Culture, is reported to have stated:

> The healthy development of the culture industry will benefit from scientific and systematic governmental administration and from the comprehensive and in-depth art [cultural] popularization. Along with the entry into the WTO, Chinese government is committing itself to functional transformation from "producing culture" to "managing culture," following the rule of art [culture], applying macro-management to create a relaxing and active atmosphere for art [culture]; at the same time, the government is zealously attracting excellent foreign art [cultural] works in order to provide Chinese audiences with a wide range of artistic enjoyment that is multilayered and multifaceted.[21]

From this statement we can see that the Chinese government not only is seeking an effective administrative strategy corresponding to the demands of new cultural development but is also interested in promoting collaborative relationships with international cultural communities. Accompanying the currency of the term "cultural industry," the government has encouraged Chinese people to discover, manipulate, and create profitable cultural products for material returns. As an important sector of culture, art in China has been called upon to respond to the new function of culture and to contribute to the development of the new industry. Various official art institutions have started to take the developing cultural industry as one of their institutional tasks. In the constitution of the Chinese Artists Association passed in 2004, article 15 says: "[we] should strengthen intimate cooperation with relational governmental branches and other social sectors to develop the artistic undertakings of our country; [we] should develop the art culture industry, according to state policy." Here, theory has come, as is often the case, much later than actual practice. Nevertheless, this formal embracing of cultural industry by the art world is clearly intended to advance the marketization of the Chinese art world.[22]

In the context of cultural industry and its transformation in China, the institutional structure of the Chinese art world has also experienced new developments. Artists are no longer collective cultural workers, but individual market agents; as such, they have assumed much greater powers, rights, and relative freedom in how and for whom to create art.[23] They can choose to be a regular state-stipend receiver maintaining an official job at an official unit, or to be an independent artist relying entirely upon the market, or both.[24] At the same time, the increasing mobility of Chinese society and the flexibility of market operations allow artists to choose their place of residence. As a result, many choose to congregate in big cities such as Beijing, Shanghai, and Guangzhou. There, they come together in artists' villages or art districts and enjoy advantages such as the ability to stay up to date with the newest experiments and theories in the field, to be better informed of the newest market trends, and to be easily contacted by art dealers and curators.

Accompanying this greater economic flexibility and social mobility, a diverse and dynamic art scene has emerged within China. Making art is no longer an official task with limitations on content and style. Instead, a wide range of choices are open to artists. If Chinese artists wish to respond to the official call by producing works that express political allegiance or positive social messages, they are still able to do so. Artists can seek patronage and recognition within the official system through established channels such as art exhibitions organized by the CAA and its local branches, official art magazines, and public museums. If they decide to make art that responds directly to the market, they are now able to engage with a flourishing international art market for Chinese art. Some artists are even more flexible and create different works answering to both contexts. The previous simplistic view of art during the Maoist period—which centered on the idea that good/healthy art serves the revolutionary aims of the Chinese communist Party and reflects the view of the masses and that bad/harmful art includes abstraction, expressionism, and the depiction of the nude—has totally disappeared in today's Chinese society. Nudes, abstractions, and expressionist works have already been appreciated as proof of openness and are celebrated as new achievements in official art. Today, hardly anyone speaks of good art or bad art simply according to established criteria of style or content. When the term "good art" is used, it does not necessarily contain an imperative sense of political correctness, but likely refers to various kinds of art, ranging from art that serves to critically interrogate Chinese society and culture to art that simply attracts attention, evokes thought, and succeeds in the art market. Certainly, the government still maintains its restrictions on artistic production that could be perceived as undermining the integrity of the Party and occasionally it can be seen intervening in the public display of this type of art. Nonetheless, artists nowadays are dealing with a much more open and tolerant social environment as the normal condition of their artistic practices.

Globalization, Exhibitions, and Transnational Art

If marketization has internally transformed Chinese art, globalization can be understood to have accelerated that process. Within China, marketization and globalization are inextricably linked forces that augment and complement one another. With globalization as a driving force, marketization has created the conditions for China to modernize itself and catch up with the rest of the world. Globalization stimulates and speeds up the process of marketization and connects the Chinese domestic market to the international one. With the aid of far-reaching marketization and the growth of cultural industries, globalization is able to exert its maximum influence on Chinese society, particularly on individual artists. Leaving out the impact of globalization on the economic and social domains, it is possible to focus on how globalization has affected the practice and display of Chinese contemporary art in China and beyond, and how Chinese artists have utilized the opportunities presented to them through globalization. Within the Chinese art world, the impact and presence of globalization can be seen not only through the circulation of new concepts and practices but also through social and market relationships that connect Chinese artists directly with their international counterparts and the whole machinery of the international cultural industries sector, including curators, critics, dealers, galleries, art journals, auction houses, and museums.

Any study of contemporary art, no matter from which regional perspective, cannot afford to ignore the effects of globalization. The whole contemporary art world is under transformation, motivated by forces generated by globalization. In her book-length study of the relationship between globalization and contemporary art, art historian Charlotte Bydler points out that since the late 1980s and early 1990s, with the growing popularity of electronic communications and transnational travel and migration, globalization has prompted new approaches to making art and displaying art, new theories for explaining art and new perspectives for viewing art.[25] In particular, the international art world has witnessed an explosion of recurrent large-scale international art exhibitions.[26] These exhibitions are often devoted to creating a global platform for transnational cultural exchanges.[27] As an effective platform for engagement with transnational cultural, social, ethical, and political issues, they have attracted increasing attention as part of today's art world, and have acquired greater power in shaping and reshaping the structure of the global art world and its relationship to politics and society.[28] Accompanying the increasing prominence of recurrent large-scale exhibitions as part of the international art world, there has been the emergence of what Michael Brenson refers to as "the Curator's Moment."[29] During the past decade, independent curators have become increasingly important in both their social role and their sphere of influence. International curators no longer operate invisibly behind the artworks they curate, but have become, as Mari Carmen Rameires indicates, the "central player in the broader stage of global cultural politics."[30] The curator of contemporary art now travels internationally, stands in front of various exhibitions, giving meanings, raising issues, interpreting artworks, and promoting what is claimed to be important for today's art as well as for society. Curators and their exhibitions have now become the principal arbiters of meaning within the global art world; and it is in relation to these conditions that Chinese contemporary art has made its presence felt and acquired its transnational status.

Emerging during the early 1990s, what is now regarded as Chinese contemporary art took a very different direction from its predecessors, Chinese avant-garde art and earlier forms of unofficial art. Chinese avant-garde art started in the late 1970s and continued to flourish as a widespread art movement across China in the 1980s in the context of Deng's reform and opening policy. As part of intellectual discourse within post-Cultural Revolution China, the movement was characterized by collective activities and an enthusiastic belief in intellectual engagement with society and political reality. The movement's peak was marked by the China/Avant-Garde Exhibition at the China National Museum of Fine Arts in Beijing in February 1989. The exhibition was an ensemble of the work of art groups and individuals working throughout China. It presented a wide range of works in various media including installation, video, and performance.[31] The exhibition was later referred to by scholars as an announcement of the end of the avant-garde art movement within China, due to two forced closings of the exhibition by the Public Security Bureau as well as the large-scale ideological and practical suppression of avant-garde art practices—part of the conservative crackdown following the Tian'anmen protests of June 1989.[32] As a consequence of the official denunciation of the Tian'anmen protests as an antirevolutionary movement, vigorous and sincere debates among Chinese intellectuals, including their critical and introspective discourse on Chinese society, came to a sudden halt. Any practice related to avant-garde art was no longer allowed in public and reviews of that art, unless highly critical in tone, were not allowed to be published.[33] This tense political situation disheartened many intellectuals, including many artists, who were committed to social change and responsibility. It was at this point that many of the artists who had been engaged in the Chinese avant-garde art movement of the 1980s left China for settings more conducive to their artistic development.

During the early 1990s, former avant-garde artists who stayed in China and some newly emerging young artists developed a very different art, one that discontinued the intellectual and political edge that had characterized Chinese avant-garde art in the 1980s. This new approach was characterized strongly by a tendency toward satire, indifference, cynicism and self-denial broadly defined under the titles "Political Pop" and "Cynical Realism," the diversity of actual art practices not completely encompassed by those two terms. Denied access to the domestic Chinese audience through public exhibitions and publications, Chinese contemporary art of the early 1990s remained largely unknown in China. However, in 1993, "Political Pop" and "Cynical Realism," together with other types of contemporary art from China, were introduced to an international audience through the Venice Biennale, one of the world's most renowned international art exhibitions.[34] These two types of art were received with great enthusiasm in the West, appearing in publications such as *The New York Times* and *Art in America*. An international market for this type of Chinese art began to develop as a result. Since the early 1990s, contemporary Chinese artists have been invited to exhibit their works frequently in long- or newly-established international exhibitions, including the Venice Biennale, Documenta, Saõ Paulo Biennial, Johannesburg Biennale and Kwangju Biennale.

In addition, a number of exhibitions devoted entirely to Chinese contemporary art were staged outside China during the early 1990s, thereby raising the international profile of contemporary Chinese art still further. In 1993 a large exhibition titled "China's New Art: Post-1989," was organized by the Hong Kong Hanart T Z Gallery. After its initial showing in Hong Kong (which, at the time, was still under British administration), this exhibition subsequently traveled to London, Sidney, Chicago, Portland, and other sites until 1997.[35] Between 1997 and 1998, an exhibition titled "China!" which presented several new schools of art by thirty-one artists from China, traveled to the Kunstmuseum in Bonn, the Kunstlerhaus in Vienna, and the Singapore Art Museum.[36] In 1998, another important exhibition of Chinese contemporary art titled "Inside/Out: New Chinese Art," curated by Gao Minglu, was mounted by the Asia Society in New York and the San Francisco Museum of Modern Art, displaying works made by Chinese artists after 1989.[37] "Inside/Out:

New Chinese Art" toured New York, San Francisco, Mexico, Seattle, and several major Asian cities and brought the most up-to-date Chinese contemporary art into direct contact with the international art community. These shows, among others, significantly increased the international profile of Chinese contemporary art, contributing greatly to that art's acceptance as a commodity on the international art market and as a focus for international academic study.

Since its inception in the early 1990s, Chinese contemporary art has been associated with international exhibitions, through which it acquires significance as a new art emerging in the global art world. Chinese contemporary art has consolidated its identity and gained its reputation as part of a process of global cultural exchange, a process that not only involves art and culture but also implicates differing political and ideological outlooks. Global trends, such as multiculturalism, transnational markets, and economic and cultural globalization, have played as important a role in shaping the current status of Chinese contemporary art as the localized political situation in China. However, Chinese contemporary art has not developed exclusively in relation to exhibitions staged outside of mainland China. Since the early 1990s transnational exchange has also introduced the concept and the practice of independent curatorship in China. This coincides with the growing prominence of individualism in Chinese society as a necessary product of a growing commercial culture and the rise of "advertised life."[38] Before the 1990s, exhibitions in China were always organized by committees made up of various officials, in relation to which the collective rather than the individual was valued. Motivated by the official call during the 1990s in Chinese society to "let China go to the world, let the world come to China," even greater efforts were devoted to improving the investment environment in order to attract more foreign capital and at the same time to raise the standard of production to meet the needs of the international market.[39] As part of a public call to be global and to participate in internationally based projects, competition was pursued in various areas of Chinese public life, including sports, science, technology, economics, and culture. Catching up with the newest practices in the international art world became an open desire. Contemporary artists and critics, who lacked public appreciation and institutional support in China, became eager to introduce the international art world to China as a way of sustaining their own existence.

In the effort to build up close or parallel connections with the international art world, independent curators (most of whom were originally art critics) have emerged within China. These independent curators have gradually asserted their position as agents of change in relation to the transformation of the Chinese art world. They have worked as intermediaries between the Chinese art world and international sponsors (entrepreneurs in many cases), artists, media, and government officials. As a result of their efforts, many short-term exhibitions have been staged through which contemporary art in China has maintained its continuity and vitality. Notable examples of such exhibitions include "The Traces of Existence," curated by Feng Boyi in January 1998 (in a suburban warehouse, Beijing), "It's Me!—An Aspect of Art Development in the 1990s," curated by Leng Lin in November 1998 (in the Workers' Cultural Palace, Beijing), "Beauty Like Materialism," curated by Zhu Qi in April 1999 (in the Art Gallery of East China Normal University, Shanghai), "Art for Sale," curated by Xu Zhen and Yang Zhenzhong in 1999 (in Shanghai Plaza, Shanghai), "Human—Animal," curated by Gu Zhenqing in 2000 (in Qingliangshan Park, Nanjing), and "Fuck off—Uncooperative Stance," curated by Ai Weiwei and Feng Boyi in 2000 (in Eastlink Gallery, Shanghai).[40]

Some of the exhibitions organized by newly established independent curators within China have been very controversial in their themes and in the form of the artworks on display. For example, in the catalogue accompanying the exhibition "Fuck off," photographic representations of artworks used living human bodies, stillborn fetuses, parts of corpses, and live animals to address themes such as sex, death, violence, politics, and power.[41] These exhibitions often had very limited circulation among small domestic audiences and were often closed by governmental authorities or received furious public criticism. Nevertheless, the exhibitions in question received a great deal of critical attention and aroused significant public discussion via informal and underground channels of distribution. Indeed, the identification of the exhibitions with notions of being underground or unofficial drew strong international attention. Curator Feng Boyi provides a vivid description of this situation:

> Banned from exhibiting their works publicly, the artists had to invite *Quanneiren* [people within the circle] to visit their shows that were held in basements, which made the shows seem mysterious. The more mysterious they seemed, the more foreign reporters came, which brought suspicious policemen lingering around. And the police presence would attract even more foreign reporters, thus resulting in art events, which would then draw more attention and coverage from the international media.[42]

This is an illustration of the complex relationship between Chinese artists and their non-Chinese audiences. International dealers, curators, and critics who travel around China seeking new trends and sensibilities in Chinese art have tended to sympathize automatically with artists participating in underground exhibitions and have tried, with greater enthusiasm, to introduce them to the global art world. As a result, many underground artists have gained considerable reputations within the international art scene and have benefited from the consequent development of a market for their art outside of China; so much so, in fact, that they have been able to rely totally on the international art market and ignore negative reception of their work in China. In developing their careers, these artists have taken the path of "going global," moving from the Chinese underground to the international mainstream.

The development of Chinese contemporary art cannot be separated from the differing contexts, international and domestic, that have promoted, nurtured, and conditioned its overall profile. Gao Minglu has argued that Chinese contemporary art was brought into the international arena by the rapid economic globalization that ensued after the Cold War.[43] It could also be argued that the globalization of contemporary art exhibitions and the art market has greatly motivated the development of contemporary art in China. With the anticipation of going global and nurtured by the international art world, Chinese contemporary art was able to develop into a prominent force before entering the cultural mainstream in China at the beginning of the twenty-first century.

Cultural Nationalism and the Pulling Back of Chinese Contemporary Art

It may seem strange to talk about cultural nationalism right after a discussion of the overwhelming impact of globalization on the Chinese art world. However, this is exactly what has happened in contemporary China, where originally oppositional forces—whether they be from West or East, past or present—have been managed to work together for either ideological or pragmatic purposes. Just like the coexistence of a planned and market economy, the seemingly opposing forces of cultural nationalism and globalization have become reciprocal trends within China. Nationalistic projects with intentions to seek and present the uniqueness of Chinese culture and civilization, to assert past glories, and to amplify present achievements go hand in hand with international projects that aim to present China as an open and modern nation, to de-emphasize cultural and political differences, and to package China for acceptance into global systems. The revival of centuries-old Confucianism and the search for the authentic Chinese spirit are trends that were seen as complementary to the huge efforts mobilized to meet the standards for entering into the WTO and to be the host of the Olympic Games in 2008. In this context, nationalism is seen as a way to circumscribe and practice globalization, while globalization is used to evoke and manipulate the sentiment of nationalism. The two terms have been promoted equally by the Chinese government in post-Deng Chinese society.[44] Their connection is only one aspect of the complexity of today's economic, social, and cultural conditions within China. Cultural nationalism, like marketization and globalization, has played an important role in the overall transformation of the Chinese art world. It essentially brings unofficial contemporary art into the scope of official art while challenging the definition of the art establishment in China.

Accompanying China's rapid economic growth and greater accessibility to the rest of the world, nationalism has gained a new appeal in many aspects of Chinese social life. The state, intellectuals who keep themselves in line with state ideology, and intellectuals who have been critical of the state all embrace nationalism as a societal necessity in order to ensure China's further development in the globalized era. Various discussions on nationalism have been organized and promoted, and have generated widespread responses within Chinese society. Political scientist Gunter Schubert has summarized this tendency:

> Nationalism is definitely a "hot" issue in present-day China. Government officials, party cadres, intellectuals of both regime-critical and regime-supporting camps, cultural conservatives, liberals, dissidents, and young entrepreneurs with populist appeal all take part in this ongoing debate.[45]

As indicated by numerous Chinese scholars, from the state's point of view the revival of nationalism is a necessary strategy for the Chinese Communist Party (CCP) to deal with problems brought about by economic reform and opening up to the outside world.[46] The Marxist-Maoist ideology which supported the founding and the consolidation of the People's Republic of China in the past is gradually losing its appeal in contemporary China. The CCP is facing an urgent task of setting up a new central ideology for pulling together people of different racial backgrounds and social status. In this particular historical moment, cultural nationalism has become a useful ideology that can help the CCP to maintain its authority in China. Professor Guo Yingjie argues:

> Having shifted away from its traditional Marxist-Maoist basis of legitimization, the CCP is compelled to reposition itself in relation to the "people" and "nation." In essence, this is the main thrust of Jiang Zemin's recent "theory of three representatives." As state nationalism is embraced as a supplement ideology, it has opened up considerable space for cultural nationalism and enabled it to articulate its own project under the protection of the official patriotic rhetoric.[47]

As Guo suggests, in recent years the party has busied itself formulating new theory in response to new situations. In 2000, the Chinese president Jiang Zeming put forward the theory of "Three Representatives."[48] Here, there is no longer political focus solely on workers, peasants, and soldiers, as was the case during the Maoist period, but instead on "the most extended Chinese people." Moreover, the centrality of class struggle to party ideology is replaced by notions of "Chinese advanced culture" and "Chinese advanced productivity."[49] The Sixteenth National Congress passed this theory as a state proposal in 2002 and it was formally added into the constitution of the PRC in 2004. The ongoing practice of economic reform has greatly changed the structure of the social order within China. The so-called masters of socialist China, the workers and peasants, whom the CCP claimed to represent, used, in principle at least, to be the dominant forces. During the past two decades, however, they have been displaced by newly emerging business, technical, and intellectual classes. These newly established classes assert an increasingly significant influence on Chinese society, which the CCP cannot afford to ignore. As a consequence, the "Chinese people" and "Chinese nation," two terms with open meanings, have been used frequently in all kinds of government speeches.

Cultural nationalism has become an effective ideology for pulling together a Chinese populace disappointed with the ideals of communism.[50] In order to legitimize itself culturally, the CCP has spent great efforts positioning itself as the inheritor and promoter of Chinese traditional culture.[51] The energetic promotion of studies on Confucianism and other aspects of ancient Chinese thought are good cases in point.[52] Since the mid-1990s, Confucius has regained great popularity within Chinese society.[53] The government has supported many projects whose aim is to articulate the philosophy of Confucius and its applicability within contemporary China. Many statues have been erected in Chinese universities to honor this ancient thinker, educator, and philosopher. The Chinese government has also set up forward-looking programs which are designed to appeal to all Chinese people and to promote the necessity of a Chinese way of developing culture as a contribution to the overall power of China.

This state-supported cultural nationalism has far-reaching influence among differing strata of Chinese society. It coincides with nationalistic sentiments circulating among intellectuals, entrepreneurs, and the public who feel resentment about the influence of western cultures, commodities, and social values on Chinese society as part of globalization.[54] The state's call to find a Chinese way of developing contemporary culture appeals strongly to these groups. They see the pursuit of national identity and cultural autonomy as a way to counterbalance the overwhelming impact of western cultures on Chinese society since the 1980s.[55] They argue that China, as a booming country in the new century, should create its own brand of contemporary culture comparable to that of the country's glorious past. And they have called for governmental and public efforts to develop national culture and arts in order to enhance national self-esteem and self-confidence.[56] It is therefore possible to see a great degree of collaboration between the Chinese government and the Chinese people, who might not otherwise agree with the CCP's political agendas. In short, cultural nationalism has become a highly influential ideology within contemporary China.

Within the Chinese art world, nothing has benefited more from a resurgent Chinese cultural nationalism than contemporary art. In 2004, the local government of Tongzhou district erected a billboard at an intersection on the way to Song Zhuang Artist Village in the eastern suburb of Beijing (fig. 1). The billboard, which carried Chinese and English texts (the bilingual sign is a very new and popular trend in China), read:

> **Welcome to**
> **[Song Village] Chinese Contemporary Artist Community**
> *A village that determines the status of Chinese contemporary art in the world*
>
> Just as Barbizon in France, the East Village in USA, Dachau and Worpswede in Germany, Song Village in Beijing, China has attracted good concerns from domestic and international circles of art and cultures due to the collection of numerous artists and enormously active artistic atmosphere. As the main body of Chinese contemporary artist community, Song Village will represent the status of Chinese contemporary art in the world.

Song Zhuang Artist Village is situated in an area on Beijing's eastern outskirts where there is convenient public transportation to downtown Beijing, inexpensive housing, and low living costs. It first began to attract artists, who came to rent local peasant houses as their living quarters or studios, in 1993. In 1995, increasing numbers of artists began to move in when the artists' colony Yuan Ming Yuan [the Winter Palace of Qing Dynasty] was banned and its residents dispersed by the government. By the summer of 2005, there were more than two hundred artists living in ordinary detached peasant houses in the Village, not including those involved in other cultural professions. The village has become a place where artists, critics, musicians, movie producers and freelance writers congregate to experience a kind of self-imposed vagrant life, free from any institutional affiliation and conventional moral restraints. At the same time, it is also a place where foreign curators and art dealers have come to search for new Chinese art in recent years.[57]

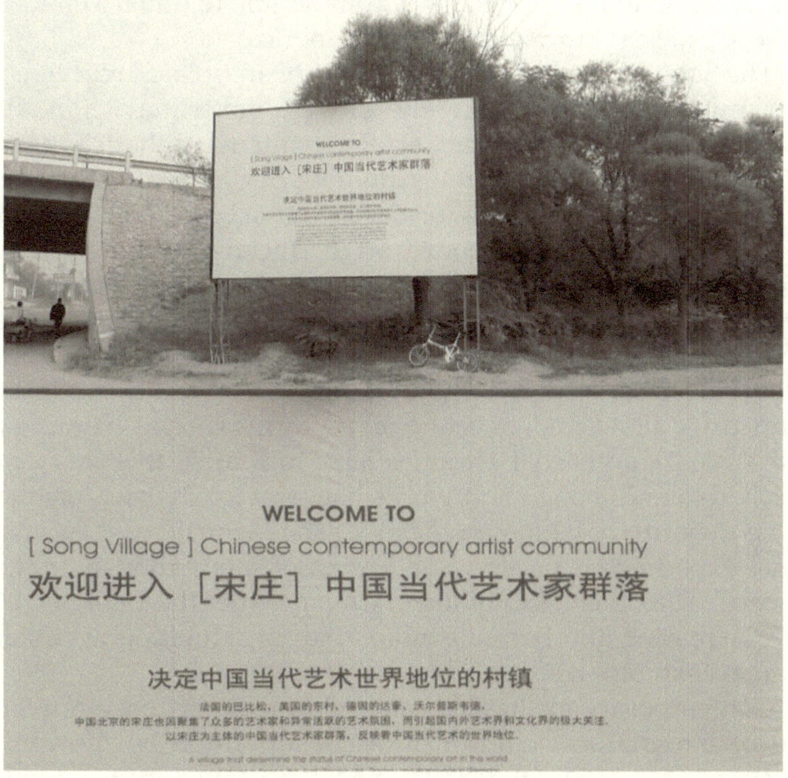

Figure 1. The billboard on the road to Song Village titled "Welcome to [Song Village] Chinese Contemporary Artist Community" (source: photo by Yu Jiantao, an artist resident in the Song Zhuang Artist Village)

The local government billboard conveys an important message concerning the current official perception of contemporary art and artists in China. A few years ago, vagrant artists who did not have an affiliation to any officially recognized unit were regarded by the authorities as a potential threat to the stability of Chinese society and their collective places of residences were thought of as problematic spaces. The government tended to adopt a suspicious and vigilant attitude toward such artists and their activities. The first artist village in Beijing was closed down by government officials in 1995; another, called East Village, had the same fate. In 2004, however, the government legitimized the Song Zhuang Artists Village by approving the official road sign marking its existence (fig. 1). Moreover, wording on the billboard exhibits a bold and nationalistic tone, describing the village as comparable to other well-known artist colonies in Europe and North America.

The Song Zhuang Artists Village is not an isolated case. It is one of many examples that show the Chinese government's modified strategy toward contemporary art. This shift in emphasis is particularly notable in relation to the exhibiting of Chinese contemporary art. Starting in 2000, the authorities in China began to lift their ban on the showing of contemporary art in official government venues. The Third Shanghai Biennale in 2000, which was sponsored by the Cultural Ministry of China and the Shanghai Municipal Government, can be seen as the first instance of this lifting.[58] The range of exhibited works included photographs, video works, and installation works, alongside conventional art forms such as painting and sculpture. As a number of critics have indicated, this was a huge step; video and installation works had previously been anathema to the majority of Chinese officials.[59] The biennale was an institutional experiment, the first application of international curatorial practice to an official exhibition in China.[60] After the Shanghai Biennale, increasing numbers of similar kinds of exhibition were staged in public exhibition spaces across China.

Contemporary art has also started to make its presence felt as part of international cultural projects supported by the Chinese government. In 2001, the Chinese Ministry of Culture assembled an exhibition of Chinese contemporary art titled "Living in Time," which was staged in Berlin as part of the China Festival during the city's Asia-Pacific Week. The exhibition was curated by Fan Di'an (a Chinese official who has achieved public prominence in recent years through his involvement in the staging of contemporary art exhibitions) and Hou Hanru, alongside the German curator Gabriele Knapstein. This was the first time Chinese authorities had organized an overseas exhibition that included contemporary art.[61] In the following year, the first Guangzhou Triennial opened at the Guangdong Museum of Art in Guangzhou. The triennial was a retrospective exhibition of underground Chinese art of the 1990s.[62] Then, in 2003, the government assembled China's first national pavilion at the Venice Biennale, choosing exclusively works of contemporary art for the pavilion.[63] A little later that year, the Chinese authorities assembled another large exhibition titled "Alors, La Chine?" [Well, What about China?], which took place as part of the China Year staged by the French government. Curated by Fan Di'an in collaboration with two French curators, the exhibition included a variety of artworks using traditional and contemporary modes of production. Through a series of exhibitions, the Chinese authorities have shown a positive and supportive stance toward independent contemporary art, including it as part of the presentation of officially supported contemporary Chinese art. As a result, the status of contemporary art in China has changed significantly in just a few years. Once an entirely underground phenomenon banned from being shown in public, Chinese contemporary art is now officially sanctioned for national and international exhibition.

What motivated the authorities in China not only to relax previous constraints but also to put considerable financial resources into supporting and promoting Chinese contemporary art? China's increasing openness to outside cultural influences, its continuing economic modernization, and the CCP's adoption of a new post-Maoist ideological strategy have all, undoubtedly, played a part in influencing this shift. In addition, however, it could also be seen as a response to surging nationalistic sentiment and the call for pulling back Chinese contemporary art. The idea of "pulling back Chinese contemporary art" has emerged as a counterbalance to the tendency of most Chinese contemporary artists to seek recognition and sponsorship within the international art world while their art went largely unrecognized in China.[64]

On October 20, 2004, at an International Academic Forum hosted by the Chinese National Museum of Fine Arts, director Fen Yuan announced that the Museum would invest 250 million RMB in artworks created by Chinese artists during the twentieth century within the next five years.[65] According to Fen, the funding was to be used to stem the flow of good Chinese artworks overseas.[66] This is almost certainly the biggest budget the Chinese government has ever invested in Chinese art of the 20th century. During the period of China's state-planned economy before the 1980s, collections in state-run museums often came at very low cost. With a rising market for Chinese art outside mainland China in recent years, increasing numbers of artists have sold their works to collectors and museums in Hong Kong, Taiwan, and countries outside China. Concerned scholars have argued that this poses a serious problem for future research into Chinese art. As a consequence, there have been calls for the setting up of domestic collections of Chinese contemporary art and for generous state investment.

Shanghai Gallery of Art, a private gallery in Shanghai, has staged a series of exhibitions showcasing the work of expatriate Chinese artists such as Xu Bing, Huang Yongping, Chen Zhen, and Yan Peiming. In August 2004, the gallery held Xu Bing's solo exhibition "Tobacco Project: Shanghai," a work that traces the history of the tobacco industry in Shanghai (fig. 2). It was the first time Xu's work had been shown in China since he moved to the United States in 1989.[67] According to the organizers, the aim of this series of exhibitions was to "pull back" Chinese contemporary art, making internationally well-known artists and their works more familiar to audiences in China.[68] In an article titled "Thinking of Pulling Back Chinese Contemporary Art," the critic and curator Pi Li discussed how he was invested in a similar idea by organizing exhibitions that would present artworks authentically—not fictionally for the purpose of satisfying an internationally fabricated image of China—as well as addressing the contemporary context of Chinese society.[69] As a consequence, Chinese artists have developed an increasingly positive attitude toward the reception of contemporary art within China. Consider here, for example, Yin Kun, a resident artist of the Song Zhuang Artists Village, who during an interview professed eagerness to open his first retrospective exhibition in China.[70] Sponsored by an art gallery owned by a Singapore art dealer, the exhibition was scheduled to open in Beijing before touring to Singapore and elsewhere. Yin emphasized that it was more meaningful to have Chinese people as the first audience for his work.[71] This is markedly different from the situation in China a few years ago, when Chinese artists tended to seek exposure for their work outside China.

It would appear that official institutions, private art galleries, and critics within China have begun to share in a unified vision, one that looks toward the pulling back of Chinese contemporary art for reasons of political ideology, national interest, institutional reputation, marketing strategy, and cultural critique. What is more, it is possible to see rising cultural nationalism as the fundamental motivation that makes this shared vision practicable and sensible. Riding the rising wave of cultural nationalism, contemporary art in China has finally achieved positive status within Chinese soci-

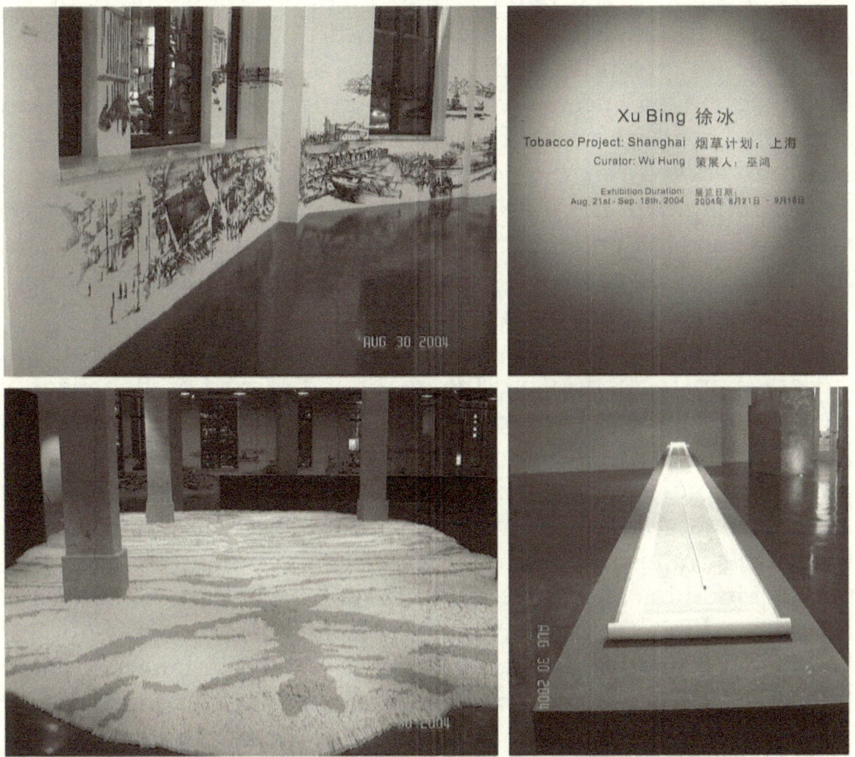

Figure 2. Xu Bing, *Tobacco Project: Shanghai,* 2004, installation (source: author)

ety. As such, the history of contemporary art in China as an underground phenomenon opposed to official art has come to an end.

Conclusion

From a sociopolitical and economic perspective, Post-Deng China has continued to pursue most of the established elements of Deng's market reform policy. What is new however are developments such as the increasing impact of globalization, the legitimizing of contemporary cultural practice and heavy leanings toward cultural nationalism, all of which can be seen as rational developments as China moves ahead following the road conceived by Deng. It is clear that marketization has been chiefly responsible for the current dynamism of Chinese society. The state sees the market economy as an effective mechanism to generate the kind of power that it needs and that it can harness, and therefore spares no efforts in promoting it. Official artists enthusiastically embrace the market not only for personal profit but also as an expression of their ideological allegiances. Avant-garde artists have, for their part, attempted to break away from state ideological control in order to secure freedom of expression. Nevertheless, many have ended up collaborating with the state to promote a market orientation for the arts in China.[72] Contemporary artists active since the 1990s have relied on the free market, especially the international marketplace, to sustain their development.

The cumulative effects of continuous economic, social, and cultural transformation and the increasing impact of globalization have greatly changed the social structure of the Chinese art world. It now operates in a different way, exhibiting a dynamism that was unseen before. A significant difference is that official organs such as the Chinese Artists Association are no longer the only players within the Chinese art world. This has brought many changes to official art in China and its relationship with other parties. As Joy Annamma and John Sherry have argued in their study of how the value of art is framed by the contemporary Chinese art market, "since the mid-1990s, the framing process has been either an independent, collaborative, or collusive one between artists and the state and between China and the West."[73] This describes precisely how the new social relationship among artists of different camps—official, unofficial, underground, independent, and international—now operates within China. The conflict between official and avant-garde art of the 1980s and underground art of the 1990s has been absorbed into a new ideology that combines the desires of being global, marketable, and nationalistic all at once.

The terms "unofficial" and "underground," which were used to refer to art outside the official political system within China during the 1980s and 1990s, have lost their historical relevance. As Meg Maggio, the director the Courtyard Gallery, an established contemporary art gallery in Beijing, and a resident of China for almost 20 years, has commented recently:

> The once underground Chinese contemporary art scene has moved well above ground. It is not only widely exhibited internationally, but is also increasingly embraced by Chinese officialdom. "Avant-garde" may no longer be the best term to describe what is happening in today's Chinese contemporary art scene. Whether one likes it or not, the hue and cry of the market is heard by all, and nearly everyone has joined the race to art world fame and fortune.[74]

In this context a new term, "un-unofficial art," has emerged, reflecting awareness among some critics and curators of the changing nature of avant-garde or underground art within China.[75] Regardless of this shift in terminology, it is clear that the Chinese art world has never been more dynamic, diverse, and spectacular, embracing at once global and national inclinations.

3

The International Identity of Chinese Art: Theoretical Debates on Chinese Contemporary Art in the 1990s

Yiyang Shao

The end of the Cold War contributed to a unification of differing political systems around the world. As one of the most rapidly changing regions in the world, China gained international attention both economically and politically as part of this unification. During the 1990s, Chinese avant-garde art was included in numerous international art exhibitions that promised the hybridity of cross-national collaboration. Among the most prominent of these international exhibitions was the 48th Venice Biennale, which took place in 1999. It featured the work of twenty artists from mainland China, the largest number of works from any nation that participated in the Biennale.

However, the West's recognition of Chinese contemporary art had no legitimacy domestically within the PRC, since China had not set up its own official national pavilion in Venice. This international recognition without Chinese internal support coincided with the increasing independence of Chinese contemporary art from international modes of production and art discourses as well as its increasing dependence on external sites of display and external sources of financial support.[1]

During the early 1990s, artworks identified with the movements known as Political Pop and Cynical Realism were exhibited internationally as exemplars of Chinese avant-garde art for the first time. Major international exhibitions of the early 1990s that showcased examples of Political pop and Cynical Realism include two held in 1993: "China's New Art Post-'89" at the Hanart Gallery in Hong Kong and "China Avant-Garde" exhibition in Berlin; as well as three staged during the following year: "Mao Goes Pop" in Sydney (a restaging of "China's New Art Post-'89"), the section "Passaggio ad Orient" of the Venice Biennale, and the 22nd São Paolo Biennale. In all of these exhibitions, Chinese contemporary art was presented as a focus for political rebellion against established authority within China.

"Political Pop" and "Cynical Realism," terms that attracted tremendous attention from the international art world, had been used internationally since the early 1990s to signify paintings and sculptures involving the ironic appropriation of socialist propaganda icons often juxtaposed with symbols of Western consumerism. The cynical realist artist Fang Lijun, for example, painted portraits of himself and his friends in the midst of executing giant yawns. Fang also created his own unique lexicon of symbols based on what might be termed "bald cynicism." Another important cynical realist painter, Liu Wei, created an irreverently cynical pictorial language centered on a series of distorted family portraits, using his own playful vocabulary to render ridiculous the solemn postures of army cadres and even the poses of his own family members. Both of their works, particularly the bizarre portraits of soldiers and war heroes produced by Liu, illustrate the world of the *Liumang* (rogue). Fang sums up their common view as follows:

> Only a stupid bastard would allow himself to be cheated time and time again. We would rather be called the lost, bored, climacteric, rogues and confused than be cheated again. Don't try any old tricks on us, for all dogma will be thoroughly questioned, negated and thrown into the rubbish bin.[2]

According to the critic Li Xianting, Political Pop and Cynical Realism are characterized by "an immersion in popular culture and a de-constructionist approach." In Li's view, the artists made cynical images "based on political propaganda of the Maoist period" as a "comment on a society in which they no longer had any faith."[3]

The "attitude of malaise adopted by the Cynical Realist artists" was moreover, argues Li, "their means of expressing their rejection of the idealism and heroism of the 1980s movements, and particularly of the '85 New-Wave."[4]

"Zhengzhi Bopo" (Political Pop) combines political themes associated with the Cultural Revolution and the formal charactersistics of American Pop Art. Li Xianting, again, provides a critical frame of reference for this movement:

> The nucleus of the Political Pop movement consists of artists from the '85 New-Wave movement who have given up the serious metaphysical concerns of their earlier work and have instead adopted a de-constructionist approach matched to a Pop technique, to execute works of comic satire which illustrate their view of influential political figures, particularly Mao, and major political events.[5]

Political Pop tends to borrow a whole range of images from the Cultural Revolution era. Stylistically, it shares the decorative effects of "red, bright, and shining," which are regarded as the basic aesthetic principles for public art produced during the Cultural Revolution. The key proponent of Political Pop, Wang Guangyi, began his *Great Criticism* series in 1990, in which he employed slogans from the big character posters and propaganda paintings of the Cultural Revolution juxtaposed with images of popular Western consumer products such as Coca-Cola. Yu Youhan's and Li Shan's respective "Mao series" followed the basic principles of Maoist art, using folk art elements such as a bright palette, reminiscent of traditional peasant New Year's pictures. Yu Youhan's *Chairman Mao Talking with the Peasants of Shaoshan* is a typical example. Yu appropriated a famous 1940s photograph of Mao taken with a family of cheerfully smiling peasants in his hometown village of *shaoshan,* and manipulated it with brightly patterned pop color, which recalled the decorative style of Chinese folk art. The simulated naïve language used by Yu satirized this important Maoist propaganda image and the whole of Mao's socialist realist art policy. Li Shan's *Rouge* Series, which he started in the late 1980s, plays directly with Mao's image in a style highly reminiscent of the flattened design of political posters during the time of the Cultural Revolution.

Li Xianting believes that the characteristic elements of Political Pop and Cynical Realism are in many ways interchangeable and overlapping, both of them being the results of consumerist culture. He comments, "In a sense, 'Mao Fever' and Political Pop are alike in that there is inherent in both the use of past icons or 'gods' to criticize, or in the case of the latter, to satirize, current reality."[6] Whether it be Cynical Realism's depiction of "*popi*" (the rogue), or Political Pop's use of consumer images and its toying with political images, the underlying trend was to express a political position, even when the work had no direct relationship with politics. Roguish humour and political irreverence were displayed in much of the work.

Soon after the first major exhibition dedicated to Political Pop and Cynical Realism, organized by the Hanart TZ Gallery in Hong Kong in early 1993, both "movements" achieved widespread international recognition as superficially kitsch forms of art that would go on to flood the international market. At the time, many critics argued that Cynical Realism and Political Pop had gained international visibility mainly for political rather than artistic reasons. In a contemporaneous review, John Clark criticized the exhibition "Mao Goes Pop" as "something of a loss," stating also that it "represents a necessary and difficult beginning." Clark pointed out astutely that most exhibitions of Chinese contemporary art "are put together by small groups with a restricted view," and that "Mao Goes Pop," which was staged in Sydney, was not a thorough attempt "to appraise the full range of visual arts activity in China or to elucidate the various types of work and their relative quality in relation to Australian values." He concludes, "Accepting value from others requires knowing what you yourself think valuable."[7]

Clark's line of argument is significant in part because it echoes the Chinese intellectual's desire to fight for the equal status of Chinese contemporary art. As part of this struggle the content of Political Pop has been criticized by Chinese intellectuals speaking from nonartistic perspectives. In an article titled "Who Plays with Whom," You You, a political dissident and writer in the Chinese diaspora, strongly criticized the exhibition "Mao Goes Pop," arguing that it represented an "opportunist" attitude expected as part of the Communist heritage:

> The ideology expressed in this work has little difference with the Communist's obsession toward power. But what makes this sort of work so popular in the West? First, because what they think about is not art, but is only about politics and media attention. With their own wishful thinking, they think all Chinese art has to have political color, so that Mao's face as political capital not only can be sold in China but also can make a profit in the West. Secondly, Chinese art has become a commodity, which the Westerner can identify with. It seems Chinese contemporary art has to find its place in the Western textbook. Li Xianting mentioned the Chinese Way in his speech, but he did not give this word an exact definition, we hope this Way is not the way of Communist thinking![8]

This article makes clear that the success of "Mao Goes Pop" was built on a residual cold war ideological antagonism between East and West still prevalent in the international news media and art world at the time. The change of title from "China's New Art, Post-1989" to "Mao Goes Pop" when the exhibition moved to the Museum of Contemporary Art in Sydney illustrated an inclination prevalent in Western institutions to stress the "dissident" aspect of such art. This enhanced the exhibition's sensationalist quality and assisted it in breaking attendance records; but from a Chinese point of view it may also have limited the voice of the exhibition to one of Western-friendly political passivity.

In another article about "Mao Goes Pop," Fan Di'an connected the exhibition with the wider circumstances of Chinese culture at the time; placing it squarely in relation to a postcolonialist theoretical framework:

> It is amazing to see how quickly and widely that post-colonialism has spread. In its early period, Pop Art was quite shocking and rebellious, and the Neo-Realism of New Generation (*xin shengdai*) was also vigorous in the 1990s and broke out of the spiritual shackles. But within no more than two years, they seemed to join together, and turned into "Pan-Pop." In essence, it fell into the Post-colonialist cultural condition, and it meant pushing forward the trend

> without anything at the heart. Mao Goes Pop showed this condition to the Western world.

In particular, Fan singled out the entrance installation *Consuming Socialism* as a typical example of Western hegemony under the power of postcolonialism:

> When they piled up everything they could get from China's everyday life, including political leaders' images, coins, public voices and public images, it almost overwhelmed all the work inside the exhibition itself—this indeed made people think. Such a little trick seemed to have handled a part of Chinese art history. This indeed gave us a warning…under the situation of post-colonialism, the independent value of Chinese culture has been completely lost.[9]

What Fan saw in relation to this exhibition is an example of how contemporary art has become a commodity when made accessible to a wide global audience. Once art becomes a commodity in the global market, he argues, "the power is once again returned to the power of the rich and industrialized countries, the gaze is perpetuated. The spectacle of the global market economy functions through commodity."[10] Chinese Pop Art can therefore be interpreted as being subject to the dominance of the Euro-American global art markets and their shaping of other cultural art forms.

Although Political Pop and Cynical Realism in exhibitions such as "Mao Goes Pop" was criticized strongly by Chinese and non-Chinese art scholars alike, it was nevertheless upheld as representative of the Chinese avant-garde at the 45th Venice Biennale in 1993. This inclusion in the Venice Biennale was widely questioned at the time, provoking intense criticism from both Chinese artists and art critics. Many saw the inclusion of Political Pop and Cynical Realism in the Venice Biennale as the choice of the West and, therefore, as one not based on the Chinese situation. The critic Yin Shuangxi argued that Chinese art was still at the margins of international achievements after 1989, when some international art institutions and media had not yet abandoned the opposing ideology of the Cold War and were constantly looking for "anti-official art."

This situation was most evident at the 45th Venice Biennial. Political Pop and Cynical Realism were chosen as the representatives of Chinese contemporary art, while Chinese experimental art, which had made serious inquiries into the daily lives of Chinese people, was not given the attention that it deserved because it lacked readily recognizable Chinese characteristics.[11]

Yi Ying questioned the genuineness of the political criticism presented by Political Pop, arguing that,

> China today is no longer what it was in the 1980s with idealist critique as its standard. The commercialization of political subject matter has made political pop into a commodity. As a result, the choice of subject for the artists does not come from political consciousness and criticism, but rather from the market.[12]

Alongside this, Wang Lin directly questioned the authority of the West to choose Chinese art.[13] He pointed out that Political Pop and Cynical Realism are similar in content to art produced in the former Soviet Union and in East Europe. In the eyes of some Westerners, China was the last bastion of the clash between the East and West; a living fossil of the Cold War. Human rights issues were still seen as the main problem in China. On the other side, some Chinese artists pretended to fit their needs into Western perspectives on political power. As a result, Chinese art remained in the opinion of many Westerners still in the past tense, at best, offering examples for Western human rights activists.[14] Overseas Chinese art curator Hou Hanru also expressed his deep disappointment at the choice for Venice:

> At the time Chinese art had undergone more than ten years of development, with so many highly qualified and meaningful artists around the world. Still, why won't those who first participated in the Venice Biennial still adopt "official" academic techniques and art conceptions to express their personal plight in desire and illusion? One of the reasons, at least, is that their work simply conveyed the mental state of the young people who have no ideals. It is a weak cynical

> state to go against invented official ideology. It is also what the Westerners who remain within the stereotyped ideology of the Cold War are interested in, are capable of imaging and are happy to "sympathize" with.... Such works in the exhibition do not show that Oliva [Italian critic Achille Bonito Oliva, the Curator of 45th Venice Biennale] understood Chinese art, but that he made a statement by this opportunity to Westerners, that he had been to China, and that the sphere of his influence had already extended to China. Then we have to ask a question: Is it a real peaceful coexistence?[15]

Due to the frequent participation of the Chinese avant-garde in international exhibitions, during the 1990s the related issues of Chinese "modernity" and "international identity" were widely discussed in the Chinese art world. In a "pan-discussion," Zhu Qingshen, Wang Lin, and Wang Nanming examined the issue of how Chinese art could confront globalization, especially American cultural hegemony, as well as how it could establish its own cultural identity.[16] Zhu Qingsheng believed that the participation of Wang Jianwei and Feng Mengbo in Documenta X (Kassel, 1997) could be seen as a success for Chinese art, after being anticipated by discussions during the 1993 Venice Biennale. Here Zhu begins by asserting that "The leading tendency of the Chinese art world is to be controlled by exhibitions chosen by the West, as well as by the external intervention of compradors, which is culturally still universal in China due to a passive colonial mentality." Zhu then goes on to cite the "China!" exhibition held at Bonn in 1996 as an example of this tendency, which, he contends, included only works satirizing China and Chinese culture.[17] Zhu also registers a deep anger "at the obstacles to Chinese artists brought about by the priority given to oil painting as well as to foreign curators," stating,

> When the master considers his creation he uses what materials he requires. If he thinks of something he uses it, but when it involves the understanding of modernization one stops short with perplexity. Modernization is a historical process, which the cultures of all countries must encounter. However, every state and nation has its own way to achieve

> it, there is no universal modernization. Chinese civilization will never become American civilization based on universal modernization unless the state was destroyed.

Based on this opinion, Zhu puts forward an argument that the state should support Chinese modern art. He warns, "If cultural creation has no capacity to generate itself then it could have no other way than that employed by the force of Euro-American internationalization based on universal principles." Zhu concludes with the assertion that "after 1997, when the aim of 'stepping towards the world' had already been reached, hope for Chinese art is aimed at its two basic supports, 'culture' and 'quality,' once again."[18]

Wang Lin, who also opposed those presenting Chinese contemporary art abroad, argued that Chinese art is facing "a real loss" after participating in the major international art exhibitions of the 1990s. In his view, the so-called "joining the international track" was only an urge to participate in the exhibitions, which involved the artists' heightened illusion of success. He also argued that Chinese participants in Venice and Documenta were being used as part of the political strategies of foreign curators, thereby becoming a "dish in the menu of a polarized Western selection." The picture drawn by Wang is vivid: powerful art dealers and artists pretentiously dressed in 1930s Chinese costumes matching the image they were supposed to have at the Venice Biennale and catering to that banquet. In Wang's view it was a great source of sadness that such a big country as China did not have its own international art exhibition.[19]

Regarding national modernization, Wang does, however, disagree with Zhu's comments that "there is no universal modernization." He warns that "without further explanation, national modernization could lead to excessive nationalist sentiment, and even to an increase in feudalism." He believes that modernization has two meanings: first, the development of production brought about by the growth of science and the rise in people's living standards, which might be referred to as "secular" modernization; and second, the degree of people's freedom. Zhu argues that we cannot see the freedom of the people in only the spirit of Western culture (thereby detaching it from nationalist attitudes) because the need for freedom as part of the historical process is not the exclusive privilege of one particular nation but the common aim of all people. At the same time, concerning China's own cultural construction, Zhu argues that it is necessary to warn against global Westernization and American cultural hegemony.

Wang Lin raises three other issues related to China's cultural identity, alongside those discussed above, which point toward the possible construction of a cultural system involving a division of rights in world culture. First, he asks: what is the objective in establishing a national cultural position as well as international status? In response Wang contends that it is spiritual freedom for the Chinese people not only to be free from the culture of feudalism but also from the culture of colonialism. For many Chinese people cultural colonialism has already become a habitual state of mind. Only under the presupposition of a liberated person can we discuss the international strategy of Chinese art. Second, at issue is the question of a specifically Chinese experience. Unlike most other Chinese art critics, Wang does not see Chinese art as belonging to the concept of the state. For him, "joining the international track" (*guoji jiegui*) is meaningful only as a communication tool between regions. In Wang's view, "Speaking from the point of cultural studies we cannot regard the Chinese experience as all one thing, and should regard it as the existential situation surrounding us as well as a spiritual experience. For individual artists, it is a concrete, detailed, genuine existential experience." Third, in the spirit of criticism, contemporary art must insist on its intellectuality. Intellectuals are a group of people who, Wang argues, stand for the progress of society in the domain of spiritual culture as well as the possibility of searching for the development of humanity. Intellectuality is represented, above all, as reflective thinking (*sixiang fanxing*) and spiritual criticism. But, as Wang sees it, criticism is different from rebellion—rebellion is normally based on the negation of reality, but criticism is based on responsibility for the future. Wang asserts that most post–1989 Chinese music and cynical realist paintings are strongly characterised by a tendency toward rebellion. He also asserts that they were weak critically, since they were aimed at the Maoist problem—that is to say, counterfeit political illusion and empty social ideals—and were therefore based on the outmoded oppositional ideology of the Cold War between the East and the West.

In the same article, Wang points out that "lack of autonomous rights pushes Chinese contemporary art in international exhibitions into an increasingly dependent status." In his view, the "contemporaneity" of contemporary Chinese art was misrepresented by contemporary Chinese art exhibitions held abroad, and that "Fed by Western art institutions, Chinese art has lost its contesting character, either against Western hegemonism, or for its own culture and system within that context." In particular, Wang seeks to emphasise differences in the role of Chinese intellectuals during the 1980s and 1990s. As Wang puts it, "In the eighties, we could raise the slogan of a new wave art, and we could have the exhibition of 'New Wave' art. But this can be seen more or less as motivated by the system." The true transformation of ideology during the 1990s, he believes, was the separation of intellectuals and the system, thus pushing intellectuals into their own specialized role. In Wang's opinion, Chinese contemporary art at that time "seemed more and more like a narrowed form of racial iconography." Wang argues that contemporary art does not depend on a single context, but comes from a mutual exchange between the context and its discourse. An audience, critic, or curator does not understand the art until they understand the specific discourse. Therefore, the more powerful nations often see third-world culture from the point of view of a tourist. This has caused Chinese contemporary art to be represented in the West as a code of Western media and international political strategy, and, as such, it has barely been involved in academic discussion as part of the whole contemporary art scene.[20]

Like most art critics and historians within China during the 1990s, Zhu Qingsheng, Wang Lin, and Wang Nanming were concerned about the lack of contemporary art venues to produce and exhibit art in China. The fact that Chinese contemporary art could be exhibited only abroad gave audiences the impression of an "art in exile." This also put Chinese curators in the unfortunate position of having to think constantly about how to present Chinese contemporary art in ways that would make sense to Western audiences. Due to its predetermined position in the mainstream of the international art market, Chinese art and culture was able to make only a passive entrance onto the international stage and its significance could not be fully recognized.

Debates on the relations between Chinese art and international art gradually evolved into an exposure of dissatisfaction about participation in international events. As a response to the extensive criticism of major exhibitions held in the West, the controversial art curator Li Xianting defended himself and the art he curated by posing the questions, "What does it mean to 'step onto the international stage'? Step onto the international stage—is this a political statement, or is it a cultural strategy? Or, is it simply artistic orientation?"[21] In Li's view, Western interest in the Post '89 New Chinese Art exhibition was due to two things strongly related to the prevailing context of the time: first, the end of the Cold War; and second, the influence of postcolonialism. For Westerners, postcolonialism is an expression born of their search for pluralism and their attempt to downplay the cultural dominance of Euro-American logocentrism. Nevertheless, as the world becomes increasingly global, the motivation of the West is still to maintain its position at the helm of world art. For this, the West requires the presence of non-Western, peripheral cultures on the Western serving plate. Under these circumstances, China's role in this dinner is that of a "spring roll." As Li would have it:

> The real reason for such a broad Western interest actually had more to do with the timing of the exhibition, as it happened at the end of the Cold War. As the last red bastion, even if it was still a bastion, China was beginning to show cracks. The art exhibited at this exhibition shed light on the cracks appearing in the cultural realm.

The question was how to make a genuinely Chinese art that would be accepted as part of the international art world. The strategy to bring this about is, Li suggests, the turning of politics to the advantage of Chinese art. Li contends, "To begin with, we will have to acknowledge the importance of the political dimension and the cultural dimension in the international art world." In the process of "stepping onto the international stage," he says, "we will inevitably lose some of our innocence/idealism." Faced with the dilemma of an international hors d'oeuvres plate, he argues "spring rolls" are politics:

> If you don't play the spring roll, there is a good possibility you will be passed over or ignored altogether. This is the harsh reality. If we want to "step onto the international stage," we need to face the facts: the international stage only wants spring rolls. There is nothing we can do to change this fact. So what do we do? We can always play the spring roll in a proactive way and to a certain degree alter the content of the spring roll over time while all the time realistically reckoning with issues of our own contemporary culture.[22]

Here, Li acknowledges that Chinese Contemporary art has to reach the Euro-American standard and that the criteria for selection may not be justified. But he also argues that Chinese art has no other choice than that of establishing its international identity by participating in more and more international exhibitions. Li looks at the fears that the changes in global power relations had unleashed during the 1990s. For him, the misery of being exploited is nothing when compared to the misery of not even being exploited at all.

Other art critics, however, warned that the misinterpretation of Chinese art in the context of the international art world of the 1990s could eventually mislead Chinese art. In a conversation with Francesca Dal Lago, Gao Minglu indicated that Western perceptions of Chinese contemporary art traveled back to China and influenced the way Chinese artists thought of themselves:

> The Political Pop movement is a good example. It actually appeared before the political events of 1989, but because of western anti-communist expectations following the fall of the Berlin Wall and the 4 June crackdown, Political Pop and the avant-garde in general received unprecedented attention after 1989, and not only in political terms, but commercially and within the context of the international museum world. Since there was an anticommunist political movement, necessarily there had to be an anti-communist avant-garde after 4 June. Ironically, Political Pop is not anti-

> communist. With more accurate observation you may notice how artists such as Wang Guangyi, for example, in fact carry some strong nationalist connotations in their work.[23]

Huang Du also observed how the power of "Western colonialism" manipulated Chinese art during the 1990s:

> Art movements such as "Political Pop" and "Cynical Realism" echoed Western colonialism and power politics after the Cold War, while serving as an example of the connection between art and commerce. Since then, pragmatism and a utilitarian outlook have spread rapidly, causing hordes of artists to blindly mimic and pursue these trends. Needless to say, such courses of action, have, so far, governed the direction of contemporary Chinese art.[24]

International identification has been a concern for Chinese modernity since the 1980s. The official slogans from "going to the world" in the 1980s to "joining the international track" in the 1990s have reverberated within Chinese artistic and cultural circles.[25] The linear view of history, embedded in Western enlightenment discourses, has been internalized to a large extent by Chinese intellectuals in the search for modernity. The replacement of historicity and spatiality with universality and temporality has meant that Chinese intellectual discourse in modernity has been inevitably reduced to a subset of the "universal project." Therefore, during the 1980s modernity or modernization, for Chinese intellectuals, was the basic means to achieve a modern, wealthy, and powerful nation-state. It was also perceived as a process whereby Chinese tradition and culture should be critically reexamined in terms of the norms and value system of Western modernity.[26] The dominant mode of thinking among Chinese intellectuals during the period was thus the dualistic notion of the West versus China, and modernity versus tradition. China's modernization increased in its intensity particularly during the mid-1980s. For some Chinese art critics and artists who were actively involved in the '85 New-Wave, it seemed that "Chinese art should be similar to Chinese soccer, in that some day it should go out of the county and enter the international arena."[27] This "Olympic attitude" was labelled by Gao Minglu as a "defensive modernity" bound up with the articulation of a national identity and subjectivity. Even though the issue of modernity had already been debated within Chinese societies, until the late 1980s the practical and theoretical concerns of this modernity were rooted in a desire for international strengthening in reaction to Western influences.[28] This situation was further explained by Hou Hanru, who asserts, "At the time of the '85 Movement (or New-Wave) of Chinese avant-garde art, the central issue that we faced was cultural and artistic modernization. Our concerns focused mainly on China's own reality, and the attempt to introduce Western modern/contemporary art and culture to influence the situation and hence to solve some urgent problems."[29] Here Hou goes on to argue that, not until the basis of society is altered by the global economic system would any real interplay or clash of the East and the West ever become possible.[30]

This discrepancy in China's ever-changing agenda had grown out of an increasingly unstable self-identity and the stagnant frame of reference known as postcolonialism, in whose terms the West, according to many interpretations, fabricates the representation of China. The artist's role in participating in the postcolonial spectacle plays into the gaze of the obvious. Guy Debord describes the spectacle very succinctly:

> The individual who in the service of the spectacle is placed in stardom's spotlight is in fact the opposite of an individual, and as clearly the enemy of the individual in himself as of the individual in others—he renounces all autonomy in order himself to identify with the general law of obedience to the course of things.[31]

Opposing this postcolonial "spectacle," young art critics like Huang Du argued that contemporary Chinese art in 1990s China had become "a part of the process of re-negotiation between the local and global" and that this very process was generating a new and constantly mutating cultural and artistic structure on a global scale. Huang saw the new trends in the art of the time as follows:

> Recent art history relating to Chinese art shows that there are a number of identifiable and fixed styles indicating that there is no continuation on from either "Political Pop" or "Cynical Realism" and that the terms cannot avoid being narrowed into historical periods. In fact, the Venice Biennale heralded the end of these movements in 1993. Certainly, contemporary Chinese art has been creating new trends, in response to sudden changes in China's social values and structure, especially with the rise of a borderless information society. In recent years many young artists constantly search for freedom through the practice of artistic creativity, dismantling the rigid authority and dominant position of socialist realism and succeed in overcoming the narrow political outlook of "Political Pop" and "Cynical Realism." Instead, Conceptual art, Installation art, Environmental art, and Performance art all impact on their work and make for a more multi-dimensional and complex response to art and society.[32]

The structural determinants of this new artistic and cultural identity were undoubtedly a reflection of economics. After 1992, with the onset of China's new market socialism on the economic front and new authoritarianism on the political front, urban society began a transformation toward a set of values that at their core were about commerce, trade, and material happiness. The significant phenomenon in China during the early 1990s was the development of consumer culture. Hollywood movies, fashion trends, the Internet, and computer culture: all things of an increasingly globalized world culture began to creep into the everyday lives of Chinese people. Japanese comic strips, Hong Kong commercial films, and other pop culture phenomena also took their place in the mainstream culture of the urban population in China. These influences continue to be visible not only in the store fronts lining the streets of today's Chinese cities but in advertisements, apparel, and even the daily headlines of the local news media. Without a doubt, this phenomenon has had a profound impact on the Chinese people's aesthetics and sensibility, and has forced artists to ponder the meaning of individual life in a society based on material desires.

The shift within the Chinese art world away from the political concerns of the 1980s to the economic concerns of the 1990s is evidence that domination by government ideology was giving way to the dynamic of materialism. The rise of individualism was a major difference between the 1980s and 1990s in China. As Huang Du makes clear, Chinese contemporary art of the 1990s reflected this difference: "The difference between the 1980s and 1990s lies in the 'disappearance of collective groups in Chinese contemporary art and the emergence of personalization and individuality'."[33] Yi Ying also saw the significant emergence of individualism in Chinese art of the 1990s when that art changed direction and began to address individual concerns, individual observations, and individual experience. However, these artistic changes took place quietly, unlike the spectacular movements of the 1980s that strove toward ideological liberation.[34]

Chinese Pop art, which developed along with the consumer culture of the 1990s, was reexamined by art historian Gu Chengfeng (editor of *Jiangsu Huakan*). He divided Chinese Pop art of the 1990s into two categories: one focused on Mao's image and popular icons of the Cultural Revolution; the other focused on the immediate social and cultural context and consumer culture. He therefore disagreed with the generally held view of the time that Chinese Pop art was specifically a form of "Political Pop." Gu believed that the non-political tendency was more obviously seen in the work of *Xinshengdai* (the New Generation) artists. He writes, "Compared to the old generation who were major participants in the '85 Art Movement, these artists worked in a more relaxed manner." For example, in Wang Guanyi's work subject and technique created focus and intensity, while in young artists' work political images became deconstructed and mixed up with disparate commercial symbols. Consider here, for example, Gong Weijia's paintings *Yaoge* (Inviting Song) and *Xingfu Shike* (Happy Moment). Like Wang Guangyi, the artist took popular images from the Cultural Revolution, creating a strong sense of displacement by transposing political symbols from *Wangpai* (Triumph Cards) and *Wushu* (Martial Arts). In a similar vein, Zhang Pin's painting *Dahu shangshan* (Beating Tiger on the Way up to the Mountain) demonstrates a comedic effect.[35] In this sense, Pop art produced by the younger generation was aimed more at individual rather than political concerns.

That the Chinese social consciousness could be cleansed so soon of the memory of the summer of 1989 and be filled anew with the fetishism of consumerism is a reality that Chinese intellectuals have confronted with mixed emotions. In a conference organized by CAFA at Shanxi in 1998, art historians and critics summarized the significance of Chinese contemporary art during the 1990s and its difference from that of the 1980s. They expressed their concerns on the late art trends emerging under consumerism.[36] Shao Dazhen observed that, overall, Chinese art in the 1990s was greatly influenced by the media and the impact of the market and was characteristic of the "emergence of neo-conservatism, pluralism, loss of center and authority." The dramatic impact of the various groups of artists and schools of art during the New-Wave art movement of the 1980s had now lost its power. Rather than revolutionary utopianism, a cultural neoconservatism that would outgrow itself as pluralism took root in Chinese society. Shao Dazhen believed that the effect of the so-called neoconservatism of the 1990s was to neutralize the radicalism of Chinese contemporary art during the 1980s. However, this was not the same as adhering to the conservative standards of passive or vulgar conservatism. He argued that the distancing and cynicism that prevailed in the new art of 1990s, which came from cultural conservatism, should not be seen as a sign of a completely negative or nihilist rejection of reality. Rather than responding to the impasse by ignoring the problem, it could be seen as a way forward involving a positive attitude to engaging with real life.[37] Wang Nanming believed that the major issue of the 1990s was how to make Chinese contemporary art accepted systematically. Yi Ying warned that the neocolonialism of the West, which was particularly emphasised by the American media, had threatened the serious intent of Chinese modern art. Huang Zhuan argued that the main aim of Chinese contemporary art was still cultural enlightenment and its fight against cultural totalitarianism, the rise of consumer culture during the 1990s having vulgarized the issue. However, he also argued that cultural relativism and nihilism do not oppose cultural totalitarianism as it appears on the surface, but on the contrary assist it and "legalize" it. Huang criticized internationally fashionable Political Pop and Gaudy Art for having covered but not disposed of the real problem of Chinese contemporary art. To call them "Avant-garde" was a tragedy for Chinese contemporary art. On the whole, the discussion at the conference indicated an internalized vision of Chinese contemporary art during the 1990s and revealed the major concerns of academic Chinese art historians and critics at the time. It testified to a pluralism that had taken shape in relation to Chinese art of the 1990s as a well as a sympathetic appreciation of values such as toleration, autonomy, rights, and equality.

In addition to the formal theoretical papers given at the academic conference accompanying the '98 Asia-Pacific Contemporary Art Exhibition, which was held in Fuzhou, some Chinese art critics and artists also made personal statements. The exhibition comprised Chinese-recognized contemporary art and some international art. At the Fuzhou conference, delegates focused on the issue of modernity in Chinese art at the end of the 1990s. The major curator, Fan Di'an, believed the problem to be one of cultural conflicts between East and West. During the conference, Fan argued, "The impulse and radical actions of taking Western art as the model was once popular among young artists. They tried to achieve individual freedom for their art by the route of modernism." Fan also warned that it was important to have a correct view of tradition. When the word "modern" becomes the artists' focus, the value of traditional art is likely to be ignored. He advocated that artists reexamine their own tradition and search for what is valuable in it "from its spirit and character instead of from the level of material and technique." Fan argued that it was the rise of mass consumer culture in 1990s that had reduced the audience's capability of appreciating beauty to a superficial level and that weakness of cultural intention and mediocrity of spiritual quality had become the common problem of many artworks. Under such circumstances he stressed the importance of cultural ideals and the cultural values of art:

> Only artists with a deep understanding of the change in China's social history and progress, with a correct view on the problems of social development, together with social consciousness and a sense of responsibility as the motive for creation, and with a decent personality and high spiritual pursuit can fulfil this historical task.[38]

At the same conference, Yi Ying addressed China's own social conditions for the transformation of contemporary art in the 1990s. He saw that "the speed of Chinese social development in the 1990s surpasses the speed of the imitation of western modern art in the 1980s. The 'demonstration of the ego' raised in the 1980s only turned out to be an imitation of western modern art styles, because society did not provide the conditions for individual independence. The social conditions of the 1990s made it possible for one to lead an individual lifestyle, and for individualization to become a potential subject of art." He also contended that Chinese artists have turned away from both multiculturalism and Eurocentrism "because the methods suggested by the ideas are not compatible with the Chinese artists' life experience in Chinese society." "Only in this moment," he argued, "can we feel the existence, and the formation, of the Chinese art language on its own terms."

Wang Lin restated his criticism that Chinese contemporary art exhibited abroad had been dominated by Western choices that interpreted Chinese art of the 1990s in terms of political rebellion. He writes, "In the 1990s, the Chinese lived in a cultural environment where pre-modernism, modernism, and post-modernism simultaneously existed," and that:

> Being a cultural giant instead of a small nation without a cultural tradition, China definitely will not be satisfied by only having a token booth in the western organized international exhibition. China is responsible for the world's future cultural development. We cannot identify ourselves with the idea that culture of the future will merely be the globalization of Western culture, not in the field of spiritual culture at least. Only in an independent, natural and spontaneous state can Chinese art create contemporary art achievements and an independent art history.[39]

Looking from the vantage point of the Sichuan Academy of Fine Arts, which is located in a relatively marginal geopolitical position, Wang Lin was more aware of regional culture. He criticized the culture of the Chinese central plains (*zhongyuan wenhua*) and Confucianism as the representatives of China and all cultures in China. The Southern culture in Shanghai, Guangzhou, and the Southwest culture, such as in Sichuan, are varied, he asserted, but are often presented as a single entity in the political and cultural center. He noted that art exchanges were often conducted through political channels. Thus art was likely to become an invisible weapon, a tool to gain political and cultural power. In contrast, regional exchanges are closer to the essence of art exchange. Regional exchange is impossible if Chinese art and culture are regarded as an integral part of the whole. For Wang the reappearance of Chinese experience can be regarded as the ratification of regional culture and its artistic value.[40]

Yin Shuangxi pointed out that the specific political situation of Hong Kong and Taiwan led to foreign choices typified by the 1993 Venice Biennale when Political Pop and Cynical Realism were chosen to represent China. He observed three characteristics of Chinese contemporary art since 1994. First, there were no more major art movements to be found. Second, there had been an enhancement of artistic personality and an elimination of any sense of authority and centrality; the artist's attention had turned from ideological critique to daily life and the public environment, and rapid changes in the market economy had forced artists to ponder the meaning of individual life in a society based on material desires. Third, there had been significant changes in art media and the emergence of multiple styles of expression.[41]

Gu Chengfeng called for idealism once again. He saw the faded remnants of 1980s humanism during the 1990s, particularly in the form of Pop and Gaudy Art.[42] But he also argued that a healthy and well-constructed cultural mechanism was still needed, even in relation to the prevailing economically directed cultural background. Idealism, he argued, is always profoundly associated with the aim of truth, goodness, and beauty. It might be adjusted and shelved in the short term. But laughing at idealism is akin to laughing at ourselves, he warned, and, moreover, that cultural nationalism could be even more dangerous than cultural colonialism.

The 1998 Shanxi conference and '98 Asia-Pacific Contemporary Art Exhibition with the conference at Fuzhou signified the emergence of an internalized vision of modernity in relation to Chinese art. A number of Chinese critics advocated the idea of a Chinese version of modernity by creating a new sense of national cultural identity. They also demanded a return of their legitimate rights as self-defined historical subjects, capable of developing their own narrative of modernity, of relating their own experience, and of mapping out their own future. This vision recognized the importance of cultural difference. At the same time, it also emphasized dialectics rather than absolute difference between the two poles, and hence went beyond confrontational logic of the self versus the other, and beyond the desire to assert its own subject position as an overpowering one. While May Fourth intellectuals during the early twentieth century could only conceive of and emulate a single Eurocentric mode of modernity, a number of Chinese art critics during the 1990s became conscious of the historical nature and cultural origins of modernity. They began to locate modernity within a global context. The absolute nature of Western modernity was deconstructed, and the myth became a reality defined in the mundane day-to-day process of Chinese modernization.

4

Oh Father, Where Art Thou? A Bakhtinian Reading of Luo Zhongli's *Father*

Stephen J. Goldberg

> Practice is a set of relays from one theoretical point to another, and theory is a relay from one practice to another. No theory can develop without eventually encountering a wall, and practice is necessary for piercing this wall.
>
> —Gilles Deleuze[1]

What possible relevance could the theories of Mikhail Bakhtin (1895–1975), working in the aftermath of the Russian Revolution, have for the painting of an artist—Luo Zhongli (b. 1948)—working in the aftermath of the Chinese Cultural Revolution? Each in his own way was obliged to make accommodations with Marxist regimes. I raise this question fully recognizing that the current state of Chinese art history in the West is woefully underconceptualized. That is to say, there is precious little theoretically informed, systematic analysis of traditional or contemporary Chinese art, and there is no culturally sensitive critical reflection on the appropriateness of Western art historiography as a narrative order of representation. This stands in marked contrast to the theoretically informed research currently conducted in the fields of Chinese literature and film studies.

Tzvetan Todorov called Bakhtin the *fondateur moderne* of pragmatics.[2] While Ferdinand de Saussure's structural linguistics limited its field of inquiry to the language system as a separate entity, Bakhtin and his circle were concerned with the study of discourse, "with the socially-situated utterance and with the structuring of linguistic form and meaning by context, and his specific views on these subjects," which Trevor Pateman observed "relate much more obviously to the contemporary literature on pragmatics...."[3] Bakhtin's writings on literature as a polyphonic, heterogeneous discourse must also be seen as being in contradistinction to Russian formalism, which attempted to distinguish the poetic use of language from ordinary everyday usage.

This chapter undertakes an examination of Bakhtin's thought, with a specific focus on his dialogical theory of "double-voiced discourse" and "addressivity,"[4] through a reading of *Father*, a painting by Luo Zhongli, an artist from Sichuan province (fig. 1). Double-voicing (here redefined as the internal bifurcation of visual modes of address) will be shown to be an implicit strategy in the artist's attempt to offer a counter-memory of the recent historical events during the Cultural Revolution (1966–1976). In so doing, Luo Zhongli's *Father* posed a challenge to the sovereignty of the Communist Party state by undermining, through a rhetorical strategy of parodic inversion, two of the principal discursive instruments by which the

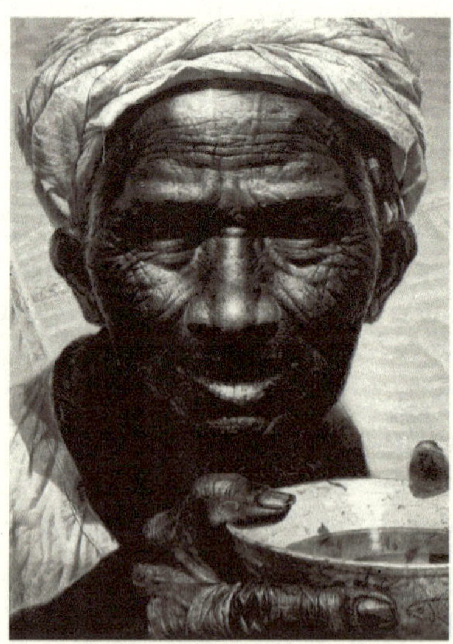

Figure 1. Luo Zhongli. *Father* (1980). Chinese National Art Gallery, Beijing.

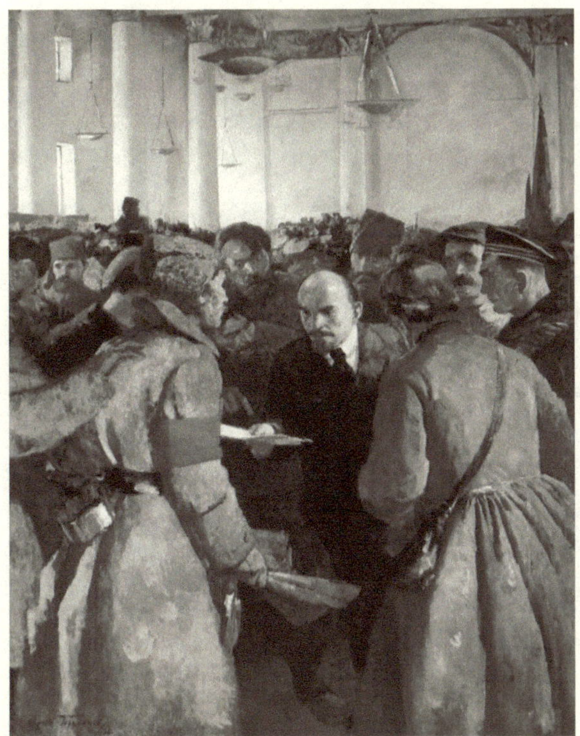

Figure 2. Aleksandr Mikhailovich Gerasimov (1881–1961). *Lenin Addressing the Second Congress of the Soviets* (1936). The State Museum in Leningrad.

legitimacy of this sovereignty was inscribed and rationalized: Socialist Realist paintings and political propaganda posters.

Sovereignty implies, in its most general sense, a stabilized system of authoritative control over a domain and its subjects, and is rationalized through the power, authority, and persistence of the discourses within which sovereignty is inscribed.[5] In China, sovereignty resides with the Communist Party state which was established by Mao Zedong on October 1, 1949.

From the inception of the People's Republic of China, the new government set about creating a new art for the new nation. It was decided that oil painting would be a primary focus, and that Soviet socialist realism would be the most appropriate model. This can be illustrated in Aleksandr Mikhailovich Gerasimov's (1881–1961) *Lenin Addressing the Second Congress of the Soviets*, dated 1936, in the State Museum in Leningrad (fig. 2).

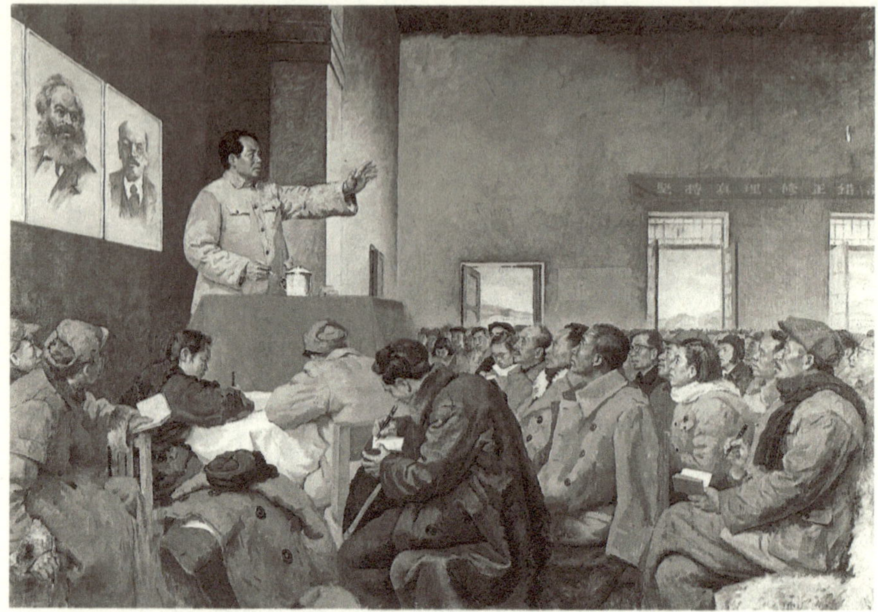

Figure 3. Luo Gongliu (b. 1916). *Mao Zedong Reporting on the Rectification in Yan'an* (1951). Museum of the Chinese Revolution, Beijing.

Young artists were sent to Leningrad to study and a Soviet artist, Konstantin M. Maksimov (b. 1913), was invited to Beijing to instruct an elite class of young painters.[6] In early campaigns, artists were encouraged to produce major historical paintings in the new manner for the state buildings erected around Tiananmen Square. Establishing both a Chinese socialist realist style and a revolutionary iconography, this group of paintings determined the course of China's artistic development for the next two decades.

Luo Gongliu's (b. 1916) *Mao Zedong Reporting on the Rectification in Yan'an,* dated 1951, in the Museum of the Chinese Revolution in Beijing (fig. 3), is one of the earliest paintings to praise and publicize the history of the Chinese Communist Party. The portraits of Marx and Lenin on the wall behind Mao serve to establish his political genealogy and authority. As a new genre, history painting interprets, legitimates, and projects the goals of the newly formed communist society, as it forges ahead independently of the authority of its own classical tradition.

Setting officially sanctioned artists to work on historical commissions was a strategy to secure the "image of legitimacy" for the

Communist Party and Mao Zedong, understandable in a society that traditionally placed distinct value on an account of their past. At the same time, sanctioning an official image of history must be read as political rhetoric rather than as mere commemoration of historical fact. It is an assertion that the all-powerful Communist Party state can control not only the present, but the past as well. For, the truth of the past is dependent on its representations in the present, and those in the present who possess the power to represent it. "Who controls the past controls the future; who controls the present controls the past."[7]

In the post-Mao era, the state as authoritative agent became increasingly destabilized as China entered into the emerging global economy during the Era of Reform ushered in by Deng Xiaoping in 1978. This has been accompanied by a growing instability (in that other dimension of what stabilizes sovereignty) as transnational cultural forces emanating from the West have rendered ambiguous the domain of subjectivity over which the party-state has claimed control. Removal of complete party control of the arts freed artists, such as the late Chen Yifei (1946–2000), trained in the realist tradition of the preceding era, to begin to experiment with new themes that questioned the construction of social reality under the previous regime.[8] Chen Yifei's *Looking at History from My Space*, dated 1979, in the Collection of Lawrence Wu in New York, is a truly remarkable expression of the kinds of critical reflections that emerged in the immediate aftermath of the death of Mao (fig. 4).

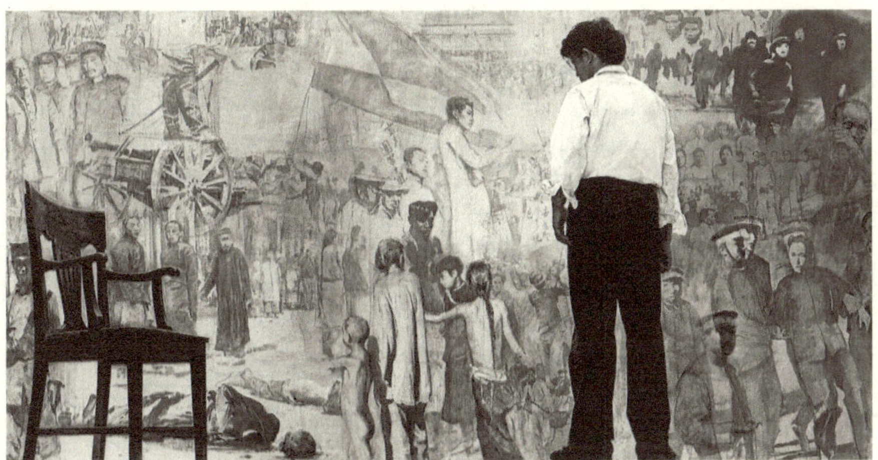

Figure 4. Chen Yifei (1946–2000). *Looking at History from My Space* (1979). Collection of Lawrence Wu, New York.

In *Looking at History from My Space*, the artist depicts himself looking back on a photomontage of the memory of horrific events surrounding the emergence of the May Fourth Movement, returning to the historical moments that led up to the formation of the PRC and Cultural Revolution. What has changed is the redemptory promise that underlay the rupture with the culture of the past, marked by the innovation and newness in modern Chinese literature, art, and culture, precisely because they refused to affirm the conditions and values that made such suffering in China possible. The standpoint we are given looking up to the figure as if on a stage, marked by the lower edge of the painting, harkens back to the heightened theatrical narrative focalization in portrayals of peasants, workers, and soldiers enforced in the early seventies under the tyrannical supervision of the arts by Mao's widow Jiang Qing. It is a truly remarkable redeployment of the representational resources developed in Chinese Socialist Realism. *Looking at History from My Space* raises fundamental issues which lie at the core of this present study. It is about history, art, and the necessity of memory in an antiredemtory age.[9]

Chinese visual culture, in the last two decades of the twentieth century, has been a contested terrain; at stake was the reality of history and authenticity of memory under the threat of state-sanctioned manipulation and erasure. Who gets to choose what to remember and what to forget, what to pass over in silence, and what to obscure?

Oh Father, Where Art Thou?

In 1980, Luo Zhongli, a relatively unknown thirty-two-year-old artist, exhibited a painting titled *Father*, a monumental portrait (227 × 154 cm) of a humble, old Chinese peasant staring out in our direction from above a rice-bowl half-filled with water that he holds in his sun-dried, leather-skin hands (fig. 1).

In the minds of the generation of Chinese viewers attending the exhibition, for whom the bitter suffering experienced during the violent and chaotic period of the Cultural Revolution (1966–1976) was still a vivid memory, the scale and frontality of this image evoked Mao Zedong's *Helmsman's Portrait* (fig. 5), an oil painting executed

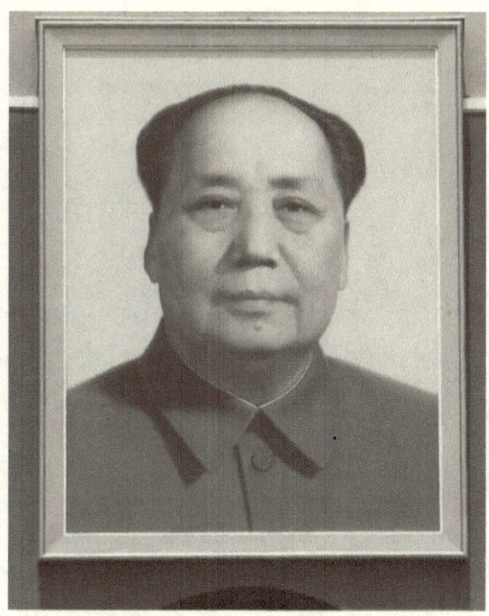

Figure 5. Mao Zedong's *Helmsman's Portrait*. Gate of Heavenly Peace, Tiananmen, Beijing.

in 1964, which hangs prominently above the central portal of the Gate of Heavenly Peace (Tiananmen). *Father*, like Mao's *Helmsman's Portrait*, is painted in a style derived in part from the art of Soviet Social Realism. It is a style of pictorial representation that was seen everywhere in the official art of the Cultural Revolvution.[10]

Returning to Luo's depiction of *Father*, upon closer inspection, there are discernible fundamental differences from Socialist Realism, indicative of the influence of the Photo Realism of the contemporary American painter Chuck Close as well as the portrayal of nineteenth-century peasant life in the paintings of the French artist Jean François Millet (1814–1875), attested to in a personal statement by the artist.[11] Painted just five years after the death of Mao, Luo was able to gain access to these alternative Western modes of visual representation during the Era of Reform that marked the beginning of China's opening up to the rest of the world after decades of self-isolation.

In that which follows, Luo Zhongli's painting will be considered not simply in terms of a structural process of cultural hybrid-

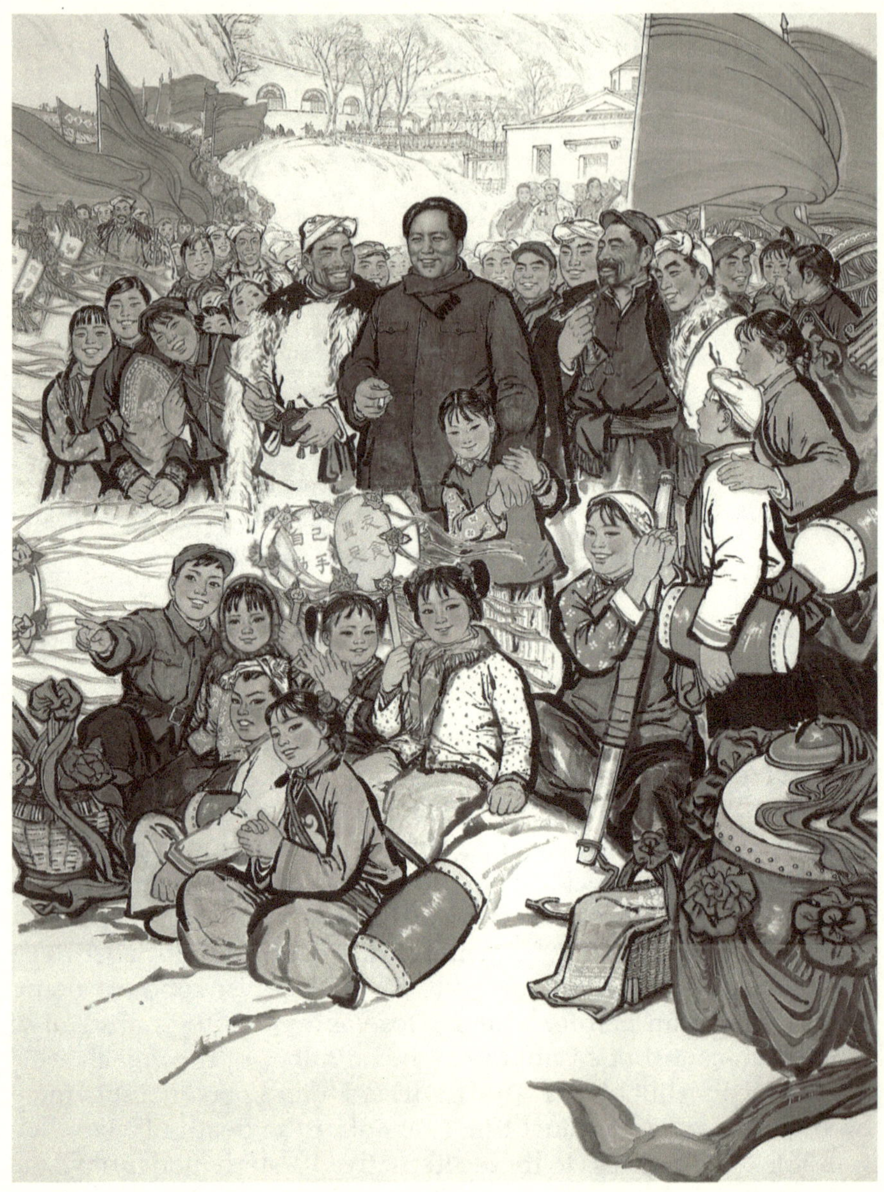

Figure 6. Liu Wenxi (b. 1933). *New Spring in Yan'an* (1972). China International Exhibition Agency, Beijing.

ization or stylistic influence, but as a historical event of cultural resistance to the legitimacy of state-sponsored political propaganda in order to address the continuing plight of peasants in rural areas of Sichuan province.

Father, as already noted, was influenced by Chuck Close's monumental portrait-paintings of ordinary people, rendered in a technique that replicates in the medium of paint the photographic process of color separation. This would account for Luo Zhongli's hyperrealistic depiction of the "heavy-knit brows over the deep-seated and darkly shaded eyes,"[12] and deep-cut wrinkles in the dark, leather-textured skin. These features distinguish Luo's depiction from the idealized representations of red-cheeked, smiling peasants made during the Cultural Revolution (fig. 6).

The themes of the peasant, the worker, and the soldier were used in posters, paintings and theatrical performances to further the political ideology and policies of Mao Zedong. As "model figures" of the proletariat, the peasant must be represented with a "sturdy, healthy body and ruddy complexion."[13] As Maria Galikowski observed, "the 'model' was typically allowed to reveal no signs of aging and had ideally to appear in the 'spring of life' (*qingchun shidai*)."[14]

In depicting *Father* with a wrinkled, craggy face and beads of perspiration on his brow, wisps of white facial hair on his chin, a single tooth in his mouth, and fingernails filled with dirt, Luo explicitly broke with just about every officially prescribed artistic convention for representing this "model" figure of the Cultural Revolution.

Luo brings to his painting a critical social dimension absent in the work of Chuck Close as well as the highly romanticized Chinese peasant paintings. This he derives, in part, from the powerful paintings of peasant life by Jean François Millet, especially *Man with a Hoe*, painted between 1860 and 1862 (fig. 7). In a revealing letter to Alfred Sensier in May 1863, Millet wrote:

> I can clearly see…the sun streaming through the clouds, in all its glory, a long way off from the earth. I see just as clearly, out there in the plain, horses steaming as they plow; then, in a rocky place, a weary man, whose grunts have

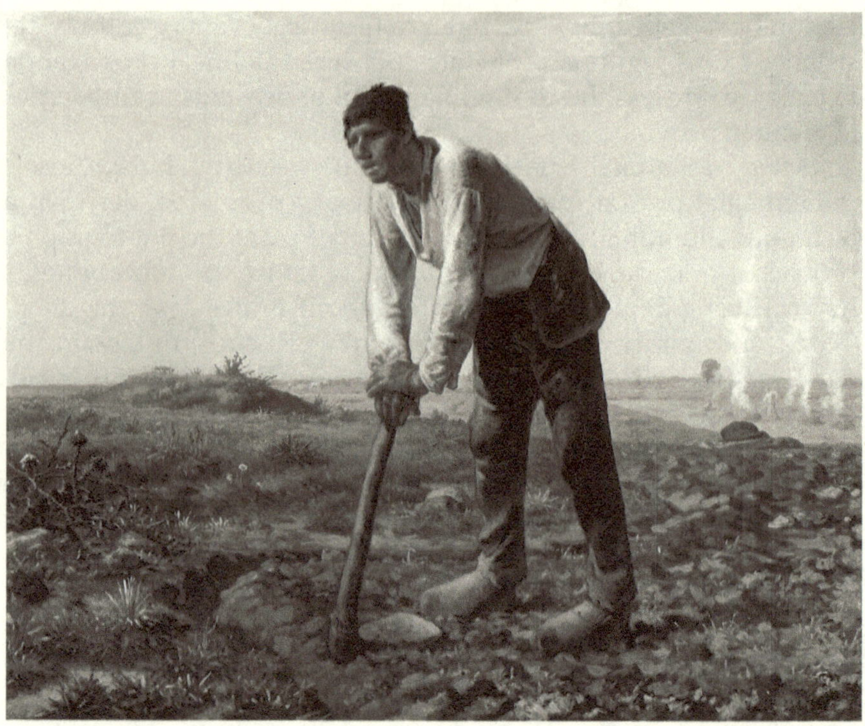

Figure 7. Jean François Millet, *Man with a Hoe* (1860–1862). J. Paul Getty Museum, Los Angeles.

> been audible since morning, who is trying to straighten up a minute to catch his breath. The drama of these things has its splendors. It is no invention of mine, and the expression "the cry of the earth" was coined long ago.[15]

In Luo's *Father* portrait as well as Millet's *Man with a Hoe* we are visually confronted with the pure brutality of peasant life set against a backdrop of parched barren earth.[16] Luo has stated that in his painting he wanted to address the failure of the Communist Revolution to improve the conditions of the peasants. In her book, *Art and Politics in China: 1949–1984*, Maria Galikowski notes the following concerning Luo Zhongli:

> Sent to work in a small factory in the Da Ba mountain range, Da county, Sichuan, during the Cultural Revolution, he had since been in continuous close contact with the peasants living there, becoming familiar with them and their lives. He recalled that a particular event in 1975 formed the basis for *Father*. He had in that year witnessed a peasant guarding a pile of dung (dung being a valuable commodity in rural areas which needs to be guarded), and the sight of this old face made a great impact on the artist, reminding him, as the peasant did, of Yang Bailao, Xiang Linsao, Run Tu and Ah Q, all fictional characters from the lower echelons of traditional Chinese society.[17]

In making this comparison, Galikowski suggests, "Luo is indicating that, in his view, no fundamental improvements have taken place in the lives of the underprivileged since the early part of this century."[18]

Luo Zhongli was a member of a group of painters known as the "Native Soil" or "Stream of Life" movement (*shenghuoliu*). The core of this movement consisted of young intellectuals in their late twenties and early thirties who had been "sent down" to the countryside. Former Red Guards growing up in the closed-off world of "New China," they had absorbed the dictum that art should "truthfully reflect life" (referring to the idealized "truth" promoted during the Cultural Revolution). But after being sent down to the countryside these young elite were for the first time in their lives confronted with the harsh realities of rural poverty and misery.

An image that comes to mind is Dorothea Lange's 1936 famous photograph *Migrant Mother,* taken in a pea-packing camp in Nipomo, California (fig. 8). Lange sought to use her photographs as tools to effect social change in response to the anguish and suffering of those burdened by the Depression and drought conditions of the Dustbowl. The difference between Luo's *Father* and Lange's *Migrant Mother, Nipomo, California,* as we shall now see, is not so much a matter of the medium employed, but rather of the rhetorical strategy deployed: "parodic inversion."

When first exhibited at the Second Chinese Exhibition for Young Artists in 1980, Luo's *Father* was extremely controversial.

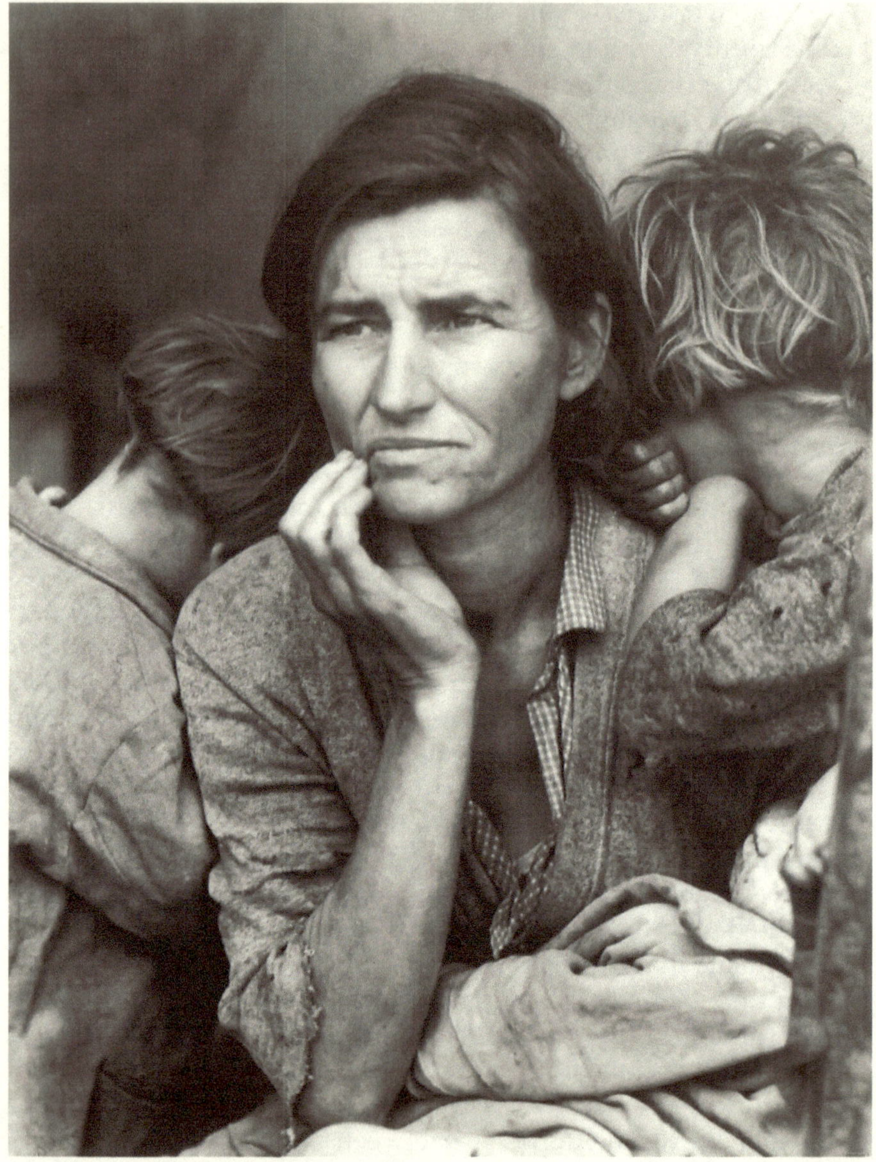

Figure 8. Dorothea Lange. *Migrant Mother, Nipomo, California* (1936). Collection of Susie Tompkins Buell.

While many viewers were so moved as to weep before the canvas, others, it is said, deplored it as "numb, idiotic," "passive, resigned, pessimistic," "ugly and deformed," "an unenlightened old-fashion peasant...."[19] Although Chinese were generally divided in their response to this painting, no one that viewed it remained unmoved. *Father* ultimately received first prize from among the works included in the exhibition.

For the Chinese spectator, there was something "foreign" and yet absolutely familiar and compelling about this hyperrealistic portrait of an anonymous old Sichuan peasant. Why render this unflattering portrayal of peasant life on a monumental scale reserved only for the portraits of Communist leaders such as Mao Zedong? This foreignness is key to understanding the meaningful connection between, on the one hand, the purposeful adoption of Western-derived imaging practices and the social value that they acquired in producing an experience of visual estrangement for viewers within the new cultural context of contemporary China.

With *Father* the Chinese viewer is subjected to that which the German dramatist and theorist Bertold Brecht termed *Verfermdungs-Effekt*, the "alienation effect," that "stressed the need in the theatre to alter the events to be presented in order to induce a critical attitude in the spectator toward what we see."[20] This has its apolitical origins in the writings of the Russian Formalist Victor Shklovsky, who termed it *ostraneniye*, "making strange."[21]

A more pragmatic or "dialogical" framing of Luo Zhongli's strategy would be to characterize it in terms of double-voicing. Double-voicing is a concept first formulated by Mikhail Bakhtin to describe the dialogical characteristic of speech. However, as Caryl Emerson notes, "the dialogic need not be exclusively verbal interaction although Bakhtin came to investigate dialogue largely in terms of the word."[22] Its use in the present context would be predicated on a conception of pictorial "style" not simply as a formal property of the painting-as-material-object, but rather in its communicative function as a mode of "visual address," what Bakhtin termed its "addressivity, the quality of turning to someone." Through the performativity of its modes of visual address, painting "interpellates" ("brings into being" or "gives identity to") its beholder *as* viewing subject, and in this way it is constitutive of spectatorial subjectivity.

Wayne Booth, in his introduction to Caryl Emerson's translation of Mikhail Bakhtin's *Problems of Dostoevsky's Poetics*, comments that for Bakhtin, the task of fiction is "to do justice to our dialogical natures," to "the essential, irreducible multi-centeredness, or 'polyphony', of human life."[23] He goes on to explain,

> We come into consciousness speaking a language already permeated with many voices—a social, not a private language. From the beginning, we are "polyglot," already in process of mastering a variety of social dialects derived from parents, clan, class, religion, country. We grow in consciousness by taking in more voices as "authoritatively persuasive" and then by learning which to accept as "internally persuasive."[24]

For Bakhtin, what is of consequence in allowing for "multi-voicedness" in Dostoevsky's novels is the articulation of the "integral point of view," the "integral position,"[25] the juxtaposition of orientations or situated expression of beliefs and values (or ideology), answerable to "the inescapably dialogical quality of human life at its best."[26]

Bakhtin recognized that "double-voicing is a characteristic of all speech in that no discourse exists in isolation but is always part of a greater whole; it is necessarily drawn from the context of the language world which preceded it."[27] It is thus never value-neutral, nor free of the intentional uses of others. However, it is in his study of prose fiction that "double-voicing" takes on a second sense, one that is of particular relevance to the work of Luo Zhongli. As Phyllis Margaret Paryas observes,

> Here double-voicing is an element discernible in discourse when the speaker wants the listener to hear words as though they were spoken with "quotation marks," expressing two different intentions at the same time. The novel is constructed almost exclusively with this kind of internally dialogized language, that is, language which contains two voices within a single grammatical construction. In *Problems of Dostoevsky's Poetics*, Bakhtin distinguishes between

> utterance spoken without quotation marks (monologic and single-voiced) and those accented with quotation marks (dialogic and double-voiced utterances).[28]

The art of Socialist Realism exemplifies monologic and single-voiced images, depicted as unaccented, without qualification or quotation marks, and is perceived by the viewer as a direct and unmediated representation of the world. It offers a hermetic, pure, and unitary depiction of its subject, without any recognition within the painting or propaganda poster that there is another perspective, a contesting or different portrayal which might be an equally valid way of addressing the referential subject. Socialist Realism represents its subject authoritatively, by suppressing the awareness of an alternative point of view which might render the depiction qualified, although its presentation is "shot through with intentions and accents."[29]

Luo Zhongli's *Father* realizes an internally dialogized pictorial discourse, incorporating multiple and counterposed modes of visual representation and address, serving to express the artist's intention indirectly and in a refracted way. Focusing on a double-voicing or internal bifurcation and dialogic ambiguity in the visual modes of address, *Father* parodies the genre of the officially sanctioned propaganda art of the Communist Party state by a deliberate inversion of the portrayal of the peasant in the manner reserved for the monumental portraits of Mao. It is a concentrated internal dialogue of two incorporated genres, Socialism Realist historical paintings and propaganda posters, through the inflection of another, the hyperrealism of the West. This enabled Luo to accomplish a more substantively sociohistorical account of peasant life, where the subject depicted is marked in class, generational, and regional terms.

In Luo's *Father*, the effect of this dialogic interaction is one of defamiliarization, which, by de-automatizing habitual perception, presented an alternative view and interpretation of peasant life, a counter-memory of recent historical events to that fostered by the propaganda posters of the Chinese Communist party-state during the Cultural Revolution. Liberated from the "monologic isolation and finalization"[30] of the previous visual regime, Luo's depiction of a peasant asks anew: Who really was the true paternal icon of the nation? Was it Mao or was it the anonymous peasant?

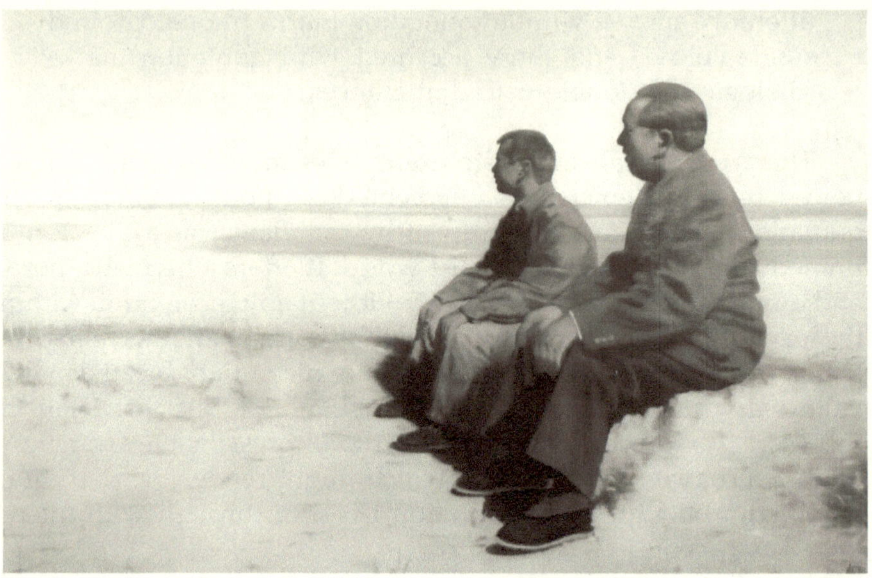

Figure 9. Yin Zhaoyang (b. 1970). *Yin Zhaoyang and Mao* (2003). Sigg Collection.

Counter-memory also, however, awakens recognition within the collective imagination of that which one was conditioned to remember to forget, the long-suffering image of the rustic as paternal icon of the nation, as emblem of China's backward rustic past and the barren, unyielding Yellow Earth depicted as encompassing *Father*. The tension and inner contradictions of the competing claims of pity and denial offer up a collective image with which to view oneself.

Here we experience what happens when official representations of history come into conflict with repressed memory. It serves to disclose the ways ideological and political hegemony are linked to the mechanism of politically enforced amnesia.[31] Luo's *Father* portrait served as well to deconstruct Mao's *Helsman's Portrait*, disclosing an *inner contradiction* between its overt *political intent* and the covert ways that he is, in fact, deified as a religious icon.

In so doing, Luo's *Father* portrait offers an alternative point of view from which to critically reexamine, reflect upon, and reassess the validity of the government's techniques and codes of political propaganda. Thus one can begin to question the legitimacy of the Communist Party's regimes of truth and power through the discursive domains of socialist realist paintings and propaganda posters. These produce disciplinary effects that condition one's sense of self or identity, one's historical memory, and one's personal conduct.

Let us fast-forward to a painting by Yin Zhaoyang (b. 1970). *Yin Zhaoyang and Mao*, painted in 2003 (fig. 9), is based on a well-known photograph from 1952 in which Chairman Mao surveys the Lower Huang He, traditional symbol of the cradle of Chinese civilization, from atop a dike. Here the artist positioned himself sitting beside Mao, and "together the two stare into the distance—like 'father and son.'"[32] The art critic Zhu Qi makes the following observations: "Now that the heroes are gone, Mao's children find themselves alone, insecure. In an age where limits get lost in vagueness and the doctrine is that everyone can make up their own rules, in an age of violent mass culture and shaky materialistic value they have to cope with the aftershocks of collapsing utopias."[33]

The soft focus and dispersed light of this scene capture a poignant, desire-laden reverie that gives expression to the existential dilemma confronting the current generation in China: the individual as well as the community are in need of a "memory story" to explain their identity and their past in order to go forward, to "live on" in the wake of the loss of the "father" (Mao). To accomplish this, Yin Zhaoyang appropriates Gerhard Richter's style of paintings that capture photographic reality, the reality of the world made visible in the photograph. In so doing, Zhu Qi observes, "the artist found his own style to create artistically convincing connections between personal history and individual subjectivity to the collective history of modern China within an updated version of the genre of history painting."[34] *Yin Zhaoyang and Mao* awakens us to the need for a sense of history that is animated by the desire to give meaning and direction to the present by finding its development in the past. It represents both a symptom and critique of the loss of authority in a society that remains nostalgic for a past that is no longer firmly grounded in intimate memory. It is a sign of the failure of the state to control not only the present, but the past as well.

5

Imperious Griffonage: Xu Bing and the Graphic Regime

Hajime Nakatani

"You know, I don't believe there's such a thing as the Japanese language. I mean, they don't even know how to write. They just draw pictures of these little characters."

—Laurie Anderson *United States Live*

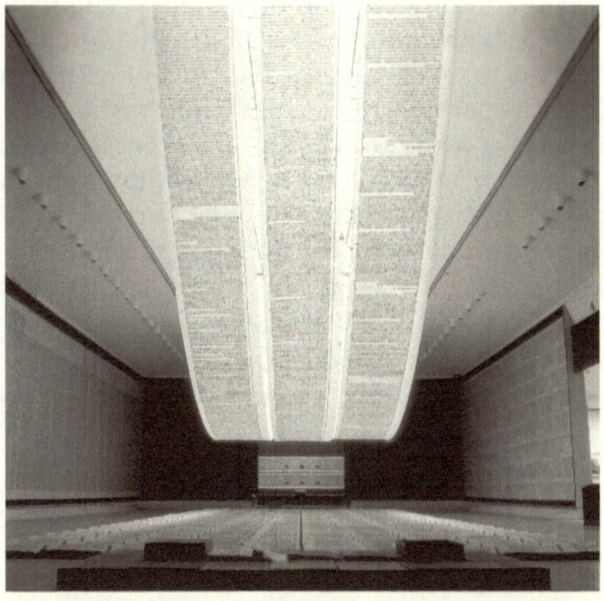

Figure 1. Xu Bing, *A Book from the Sky*, 1987–91, hand-printed books, ceiling and wall scrolls printed from wood letterpress type using false Chinese characters, installation view, *Three Installations by Xu Bing*, Elvehjem Museum of Art, University of Wisconsin-Madison, 1991–92 (artwork © Xu Bing)

Chiasmus

I'd like to broach my discussion with a scene of writing. The setting is a primary school classroom late in the tumultuous decade of the Cultural Revolution (1966–circa 1975). A young teacher is copying from a textbook onto a blackboard. The text being copied is of course studded with obligatory tributes to the Party and shone through by the rising sun of Maoism. Several dozen heads nod up and down as students earnestly copy the teacher's copy of the printed text. As striking as the mute intensity of this graphic litany is the low but persistent noise of chalk and pencils, whose incessant hitting of the board and scratching of the pages, set against the speechless background of the collective endeavor, achieves an almost claustrophobic intensity.

This is one of the recurrent scenes of writing in Chen Kaige's *The King of the Children* (孩子王 1987), a memorable film about a young teacher sent down, like many of his generation, to the marginal southern province of Yunnan during the Cultural Revolution.[1] Awaiting the idealistic young man there is the harsh reality of the poverty-stricken local school, where textbooks are in critical shortage. Compounding the situation is the pedagogical directive of the local party, which confines teaching to the verbatim transmission of Party-sanctioned textbooks. Baffled, but with no alternative, the young teacher at first reluctantly conforms to the status quo. But the force of the scene goes beyond these local circumstances to comment on a more general condition of cultural transmission. The pedagogical model here is ultimately that of writing that writes itself, teachers and students alike inserted in this tautological circuit as its mere linkages. With a sensory tangibility that overrides even the ideological content of the texts being copied, writing repeat-

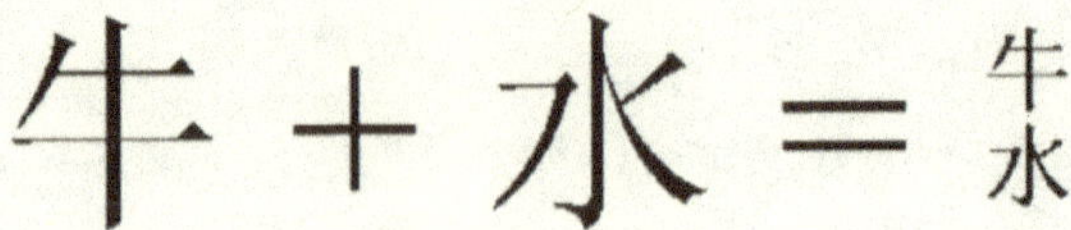

Figure 2. Structure of "Cow-Water" Pseudocharacter

edly summons and subjugates bodies to the scene of its self-perpetuation. The profound complicity between the operation of power and the physical act of writing is a crucial component of what I call the graphic regime. Perhaps elsewhere as well, but especially in China, the sheer physicality of writing has continuously defined the ground parameters of what culture is. The revolutionary era was no exception.[2]

But there is another layer to *The King of the Children*'s scene of writing. For the noise permeating the room comes not only from the scratching and scribbling of writing but also from the tramping of the herd of cows strolling in the vicinity of the school yard, long shots of which repeatedly cut into the film to profoundly inflect its meaning. One day, while routinely copying the textbook, the teacher inadvertently mixes in a nonexistent character consisting of the graph "cow" above the graph "water" (fig. 2). In a later account to the children, the teacher tries to explain his miswriting by evoking a piece of folk knowledge: cows are stubborn, nonsubmissive animals, yet one can subdue them with one's urine, because they love salt madly.

Rey Chow interprets this event of miswriting as a subversive intrusion of nature into the hegemonic text of culture, an intrusion that threatens the closure of the teacher's national subjectivity by exposing—via scatological insight—the dirty truth of culture as senseless subjugation.[3] Chow is certainly correct to stress that miswriting here conjures up the threat of nature's disruption of the text of culture, but I want to raise one simple observation against this otherwise perceptive reading. Namely, even as it disrupts culture's text, *nature also writes*—albeit in gibberish. Not unlike the overlay of the cows' steady, stomping noise that competes with the scratching sound of inscription, nature (figured here in the overbearing bovine presence) momentarily overtakes the teacher's inscribing hand to furtively drop its own mark amid human syntax. In other words, this intrusion of nature produces not a sheer negation of writing, as Chow seems to suggest, but *another* writing—a bovine script as it were—that insists in its peculiar graphic presence.

We encounter this same alignment of nature with writing again when the mute cowherd—who acts in the film as the

> personification of nature and who rejects with stubborn silence the teacher's well-meaning offer to instruct him in how to write—intrudes on an empty classroom to compose his own mysterious script on the blackboard. The singular cryptogram, thrown together with cow dung and leaves, mimics the act of writing without achieving semantic efficacy. Yet the mute, material insistence of this script lends it a powerful mystique, one that transfixes the teacher and the camera alike in a moment of semiotic abandon.

Thus in *The King of the Children*, the line that separates nature and culture does not run between writing and its absence. Rather, it lies between the lexicographically sanctioned writing of culture and nature's own script. Writing as such thus straddles the great nature-culture divide, dictating to the two sides the terms of their negotiations. It is in this absolute, totalizing sense that I will speak in this essay of a graphic regime. With the term, I want to evoke the ways in which writing serves not only to transcribe a world existing out there but to actively shape its implicit order. In a nutshell, the graphic regime is the world conceived *as* writing, a cosmo-graphy in the literal sense of the writing of the cosmos. It is the site in which writing as nature of culture and writing as culture of nature recognize their own chiasmic likeness in each other.

Notwithstanding its successive inflections and refigurations, an enduring equation between the conceivability of order and the envisioning of the world in the likeness of writing appears to persist through the long and variegated history of China. Scholars are increasingly turning their attention to the perennial role writing played in defining the fundamental outlook of early imperial order and lending to it some of its most salient and enduring characteristics—e.g., the formidable imperial bureaucracy and its massive textual output through which the polity was rendered accountable and manageable, the ideological centrality of scriptures and commentaries not only in Han and post-Han Confucianism but also in religious Daoism and later in Buddhism, and the cosmological authority accorded such graphic systems as the *Book of Changes* (*Yijing*).[4] Indeed, writing as such was deemed to be the creation of ancient sages, the privileged cosmo-graphic matrix through which later rulers were to know the world and to enact its implicit order.

With some notable exceptions, this growing scholarship tends to relegate the persistent nondistinction between writing and world to the status of instrumental irreality—i.e., ideological apparatuses and phantasmic formations of power serving at once to mask and to facilitate the imperial state's real-political interests and desires. Such an instrumentalist account of the role of writing in the formation of Chinese imperial order, which also finds echoes in well-known media-historical theories on the intersections between writing and complex polities elsewhere, may have its own usefulness, but it also risks to foreclose insights into the more subtle and deep-seated complicity between imperial order and the graphic regime.[5] At this deeper level, the relationship between writing and the empire needs to be reversed. Namely, rather than writing simply serving the imperial state as its communicative and political medium, successive imperial dynasties inserted themselves in a world always already conceived as writing. It may even be argued that, in a sense, the dynasties themselves served as instruments for the graphic regimes' blind self-perpetuation.

It is the positivity of such a graphic vision that needs to be fathomed. But how is it possible to insert ourselves into such an unfamiliar vision? My essay is a modest attempt to grope for a point of entry through the works of Xu Bing (b. 1955), the prominent Chinese artist who has been at the center of contemporary Chinese art's quick rise to international prominence since the 1980s and whose oeuvre constitutes one of the most poignant contemporary attempts to reenact the experience of the graphic regime. Xu's extraordinary work confronts the beholder with a series of perceptual questions and paradoxes. Patiently tackling each of these graphic exercises will bring us to the threshold of another history of writing, no doubt punctuated by numerous shifts and ruptures, whose historical grammar is not yet readily available to us. If in the course of this exercise I give the impression of positing an ahistoric and monolithic regime, it is only as a preliminary approximation, one that a fuller historical account may subsequently reinstate to its originary disunity.[6]

Graphic Procreation

> Language is a virus from outer space.
> —attrib. William S. Burroughs

The intersection of writing and nature that informs Chen's film has also been a central preoccupation in Xu's works. For example, the *Character Landscapes* (2000) are presumably sketches of actual scenes, but Xu uses Chinese characters instead of natural forms to render the landscape in front of him (fig. 3). As if to actualize the modern (and predominantly Western) mythology of the Chinese pictograph, wherein characters are deemed to put forth more or less schematic likenesses of the things they stand for, Xu "depicts" a tree using the graph "tree" (*shu* 樹) and a rock using the graph "rock" (*shi* 石). At stake here, however, is not whether the notion

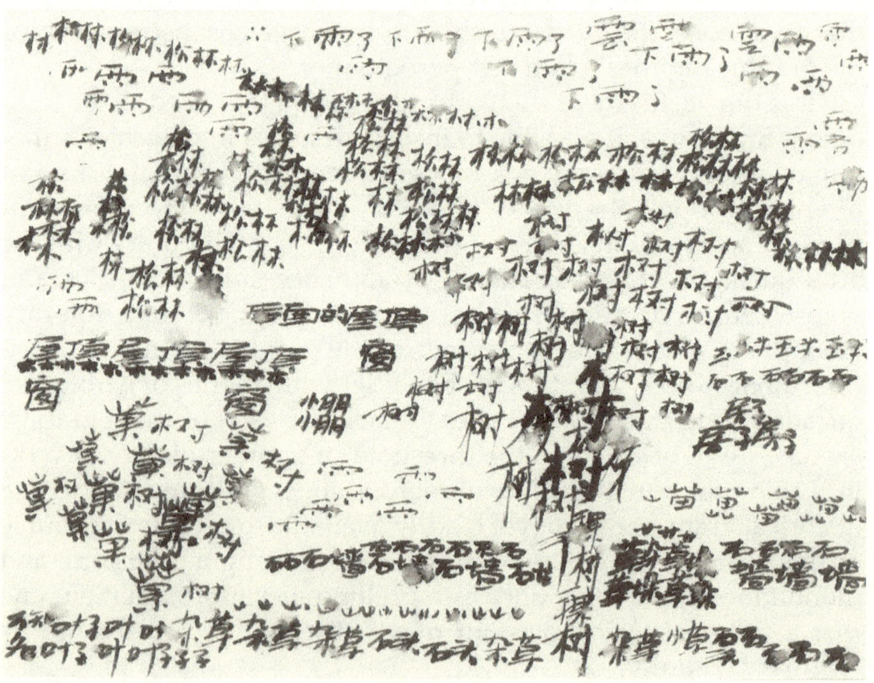

Figure 3. Xu Bing, from *Landscript Sketchbooks*, 1999–2000, ink on paper, 4 1/2 × 5 7/8 in. (11.3 × 15 cm) (artwork © Xu Bing)

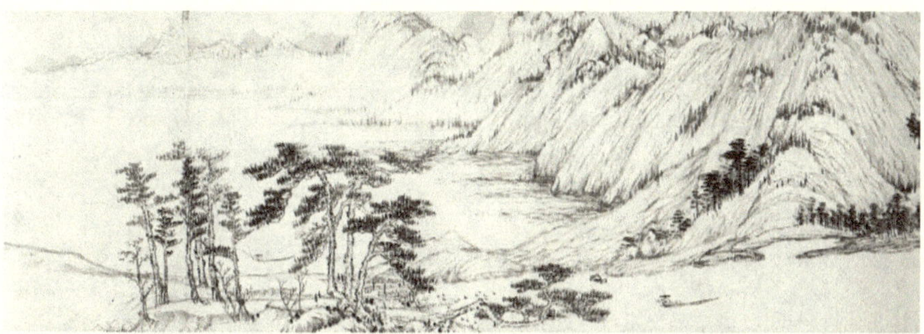

Figure 4. Huang Gongwang, *Dwelling in the Fuchun Mountain*, ca. 1350, detail of handscroll, ink on paper, 13 in. × 20 ft. 10 3⁄4 in. (33 × 636.9 cm). Collection of the National Palace Museum, Taiwan (artwork in the public domain)

of pictography offers an adequate characterization of the Chinese script, nor even whether Xu Bing believes such to be the case.[7] In fact, the pictorial convincingness of these written landscapes owes less to the resemblance between shapes of objects and of graphs than it does to the prominent calligraphic strokes delineating them, serving to place Xu's landscape squarely within the parameters of classical ink painting. In place of the pictographic myth, the works actualize another deep-seated cultural impulse: the myth of landscape as calligraphic formation, perhaps best exemplified by Huang Gongwang's fourteenth-century masterpiece *Dwelling in the Fuchun Mountain* (fig. 4).[8] The conception of the calligraphic stroke as embodiment of nature's immanent forces and articulations, one that governed post-Song dynasty landscape painting, is here rendered literal by embedding calligraphically traced graphs in real landscapes, thereby returning writing to its natural matrix.[9]

Xu's breathtaking installation *American Silkworm Series* also activates the affinities between writing and nature's pattern, albeit perhaps in the opposite direction (figs. 5–6). The association here between braille and the patterns of eggs laid on the surface of the open pages is evident.[10] Less evident is the analogy between text and texture evoked by the delicate overlay of silk, at once masking and echoing the printed text beneath it. By capturing the moment of intersection between the pattern of nature and the pattern of culture, this evolving overlay realizes the enduring idea of *wen* (文),

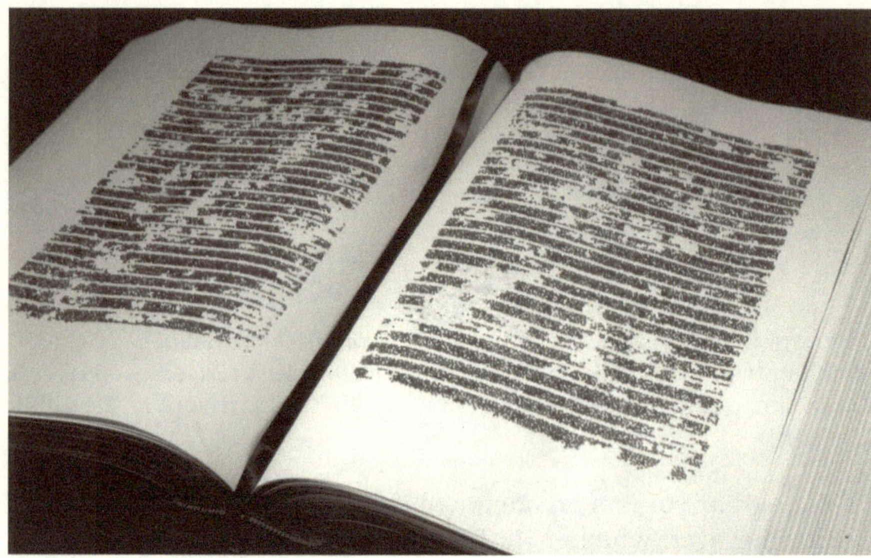

Figure 5. Xu Bing, *American Silkworm Series 1: Silkworm Books*, 1994–95, live silk moths laying eggs on blank books, book 13 × 11 × 2 in. (33 × 27.9 × 5.1 cm) (artwork © Xu Bing)

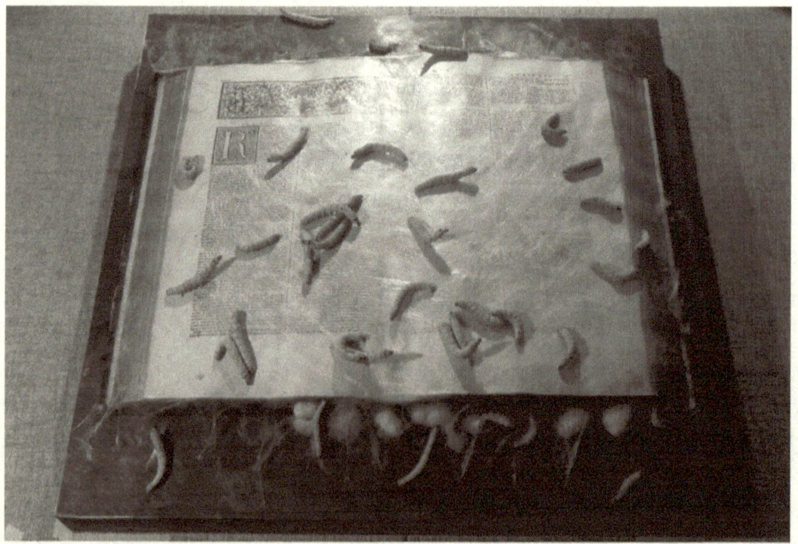

Figure 6. Xu Bing, *American Silkworm Series 2*, 1994–95, live silkworms spinning silk on objects, including a laptop computer, newspapers, a Bible, computer paper; dimensions variable; installation view, *Xu Bing: Language Lost*, Massachusetts College of Art, Boston, 1995 (artwork © Xu Bing)

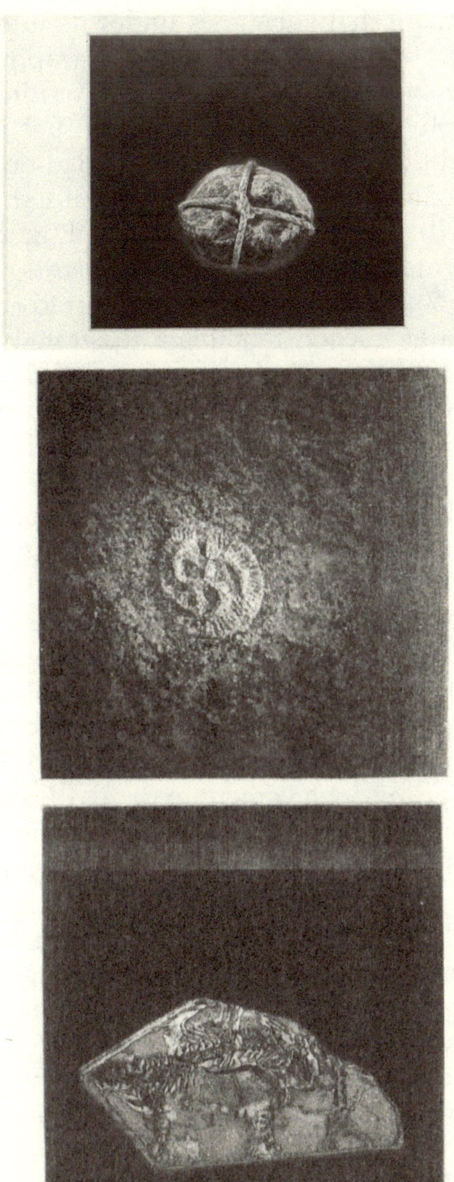

Figure 7. Xu Bing, *Pebble 2*, 1987, etching and mezzotint on paper, 19 1/4 × 20 1/2 in. (49 × 52 cm); *Fossil 1*, 1987, etching and mezzotint on paper, 19 1/2 × 19 in. (49.4 × 48.4 cm); and *Moment 1*, 1988, etching and mezzotint on paper, 9 1/2 × 9 1/2 in. (24 × 24 cm) (artwork © Xu Bing)

the signifying design that subsumes under its universal legibility an eclectic array of patterns, including the graphic configuration of the script, the syntactical articulation of writing, ritual's measured choreography of the human body, and such natural patterns as the stripes and dots embellishing the myriad flora and fauna of the world.[11] Bringing these disparate cases of *wen* together is the idea of a nature that writes itself, which, as Eugene Wang points out, already informed Xu's early interest in fossils and rough petrified surfaces (fig. 7).[12] Yet the silkworms' effort to envelop the book of culture in a huge cocoon remains a frustrated one, since silkworms are incapable of forming cocoons on flat surfaces, thus holding the interweaving of nature and culture in a prolonged state of suspense.[13]

Yet the deconstructive project of these works, seeking to blur the entrenched divide between culture's text and nature's texture, is couched in a characteristically postmodernist gesture of provisionally accepting the divide in order subsequently to transgress it, a gesture that perpetuates the divide even as it continually displaces it. We need to turn our eyes to an earlier work of the artist to find actualized the condition of a graphic regime that is truly indifferent to an ontological schism between textual meaning and texture of being. A landmark of Chinese experimental art that remains the artist's most intriguing achievement to date, *A Book from the Sky* 天書 is monumental precisely for the cosmic megalomania of its arrangement (fig. 8).[14] The mirroring and echoing among the ample scrolls hanging from the ceiling, the open volumes lined up on the floor—which faithfully reproduce the typographic and xylographic conventions of traditional Chinese book-printing and book-binding, down to the formats of front page, interlinear commentaries, marginalia, and table of contents—and the panels surrounding the large but nonetheless claustrophobic space of installation reenact the familiar Chinese cosmological trinity of Heaven, Earth, and Man (figs. 9–10).[15]

I hasten to qualify that I do not propose the cosmological model as the work's static and definitive allegorical meaning. Instead, I want to suggest that the cosmological setup constitutes a matrix in the root sense of the term, a productive configuration, a deployment of elements generative of a world. The cosmology of *A Book*

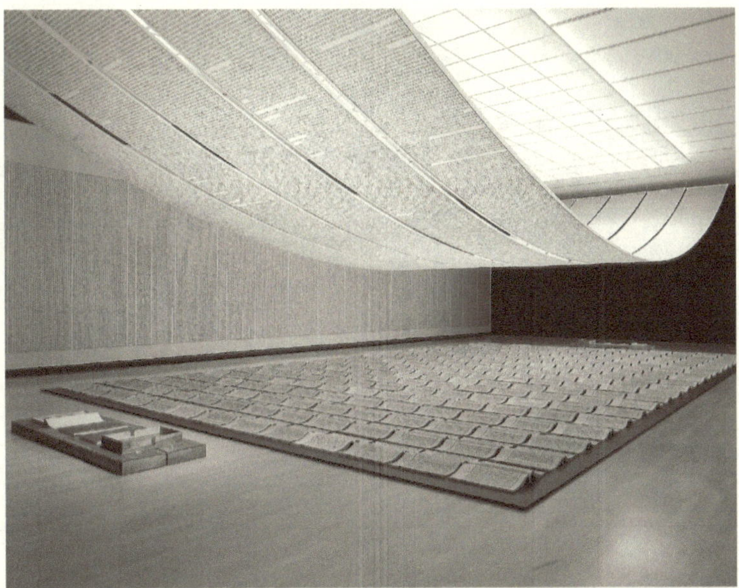

Figure 8. Xu Bing, *A Book from the Sky*, 1987–91, hand-printed books, ceiling, and wall scrolls printed from wood letterpress type using false Chinese characters; installation view, *Crossings*, National Gallery of Canada, Ottawa, 1998 (artwork © Xu Bing)

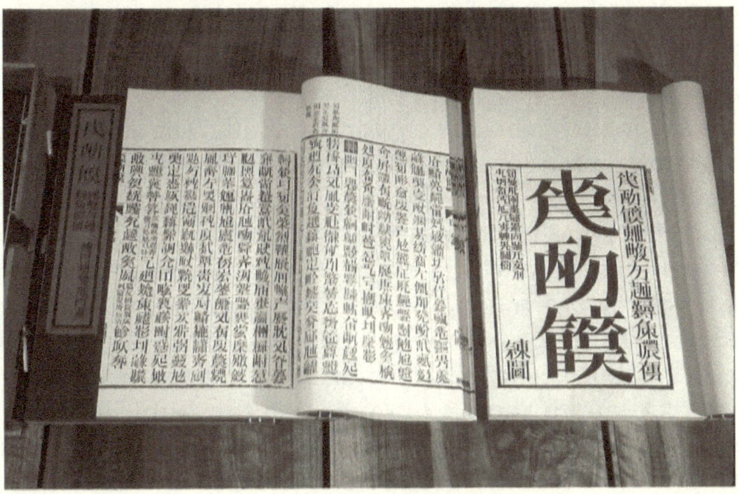

Figure 9. Xu Bing, *A Book from the Sky*, 1987–91, detail of one set (four volumes) of hand-sewn, thread-bound books printed from woodblock and wood letterpress type using false Chinese characters, ea. closed vol. 18 1⁄8 × 11 3⁄4 in. (46 × 30 cm) (artwork © Xu Bing)

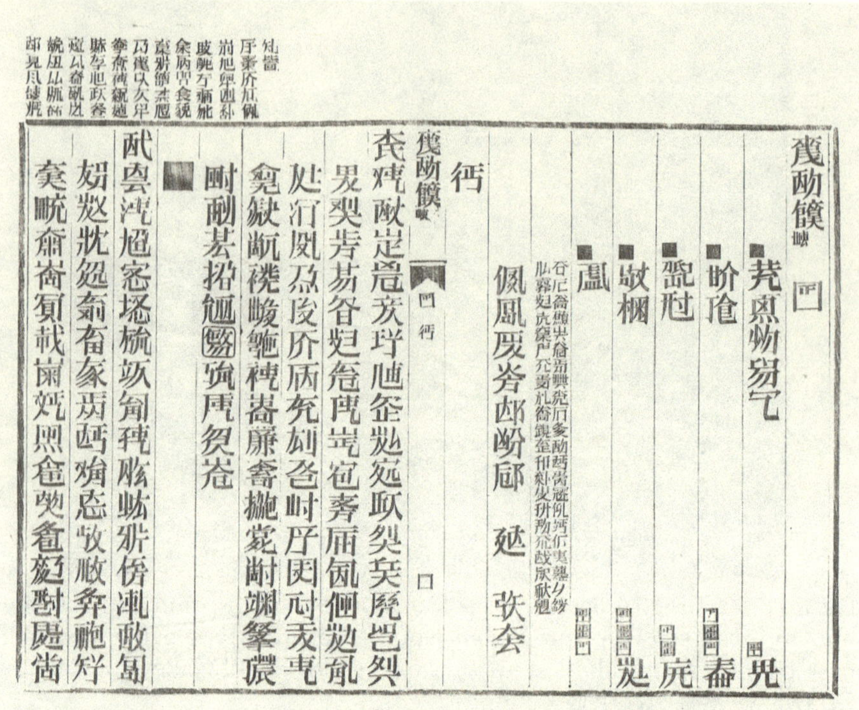

Figure 10. Xu Bing, *A Book from the Sky*, 1987–91, detail of last page of table of contents and first page of text of volume 1 (artwork © Xu Bing)

from the Sky is such a matrix of world-making, ceaselessly spinning out questions, paradoxes, and, more than anything, writing. For the creatures crowding this fertile cosmos are countless graphs, or more precisely, pseudocharacters—"characters" that are generated through painstaking and exhaustive recombination of existing character-parts and fragments. For example, the pseudocharacter shown in figure 11 consists of three distinct parts or elements, two of which (木 and 寸) are real characters in themselves and can also form parts of more complex graphs; the third unit in the middle is produced by eliminating one stroke from an existing character (which is also commonly used as component complex characters). It is important to note that even as he thus tweaks and recombines existing units, Xu adheres closely to the fundamentally modular structure that governs the morphology of the Chinese script (the

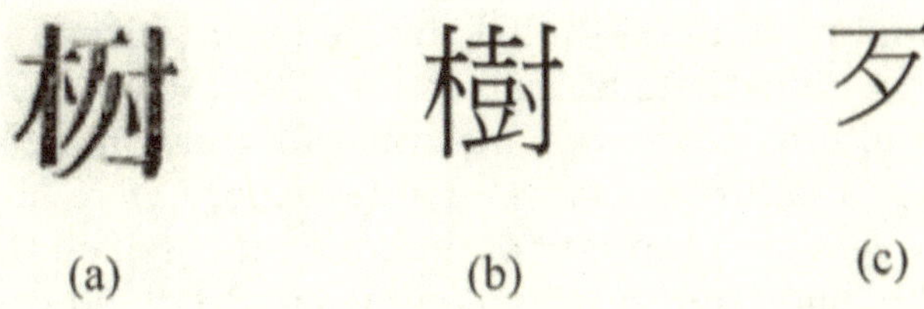

Figure 11. Structure of a pseudocharacter (diagram © the author)

real one), whereby a limited number of simpler units—some of which form characters in and of themselves while others do not—recur in more complex graphs.[16] Thus, against all appearance, the artist's method does not contradict the formal principles of the Chinese script; it radicalizes them.

The similarity this combinatorial operation gone wild bears with the scene of (mis-)writing in *The King of the Children* is unmistakable. Just as in the film nature reshuffles existing graphs to improvise its own writing, here the cosmic matrix defines a peculiar space, a cosmo-graphic machinery disarticulating and rearticulating culture's writing into a swarm of illegible but strangely compelling graphs. At the same time, the difference between *A Book from the Sky* and *The King of the Children* is also significant. For if nature in the film disrupts the coherence of culture's text from outside, from beyond the confines of the classroom, the cosmos of Xu's installation is indifferent to such a division between inside and outside or even between nature and culture. It is a space permeated by the force of writing as such, a space in which nature's disunifying operation has been generalized to such an extent as to become integral to the cosmo-graphy's inherent operation. If *A Book from the Sky* is indeed a utopia, as Stanley Abe put it in a rather liberal adoption of Louis Marin's conception of the term, it is in the latter's specific sense of a space that neutralizes oppositions, a cosmos where the chiasmus of writing between the culture of nature and the nature of culture is a plain reality.[17]

That a vision of a natural writing figures in the works of these two contemporary artists is certainly not a coincidence.[18] The two were not immune to the so-called culture fever (*wenhua re* 文化熱) that gripped Chinese intellectuals in the 1980s, when the catastrophe of the Cultural Revolution that was still fresh in memory and China's alleged failure to achieve modern glory were both attributed to the overbearing weight of the country's ossified tradition.[19] Nor were the many others who likewise engaged and continue to engage in artistic reflections on the Chinese script, such as, to name but a few: Gu Wenda, whose monumental calligraphic piece in an ancient script type called "seal script" (*zhuanshu* 篆書) is, as Wu Hung points out, illegible twice over: first, because the antiquity of the script type renders its meaning unavailable even to most Chinese beholders, and second, because the characters are all wrong one way or another (fig. 12);[20] Qiu Zhijie, who arduously copies the

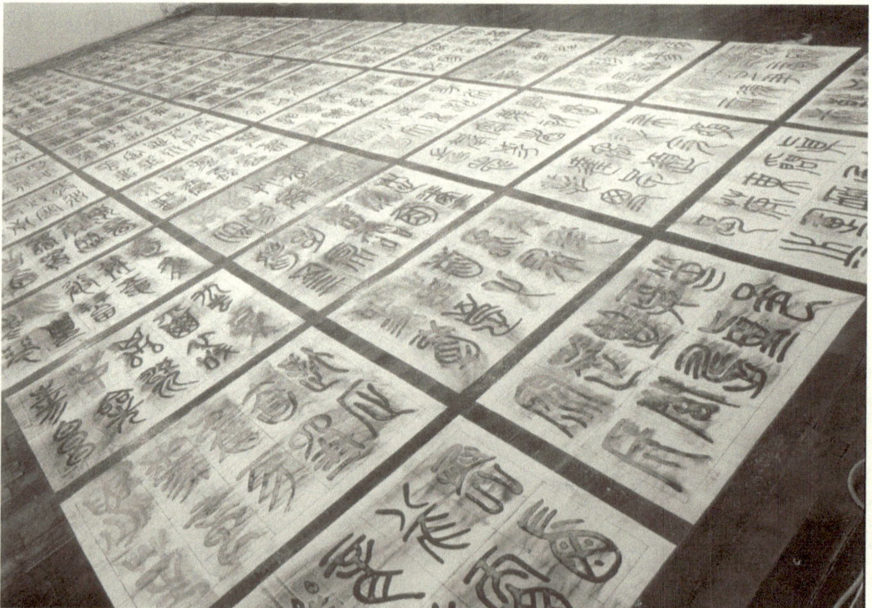

Figure 12. Gu Wenda, *Mythos of Lost Dynasties A Series*, 1983, pseudo-seal scripture in calligraphic copybook format, ink on rice paper, silk border mounting, ea. 24 × 36 in. (61 × 91.4 cm) (artwork © Gu Wenda)

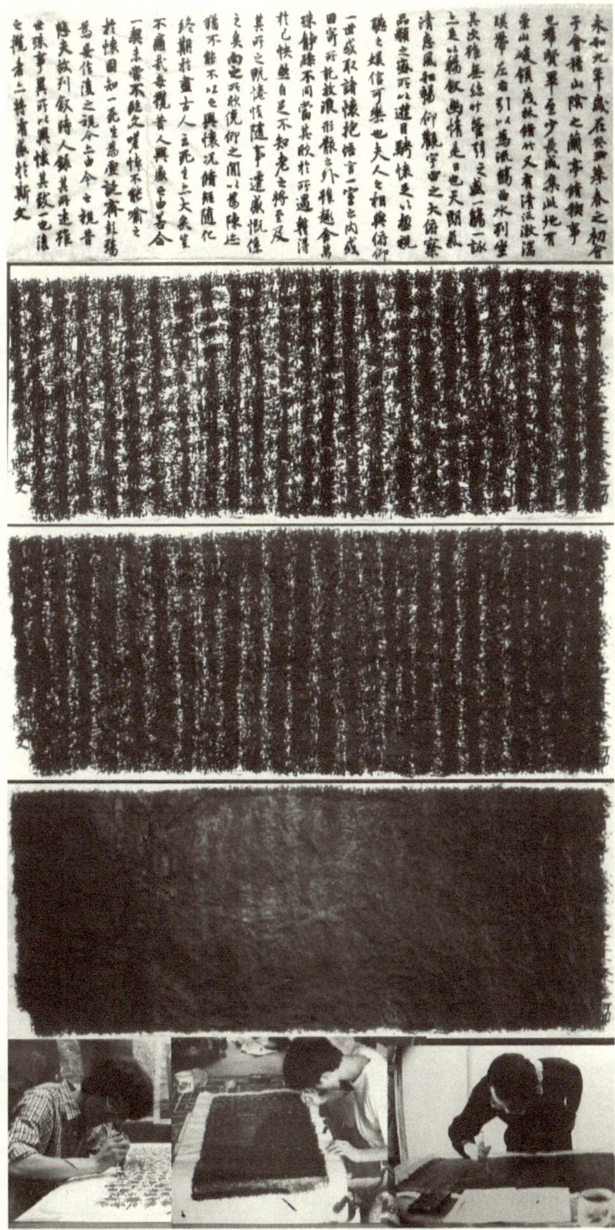

Figure 13. Qiu Zhijie, *Writing the "Orchid Pavilion Preface" One Thousand Times,* 1990–94, installation with video documentation, ink-on-paper calligraphy, approx. 16 ft. 6 in. × 16 ft. 6 in. (500 × 500 cm), calligraphy 29 1⁄2 × 70 7⁄8 in. (75 × 180 cm) (artwork © Qiu Zhijie)

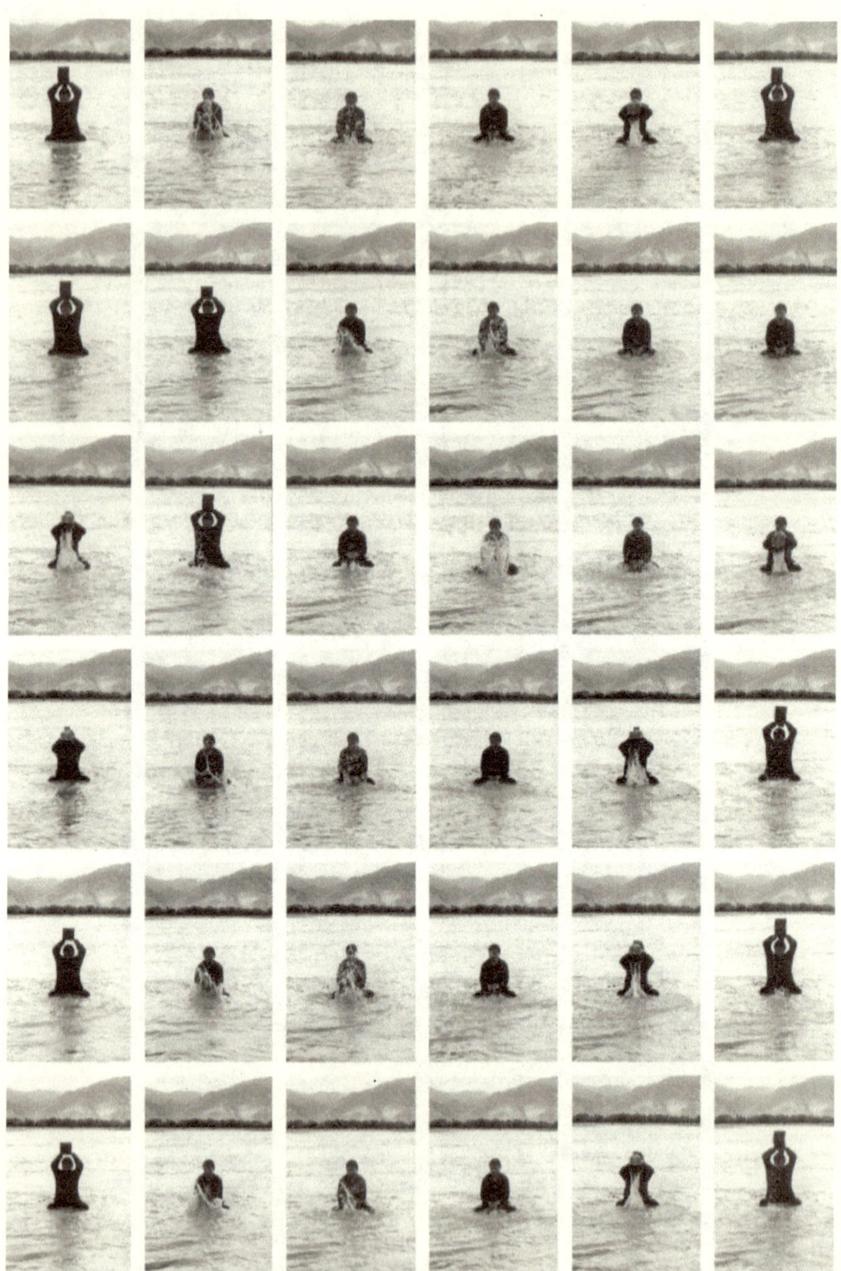

Figure 14. Song Dong, *Printing on Water*, 1996, performance in the Lhasa River, Tibet, one set of 36 chromogenic prints, ea. 24 × 20 in. (61 × 51 cm) (artwork © Song Dong)

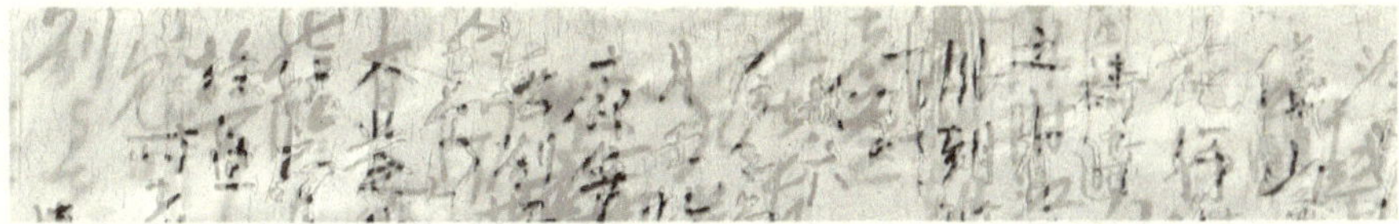

Figure 15. Wang Tiande, *Digital 06-CL02*, 2006, Chinese ink on Xuan rice paper, burn marks, 14 1/2 × 118 7/8 in (36.7 × 302 cm) (artwork © Wang Tiande)

Orchid Pavilion—the most authoritative work of traditional calligraphy—a thousand times over the same sheet of paper, in a cynical self-cancelling endeavor culminating in a plain black block of ink (fig. 13); Song Dong, whose no less poignant performance engages the artist in a repetitive effort—all the more compulsive for its futility—to imprint the surface of water with a large woodblock carved with the character "water" (fig. 14);[21] and Wang Tiande, whose exquisitely layered work covers a seemingly conventional piece of calligraphy—though barely legible and forming no readily comprehensible writing—with an overlay of a "negative calligraphy" as it were, "written" with lit cigarettes used to burn holes (or "dots," in the spirit of the work's title) into the paper (fig. 15).[22] It would be a tempting exercise of cultural history to examine the different ways in which writing figured and continues to figure in these and other artists' and authors' intense reflections on what many of them conceive as the prison-house of Chinese civilization—albeit with acute ambivalence. But the primary concern of my essay is not to contextualize the works in their immediate epochal background, but instead self-consciously to buy into and to attempt to inhabit the underlying graphic vision that they seem to simultaneously loathe and embrace. My goal here is to use *A Book from the Sky* as a heuristic entry point into the Chinese graphic regime, so that we may begin to get a feel of this vision from the inside.

Such an interpretive gesture of inhabiting would seem to be particularly appropriate for a work like *A Book from the Sky*, itself the product of the artist's prolonged act of vicariously inhabiting the cosmo-graphic space subsequently materialized in the installation. The fact that the artist immersed himself in a yearlong retreat away from the commotion of the late 1980s cultural scene into the solitude of his studio to design and to carve the pseudocharacters

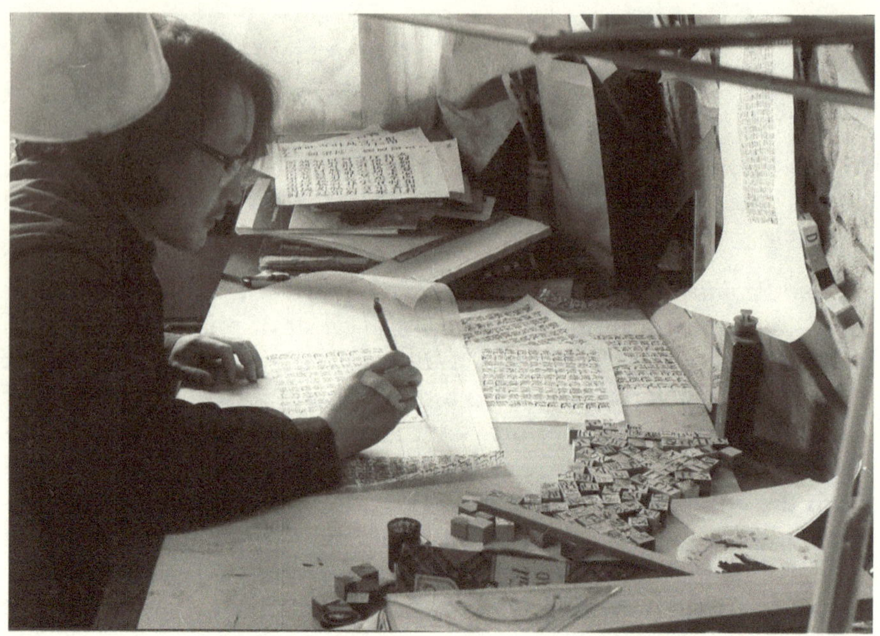

Figure 16. Xu Bing creating fake characters for *A Book from the Sky* at his studio, 1987 (photograph © Xu Bing)

is by now something of a legend (fig. 16).[23] Instead of resorting to a facile narrative of spirituality and the lonely artist, I want to suggest that the long retreat was marked by the artist's *possession* by the cosmo-graphic vision. By "possession" I mean quite literally the conversion into an agent of the vision: Xu became the catalyzing agent for the cosmo-graphic space in which graphs procreate by crossbreeding and regenerating in new combinations. Methodically and exhaustively, the artist precipitated this graphic orgy to give birth to the countless pseudocharacters.

If this sounds like a figment of a fertile imagination, the imagination turns out to have canonical backing. In the postscript to the still-authoritative ancient dictionary *Shuowen jiezi* (說文解字), compiled by the scholar Xu Shen (許慎) in the Eastern Han dynasty (25–220 CE), we find the following passage:

> 文者物象之本。字者言孳，乳而寖多也。
> The simple graph (*wen* 文) is the fundamental image of things. The complex graph (*zi* 字), on the other hand, means "to give birth" (*zi* 孳). It procreates and multiplies.[24]

Xu Shen's distinction between *wen* and *zi* was essentially a morphological one, intimately bound up with his famous "Six Laws of Character Formation" (*liushu* 六書), in which he classified the morphology of complex graphs into six basic structural patterns.[25] *Wen*, on the one hand, is morphologically simple, forming an indivisible graphic unit that purportedly entertains an iconic relation to the shapes of things.[26] *Zi*, on the other hand, is composite, consisting of two or more simpler graphs combined according to one of the six morphological patterns. The above passage thus serves to highlight an unexpected connection between what is usually taken to be a purely classificatory system of existing characters and a notion of graphic fertility, thereby further entrenching the radical collapse between nature and culture.[27] The totality of existing graphs is the product of a regulated process in which simpler graphs mate to form complex ones, and it is such a law of procreation that grounded the classification system of Xu Shen's dictionary.

Evidently, the corpus of actual graphs is always enmeshed in the messy history of words and their uses, and the referential responsibility of Xu Shen as lexicographer inevitably frustrated his project to uncover a coherent system of graphic fertility beneath the daunting heterogeneity of existing characters. This impossible dream, however, also proved to be a tenacious one, resurfacing throughout Chinese history in a multitude of cultural milieus and metamorphosing into myriad forms of character interpretations.[28] Placed at the tail end of this curious genealogy, Xu Bing's grand cosmo-graphy may perhaps be seen as the delusory realization of the millennia-old, frustrated dream, one finally actualized by allowing pseudocharacters to devour the entire cosmos.

Nonsense?

Such a reading of *A Book from the Sky*, however, flies in the face of the prevailing interpretations that perceive the work under the sign of sterility rather than fertility. Virtually all critics unconditionally accept the ground characterization of the pseudocharacters as *nonsense* writing.[29] Thus, allegorizing critics read into the evacuation of meaning an essentially political, critical intent, one targeting the oppressiveness of either culture in general, the Chinese tradition more specifically, or the Communist regime.[30] The anti-allegoricists instead recognize in the "nonsense" characters the realization of the "open text," the archetypally postmodern figure of the freedom of the reader.

Such a convergence of what are otherwise diametrically opposed readings is enough to alert us to an entrenched interpretive paradigm operating beneath the apparent divergence. Uniting these readings is the familiar communication model of meaning, a model defining meaning at the intersection of intention and reception. The two readings simply highlight one or the other end of this communicative chain. But falling through the cracks of such a communication-centered model is the agency of the graph, its intrinsic capacity to produce and reproduce itself and its signification. It is symptomatic that the prevailing interpretations fail to closely examine *A Book from the Sky*'s pseudocharacters in their concrete forms and structures, instead glossing them over abstractly as at once meaningless, painstakingly crafted, and beautiful. But it is precisely the tangible being of individual graphs that propels Xu's cosmo-graphy, their vitalistic capacity orchestrating the work's vortex of graphic procreation and regeneration.

A closer look at the graphs reveals their profoundly riveting nature, as illustrated by the enthralled viewer at the first public show of the work in Beijing in 1988 (fig. 17). For those familiar with the Chinese script, to look at Xu's pseudocharacters is a tantalizing experience, one that mixes enchantment with frustration. The graphs frustrate because they are meaningless in the precise sense that they fail as "logographs," as modern linguists put it (in emphatic opposition to the notion of the ideograph).[31] Xu's pseudocharacters fail as writing not because they do not correspond to meanings directly (the real Chinese script does not do so either), but because they do not correspond to any known words and are hence bound to remain unpronounceable and unfathomable. Yet the same failed characters enchant because the un-logographic pseudocharacters are nonetheless perpetually on the cusp of signification. That a graph devoid of lexical support can nevertheless be compelling is one of the most intriguing insights that Xu's work brings about.[32] The task of distinguishing combinations of elements that somehow make sense as graphs from those that do not was a central preoccupation of the artist during his yearlong seclusion. At stake here

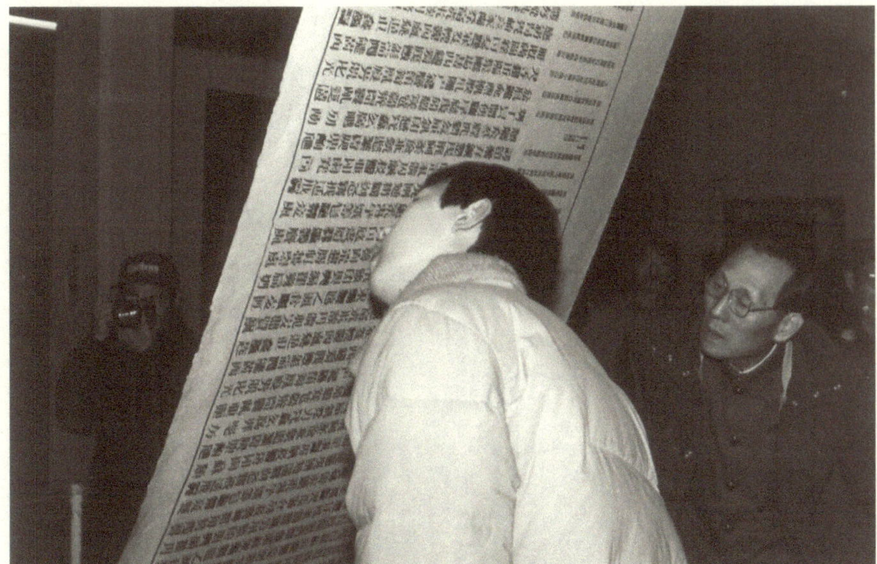

Figure 17. Visitors viewing *A Book from the Sky*, 1988, China Art Gallery, Beijing (photograph © Xu Bing)

is thus not an extraneous consideration for aesthetically pleasing forms unrelated to semantics as such, but rather a sensibility that presumes an intrinsic connection between morphology and meaning, something akin to the ideographic fantasy that modern linguists took such pain to discredit.

In his insightful treatise on the Chinese art of writing, Jean-François Billeter emphasizes that a well-formed character should possess an organic autonomy: "Like the organism, which in the realm of nature is a relatively complete and closed system, independent of its surroundings, the character has to constitute, in the realm of forms, a system that is relatively complete, closed and independent of the surrounding space; by its form, it should be the equivalent of a living being."[33] To achieve this goal, the writing hand needs to adhere to several formal rules, such as: (1) to fit the character in an imaginary square (as opposed to the roman alphabet, which unfolds across a horizontal line); (2) to give the character a center of gravity; (3) to give the character a "silhouette," as clean an outline

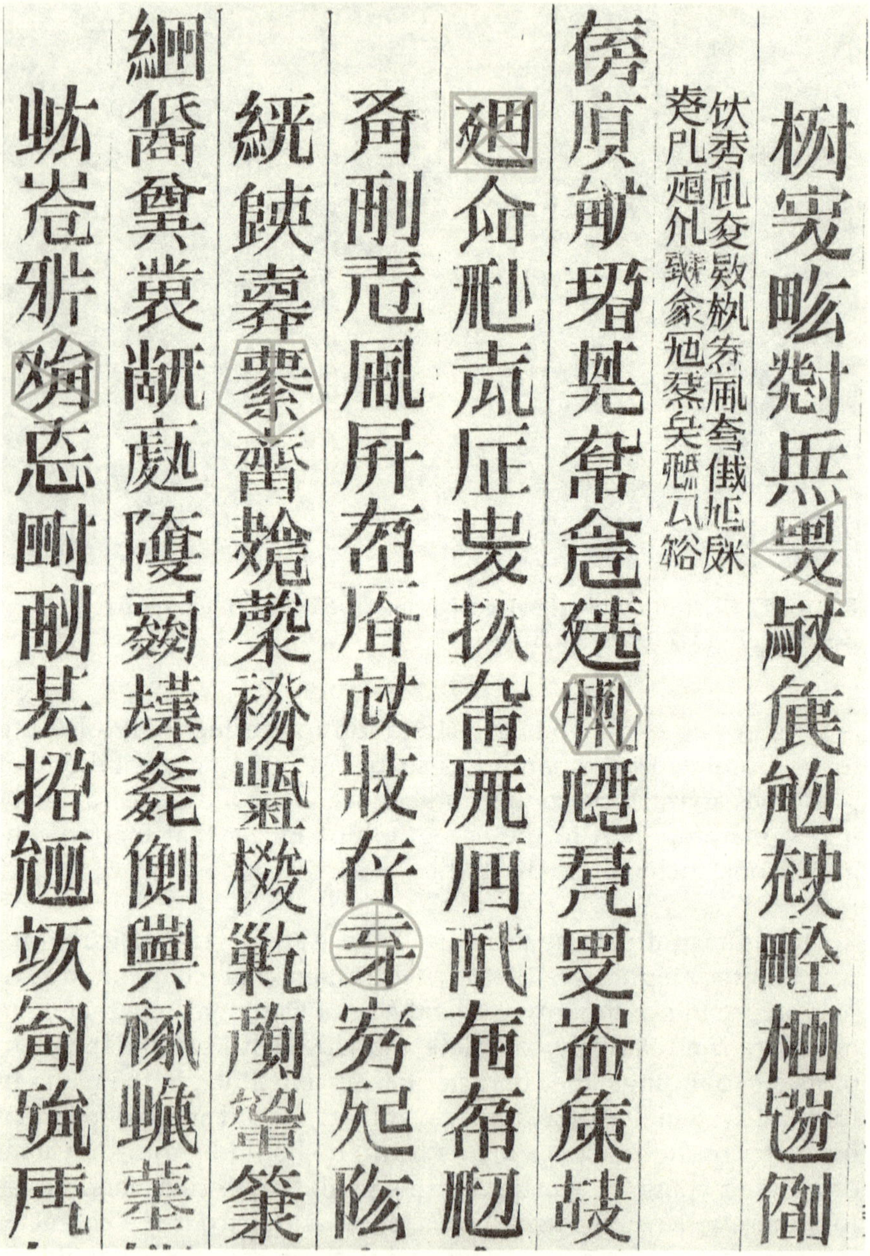

Figure 18. Xu Bing, page in *A Book from the Sky*, 1987–91, with red marks added by the author (artwork © Xu Bing)

as possible; (4) to integrate the distinct parts of a complex character by adjusting the relative size and density of the different parts. While Billeter's rules apply primarily to calligraphy (i.e., handwriting), they provide useful yardsticks to measure the well-formedness of printed characters—and, indeed, of Xu's pseudocharacters as well. Their morphological soundness and general conformity to the organic morphology of real characters become apparent when one simply marks their outlines and centers, as in figure 18.[34] These centered, proportioned, and clean silhouettes are what lend body to characters and pseudocharacters alike, what Billeter aptly calls the character's "body sense."[35]

Further extending the organic and naturalizing analogy, we may compare this experience of significant form to that of the face. Well-formed graphs congeal into a countenance, whereas ill-formed ones do not, and this unity of mien is what confers a halo of meaningfulness to Xu's pseudocharacters. At the same time, the physiognomic expressivity of graphs frustrates the beholder, because their evocative aspects refuse to conform to the fixity of the lexicon. They cannot be named. This is probably what the artist meant when he said that his pseudowriting has a face but has no voice.[36]

The face, the philosopher Georg Simmel suggests, is the empirical paradigm for synthesis.[37] It is the experience of the Kantian "unity of multiplicity" in the here-and-now of perception, one in which the vagaries of constantly moving parts crystallize, immediately and tangibly, into the coherence of a countenance. To recognize a graph in the outlandish recombination of graphic parts is an experience comparable to such a physiognomic recognition. This is a pregnant analogy, especially because much of the meaning the viewer finds in Xu's graphs in fact derives from the multitude of associations triggered by their components as well as their overall shapes. Character elements incorporated in the pseudocharacter evoke a quality (e.g., "water," "sharpness," or "enclosure"), and similarity with existing graphs add further layers of connotations, both semantic and phonetic. A pseudocharacter "makes sense" when the myriad of connotations without denotation congeal into the coherence of a mien.

Some examples are in order (fig. 19). The first character is a rather obvious example of a successful semantic convergence of parts, showing the character for "flame/aflame" (炎) sitting above the character for "death" (死). The next pseudocharacter is somewhat more subtle, seamlessly fusing two existing characters into a graph that evokes an equally successful semantic fusion: the character *bing* (兵) stands for "soldier" and *shu* (庶) for either "numerous" or "common, lowly"; their combination suggests something like a swarm of foot soldiers, an association reinforced by the increased number of dots at the bottom. The third and most poignant example combines the common element (or "key," *bushou*) that is often found in characters having to do with the flesh (月). On the right is the character for "to press, to crush, to flatten." The painful pseudocharacter that results from their combination would probably be pronounced something like *ya* or *zha*, following the character on the right, since in existing characters of the same structure, the right-side elements usually bear phonetic information. The "sound(s)" further reinforce(s) the painful "meaning" of the pseudocharacter, since it puns with a host of such similar words as "to push" (*ya* 押), "to (op)press" (*ya* 压), "to squeeze" (*zha* 搾), "to explode" (*zha* 炸), and so on.

Such an analysis necessarily remains tentative, given the more or less subjective nature of such associations. My point is not to

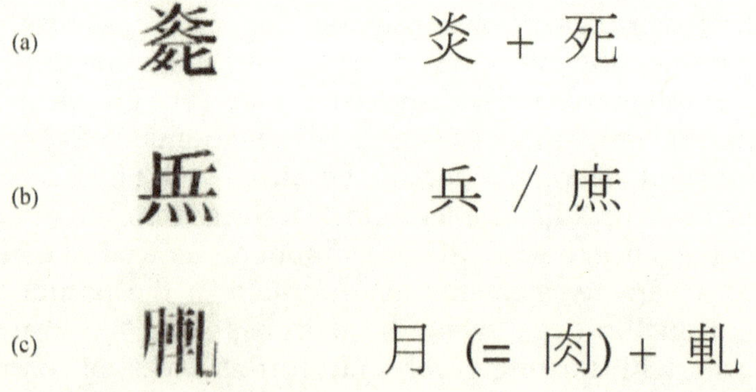

Figure 19. Semantic and phonetic "resonances" of pseudocharacters from Xu Bing, *A Book from the Sky*, 1987–91 (artwork © Xu Bing; diagram by the author)

claim that the above exhausts the whole gamut of semantic and phonetic associations that may have crossed the artist's mind as he designed each pseudocharacter or may cross the mind of the viewer plowing through the arcane graphic terrain. My aim is rather to suggest that the myriad associations evoked by Xu's little square graphs seem to gravitate toward a certain kernel, as much semantic and phonetic as morphological. The body of the character is a signifying one as well, albeit more like a face than like a name.

This immanence of meaning in the body of the character might have been what Paul Claudel had in mind when he famously stated that whereas alphabetic writing flees across the horizon, characters always face us. With this pithy formulation, he makes it abundantly clear why the agency of the graph in *A Book from the Sky* is fundamentally at odds with such poststructuralist figures of graphic materiality as Jacques Lacan's "agency of the letter" or Jacques Derrida's "trace," notwithstanding the insistence of some critics to the contrary. For what these poststructuralist figures variously seek to evoke is a presence of absence, a flurry of fugitive associations rapidly shifting from one sign to another to form what Lacan called the metonymic chain.[38] In contrast, the web of associations deployed around the pseudocharacter is *immanent*: just as the coherence of the multitude of movements animating the face is inevitably felt to be the expression of a coherent interiority, the numerous associations crowding the pseudocharacters are felt to spring from its inner kernel. If poststructuralist signification inhabits the interstices between signs, the signification of the pseudocharacter instead emanates from within the fertile center of the graph's tangibly compact being. Despite its insistent deconstructive gestures (and *pace* Derrida's critique of the book as containment of the trace), poststructuralism remains a thinking of the book, the linear discourse (albeit multilinear), the fugitive breath of meaning.[39] The Chinese graphic regime, in contrast, is the regime of script, graphic faces whose countenances and constellations maintain their unique and block-like coherence even as they respond to and intersect with one another. John Lagerway's insightful remarks on the unity of the cracks on ancient oracle bones, Daoist scriptures, and Chinese writing applies equally to Xu's pseudocharacters: "[The cracks] remind us that the original Chinese text is not linear and does not constitute a book.... Cracks on oracle bones and Taoist real writs do not represent...something outside of themselves; they are disclosures of patterns (*wen*), revelation of structures (*li*)."[40] Xu's "books" are in fact such heavenly writs (as the Chinese term *tianshu* may be rendered), for which the linear closure of the book remains alien.[41]

A phenomenon as mundane as the pun may offer a better approximation for the signification of the pseudocharacters than the trace or the metonymic chain, for its associative effects are inexorably entangled with the palpable stuff of words. Xu's pseudocharacters emerge at the intersections of graphic puns: morphological resemblances, repetitions, and overlaps converging on each of those curiously evocative ciphers. Such a collapse between signification and pun also finds interesting historical analogue in one of the peculiarities of early Chinese commentaries and lexicographic works that continue to perplex the modern Sinologist. For a similar drive to anchor meaning in the tangible thickness of the written word governs the predilection for paronomastic glosses in Han dictionaries and canonical commentaries.[42] In these curious glosses, similarities in sound or shape equally constitute the basis for punning understood broadly. For example, a passage from the Han Confucian text *Bohutong* (白虎通) expounds on the compound term "ancestral shrine" (*zongmiao* 宗廟) via auditory proximity: *zong* puns with the word "to respect" (*zun* 尊) and *miao* puns with the word "countenance" (*mao* 貌).[43] The commentary thereby derives the core function of a shrine (i.e., "the place to house the image/face of the ancestor for worship") from the graphs' auditory associations.

Some may question my direct linkage between Xu's pseudocharacters and the Han paronomastic glosses, pointing to the difference of perceptual registers separating the two. A pun, after all, is about sound, which is one sense that is presumably renounced in Xu's graphs. It would then appear as though the Han exegetes, unlike the contemporary artist, resorted to speech as their primary matrix of associations. To infer thus, however, would be to smuggle in a quintessentially modern presupposition about language and its relation to the senses. Sense discrimination is irreducible for linguistics because the modern and/or Western definition of what properly belongs to language centrally turns on it. The massive body of deconstructive critiques in the wake of Derrida's *Gramma-*

tology has brought to light the overdetermined nature of the speech-script distinction, allied with global claims about signification, subjectivity, and the *logos*. Han exegesis compels us to suspend this dense cultural formation and to turn our eyes to an equally dense but different cultural formation, one that centers on the graph as multisensory block-unit of signification. Sound then ceases to index the ontologically autonomous sphere of speech, distinct from the realm of writing, instead neighboring shape as an equally constitutive component of the discrete graph-word. This is why in Han canonical commentaries, just as in Xu's work, paronomastic glasses are found side by side with glosses that treat characters as rebuses. For instance, the word "loyalty" (*zhong* 忠) is explained in another Han-dynasty text as "one whose heart-mind (*xin* 心) holds one center (*zhong* 中; puns with 'loyalty')."[44] The combination of these two graphs indeed yields the graph for "loyalty" (fig. 20). Here, as in *A Book from the Sky*, no firm line separates visual similitude and intersections from auditory ones; together they form the tangible stuff of the written word to which Han commentators and contemporary artist alike seek to anchor all meaning.

The logic of similitude underlying the puns of ancient commentaries may appear to lend support to the notion of pictography, as some have attempted to show.[45] The pictography hypothesis, however, fails to capture the real magnitude of the authority accorded to writing in early Chinese reflections. In fact, one-to-one corre-

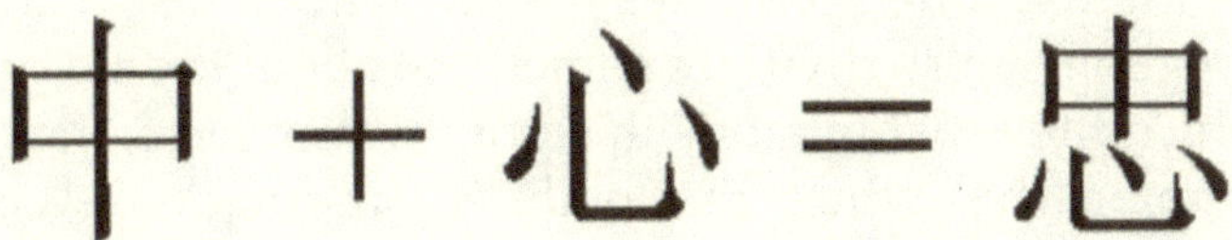

Figure 20. The structure of the character for "loyalty" (*zhong*) (diagram © the author)

spondences of whatever type between individual graphs and real things appear to have been only of marginal, ad hoc significance for the ancient Chinese reflections on writing.[46] That writing encapsulates the immanent order of the world was a given that required no further justifications. In this sense, writing formed an essentially closed system. If a certain notion of likeness nonetheless legislated the relationship between writing and the world, the vector pointed in the opposite direction. Instead of likeness anchoring writing to the world, it was the world that was invested in writing and transfigured into its likeness. Facts of writing were ipso facto facts of the world, but not necessarily the other way around. Hence the perennial importance of the pun. The dazzling choreography of graphic mirroring and resonance orchestrated by puns at once defined processes of signification and of the world, rendering moot the distinctions between meaning and being and between nature and culture.

Toward a History of the Graphic Regime

It is this sense of total closure, the claustrophobic autonomy of the Chinese cosmo-graphy that Xu's *A Book from the Sky* captures with such poignancy. The world of real things evaporates there, leaving a world composed only of writing. Bringing the collapse of meaning and being to its absurd but logical end, its ten thousand graphs supplant the ten thousand things of the universe to enact a mad dance of a cosmo-graphic system that blindly turns on itself but articulates nothing. What we witness in the universe of *A Book from the Sky* is the modus operandi of the graphic regime laid bare, the stubborn operations of the regime qua naked regime.

But if the work demonstrates the fundamental structure of the graphic regime, it also divulges something about the singular manner in which the artist inhabits this graphic universe, the marginal vantage point from which the totality of the regime's empty automatism becomes visible as such. It is a marginality that reminds us, for example, of the awed and perplexed gaze the peoples at the margins of Chinese civilization might have cast on the graphic universe of the Chinese "center." In particular, it is reminiscent of the Xixia script (as many have noted when first confronted with a page from Xu's *Book*), invented in 1036 CE by the first ruler of the inner

Asian kingdom of Xixia (fig. 21).[47] The Xixia script is one of many Chinese-inspired writing systems invented at the four corners of the East Asian cultural sphere (e.g., Vietnam, Mongolia, Manchuria), where possessing a script of one's own satisfied far more than a people's practical communicative needs; it was tantamount to a claim to membership in civilization and, hence, the expression of the burning desire to possess an imperial cosmo-graphy of one's own. It is tempting to imagine the artist inhabiting the graphic regime like an eleventh-century Inner Asian "barbarian" might have done, devising a graphic universe all his own, but which turns up as hostile and inhospitable as the one he mimics. In fact, something of this hostility is captured in one of the few ways in which Xu's pseudocharacters sometimes deviate from the morphological norm of real characters, namely in their excessively complex and aggressively thistly shapes, characteristics prominently featured in the Xixia script as well (fig. 22). The pompous prickliness of Xu's over-

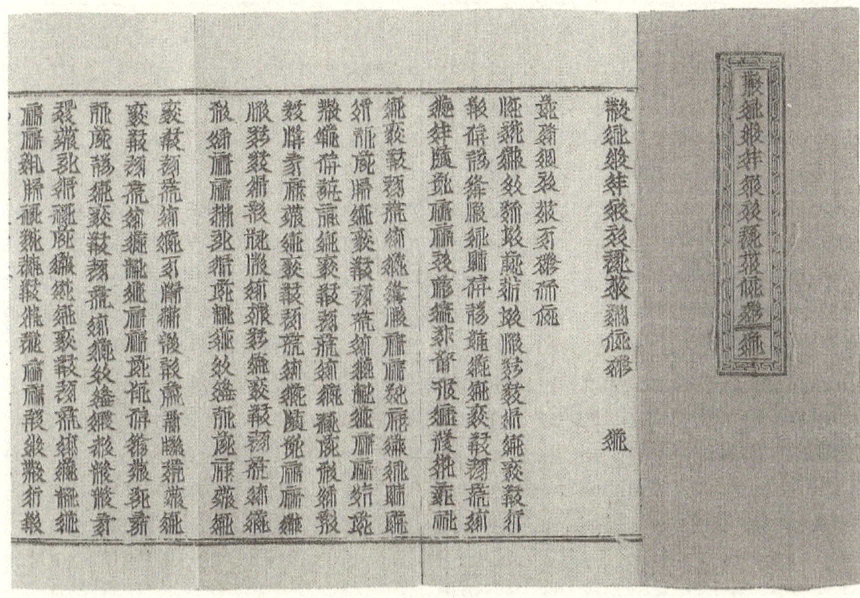

Figure 21. Cover and first pages of the *Huayan Sutra*, translated into Xixia, mid-fourteenth century, wooden movable-type print, concertina binding. Collection of the Department of Literature, Kyoto University (artwork in the public domain)

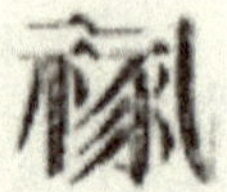

Figure 22. Xu Bing, character in *A Book from the Sky*, 1987–91 (artwork © Xu Bing)

loaded pseudocharacters captures something of those (pseudo-) empires' admixture of yearning for and fear of China's towering cultural presence. Nietzsche might have perceived in such an ambivalence the *ressentiment* of the marginal kingdoms toward China's towering cultural presence—albeit a militarily rather vulnerable power—most emblematically embodied in the intimidating universe of the Chinese script.

As tempting as this possible alliance with the geocultural margins of the Chinese civilization may be, however, this is not the only form of marginality *A Book from the Sky* evokes vis-à-vis the graphic empire. Indeed, one of the less assertive—and perhaps less deliberate—ways in which some characters of *A Book from the Sky* deviate from the norm may turn out to be symptomatic of the actual vantage the work tacitly assumes vis-à-vis the regime. Unlike the graphic overload of those Xixia-like characters, these other characters peculiarly lack density, as gaping white holes upset the otherwise finely calculated graphic poise and equilibrium of Xu's pseudoscript. Their graphic sparseness brings to mind the hollowness of the modern "simplified" (*jianti* 簡體) characters, the official script of the People's Republic of China, systematized by the Communist government in the 1950s and based partly on traditional forms of calligraphic and typographic abbreviations (fig. 23).

The establishment of simplified characters, with their fewer strokes and radical reduction of formal complexity, was aimed pri-

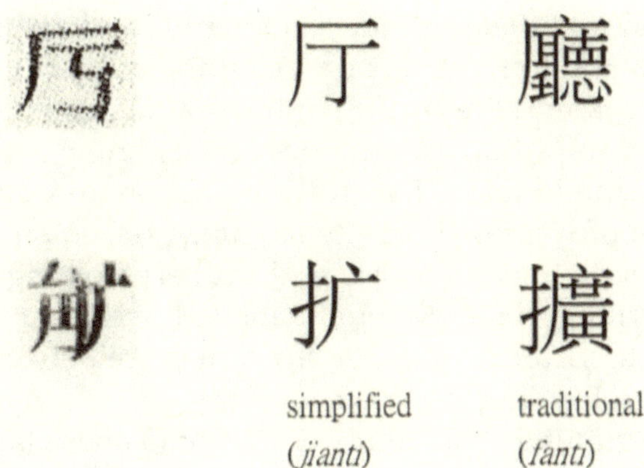

Figure 23. Xu Bing, detail showing similarities between pseudocharacters and "simplified" (*jianti*) characters in *A Book from the Sky*, 1987–91 (artwork © Xu Bing)

marily at promoting literacy by making the script easier to memorize; seen more broadly, however, the simplification of script dovetails with the language-reform movements that sprang up in the wake of the Republican Revolution of 1911 and the collapse of the Qing dynasty it brought about. Proposals for simplification continued to figure prominently in most intellectual and policy debates on and programs for the modernization of Chinese society and culture. The radical proposals variously sought to unburden the Chinese language of its heavy graphic baggage by abolishing the characters and replacing them with alphabetic romanization, by inventing some artificial phonetic script more suited to the Chinese language, or—in extreme cases—by abandoning the language altogether and replacing it with Esperanto.[48] Despite their diversity, the radical and often fantastic proposals and polemics all aimed at breaking out of what modern intellectuals perceived to be a stiflingly dense and massive scriptural burden.

By unassumingly dropping graphs and graph-parts evocative of modern simplified characters on the otherwise emphatically "traditional" pages of his books, Xu Bing advertently or inadvertently acknowledges the work's underlying affinity with this modernizing desire to stand outside the closure of the graphic empire. At the same time, the almost seamless way in which these anomalous graphs blend into their antique typographic and xylographic environment has the ironic effect of recouping modern (anti-)graphic sensibility back into the closure of the graphic regime, thereby betraying the surreptitious persistence of the regime at the very heart of linguistic modernism. For in their passion and obsession with the negation of writing, both the language reformers and the contemporary experimental artists end up perpetuating the very authority of writing that they sought and still seek to undermine—so much so as to virtually collapse the difference between reforming writing and reforming language.[49]

Such ambiguities and ambivalences of Chinese linguistic modernism are what *A Book from the Sky* crystallizes in its absurdist magnificence. It is here that we begin to confront the historicity of the work in the strict sense of the term. For in its very ability to expose the graphic regime as a system that articulates nothing but its own operations, it acknowledges its own fundamental modernity. *A Book from the Sky* is a modern allegory in the sense in which Walter Benjamin defined the term: an allegory of the allegorical apparatus as such. If the graphic pun and paronomastics of the Han commentators and lexicographers served to invest lexical meaning in the palpable density of graphs, it is by divesting the graphic regime of its entanglement with the lexicon that *A Book from the Sky* presents cosmography in its bare systematicity. No longer a fact of the world, the work becomes a world apart—a utopia—where cosmo-graphy is exposed as what it always was but never recognized itself to be: a regime.

The visibility of the regime qua regime afforded by a work like *A Book from the Sky* is what enables us to conceive a history of the graphic regime. In the optics of this privileged perspective, the history will figure as a history of blindnesses, a history of a regime that persisted in misrecognizing itself as the world. But if the efficacy of a regime is predicated on such an entrenched misrecognition, the insight of Xu's *Book* perhaps also signals the beginning of an end. In a sense, and despite fervent cultural and political effortsover more than a century to modernize the Chinese language, the modernity of Chinese writing is just beginning, and we do not yet know what new forms of articulation between writing and the world will emerge in what promises to be a protracted process of ending. Yet, insofar as its trajectory will be a function of the sedimentary graphic investments of the world that it will have to undo, the history of the graphic regime remains a history of the present.

6

The Discursive Formation of the Role of the Independent Curator in Taiwan during the 1990s

Po-shin Chiang

Translated by Michael Fei

The purpose of this essay is to analyse how Taiwanese art has developed over time in the context of the international contemporary art exhibitions held in Taiwan since the 1996 Taipei Biennial. The exhibitions included in this discussion are "River: New Asian Art—A Dialogue in Taipei" (*Heliu: Xin Yazhou Yishu—Taibei Duihua*) (1997) curated by J. J. Shih [Shi Ruiren]; "Lord of the Rim: In Herself/For Herself" (*Penbian Zhuren: Zizai Ziwei*) (1997) by Yuan-Chien Chang [Zhang Yuanqian]; and "Site of Desire" (*Yuwang Changyu*) (1997), a Taipei Fine Arts Museum (TFAM) Biennial, by Fumio Nanjo.

Before the 1990s, the organizing of exhibitions within Taiwan was almost exclusively the preserve of museum professionals. There were until the 1990s only a few instances of Taiwanese art critics participating in the curating of exhibitions. In the early 1990s, art critics became more actively involved in organizing contemporary art shows within Taiwan. Examples of contemporary art exhibitions within Taiwan during the 1990s whose organization involved Taiwanese art critics include: "Time Duration" (*Zuopin Zhong de Shijianxing*) (curated by Hai-Ming Huang, Dimension Art Center [*Dimen Hualang*], Taipei, 1991); "Access to the Summit" (*Meixiang*

Dianfeng) (by Hsing-Yueh Lin [Lin Xingyue], G Zen 50 Art Gallery [*Ji Chan Wushi Yishu Kongjian*], Taipei, 1991); "New Art, New Tribes: Taiwan Art in the Nineties" (*Taiwan 90's Yishu Xin Guannian Zuqun*) (by Yung-Chih Lu [Lu Rongzhi], Hanart T Z Gallery [*Han Ya Xuan*], Taipei, 1993); and "Installations in the Apollo Building" (*Zhuangzhi Aboluo*) (by J. J. Shih, Apollo Building, Taipei, 1993).

Most of these exhibitions were curated by art critics at the request of private art galleries, with the aim of improving the galleries' professionalism through the input of the critics' discursive capabilities.[1] The involvement of independent curators[2] in the organization of contemporary art shows has attracted widespread attention and interest from both public and private institutes within Taiwan since 1996. Government-run art museums have held large seminars inviting curators from across Taiwan and around the world to address topics related to the organization of contemporary art exhibitions.[3] Curatorship has since evolved into an independent field of knowledge and expertise within Taiwan.

If we accept Michel Foucault's view of discourse and power, we should be keenly interested in, and alert to, the emergence of the professional independent curator within Taiwan since the late 1990s. As Foucault makes clear, actual uses of the panoptic central observation tower conceived by the English philosopher Jeremy Bentham (1748–1832) had started to diminish by the end of the nineteenth century. Bentham's panopticon can nevertheless be understood to have presaged the increasing prevalence of disembodied forms of social organization and control involving surveillance, self-discipline, and decentralized power as part of the development of modern urbanized societies. By inviting six curators to organize the 1996 Biennial for the TFAM, the government-run art museum gave up the interpretative control which it had retained for many years and distributed it within an extended organizational arena of observation and (self-)discipline. As part of this shift, Taiwanese art was no longer the predominant subject advocated by art museums. Rather, it was reduced to being one object of reference among others, as part of a moralizing education apparatus attached to the staging of "international exhibitions." Curators produced and reproduced their versions of Taiwanese art within an anonymous, decentralized operating strategy. The question therefore arises as to what kind of subject position has been created as part of the discursive formation process associated with the organization of contemporary art shows in Taiwan—is it "Asian-Pacific" or "Asian" or "Chinese"? And what kind of evolutionary changes has Taiwanese art experienced under the multiple pressures from different international blocs?

In the following paragraphs, I shall conduct a genealogical review of the curatorial discourses. I shall try to reveal the derivative and connective power relations between the spatialization of curatorial discourse and curatorial discourse per se, as well as the process of discursive formation in which Taiwanese art is produced and reproduced. First, I shall analyse the origin of and the backdrop for Taiwanese curators organizing international contemporary art exhibitions in Taiwan since 1996 with a preliminary discussion of the spatialization of curatorial discourse. Second, by focusing on two international modern art exhibitions held in Taiwan in 1997, I shall examine and compare the international mappings depicted in curatorial statements for those shows, and how the subject position of Taiwanese art has been addressed. Finally, I shall explore how the identities of artists from different nations were interconnected by curators using the concept of a geographic sphere. Also, I shall discuss how Taiwanese artists have been positioned in such social sites, and what impact the curatorial model in question might have on art creation.

Part One

> I am willing to shoulder the original sin of Taiwanese society and culture
> By resigning my post as the Director of the Taipei Fine Arts Museum,
> To end this counter-strike launched by evil forces in the art circle,
> And the vicious farce therein derived.
>
> —Chen-Yu Chang [Zhang Zhenyu]

The above four-line statement was made on 7 May 1996 at a press conference held in a meeting room inside Taipei City Hall.

The person making the statement was Chen-Yu Chang, director of the TFAM at the time.[4] During the month prior to his resignation, Chang's performance in his official capacity as director of TFAM had come under intense scrutiny both within and outside the museum, resulting in a number of public events lashing out at the TFAM's managerial system. These included the Decoloring Group's (*Chuse Xiaozu*) signature campaign, a political skit and declaration about Saving the TFAM, an artists' boycott of exhibitions, as well as conflicts between the city government and legislature. For the TFAM, these events not only indicated the failure of its established approach toward collecting and exhibiting art, but also symbolized a serious challenge to the authority of government-sponsored art institutions.[5]

What did the words "the original sin of Taiwanese society and culture" refer to? What did Chang mean by "counter-strike launched by evil forces in the art circle"? Prior to the 1990s, government-run art museums had devoted their efforts to studying and promoting Taiwanese art on two primary fronts. First of all, with the advent of the localization movement in Taiwan's art circle,[6] government museums offered in succession a series of grand exhibitions to sift through the art history of Taiwan. These exhibitions, which include "Exhibition of 300 Years of Taiwan Art Works" (*Taiwan Meishu Sanbainian Zuopin Zhan*) by the Taiwan Museum of Art (co-curated with the *Hsiung-Shih Art* [*Xiong-Shi Meishu*] *Monthly*) in 1990, "Retrospective Exhibition of Western Art in Early Taiwan" (*Taiwan Zaoqi Xiyang Meishu Huigu Zhan*) by the TFAM in 1990, and "Taiwan Art 1945–1993" (*Taiwan Meishu Xin Fengmao* 1945–1993) by the TFAM in 1993, laid the foundation for art museums to become an authoritative voice in Taiwanese art studies. However, as indicated by the titles of the exhibitions in question, museums had not yet reached a consensus on how to define Taiwanese art and how to divide Taiwan's art history into distinct developmental periods. Consequently, this caused difficulties in selecting artists and their works for exhibition.[7]

Second, government museums played another important role in steering the development of Taiwanese art by hosting art competitions. Take, for example, the TFAM, which organized a series of exhibitions every two years beginning in the 1980s, exhibitions such as "Contemporary Painting Trends in the Republic of China" (*Zhonghua Minguo Xiandai Huihua Xin Zhanwang*) and "Contemporary Art Trends in the Republic of China" (*Zhonghua Minguo Xiandai Meishu Xin Zhanwang*). Although in 1992 the wording of the titles of these exhibitions was changed from "Contemporary Trends" to "Biennial," and from "the Republic of China" to "Taipei," the competitive nature remained unchanged. The purpose of the art museums in organizing such competitions was to "carry forward the creative and experimental spirit" and to "strive to be the symbol of new art in Taiwan."[8] In spite of these stated aims, the selection processes employed in the staging of the exhibitions in question became a focus of public concern. As a result, the TFAM felt it necessary to make clear that the selection processes it was using had made "adjustments" and "breakthroughs" compared to previous processes in terms of the appointment of panel members, decisions on panel composition (foreign vs. local members), the arrangement of selection stages, the categorizing of art forms, and even in the determining of criteria for selection. Notwithstanding these achievements, the museum could still not avoid being besieged by critics with questions and comments.[9]

Under such circumstances, the notions of "original sin of society and culture" and "counter-strike by evil forces" might fail to provide an explanation for why Chang had felt the need to resign his position as director of the TFAM; nevertheless these notions still possess specific historical connotations which require further elaboration. These connotations have to do with the ways in which Taiwanese art museums have identified Taiwanese art. Whether this involves endowing Taiwanese art with an academic standing through art history exhibitions or distinguishing the current trends in Taiwanese art through art competitions, it is impossible not to be involved in "dividing practices" while exercising such powers.[10] In other words, when exhibitors are accepted as part of the selection process and given the opportunity to showcase their talents, others who fail to meet the standards will inevitably feel rejected or excluded. This is the outcome of the eliminating function of competition. Moreover, the distinction between those who are accepted and those who are rejected may result in protests and challenges to authority by those rejected.

Although "original sin" and "counter-strike" sound somewhat portentous, we should still take the four lines of Chang's resignation statement seriously. These words represent the unique "literature of martyrdom" that prevailed in Taiwan's art community during the 1990s. While this kind of literature implies a form of confrontation, it transforms the final sacrifice of the martyr into a ritual performance, one involving a declaration in the presence of an audience.[11] The press conference held by Chang was in effect his personal exemplification of this literature of martyrdom. By resigning, Chang sought to declare his authority through a public act of self-sacrifice. His declaration was a public pronouncement of museum policy which had the intended effect of causing his audience to feel awe and conviction toward art museums.

The 1996 Taipei Biennial opened in June, immediately after Chang's resignation in May. By adopting the form of a curated exhibition with the theme "The Quest for Identity" (*Taiwan Yishu Zhutixing*), the established chain of competitive exhibitions at the TFAM was discontinued. The 1996 Taipei Biennial was divided into three parts. In the "Genealogy and Archives" section, curators attempted to shake off the ideological confusion of national and ethnic groups by tracing the origin of Taiwan's art history to cultural relics of the archaeological period. The purpose was to establish a historical perspective for art. Four curators—Hong-Ming Tsai, Jiun-Shyan Lee [Li Junxian], Tung-shan Hsieh [Xie Dongshan], and Kuang Lu—were invited to organize the "Contemporary Issues" section, with the expectation that the exhibited works would reflect the country's multifaceted cultural outlook and build an ideal Taiwanese art identity in the minds of those who saw it. Furthermore, the curators also included the public's voice in the "Experiencing Taipei" section. When viewed as an overall curatorial conception, the 1996 Biennial was made as inclusive as possible.

Criticism of the exhibition by art critics, however, focused not on its inclusivity but on the mechanism and method used in curating the exhibits.[12] Chien-Hui Kao [Gao Qianhui] questioned the relationship between discourse and power set against the "power of art interpretation."[13] Using the concept of a "war machine," Hai-Ming Huang further deciphered the power game of art museum curation. According to Hai-Ming Huang, curatorial discourses "stood as the real core of the exhibition" and, as such, "revealed new issues."[14] After analyzing statements made by the curators, Huang stated that the "generation of meaning was no longer dominated by artists, nor by certain kinds of scholars. Artworks became potential battlefields and war machines, and so did art museums.... The method of exhibiting and related issues made the hidden relations between art and knowledge/power more apparent."[15] In other words, the power to exhibit was not owned by the art museum, its director, or any other individual. Rather, there was a dispersed set of relationships for executing and exercising the disposed power as well as contestation of authority across that set of relationships.[16]

Seen in this light, it is possible to elucidate the workings of the 1996 Taipei Biennial in relation to Foucault's theory of Panopticism. According to Bentham's theory, prisoners should be kept in small cells in an annular building. A tall, central observation tower stands at the center of the annular structure. Each cell has two windows, one on the inside and the other on the outside. The outside opening allows light to come into the cell, while the inside opening enables the warder to watch every prisoner from the tower by the effect of backlighting. An inmate locked in such a cell will be thoroughly observed, but he or she has no way of seeing the observer. In contrast, the observer in the tower can see everything without ever being seen. Huang's argument that "a 'center' appears to exist but actually does not" implies this reversion of visibility.[17] Since traditional monarchical power is visible, with its dazzling spectacle projected everywhere and at all times, the masses stand in invisible shadows. In Bentham's model, power itself seeks invisibility and the objects of power, on which power operates, are made most visible.[18]

From this perspective, the "subjectivity of Taiwanese art" symbolized the demise of the traditional subjects of power within the Taiwanese art world. Government-run art museums surrendered their long-held power of interpretation, and distributed it to individual curators as part of an extended network of power. "Taiwanese Art" stopped being the supreme subject upheld by art museums, and became instead an object of reference concealed within a curatorial apparatus. Armed with the power to translate an individual into a subject, curators were able to operate the "government of individualization."[19] Under such a theme, the 1996 Taipei Biennial was organized into three sections. Among these, the section titled "Contemporary Issues" was further divided into four subsections, each of which was again divided into four to six programs.[20] The curatorial apparatus distinguished and identified the visibility of exhibitors and their artwork in a measured and hierarchical manner. It blended discourse and creation into one image, ultimately constructing a discursive space with isolated sections.

In a manner similar to Bentham's Panopticon, this curatorial apparatus opened up regimes of light in which far and near, dark and bright, visible and invisible are assigned as categories of interpretation. Deleuze picked up Foucault's concept of a "diagram" to explain the social field map illustrated by such an apparatus.[21] In Deleuze's view, a diagram is a map representing the intensity and density of power relations. He writes, "It makes history by unmaking preceding realities and significations, constituting hundreds of points of emergence or creativity, unexpected conjunctions or improbable continuums. It doubles history with a sense of continual evolution."[22]

Since the 1996 Taipei Biennial, the previously monarchical diagram of competitive exhibitions has been dismantled and replaced with a new diagram of discipline. All power relations in the diagram remain in an unstable, multiple and scattered status, "but at each moment move 'from one point to another' in a field of force, marking inflections, resistances, twists and turns, when one changes direction, or retraces one's steps."[23] Between those points, the curatorial apparatus depicts, using the strategy of anonymous operation, numerous diagrams overlapping and expanding into each other while generating and copying the imaginative standing of Taiwanese art. Not only do these diagrams have disciplinary functions, the endless process of their manufacture also mirrors the history of Taiwanese art's continual evolution in relation to its differing geographical and spatial significances.

Part Two

During the mid-1990s, the TFAM initiated a number of exhibitions designed to promote international art exchange. Among these, "Art Taiwan and Identities: Art from Australia," held in 1995, was considered to be a success story for "internationalization." This was the first time that Taiwan's artwork had toured four major Australian cities with equal terms and conditions and under the name of Taiwan. Australia, at the same time, shipped some of its artwork to Taiwan for exhibition.[24] With the success of this city-to-city diplomacy targeted at the Asia-Pacific region, the 1996 Asia-Pacific Triennial organized by Australia was highly anticipated.

Although invited to take part in the Triennial under "Taiwan," that name was replaced by "Taipei" in the Triennial directory. Works by Mingtse Lee [Li Mingze] from Kaohsiung [Gaoxiong] were featured in the exhibition along with those of other Taiwanese artists. In a critical review of the exhibition, the Taiwanese section of the Triennial was described as "voiceless art from Taiwan" and as "an unfocused gathering." "Do Taiwanese artists really care about being voiceless? Do we really care about our position in the Asia-Pacific region?"[25] "Is this a helpless end under political interference? Or, are there no competent curators in Taiwan? This serves as an alert for us to take part in international activities."[26]

These reflections carried certain implicit messages for the Taiwanese art world. First of all, Taiwan should not give up its crucial right to speak out independently, as the importance of the Asia-Pacific region grows. Second, Taiwan should begin to rethink its position in international exhibitions, moving from a linear back-and-forth operation between nations to a strategic alliance between regions. Finally, the demand to have international events organized by Taiwanese curators should start to gather pace. The underlying hope was to frame Taiwan's own operational strategy and diagram in handling international exhibits through "active curation" rather than just "passive involvement."

Since then, Taiwanese art's internationalization program has entered a new phase. The advantages of setting up an international art exchange site locally include the fact the local curators can play a leading role in deciding the theme and content of an exhibit, as well as who gets invited. Local critics can monitor the artistic standard of an exhibition in a timely fashion, to enhance the initiative of Taiwanese artists and win more recognition. Consequently, the year 1996 can be viewed as a critical milestone in the internationalization of Taiwanese art. International contemporary art exhibitions put together by Taiwanese curators have started to gain global attention ever since.

To further its internationalization strategy within the Asia-Pacific region, during 1997 Taiwan curated two important international contemporary art exhibitions. J. J. Shih organized one with the title "River: New Asian Art—A Dialogue in Taipei"; another, "Lord of the Rim: In Herself/Far Herself," was organized by Yuan-Chien Chang. The two key curatorial focuses of the "River" exhibition were "New Asian Art" and "Dialogue in Taipei." Born out of a "Taipei County Art Exhibition" (*Taibeixian Meishu Zhanlanhui*), the "River" exhibition followed the curatorial principle which had been in place within Taiwan since 1994. It also attempted to explore the humanistic significance of the Tamshui [Danshui] River, and to discuss "New Asian Art" from the Tamshui area by artists from Japan, Taiwan, Hong Kong, the Philippines, and Vietnam. Unlike previous Taipei County art events, the curator attempted to look at the Tamshui River as a "discourse site," rather than as a "discourse topic" per se.[27] All of the pieces exhibited, except for three outdoor works, were displayed concurrently at four locations: the Taipei County Cultural Center (*Taibeixianli Wenhua Zhongxin*), the Dimension Endowment of Art (*Dimen Yishu Jiaoyu Jijinhui*), the IT Park Gallery (*Yitong Gongyuan Hualang*), and the Bamboo Curtain Studio (*Zhuwei Gongzuoshi*). In the curatorial statement accompanying the exhibition, this arrangement was described as "a dialogue at four alluvial mouths of one river system." As he sketched this "highly friendly/low cost exhibit environment," Shih's concerns were the low visibility of the artworks being displayed in the Tamshui area and a number of consequential aesthetic and technical problems.[28] In other words, the arrangement was designed to cope with technical issues such as security and to meet practical requirements.

In addition to technical and practical considerations, the efficiency and function of the curatorial apparatus were also key to the planning of the exhibition. First and foremost, artworks were spread across multiple locations around Taipei City and County, in the "hope that the works of the hosts and guests would be compared alternately to generate a brainstorm involving both local and visiting artists."[29] The curator organized the exhibited works to be shown in scattered locations, including sites belonging to different kinds of organization, such as government offices, private institutions, and marginal organizations. This arrangement demonstrated the detailed thinking involved in planning the entire exhibition. The curator's capability and efficiency were also established by the ceremonies and by the networking events held during the exhibition, which allowed institutional representatives to meet and communicate.[30] Numerous supporting activities were also scheduled to take place among the exhibited works in the various exhibit locations. Artists talked about their creative endeavors at seminars. Local and visiting critics and curators shared their common experience in workshops. Volunteers received training and visitors enjoyed guided tours. Through all these activities, exhibition participants learned from what they observed, made friends with other participants, and shared their experience; they also identified their position in the event as a whole and connected with the exhibition theme.

Despite its stated aims, this exhibition appears to have provided a preliminary framework for a separate system.[31] Bentham's prison design plan involved setting up several isolated activity areas with multiple functions between prison buildings. The "River" exhibition strove to establish communication and dialogues, without the participants being totally isolated. However, the separation of event sites which took place as a result of technical, functional and practical considerations also gave the curatorial apparatus the functions related to cognition and education. Indeed, the formation of meaning was a function accentuated by the curator:

> It has been our expectation to extract and develop more concepts of contemporary thinking, being joined by other Asian artists in discussing artistic creation with reference to the topic of the "River".... These exhibits let the living water of art flowing from our own and other Asian lands wash toward the Taipei basin, leaving a deposit of organic soil to grow the landscape of contemporary Asian cultures and nourish the local artistic fields.[32]

Through this dialogue in Taipei, Taiwanese and even Asian contemporary art have been given a new look, and the curatorial apparatus has been given the functions of forming meanings and generating ideas.

The decision process for selecting artwork for the "River" show involved both international invitations and domestic collection. Among the invited international artists, Japan's Ichi Ikeda and his "Arching Ark" were at the top of the list. Ikeda installed concurrently, both in Taiwan and Japan, two "sailing" vessels to carry water containers, symbolizing the future interflow of culture. As described by the artist, "there are many islands, big and small, lined up in an arcing pattern between Taipei and Kaseda, as if the two cities are connected in a arc."[33] The curator of the exhibition decoded Ikeda's creation as follows:

> It was a boat-like installation made of bamboo and wood. At the opening ceremony, it was a stage for the artist to perform a water-friendly ritual. In the following days, it was moved to an outdoor square to be worshipped as a religious instrument on a primitive altar. In a ritual process of symbolizing global cultural integration with the idea of "water returning to the ocean," it played a critical role as "Spirit Carrier."[34]

In these events designed to shape a new Asia, the audience could view the boatlike installation, worshipped as a religious object, after taking part in the opening ceremony of "Taipei Taking Off" (*Taibei Chuhang*). The curator believed that "they are simultaneously participating in a conceptual event that marks the Great Harmony of the cultures of the world."[35] There were also other pieces in the exhibition that emphasized audience involvement or a ceremonial process.[36] As coordinated by the curatorial apparatus, the audiences and artists interwove a world of shared experience through conversation, observation, and the sharing of feelings, memories and imagination. However, this "New Asia" involved only Taiwan's neighboring countries, indicating that the contemporary art of nations other than those of East Asia remained unfamiliar and distant to Taiwan. With Japan at the top and Vietnam at the bottom, the "New Asia" resembled a pilgrimage route for colonies to deliver tribute to their suzerain. As such it opened up a unique area for contemplation relating to "New Asian Art."

Soon after the "River" show, another important Taipei international contemporary art exhibition was under way. Sponsored by the city government of Hsinchuang [Xinzhuang] and curated by a female curator, the exhibition "Lord of the Rim" invited seven female artists from the United States, Japan, Korea, and Taiwan to explore issues involving identification and social status, such as gender and class (the U.S. artist invited to participate was the groundbreaking maker of women's art, Judy Chicago). Metaphorically, the "Rim" implied the marginal position of those females who were part of the working class and who lived on the rim of the Taipei and Pacific Basins. "In Herself/For Herself" was a theme conceived by a female curator in the hope of "generating discourse about decentralization" with the participation of female workers from Hsinchuang.[37] This exhibition, within many interactive projects, was successful in facilitating dialogue between local and foreign artworks.

In contrast to the "River" exhibition, which made grand statements about the reshaping of New Asian arts, statements accompanying the "Lord of the Rim" exhibition sought to elaborate on the curator's personal experience from a feminized perspective. Chang Yuan-Chien [Zhang Yuanqian] presented a curatorial vision that started out from her experience of living and working in New York and Tokyo for five years before moving back to Taiwan. From this starting point she then narrowed her focus to concentrate on the geographic relationship between Taipei and Hsinchuang, where "Lord of the Rim" was held and which she referred to as "Twenty minutes from Taipei by car" and "a very unique town."[38] She then went on to cite the analytical comparison presented in the *Studies of the Immigrant Population in Taipei County* (*Taibeixian yiru renkou zhi yanjiu*) (1993) by the sociologist Hsin-Huang Hsiao [Xiao Xinhuang], highlighting differences between the city and county of Taipei. Starting from the first two paragraphs of this study, Chang plotted out a discursive strategy of core versus rim, as she moved around the wider geographic setting of her exhibition. Her curatorial discourse shifted continuously from the Pacific Basin to Hsinchuang and the Taipei Basin.

In Chang's eyes, a collection of randomly disposed "materials, machines, and half-finished products," as well as "forms of manual labor" and "residential and factory spaces," constituted the primary cultural characteristics of Hsinchuang's landscape.[39] At the intersection of these three characteristics sat the textile and garment industries of Hsinchuang. Chang's curatorial statement then presented the leading protagonists of the exhibition: "The majority of human resources in the textile and garment industries are composed of women, whose pursuit of self-consciousness and self-identity coincides, though through different approaches, with the self-perfection of a marginal community. Seven female artists have been invited for that reason."[40]

However, in spite of this open gender bias, it would be a mistake to reduce the significance of "Lord of the Rim" simply to a debate over gender politics. The exhibition also touched, as Chang herself makes clear, on "issues not unfamiliar to contemporary art, such as the elite versus the masses, craft versus pure art, individual creation versus mass production, and aesthetic space versus social space."[41] Through a writing tactic of constantly searching for differences as part of a landscape of close interconnections, Chang gave shape to a wider vision signified obliquely by the term "In Herself/For Herself," which made up the subtitle of "Lord of the Rim."

If the redrawing of the New Asian art diagram as part of the staging of the "River" exhibition drew on the potential function of the contemporary art exhibition as an educational platform, the planning of "Lord of the Rim" also served to re-draw the disciplinary diagram of the factory apparatus in Hsinchuang. Following the theme of "In Herself/For Herself," four of the female artists invited to participate in the exhibition started the production of their exhibited works by interviewing the women of Hsinchuang. As Chang indicates, the artists asked the women "about the relationship between clothes and the body, between humans and the body, and between labor and management, as well as asking about the power structure of gender in their industry."[42] The artists then extracted material from their interviews to create works echoing the exhibition theme. The curatorial apparatus relied on frequent interviews and interactions in an attempt to highlight the collective suffering of women and develop sisterlike friendships between female artists. The artist Mali Wu took steps to weave a "Story of the Women of Hsinchuang" (*Xinzhuang Nüren de Gushi*) with the participation of local female workers. Shimada Yoshiko invited local women to work collectively on the sewing of "1000 Red Knots" (*Qianren Zhen*) (fig. 1). Lichuan Huang [Huang Lijuan] encouraged collective par-

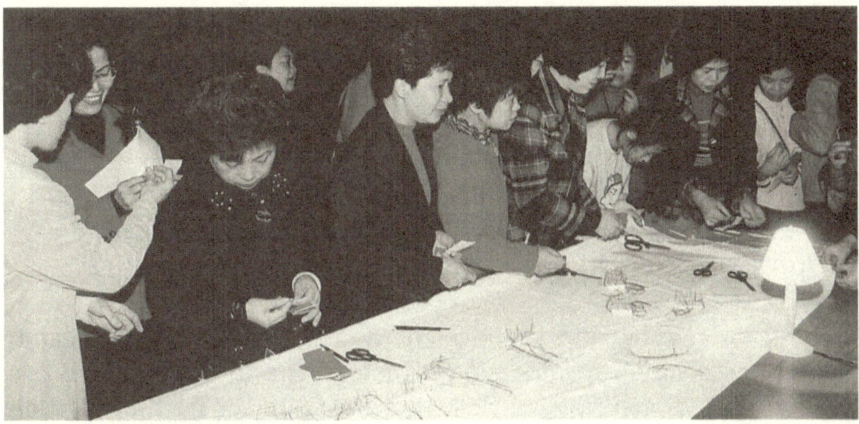

Figure 1. Japanese artist Shimada Yoshiko invited local women to join her in sewing "1000 Red Knots" at the exhibition "Lord of the Rim: In Herself / For Herself" (1997).

ticipation in her workshop, titled "Yarns of Remembrance" (*Shaxian Yiwang*).

All these works can be seen as partial reproductions of the disciplinary diagram of the factory apparatus. However, by inviting the artistic collaborations described above "Lord of the Rim" can be understood not to have simply reproduced that diagram, but to have challenged and criticized the power relations implicated within the working structures that it mapped.

The curatorial apparatus set up by Chang can also be understood to have functioned effectively as a critique of artistic production. The power of feminist art has been constantly reaffirmed by the tendency toward collaborative working among many of its participants (the joint efforts of women in the process of crafting artworks) as well as the use of artworks and the process of their making to celebrate female life. Ying-Ying Chien [Jian Yingying] highlights the unique rituals and events that were carefully organized by Chang as part of the staging of the exhibition. Chien writes, "They let the works of nonlocal artists take root and become localized, while providing treatment and blessings for the injured soul, body, and land."[43]

If the "River" show ran the implicit risk of presenting art as an object of ritualistic veneration "suzerainty," "Lord of the Rim" adopted this stance in a self-concious and wholly undisguised manner. The beginning of Chang's curatorial statement, published in *Artist* (*Yishujia*) *Magazine*, states:

> In "Lord of the Rim," seven female artists from the Pacific Rim will join in this dialogue with Hsinchuang. The six Asian artists in the group salute Judy Chicago, and hope the presentation will "inpire people to care for their cities."[44]

The feminist ideas and practices of Chicago, who long ago established her position in modern art history, are undoubtedly representative of pioneering work in the field. In her curatorial statement, Chang talks about Chicago, saying that "her participation in this exhibition can be seen as a declaration of intent, as well as providing our theme with some historical context."[45] To have "Judy gather with Asian artists to exhibit in Hsinchuang makes a fairy tale in exhibition culture come true."[46] This framing of "historic context" traced the exhibition's headwaters to, and made a connection with, the first generation of feminist art. The "declaration of intent" linked the exhibition to the American feminist art movement, stating a clear position for the exhibit in terms of its ideas and practices. Chicago responded to the "fairytale" by sending some of her older works to the exhibition. She did not join the collective creative process in Taipei County, but held a simultaneous solo exhibition in Taipei City. The curatorial apparatus originally planned to showcase only Chicago's older pieces, without her participating in the collective events, with an intention of bringing "historic context" and a "declaration of intent" into play. This plan, however, aroused criticism for "not considering the uniqueness of the exhibiting site by showing only older works."[47]

Chicago's art featured mostly "white, middle-class, educated women."[49] Even without taking this into account, the intense contrast between the exhibiting sites of the simultaneous exhibitions—a commercial gallery in Taipei versus the City Cultural Center of Hsinchuang—broke the multilayered arrangement which had been put diligently into place by the curatorial apparatus. All the strategies defined in the curatorial statement to differentiate between social classes, and between urban and rural and high and low art, collapsed. The evolution of the Rim diagram, which turned from the other end of the Pacific Rim and eventually returned to its origin, had been substantially compromised.

In both the "River" and "Lord of the Rim" exhibitions, the curatorial apparatus strove to create an atmosphere for international art dialogue by identifying a theme of shared vision and partnering with artists from areas of geopolitical significance. However, the diagrams prepared by both the "New Asia" and "Pacific Rim" apparatuses preset a ritual subject. All participants, including artists, audience members, staff, and curators, were invited to a sacred ritual site. As a space of liminality, as defined by Carol Duncan, the curatorial apparatus triggered a moment where morality and rationality were disconnected.[49] The participant shook off the burden of secularity and the real world, and collectively fulfilled the meaning intended and recalled by the exhibitions through various spiritual rituals and imaginary actions. The role or function played by the audience was to take part in a flow of symbols and meanings. Yet Taiwanese art, while standing in this flow, still had its own blind spots.

Part Three

Subsequent to the "River" and "Lord of the Rim" exhibitions, there was another contemporary art show in Taiwan that sought to adopt an international curatorial approach: the 1998 Taipei Biennial. According to Mun-Lee Lin [Lin Manli], director of the TFAM at that time, this was the first international biennial organized in Taiwan by an international curator (Fumio Nanjo) with a clearly defined theme and an intentional Asian perspective.[50] The exhibition took the concept of "Site of Desire" as its theme. In an essay consisting of a mere five hundred words, Nanjo briefly described his curatorial motive for taking "desire" (fig. 6) as a keyword for the exhibition.[51] However, as Nanjo chose not to elaborate on the connection between the theme and the exhibited works, or on the interconnectivity between the artworks, the exhibition was repeatedly questioned by Taiwanese critics during its showing.[52] It was three months after the exhibition had ended before Nanjo finally extended his essay into a curatorial statement published in a special publication for

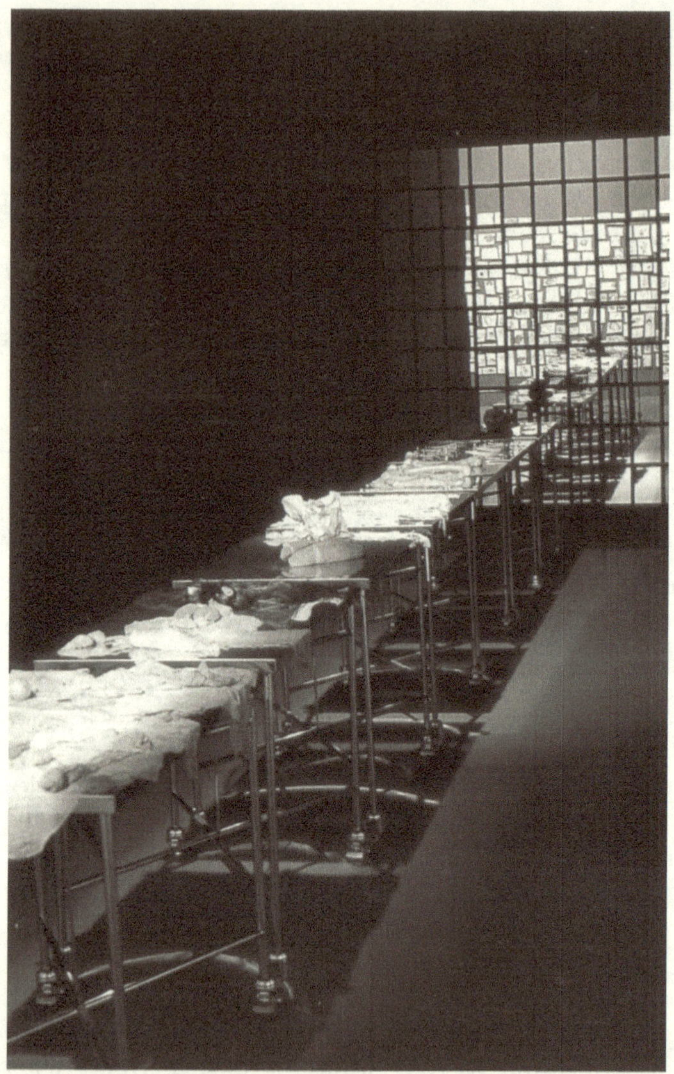

Figure 2. Liu Shih-Fen, *The Multiple Sophism of Skin and Membranes,* 1998. From the 1998 Taipei Biennale *Site of Desire* (courtesy of the Taipei Art Museum)

the biennial. In this statement, Nanjo first listed a number of factors that might stir human desires and then pointed to the phenomenon and possibility of targeting Asian cities as sites of desire. As for the meaning of his statement's title, "Palimpsestus Urbanus" (Palimpsest Urbanism), he provided the following explanation:

> During the European medieval period, parchment was a rare, expensive commodity. A palimpsest refers to a parchment that has been used, scraped, and reused. With time, there were instances where the previous texts became faintly visible through the surface layer of writing. Here "urbanus" is the Latin term for "urban." This term also carries the meaning of "urbane," a term used in modern English to refer to a person who is refined, educated, polished, or one who is multitalented and knowledgeable, or—at times—one who is shameless, audacious. While unquestionably the active development of Asian cities has been brought about on the one hand by modern western technology, democratic philosophies, and economic systems, on the other hand, lower layers of distinctive traditional cultures and traditions still remain. In the midst of contemporary cultural symbols, these traditions are either clearly revealed, metaphorically manifested, or suppressed. Thus, metaphorically, these city phenomena are like giant palimpsests.[53]

Although somewhat oblique in its phraseology, this explanation may nevertheless help us to understand how the contextual interrelationship between Asia and other issues was addressed and connected as part the curatorial discourse involved in the staging of the Taipei Biennial. As a medium of signification, palimpsests assumed the same metaphorical importance as the scope of Asia defined by the curator. Nanjo writes, "The Asian city is both a labyrinth of desire and a many-layered palimpsest."[54] Here, it can be assumed that the word "urbanus" refers to a kind of new urbanism that was perceived by Nanjo to be a salient issue in tackling the cultural and political significance of globalization. The connotations of many of the terms used in Nanjo's statement relate to the key theme of urbanism but are not otherwise interrelated, suggesting an open style of writing commensurate with the polysemy of the palimpsest. Throughout his statement, Nanjo was apparently attempting to develop a multilayered and multidimensional discussion space around the exhibition theme, rather than interpreting the show from a single persepective. What diagram, then, would the curatorial apparatus of the Taipei Biennial draw in relation to this palimpsestic interpretative approach?

Another focal point emphasized by the TFAM for the biennial was its appeal to an Asian perspective; an approach different from those adopted in biennials held in other countries. What was an Asian perspective? "The Biennale was organized with a regional focus and artists were chosen specifically from the spaces of Japan, Korea, China, and Taiwan, which make up East Asia. Despite the vast geographical area and seemingly disparate cultures of this region, shared historical experiences create common identities. More importantly these areas also share a similar fate as they face the onslaught of Western capitalism and culture in the process of modernization," explained Mun-Lee Lin.[55]

The reason behind the selection of the four East Asian nations for the biennial, as explained by the TFAM, was their shared cultural heritage and similar experiences in facing the impact of Western modernization. Was this common experience shared by people only from these East-Asian areas? Was it not shared, for instance, by people from Singapore? Was it appropriate to put Japan, an economy structurally equivalent to that of the United States and Europe, on the same footing with the three other developing nations, in terms of its indigenous experience of modernization? In applying what was in effect a dialectical interpretative framework involving tradition versus modernization, a tendency toward over-simplification was, perhaps, unavoidable. Nanjo echoed the TFAM's policy in the short essay published before the exhibition. "Tradition is being reexamined and reborn as well as being creatively transmitted. Western modernity is learned from, studied, copied, and denied."[56] This idea was further elaborated upon in Nanjo's post-exhibition curatorial statement:

> Originally, Modernism advocated formalism and the universal and was indifferent to such cultural questions as context, difference, locality, and tradition. For this, Modernism has been justifiably criticized. However, the question remains: how does the vernacular art which needs to be inter-

> preted according to an individual cultural context become a language universally accepted among other cultures? Given the diversity of arts which are born in a multiplicity of contexts, including those of the West, in the future will we gain an understanding of those various arts only through translation, in the same manner as we read a translated book?[57]

The curator appeared to share the same Asian perspective as the TFAM in questioning and criticizing Western modernism and its advocated universality. However, when speaking of Asian modernization, Nanjo believed that "the regions of Asia have not experienced a unified form of Modernization. Modernization has progressed in different ways, depending on the cultural and social conditions present in each country."[58] In other words, modernization could not rationalize the great differences as well as similarities between the regions. He explained why artists from China, Japan, Korea, and Taiwan are linked together despite their differences: "It is because they share two common experiences, one being Confucianism and another being Chinese characters, which are or were used by all of them."[59] In Nanjo's mind, it was Confucianism and Chinese characters that connected the East Asian nations. But what kind of role did modernization play in the artistic system centered on Chinese culture?

Arguably, the Asian diagram depicted by Nanjo continues the tradition of modern Japanese thought since Okakura Kakuzo (1862–1963), who advocated the concept of "Asia as One" in his text the *Ideals of the East* (1903).[60] This concept was a unique preoccupation of the Japanese people during the twentieth century as part of the country's constant shuttling between thoughts of "leaving" and "leading" Asia. Such thoughts were, in part, an ideological response of modern Japan to Western invasion. The resulting "Asia Complex," which differs fundamentally from the outlooks of other Asian nations, should not be separated from discussion of Japan's modernization.

Japan has taken a path different from other Asian nations in its drive toward modernization. Looking back at the development of modern Asian history, it is clear that Japan attempted to transcend China in completing its own modernization project. During the process, Japan's intention was to replace China and become a modern power contending with the West. Consequently, regional order in Asia was held in the hands of China, Japan, and the Western powers. A recent study of the East Asian tributary system by Hamashita Takeshi offers an appropriate perspective for looking at these historical circumstances. As a scholar specializing in the modern economic history of China, Takeshi suggests that no nation-state has ever existed in East Asia. The historical experiences of the region were composed of transnational trade networks based on tributary routes. Within the context of an internationalized geographical order with China at its center, use of the Chinese language was not exclusive to China. Both Korea and Vietnam once believed that they were inheritors of Chinese tradition. Japan's modernization can be viewed as a process in which Japan tried to break down the relationship of "paying tribute and receiving a grant," in order to lead the cultural-linguistic Chinese region. Such concepts as "leaving Asia for Europe" and a "Greater East Asia Prosperity Sphere" were established in reaction to the historical system of China versus barbarians. The purpose was not to destroy the system, but to displace China and take over its central position within East Asia.[61]

From this perspective, we can see that Japan has actually carried out its modernization program within a highly unstable international order. In its drive for modernization, "Asia as One" has never been a fixed concept. Rather, it has been constantly adapted, in both its role and scope, to a changing international order. For example, the concept was used as the foundation for expansion theories, such as the Greater East Asia Prosperity Sphere. Japan has, therefore, experienced a unique process of modernization.

In his curatorial statement, Nanjo criticized Western modernity and modernism. At the same time he posited an interconnection between the four East Asian nations on the basis of their shared Chinese culture, but without addressing the stated theme of the Taipei Biennial—"Site of Desire"—in a specific and in-depth manner. As a result, Nanjo's curatorial concept was left in a vague and somewhat precarious position. It is understandable that the TFAM did what it could to integrate Taiwan into a wider East Asian region through a strategy of finding common cultural-linguistic ground across national-cultural boundaries as part of the transformation of the Taipei Biennial into an international event.[62] What is regrettable, however, was that Nanjo failed to support his statement with more detailed and convincing arguments and that he disregarded fundamental differences between the geographic regions of East Asia.[63]

In addition to the emphatically Asian perspective of the 1998 Taipei Biennial, it was also the first international exhibition organized by a non-Taiwanese curator at the TFAM. The inviting of an overseas curator to organize an exhibition at TFAM marks a definitive change in the development of the Taipei Biennial. The TFAM improved its approach toward the gaining of curatorial experience, knowledge, and expertise by moving from learning by doing to "learning by interacting." Apart from being involved in research programs undertaken by international curators and in the production plans of international artists, in recent years the TFAM curatorial apparatus has actively gathered state-of-the-art information from overseas to enhance its processing techniques. Mun-Lee Lin has accentuated the positive implications of working with international curators:

> While it is not unusual for overseas art museums and institutions to work with curators from different nations, it is still a breakthrough for the TFAM to join hands with international curators. To achieve a more competitive future for Taiwan in the international art arena, we need to have extensive international connections, work more closely with international curators, and prepare more actively with our own curators. All these efforts, which supplement each other, should be carried out simultaneously and with urgency. The cooperation we have experienced between the TFAM and international curators provides not only an excellent opportunity for the museum staff to observe and learn, but a multilayered discussion space, as presented through exhibition, for Taiwanese society as a whole.[64]

Local critics approved of the international perspective of the Biennial in terms of who was invited to exhibit and how exhibiting space was arranged and planned.[65] Their attention focused on how curators were chosen by the TFAM, how exhibits were handled by international curators, how experienced those curators were, and how much expertise could be transferred to Taiwan.[66] The core value of the changes in approach toward curating, which were fundamental to the 1998 Biennial, centered on questions as to whether the local curatorial apparatus had acquired better capability in exhibition development and product innovation after importing internationally recognized expertise.

There is little to be found in the TFAM's documentation relating to the technical aspects of curating the 1998 Biennial. Only a short description was offered in Nanjo's curatorial statement regarding his chosen theme for the exhibition. Nanjo did, however, briefly reveal the process used to select artists for the exhibition in a media interview:

> The first step was to conduct a field survey, followed by visits to artists. When the theme was decided, I immediately asked the artists to put forward their creative ideas for the show. I spent a full day in Taipei meeting publicly with those artists who were not yet chosen for the exhibition, making sure that no one who deserved a spot would be left out. Thirty-six artists showed up in Taipei with their portfolios for an interview. In total, I studied the works of about fifty artists. Similar procedures were followed in other locations. Most importantly, the proposals submitted by artists had to properly match the requirements of the theme.[67]

This selection process was different from those adopted by the curators of the 1996 Taipei Biennial and of the "River" and "Lord of the Rim" exhibitions. Based on his own knowledge and experience, Nanjo first sent invitations to those artists whose works he believed were appropriate for the show. Unlike the previous three exhibitions, the 1998 Biennial departed from the established process of calling for artists to submit their portfolios by advertising in magazines. On 14 January 1998, the curatorial team announced an "Open Interview" in the *United Daily News*: "Any artists interested in sharing their creative thinking face-to-face with Fumio Nanjo, please prepare a portfolio with slides and documentation of five to ten works created in the last ten years." Each candidate was to be given an opportunity to meet with Nanjo personally at the TFAM after an appointment was made with the museum. It is understandable that a visiting curator had to rely on an open interview to deal with the disadvantage of not being fully engaged with local artists, in an attempt to ensure that nothing worthy was left out.

What deserves further exploration is the role played by the curatorial team during the entire interview process. If we compare the different ways the two biennials called for artists, we find that the interview announcement was actually a strategy of condescension to mobilize artists for collective participation.[68] With the enthusiastic slogan "Let's work together to create art for Taiwan," the 1996 Biennial called on artists to send their portfolios to the organizing committee and join the team of Taiwanese art creators.[69] In the 1998 interview announcement, however, artists seeking a place in the exhibition encountered the statements: "TFAM has invited internationally acclaimed Japanese curator Fumio Nanjo to take charge of selecting and curating" and "Although he has been in contact with a number of Taiwan artists, Mr. Nanjo is anxious to find more works by Taiwan artists." A difference of position in social space was suggested in these sentences. The announcement invited artists to share their creative thinking face-to-face with Nanjo. The sharing of ideas with an "internationally acclaimed" curator—a decision maker with a high position in the social order—translated a fierce selection process into a peaceful, humble, and charitable event. When the distance between Nanjo and the artists was removed symbolically, the curator was able to reap the accumulated benefits resulting from his increased social proximity in conducting interviews.

During the interviews, the curator reemployed the skills perfected by his predecessors hundreds of years ago. Imagine the procedures a collection custodian (called a "curator" then) had to go through in the old days as he sat in a dim corner of a museum warehouse to scrupulously review and read through documents. At his disposal were the materials in the warehouse, some of which could be included in the existing collection system. In rare cases, some artifacts might not be readily added to an existing category.

The naming, categorization, and organization of artifacts into explanatory taxonomical systems is a principal responsibility of, as well as a challenge to, museum curators. Well-informed curators have played a key role in the production of knowledge and the managing of new orders of display. While existing taxonomical systems allow us to understand the significance of objects, their institutionalization also places restrictions on the recognition of overlooked artifacts and meanings. How does a curator decide which artifacts should be included in a taxonomical system and which should be left out? Does the supposed objectivity of the process of selection conceal a tendency on the part of museums to shape the truth as they see it?[70]

Up-to-date curatorial techniques imported into Taiwan during the 1990s transcended established notions of museological ordering and display. During face-to-face sessions involving the sharing of creative ideas, curators began to identify topics that artists were expected to take as a starting point for the expression of their desires. As the criteria for exhibition set down by curators required that "proposals submitted by artists had to properly match the requirements of the theme," artists often found that they had to remold their thinking and practice to fit the given themes. As such, the curatorial process could be said, despite its apparent openness, to conceal disciplining techniques designed to guide the behavior of artists.[71] It is possible to catch a glimpse of how these disciplining techniques worked in an account given by one of the artists chosen to exhibit at the 1998 Taipei Biennial. Shih-Fen Liu [Liu Shifen] states that before her interview with Nanjo she was unclear about her own characteristics and strengths as an artist, or where she was heading with her work. "I have no clue why he picked me. I hadn't even made one single piece of exhibition or installation art before," she recalls. Nanjo stated during his meeting with Liu that her work had made him extremely nervous, so much so that he almost had a breakdown. This was something that Liu had not considered—the preciseness of the emotional effect of her chosen materials. Suddenly, the artist became aware of a new dimension to her work. Nanjo asked her to make an exhibition proposal related to the theme of desire. What Nanjo said unlocked a crucial door for Liu allowing her to rethink her attitude to creation and presentation. After her discussion with Nanjo, Liu began to use a new material, one that would be the starting point for a series of new and successful works. That material was bone.[72]

What causes an artist to move from a two-dimensional form of art to the unfamiliar territory of an installation?[73] The above account suggests that an interventionist/interactive curatorial process has the potential to redirect an artist's outlook and practice. An exhibition site turns into a laboratory for artistic creativity and learning. An artist's practice becomes intimately tied to the chosen theme of the exhibition in question and even becomes a key component for identifying the future direction of their work.

Seen from another point of view, however, through this process artists are also turned from creative agents into resources at the disposal of the curator. No longer does the curatorial apparatus passively accept what artists have to offer. Instead, it actively demands that what artists produce is made appropriate to the theme of the exhibition. What needs to be taken into account in this regard is the utility of the artist. In this sense, curatorship also means determining and constraining an artist's range of behavior. As the curatorial apparatus spatializes its subjects, artists are archived, labeled, categorized, and even directed as part of a categorical system determined by curators. An artist becomes a trained and self-disciplined docile body.

In Foucault's view, "The body is directly involved in a political field; power relations have an immediate hold upon it; they invest it, mark it, train it, torture it, force it to carry out tasks, to perform ceremonies, to emit signs."[74] Thus, body, power, and desire are all implicated in the biopolitics of curating. By defining the theme, the curatorial apparatus exerts its desire to temper, train and condition the body. Most works included in the 1998 Taipei Biennial were forms of installation art. Nanjo states that there were more than ten pieces involved in the exhibition that were completed as site-specific. He argues that site-specific works fit into an exhibiting space extremely well, and could even accent the architectural features of a museum building. Hai-Ming Huang spoke highly of Nanjo's detailed spatial thinking in organizing and planning the exhibition space.[75] Even so, some critics still had questions about the exhibited works. J. J. Shih, for example, thought that many works had been presented in a comedic spirit. Yung-Chih Lu suggested that most works on display showed a sweet and supple attitude of submission toward material desires, and a pleasant sense of security under cultural authority.[76] Chien-Hui Kao criticized the TFAM for attaching too much importance to Nanjo's curatorial experience while downplaying his curatorial ideas, leaving the site of desire as a "trap" in which Taiwanese artists spun around such social issues as sex, death, violence, and eschatology.[77] In this respect, it seems that the East-Asian diagram of international curating had tamed Taiwan into an obedient but nevertheless productive position.

Conclusion

In the same year that the 1998 Taipei Biennial was held, another exhibition titled "Inside Out: New Chinese Art," curated by the Chinese scholar Gao Minglu, took place in the United States. This showed the latest achievements of Taiwanese art in a different curatorial context from that of the Taipei Biennial. The exhibition, comprising works by artists from mainland China, Hong Kong, and Taiwan, presented the art history of mainland China without mentioning that of Hong Kong or Taiwan.[78] In Gao's opinion, the word *huaren* (Chinese) used in the exhibition title was a political compromise. He did not like the connotations of "low-class" and "marginal" that were suggested by the word.[79] In this sense, the subject position of "Taiwanese Chinese" in the exhibition was the same as that of "Singapore-Malaysian Chinese" or "European Chinese." *Huaren* here refers simply to the different dialect groups of immigrant Chinese settled in different regions. These Chinese share a common past with China; some might have specific languages, but they do not have their own history and identity. In Taiwan, as the localized movement in Taiwan's art community faded away during the early 1990s, Chinese art discourse emerged with ethnic identity as a strategy. Its development can be traced by looking at the shift in the market focus of painting in Taiwan, the growth and decline of art magazines, and the fever for China's avant-garde art. Further studies, beyond the scope of this present essay, are required to address the subject in greater depth.

Exploring, analyzing, and comparing regional art, whether it be Asian, Asian Pacific, or East Asian, has been the key focus for international contemporary art exhibitions in Taiwan. Historically,

Taiwan has looked to European and North American art in its quest to apprehend and understand contemporary art in an international context. How can this narrow-minded view of art be expanded? Although the analysis put forward here has taken into account the role of curators, artists, artworks, and sites of display, it is the purpose of this essay neither to make aesthetic value judgments nor to conduct empirical research on them. Moreover, the present discussion about the subject position of Taiwanese art does not imply that curatorial practices will necessarily induce defects or blind spots. Compared with previously established ways of organizing exhibitions, present-day curatorial practices within Taiwan offer distinct advantages in terms of utility, functionality and flexibility. The concept of curatorial practice has been brought within a more precise frame of analysis in an attempt to go beyond a dependency upon the sole authority of the curator. It is also anticipated that the current, somewhat static method of visual art criticism within Taiwan, which emphasizes the reception of artworks during the time of their exhibition, will be expanded to encompass a dynamic strategic analysis including pre-exhibition operations. Similar to the case-study approach frequently used in teaching business management, this dynamic method may help curators to reflect productively on their practice. Within the curatorial system, sponsors, artists, gallery staff, audience members, and curators are all participants in an exhibition. Each individual participant has a little power. In the center of power stands the curator responsible for an exhibition's guiding curatorial concept. We can view, through an analysis of curatorial discourse, how the exhibiting space, works, and bodies are deployed in relation to artistic creation.

Taking curatorial practice as a frame of critical reference allows us to see how power is exerted and distributed in the exhibiting of artworks. Nevertheless, certain questions remain: does curatorial practice aim at creating a space for artistic creation or for the exhibition as a creative entity in itself? How could interactive curatorship become the dominant approach toward the organizing of Taiwanese contemporary art exhibitions in such a short space of time? How does it relate to the concurrent popularity of installation art? Are there other other ways of curating the contemporary art show? All of these issues require further study.

7

Encircling the City: Peasant Migration in Contemporary Chinese Media

Ping Fu

Rural China serves as a barometer of Chinese political and historical weather. The notion of rural China is rooted in the Chinese mentality and has navigated and shaped national policy making and individuals' words and actions over China's long history. Chinese rural cinema occupied a dominant position in the screenscape of mainland China after the People's Republic of China (PRC), or *New China*, was established in 1949. However, the rural theme no longer enjoyed prominence in Chinese cinema in the last three decades of the twentieth century. Since 1978, China has rapidly and vigorously shifted from a planned economy to a market economy. The economic revolution has brought about unprecedented changes. One of the changes is that market forces have fractured the system that kept farmers pinned to their land for four decades. In the economic reform era, Chinese farmers became one of the vital forces in the construction of these changes with a scenario that veered toward a near-total reconfiguration and reconstruction of a long history of pro-village ideology, and postulated a new pattern of the rural-urban dynamic in present day China. Enjoying this rare opportunity, farmers first expanded and relocated roadside or small-scale businesses to the city, and then continued to fill various gaps in the city job market, as cinematically represented in the films discussed in this article. The migration of about two hundred million farmers to the city is one of the most striking social phenomena today.[1] Forceful modernization and irresistible globalization have blurred the line between the country and the city and renewed Chinese urban vitality and visibility. The extended urbanization of the rural area, on the one hand, brings about many positive changes in the country, but on the other hand, poses a new challenge to farmers, uprooting them from their farmland. *San nong wenti* (the issue of farmers, countryside, and agriculture), a rhetorical expression concerning Chinese farmers, frequently becomes the headline of various news media in China. The dislocation of farmers and the rupture of their tradition have appeared as urgent issues in the Chinese government's agenda and have also caught the full attention of scholars and experts in the field. For the first time since 1949, the Chinese government considered that finding solutions to the issues/problems of Chinese migrant farm workers was an urgent need for the realization of the concept of scientific development,[2] a necessary demand of constituting a socialist harmonious society, and a strategic mission in constructing a unique Chinese socialism.[3]

This article aims to conduct a survey of Chinese rural cinema under the theme of the uprooting of the peasantry. Briefly tracing the evolution of Chinese farmers' social and political status and the trajectory of their cinematic portrayals from the birth of New China till the present, the article outlines farmers' positions within the Chinese social and political diagrams and examines how the agenda of Chinese farmers is closely associated with the state's policy making. Along this line, the article examines the cinematic and media representations of the rural-urban embattlements and dialectics through a selection of acclaimed Chinese films and other media work regarding farmers in the period from the 1950s to the present. This study also tries to define the vagrant and vigilant positions of Chinese farmers in both urban and cinematic spaces of contemporary China and to respond to the following three questions: How did the political and historical dimensions circumscribe the cinematic configuration of both urban and rural spaces in the films in the period from the 1950s to today? How has the act of the farmers' encircling of the city enriched and enlarged the film genres of both Chinese urban cinema and rural cinema in terms of cinematic aesthetics and meaning production? How did Chinese filmmakers understand and present changing operations and ideologies on the rural-urban paradox and the local-global paradigm depicted in the studied visual materials?

Farmer Mobility Caught In-between

The rural-urban dichotomy has a long history in China. As some Chinese historians have pointed out, the narrative of a peasant-based Chinese revolution has dominated the history of modern China. The idea of a pro-village revolution throughout most of the twentieth century has tended to relegate urban history to a subordinate role in the grand narrative of modern China.[4] However, farmers, who had been one of the core forces and resources of the Chinese Communist Party (CCP) in the revolutionary era, before the establishment of the people's Republic of China, and had been one of the major groups to help construct New China, had not been able to find their own positions in urban space until the twenty-first century.

In the later 1940s and early 1950s, farmers were given land in recognition for their support for the CCP. But they never received titles and, by 1958, all their productive property and all their land had been collectivized without any compensation. From the 1950s to the early 1970s, the government's rural-urban policies and regulations banned farmers from entering the city. The largely glorified heroism that had been ascribed to Chinese farmers in the bygone revolutionary age gradually faded out in the late 1950s, and their roles became much more limited, functioning solely within the territory of the countryside, although farmers had been politically elevated as so-called educators of the sent-down youth during the ten years of the Cultural Revolution, from 1966 to 1976. One of the primary reasons for these phenomena is that the Chinese state leaders shifted their attention from the country to the city after 1949, prioritizing the need for building the state economy.[5] For instance, in the late 1950s, the first generation of Chinese leaders imposed a *people's commune* (*renmin gongshe*)[6] system on agriculture and farmers to expand food production at a rate greater than population growth. The celebration of the people's commune had been extended to the urban space and formed a symbolic act of farmers' encircling the city since 1958. Following the establishments of the rural people's commune, the *urban people's communes* (*chengshi renmin gongshe*) emerged in the late 1950s. By July 1960, there were 1,064 urban people's communes established in 190 big cities in the PRC. The CCP believed that the urban people's commune had three advantages. First, it was the fundamental form and organization of socialism and the best way to advance China from a socialist society to a communist one. Second, it reflected the characteristic of the Chinese revolutions and developments, which were moving from the rural to the urban. Third, it had shown many advantages for building up a socialist China.[7] The urban people's communes were under the leadership of the CCP-centered *neighborhood committee* (*Juweihui*) in the city, which was normally composed of retired senior people, including government officials, workers, housewives, and migrant farmers.

A group of films produced in the period from 1949 to 1966 exhibited farmers' roles and their anticipated influences in New China. For instance, *Five Golden Flowers* (Wuduo jinhua, dir. Wang Jiayi, 1959) presents a romantic comedy of one Chinese ethnic young man's encountering five Chinese ethnic girls who have the common name of Jinhua (golden flower), and their enthusiastic engagements in the people's commune; *Li Shuangshuang* (Li Shuangshuang, dir. Lu Ren, 1962)[8] displays the tears and laughter of a farmer couple who participate in collective farming in the people's commune; and *The Young People of Our Village I & II* (Women cunli de nianqingren, dir. Su Li, 1959 and 1963)[9] showcases a group of young villagers who try to solve the irrigation problem for their commune. One of the representative films of the rural genre of the period is *The Spring Is Always Colorful* (Wanziqianhong zongshi chun). Helmed by noted film director Shen Fu and produced by well-known Shanghai Film Studio in 1959, *The Spring Is Always Colorful* portrays a group of ordinary housewives who have newly migrated to the city from the countryside to accompany their husbands, who became employees of urban factories. Unwilling to be jobless housewives in the city, they enthusiastically gather themselves and provide sewing, daycare, and other routine daily services to the local community in their rural manner. The film well illustrates the model of and real practice of the urban people's commune under the watch of the neighborhood committee. Although *The Spring Is Always Colorful* is generally categorized as a city film showcasing Chinese women's participation in the early stage of socialist construction and its temporal structure of the film indicates a political reaction to the doctrine of "encircling the city," the formal representation of the rural elements in the film, including the rural women and their beloved *commune,* a special metaphor of Chinese rural life, through choices of cinematography, a bright color palette, montage, and close shots of the rosy faces of the rural women characters, all seem to exhibit and encourage a nostalgic response to the pro-village ideology. The disjuncture between the pictorial aesthetics and thematic narrative of the rural in the city bespeaks both the social and cinematic factors that farmers' mobility and its corresponding representations are caught in between. Such *caught-in-between* illustration problematizes the viewer's experience of "encircling the city." The filmic depiction of these rural housewives did not mean to showcase their dislocation from the rural spaces and their frustrations arising from the urban challenge they encountered. Rather, the film represents them as a much-needed labor force that effectively fulfilled the call of the CCP to shift from the country to the city and participate in the socialist construction. Instead, what *The Spring Is Always Colorful* praised and confirmed was not the farmers' migrations in particular but the farmers' participation in building up a New China in general, just as they were metaphorically glorified as colorful flowers blooming in the spring of New China. At the end of the film, a rapid forward zoom on a well-framed photo of all the principal women characters smiling like blooming flowers jump-cuts to signature scenery of metropolitan Shanghai with two gothic and byzantine architectural structures in the center of the screen. The two Western structures signify the past colonial history of Shanghai. They are the tokens of *bourgeois elements* (*zichan jieji yinsu*). Before the establishment of New China, to be more precise the urban people's commune, the city had been long criticized and repressed for its bourgeois features and decadence. The juxtaposition of the rural female images and the two colonial signifiers symbolically declares that the country is encircling the city, but who or what was in charge or praised for this encirclement remains unclear in the film. The reasons for such an ambiguous cinematic representation of farmer migration were multiple. First, an open praise of labor mobility shown in the film would conflict with the government's restriction on floating populations. Under the planned economic system, people could not move from place to place as they wished. On the contrary, "forced migration or population floating happened sometimes due to particular political purposes."[10] Second, an obvious confirmation of farmers' active and leading roles in the urban settings would deconstruct the new principle of letting the city lead the rural that Mao Zedong set for New China. Third, there were no clear criteria from the government for filmmakers, writers, and any cultural workers on how to configure new types of farmers' images, how to evaluate their values in a new social environment, and how to enliven their bygone heroisms in the urban-based social space, through cinematic, literary, and artistic representations in general under the newly issued and enforced pro-city policy and an as-yet-to-be-formed urban ideology.

Runaway Farmers and the Economic Reform

The second generation of Chinese leadership, signified by Deng Xiaoping, an eight-time cover figure on *Time* magazine,[11] initiated China's astonishing economic reform in 1978 and steered China away from its Leninist and Maoist organizational straitjacket into a wider world of technological growth and international trade. He introduced a new economic dynamism with his striking phrase that it did not matter whether a cat was black or white; as long as it could catch mice, it is a good cat. Deng also identified other areas, including the education and military systems, where changes had to be made for China to become a world power. The economic revolution changed the planned economy to a market economy and loosened rural and urban ties. Thus, Chinese farmers started crossing the boundary between the city and the country with relative freedom, becoming the primary force behind the enormous success of the reforms in the early years. Chinese filmmakers and writers immediately revealed their corresponding reactions to farmer migrations and labor mobility in this economic transformation in their films and literary works. However, while treating farmers' migration or "runaway" (*chuzou*)[12] from their homeland, many filmmakers neither posted their criticisms nor extended their praise to the migration movement of Chinese farm workers in the early stage of the reform era. Many filmmakers were uncertain in light of this unprecedented economic reform as to how to politically define farmers' running away from their homeland and the agricultural geography on screen. The following films, to a certain extent, reveal ambiguous attitudes toward Chinese farmer migration: Wang Xinyu's 1982 *Chen Huansheng Entering the City* (Chen Huansheng shangcheng); Hu Bingliu's 1983 *Country Couple* (Xiang yin); Wu Tianming's 1987 *Old Well* (Laojing); and Zhou Xiaowen's 1994 *Ermo* (Ermo), to name just a few.[13] All these films illustrate farmers' encounter with the city and their anxieties and yearning for the city, and share a common theme that the city is no longer a taboo. The utopia of urban abundance and modernization become a persistent feature in the early cinema of the reform era.

One of the early films reflecting the runaway theme, *Life* (Rensheng), directed by Wu Tianming and made in Xi'an Film Studio in 1984, exemplifies such uncertainty and contradiction. Adapted from the novel of same title by Mao Dun Literature Award–winning author Lu Yao,[14] *Life* is a heart-tugging love story and a tale of a young village man's ups and downs associated with his city dream. A young rural schoolteacher, Gao Jialin, has lost his teaching position to another young man whose father has political clout. The defeat forces him to resume his role as a farmer and assist his elderly father with farm work. His misfortune though finds the sympathy and heart of a beautiful and caring village girl. Gao Jialin is moved by her pure love and dates the girl while he continues to maneuver to run away to the city for better living and social conditions where he can pursue his dream of becoming a writer. No sooner has he landed a job in the city than he abandons the village girl for a city woman. In the end, Gao Jialin breaks up with the city girlfriend when he is forced to withdraw from his city job due to political reasons, and the village girl has married another farmer upon Gao's second return to the rural home.

Life, screened nationwide, had a high profile after its release in 1984, including the winning of the Best Film and Best Actress awards at the People's Hundred Flowers Awards of 1985. Its cinematic aesthetics, including a saturated rural mise-en-scène and fascinating long takes and long shots over the northwestern geography, plus the actress's vivid and passionate performance of the village girl, convincingly wakened a pro-village ideology and launched heated debates among critics and common viewers on the topics of morality, traditional values, man's responsibility in relationships, the position of love, and the rural-urban dichotomy. The male protagonist, Gao Jialin, became the core target of all sorts of criticism, mainly for his moral misconduct in abandoning the village girl. Interestingly, among all the viewers' responses, almost no single voice defended or justified his city pursuit and his desire for more education, knowledge, and opportunities for uplifting himself. The pro-village ideology was embedded in the extolling of traditional values and virtues that the village girl represented—endurance, kindness, tenderness, thoughtfulness, unselfishness, and all the other humanistic qualities. That the film offered its audience a viewing pleasure of the rural space enhanced and enriched the praise of the rural. Under this awaked pro-village mentality, the city was completely repressed, as was the image of the rural young man who longed for the city. The pro-village rhetoric was also acute in my conversation with the film director Wu Tianming, as shown in the following.[15]

> Fu: "How do you define *Life* in terms of film genre?"
> Wu: "It is a rural film."
> Fu: "What about the image of the city and other urban elements that significantly sustain or constitute the story of Gao Jialin?"
> Wu: "They only play a supporting role in my film."
> Fu: "In what way?"
> Wu: "The city functions as a contrast to the countryside. With this contrast, we are able to see the beauty of the countryside and the acclaimed humanism and morality appearing in the rural people. I always love the countryside."
> Fu: "To follow your view, can we call *Life* a melodrama of morality? Many viewers' responses to *Life* centered on the issue of morality as represented in the film. Could you reflect on this?"
> Wu: "You (the audience) may think the film a melodrama of morality. To me, it is a film of the rural-city dichotomy and interaction in the reform era."
> Fu: "It seems to me that the city itself and every element and every figure related to the city or within the urban setting appear to be very negative and thus repressed in the film.

> For instance, Gao Jialin's city girlfriend, the city officials, even the cinematography shows limited or fewer aesthetic merits of the city in comparison with the rural counterpart."
> Wu: "You made your points. I do regret that I did not add a little more weight on the image of the city. If I redo the film, I will also decrease moral judgments imposed upon the character Gao Jialin, and justify his desire for education and knowledge."

The conversation reveals the uncertainty about the rapid social changes that many filmmakers had during the early stage of the reform era, and also in part offers a rationale for the cinematic ambiguity reflecting the relation between the rural and the urban, including, as well, the runaway farmers.

In the late 1980s and early 1990s, a striking number of films about rural migration, and the plight of female rural migrants in particular, appeared on screen, counterintuitively focused more on economic reform than on gender issues per se. Peng Xiaolian's 1987 *Women's Story* (Nuren de gushi), one of the earliest films about rural women seeking business opportunities in the city, attracted the attention of international film critics for its portrayal of women's changing role in the labor force. And Zhang Liang's 1990 film, *Working Girls from the Special Economic Zone* (Tequ dagongmei), told the story of a group of rural women becoming employees of a joint-venture electronic factory in Shenzhen, the Special Economic Zone near Hong Kong.

The award-wining film *Ermo* (Ermo, dir. Zhou Xiaowen, 1994)[16] offers a paradoxical example of runaway farmers' mobility from the rural. The film showcases a female farmer named Ermo's desperate pursuit of the largest television set displayed in a city department store. She makes frequent trips to the city, setting up a roadside business to sell her homemade noodles, working in a city restaurant, and even selling her blood in exchange for a television. In the film director's words, the film is about "a peasant's pursuit of a new lifestyle and her wish for upward mobility" and a "search for modern civilization."[17] However, the efforts and hardships that Ermo encountered and endured in order to possess a giant-sized television, a symbolic signifier of "the global village"[18] and a typical example of "commodity-on-display,"[19] showed her pathetic craze for and blindness in catching up with the commercial trend and thus dehumanized her entire "search for modern civilization."

Similarly themed films produced in the reform era delineate how new urban culture, enlivened by the state's open-door policy, usher in a new urban space that has been socially reconfigured in relation to transnational capital and globalised cultural practices. The corresponding city-country dichotomy reflects new political assertions, ideological underpinnings, historical conditions, social transformations, and cultural practices and negotiations. The farmer's urban experience portrayed in *Ermo* illustrates ambiguous and sometimes contradictory mentalities or attitudes toward the ceaseless emergence and progression of modernization and modernity. The cinematic representation of an underlying country-to-city (im)migration craze shows the transformation of the city itself. As shown in the film, the city has been the major node of the state's and each individual's interactions with other societies and cultures around the globe. Structures of local identity, social class, institutions of social integration, and practices of consumption have all been shaped by the interplay between local and global trends, developments, and images. In short, the cinematic representations of the runaway farmer in the 1980s show that farmer migration to the city is no longer an individual effort but the result of massive actions. These later farmers' motivations for running away are oriented more around money than around looking for an education opportunity or for a better career, as shown in *Life.*

Global Outlook and Local Legitimacy

The cinematic theme and representation of farmers being uprooted was enlarged and enriched at the turn of the century, as the farmer migration became not an individual act but a mass movement where it now appears that the collective movement justifies the migration. These films show various rationales for farmers' runaway from the country to the city, with their running away now cast in a global context. For instance, *Balzac and the Little Chinese Seamstress* (Xiao Caifeng, dir. Dai Sijie, 2002), adapted from the bestseller of the same name, shows a village girl tailor's transformation. Two sent-down educated youth teach the girl tailor how to read, write, live, and love, and how to make fashionable clothes from the works of Balzac. In the end, the young tailor decides to walk out of the mountainous village to find a new life. When the two young men inquire about what made her leave, the little seamstress responds, "Balzac." That French literature awakens a Chinese rural girl's desire for change as manifested in the film simplistically contextualized and confirmed the global influence on the migration movement and the national progress as well. Up to this point, the subjects of the city and the historical past were the sole external measures of the shift from transparency to opacity and therefore to simultaneity and simulacra, entailing an act of "integrating (China) into the world community" (*Yu shijie jiegui*), representing a tangible instance of globalization in China, and becoming operational, particularly on the screenscape.

Zhang Yimou's most down-to-earth film, *The Story of Qiu Ju* (Qu Ju daguansi, 1992),[20] features a stubborn rural pregnant woman Qiu Ju entering the city and looking for justice for her husband, who has had a dispute with the village chief. On the one hand, a rural woman's quest for legal help in the city politically legitimated a farmer's entering the city. On the other hand, this cinematic instance decreased if not diminished the image and imagery of endangered urban space, and transformed the long-time ideologically repressed city into a site of hope and a rosy shelter for farmers. Furthermore, *The Story of Qiu Ju* seems to convey that the reform in theory allows individuals restitution against government abuse, and brings about China's installation of a judicial code. Qiu Ju's "runaway" witnesses the changing operations and ideologies around the rural-urban paradox and the local-global paradigm as well as a developing juridical reality.

As suggested in the film's title, *A Beautiful New World* (Meili xin shijie, dir. Shi Runjiu, 1998) displays a rosier picture of a farmer's dream coming true in the city. The film tells a story of a male farmer who wins a luxury apartment in a not-yet-built high-rise building through the lottery. Winning the lottery allows him to become a temporary city dweller and offers him opportunities to find a city fiancée. The final episode in the film presented satirically the farmer's rosy urban dream of becoming a permanent urban citizen and living in a top-level apartment of the apartment building. A low-angle shot shows the farmer standing on the construction site and embracing his city sweetheart under the heavy rains while they wave to their to-be-built urban home. The lottery, the to-be-built urban apartment, and the relationship with an urban girl seem to suggest the farmer's legitimacy in his urban dwelling and identity. However the heavy rain expresses a constellation of sensibilities that question the probability and possibility of his ultimate settlement in the city, and thus remind viewers of the growing concern for the dislocation of farmers and the issues and problems associated with the dislocation.

Moving into the new century, the representation of farmers' migration to the city has been inspired and affirmed by a TV commercial, "Your heart determines your stage" (Xin you duoda, wutai jiuyou duoda).[21] This TV commercial was produced and broadcast at the beginning of the twenty-first century by China Central Television (CCTV), the top Chinese official television network. A high-angle bird's–eye-view shot of a village scene is followed by a cut to a full view of a village girl in typical rural attire dancing alone in her rural home, the camera continuing to show a vast platform in front of a high-rise office building. In the blink of an eye, the platform dissolves into a stage, where the rural girl is waltzing with an urban, white-collar man. A zoom-out displays more pairs of dancers joining in the dancing carnival, and the subtitle "Your heart determines your stage" pops onto the screen; the commercial ends with the rural girl standing on the stage, her back to audience, the camera panning/glancing at the city below her. The slogan not only justified the farmers' encircling the city, but also became a motto and a part of a very popular public rhetoric for the youth.

With the increasing flow of peasant workers into Chinese cities, relevant problems turn up as constant obsessions. Recently, the Chinese government offered protection and services to this special group in the work force that has been much in need of enormous and lasting urban construction projects. An example is the creation of a farm workers' chorale at the 2008 Chinese New Year's gala, the most popular show entertaining Chinese audiences every Chinese New Year's eve. Led by a farmer rising star, Wang Baoqiang, the farmer singers voiced their urban dreams and announced their relocations from farm land to the urban zone, and trumpeted their newly obtained status as urban workers, which seemed to suggest a legitimacy to their being uprooted from the country to the city.

Conclusion

These cinematic and media examples of Chinese farmers and their active adjustments to, and sometimes precarious positioning by, the enormous social changes in contemporary China bespeak changing operations and ideologies in the rural-urban paradox and the local-global paradigm in Chinese political and social contexts. This article shows that the force of globalization and domestic economic demands have changed or moderated the long-time prevailing pro-village ideology. However, these changes do not seem to lie in farmers' longing for a realization of their urban dreams, though as shown in the films discussed above, Chinese farmers have taken every initiative to change their lives amid the state policy changes. Rather, all the transformations have been heavily charted by the Chinese government's political and economic decisions and measures, which embody all sorts of new governmental ideologies and assertions to keep up with both local and global changes and to meet domestic and world demands. The corresponding productions of film and media have followed this trajectory. In this sense, the representation of Chinese farmers on screen is not a mere product of mass-based cultural production, or an effective act of serving the common people, but a resounding echo of Chinese political and economic transformation under the rubric of searching for and building a modernized and globalized China.

As shown in my study, the cinematic subjects and representations of Chinese farmers and rural migration are extensively linked to many social, political, and cultural aspects of Chinese society, which have largely diversified Chinese rural cinema. This ever-emerging diversity is a warning and a reminder to any cultural worker that hybrid Chinese rural themes and rural cinema highlight the need to adjust our critical focus on Chinese farmers on screen and the Chinese rural cinema genre, including their forms and meanings, and their aesthetics and social connotations, in order to account for the problems and pleasure of our viewing experience. Either a pro-village mentality or a pro-city stand will blur our view of seeing a now-hybridized China, and a contemporary hybridized rural China in particular. Chinese farmers, who comprise about 60 percent of China's 1.3 billion population, both on- and off-screen, force us to reflect critically upon notions of human equality, individuality, mobility, locality, urbanization, modernization, and the local and the global in a rich and complex way. They have been the vital force behind China's present economic prosperity and will continue to play the role, but many of them are struggling with their basic survival both in the countryside and the city, fighting for fair wages, health care, children's education, and so forth. To look closely at who they are, what they need, and where they are inside China's sociocultural landscape is not only to plot the trajectory of Chinese rural cinema but also to attempt to describe the momentous changes happening every day in the lives of the world's largest class of a now-hybridized, rural proletariat—Chinese working class farmers (*nongmin gong*).

8

Between Realism and Romanticism: Queering Gender Representation in Cui Zi'en's *Night Scene*

Megan M. Ferry

Filmmaker Cui Zi'en's treatment of male prostitution in *Night Scene* (*Ye jing* 2005) intervenes in the bodily configuration of sexualized individuals in post-Maoist society. His look at the Chinese male prostitute in this experimental documentary underscores the male body as caught within the intricate web of a market economy that drives labor and desire, while destabilizing and reframing assumptions about gendered bodies, labor, and commerce in contemporary China. His work concentrates on reexamining queer bodies in the context of male prostitution. He does this through the metaphor of the fish, which echoes strongly Yang Zhenzhong's video installation, *Fish Tank* (*Yugang* 1996). In the same destabilizing manner as Yang's work, Cui's film disorients and conflates human bodies with fish when following the different narratives that weave in and out of the film. By focusing on the basest of the larger gay community, Cui's film challenges the abjection that informs perceptions of both gay men and prostitutes, thereby reframing mostly through testimony subjectivities otherwise rejected or demonized in society. The film also explores the limits of gay male body commodification for the construction of a society that is more tolerant of difference.

In "We Are Not Fish, We Are Not Mouths, We Are Not Queer," Cui speaks to the liberating effects of queer theory against mainstream, hegemonic culture.[1] Cui sees Yang Zhenzhong's work as defying the negative effects of social categorization. *Fish Tank* juxtaposes three television sets placed submerged within, emerging from, and above a fish tank. The video running on the screens showed lips looking fish-like that repeat the phrase "we are not fish, we are not fish." The bubbles emerging from the lips make it hard to distinguish between human mouth and fish mouth.[2] Cui sees Yang's work as evocative of other human orifices and contends that they are distinguishable only in the way in which they are used. For Cui, the metaphor of the fish aptly depicts the problem of the historical classification of sex/gender categories that in the very process of naming speaks of the exclusiveness of binary oppositions. In taking up Yang's word play "we are not fish," Cui destabilizes sex/gender categorization in order to find a new common denominator to "work out a new domain of human desire, or in other words, to use the methods of liberation to mold love, sensory capabilities, and desire into a new internationale."[3]

Inspired by the work of U.S. theorist David M. Halperin, Cui believes that queer theory breaks from sex/gender binarisms. What he takes from Halperin is an interest in how queer theory has formed a broader framework that recasts human relationships, laying open the potential for new forms of social existence, values, and interconnectedness. Cui is not interested in seeing queer culture as an appendage to existing mainstream culture. Rather he seeks to transform culture itself, or at least, to call into question the way in which culture, especially sexual culture, is represented. He does so by finding ways to express sexuality outside the existing negative language and framework of heterosexual normativity.

Instead of portraying homosexuality as alienated within China's social economy, *Night Scene* creates an alternative forum for the expression of male gay subjectivity.[4] It recasts the hitherto perception of male homoeroticism as operating outside the social norm by focusing on male prostitutes' participation in China's new market economy. In the film, these sexual subjects engage in and are engaged by the institutional languages that dictate subjectivities in consumer culture. In fact, the film links male prostitution and sexuality to dominant forms of social production and consumption by illustrating the entrepreneurship of prostitution, its relationship to individual development within a capitalist framework, and the buying power of upwardly mobile gays. Yet such a representation does not mean that the film reproduces wholesale market economy structures, but rather it both subverts and enriches their sexual normativity. As Inderpal Grewal and Caren Kaplan illustrate, new consumption patterns and media technologies created by capitalism also create new subjectivities that throw into question the established models of who belongs to a society and what rights she is accorded.[5]

Night Scene interweaves expert opinion with the realities of male sex workers working in a nightclub and the fictionalizing of a homoerotic relationship. These contrasting narratives are punctuated by the presence of fish and the refractive influence of glass and water. Prostitutes are filmed either next to or behind the aquariums lining a gay nightclub, where human relationships are joined to the symbolism of fish; some of the expert voices are situated in a similar destabilizing relationship; and the fictional relationship occurs in the context of fish and bird market. Although critical of normative sexual discourses, Cui also questions an upwardly male gay enterprise that aligns itself with commodified culture and embraces a new market economy that continues to essentialize sexuality. His film draws our attention to sexualized and gendered bodies, not as innate manifestations of an individual but as socially constructed byproducts of capitalism. Although the film does not critique capitalism directly, it examines desiring male subjects within capitalist exchange and the value of that constituted desire.

Against Categories of Gender and Representation

Since Deng Xiaoping's "reform and opening" policies of the 1980s, gender norms articulated through the Chinese state, media, and some academic circles, reiterate that males and females are different from each other. These norms have been revised from the masculine and feminine essentialist paradigms of socialism.[6] L. H. M. Ling reads in these discourses a culture of hypermasculinity, the byproduct of which is the fetishization of women.[7] In the words of Sheldon Lu, the mass media constructs a masculine subjectivity such that men reap "romantic triumph and global financial success" with a newly found sexual and business confidence.[8] Both Ling and Lu see these reified gender roles emerging as part of a transnational, capital-intensive drive for upward mobility. Men and women feel the pressure to realize the new social roles that lay claim to their supposed innate characteristics as soft and feminine, strong and masculine. Yet China's ever-increasing involvement in the global economy does not stop men and women from feeling bewildered, if not "besieged," by the plethora of media representations professing the natural qualities of such heterosexual gender distinctions.[9]

In "Qualities of Desire: Imagining Gay Identities in China," Lisa Rofel claims that public discourses emerging in the post-Mao era presume the naturalness of a gendered and sexed humanity.[10] The new consumer culture is the force behind this new definition of the sexed/gendered individual, with its promises to address the inherent desires of those formerly repressed by the socialist state. Such rhetoric posits capitalism as an economic and political system that comes closer to responding to a perceived "natural humanity" than any other system.[11] Yet this system presupposes qualitative differences between individuals based on heteronormative distinctions. According to Rofel, Chinese gay men's desire for cultural belonging both within China and within a transnational gay context puts them in a complex situation, given that normative assumptions about sex define cultural belonging in China, and hegemonic assumptions about culture make transnational gay identification equally problematic.[12] For many gay men traditional family structures and fixed gender categories do not include being gay as an option. Conversely, the transnational gay community led by U.S. and European political agendas do not meet the needs of local realities at home.

As a critique of the purported "naturalness" of sexual difference, its systematic categorization, and exclusion of gay identity, Cui reflects upon how such difference has been constructed. Sexual orientation is not the only classification Cui reworks in his film. While the International Movie Database categorizes *Night Scene* as drama, the film is framed as a documentary whose narrative is destabilized by dramatization as well as cinemtography. His film purposely conflates genres and their attendant assumptions about representation in order to breakdown the technology structures responsible for framing subjectivity on the screen. Chris Berry writes that documentarians in the 1990s, like the feature filmmakers of the

1980s, were fascinated with Chinese ethnic others, suggesting that their representations reflected the sense of alienation filmmakers themselves felt in contemporary society.[13] Offering the term "on-the-spot realism," Berry argues that this documentary style reflects an unscripted spontaneity that attempts to get closer to a sense of reality, "giv[ing] (or appear[ing] to give) the ordinary people a direct voice, which enables (or appears to enable) them to speak directly to other ordinary people."[14] In contrast to "on-the-spot realist" films, Cui's *Night Scene* not only disrupts assumptions about normativized sexuality, it also purposefully mixes both fictional and documentary elements in order to question the scaffolding leading to such sex/gender assumptions, and hence throws into question how reality gets documented. He positions his subjects and his camera behind, next to, and in front of Yang Zhenzhong's proverbial fish tank to deconstruct preconceived assumptions of sex/gender and the filmic register of such performative realities.

Night Scene makes visible the lives and narratives of young men selling their bodies through a mixture of filmic genres: documentary, feature film, and what he calls the *huiyi taolun* or "roundtable." The genres straddle the divide between a clinical and sociological examination of male prostitution, a fantasy narrative about male homosexuality as a manifestation of innate desire, and a multilayered testimony of personal adjustment. Both the documentary and fictional idioms are destabilized by moving fish, whose metaphoric presence highlight the ventriloquy of both genres as products of capitalist enterprise, though each functions differently: one as an examination of purportedly real subjects, the other an examination of romantic idealism. The documentary confers a sense of authority to narrate and to provide testimony of male prostitution, presuming an unmediated and direct link between interviewee and audience. The documentary style employs talking heads, direct cinema-type filming, and testimony to create a web of multiple meanings surrounding gay personhood. Yet the subjects are often filmed through aquariums, or positioned to look as if they are the fish in the tank, which refract the traditional relationship between audience and filmed subject of most documentary films. While documentaries often employ reenactments or recreations to create an indexical bond between text, image, and the viewer's comprehension of the historical moment at hand, the fish anchor the interviewees' testimony while at the same time dislocate how we come to know (about) prostitution and homosexuality and the correlative assumptions assigned to their social positions. Fish play a role in the fictional element too, as their contained buoyancy reveals the fragility of upwardly mobile dreams of blissful domesticity. Ultimately Cui refuses to mark either male homosexuals or male prostitutes as abject citizens. The two genres use male subjectivity paradoxically to both embrace and resist China's liberal market economy. Finally, Cui intersperses these two genres with discreet moments in the everyday lives of the prostitutes, thereby allowing us to consider what a community unencumbered by categorizations would look like. Before examining these aspects more closely I first want to look at why Cui chooses prostitution as his film's subject.

Sex Workers

Jean-François Lyotard argues that the exchangeability of the prostitute's body for currency signifies a drive for economic and political capital, not to mention social recognition.[15] The prostitute constitutes part of the circuit of exchanges through earned wages. It is money that brings this subject into the social economy since she does not enter it via motherhood or through a state-sanctioned marriage. Pan Suiming's findings on female prostitution in contemporary China suggest that there is a social acceptance of prostitution; however, it operates under a hierarchy, with the assumption that only the poor or destitute are prostitutes, whereas women of the middle and upper classes who engage in sex exchange are considered as participating in romances.[16] While the sexual acts the two types engage in may be the same, they are differently named and therefore differently valued.

Attention to sex work in China became publicly visible thanks to the work of social workers and sociologists who reemerged as credible scholarly agencies in the post-Mao era. Largely sharing the state's view of prostitution, these researchers legitimated the study of the problems of sex work, thereby enabling their own return to the academic profession and validating the othering their subjects' new framing exemplified.[17] They examined the social conditions and motivations of prostitutes to find solutions for what they saw as a national problem, concluding that the risk of sexual diseases imperiled the health of the nation, a nation whose condition would improve once China's economy could support all its citizens.[18] Filtered through the academic lens, prostitutes were portrayed as objects of either disgust, disdain, or, in contrast, sympathy. Similarly, media coverage of gay men in China has painted an equally alarming image of them as "promiscuous, doomed by AIDS, and a menace to society."[19] Such discourses paint the prostitute and gay man as blemishes on the fabric of China's modernity project, whose natures can be redressed, contained, and redeployed through academic discussion and study.

As an academic at the Beijing Film Academy, author and film director Cui Zi'en subverts and enriches this perspective of male homosexuality and male prostitution in contemporary China. Despite his own marginal and tenuous position within the academy he has been able to use his status to speak out within China as well as in transnational venues on his various invitations to lecture abroad.[20] Instead of marking either prostitution or homosexuality as pathologies, he seeks to remedy the paradigms that hierarchize social roles and sexualities.

Cui positions prostitution within the political economy of romance through the mixed use of documentary and feature film genre elements in order to make manifest how heteronormative class structures segregate the gay community and inform the language of social and economic participation. He does so in order to contend with several discourses that equate prostitution and homosexuality with social deviance, reflecting a more general concern for quality (*suzhi*), a term that has emerged in recent decades to cover everything from the quality of service and goods production to social behavior. Among the gay male community in Beijing the term is used to express anxiety about young male prostitutes coming from the countryside "to pollute city life with their transgressions of the social divisions between masculine wealth and masculine love, between urban propriety and rural excess, and between proper and improper expressions of gay identity."[21] This anxiety segregates the gay community by privileging a distinctly urban bourgeois outlook and fearing the presence of rural migrants who threaten such an outlook. On the deepest level urban-born gay men fear having homosexuality associated with prostitution because the latter is marked rural, effeminate, and lower class. Cui seeks to break from this view by destabilizing such gendered binaries.

Narrating Experience

The film's documentary narrative frame follows actual male sex workers in Beijing, as well as experts who work with or on behalf of the prostitutes, who all offer testimony to their experiences. The interviewer's presence and questions remain off camera, and the interviewees' responses participate on the level of social discourse that Chinese prostitution has been accorded in the last two decades. Several framing registers connect us to the truth-claim of testimony in different ways. These registers challenge the consequent notions of authentic subjects and a priori knowledge about individual experience that the documentary genre presumes and proffers. For instance, *Night Scene* highlights both the inadequacy of film to capture authenticity and provide a complete picture of reality and its adequacy in mining the many discourses that lay claim to the definition of both gay subjectivity and its insertion into modern capitalist societies. Its incorporation of visual elements, such as the fish, and camera positions compel one to consider the performative aspect of one's social role, that is, the constructed nature of *being* social.[22] In other words, the film does not satisfy a conventional need to know about the lived experiences of gay male prostitutes but rather questions the process by which we come to know about individuals and make assumptions about inherent (sexual/gendered) human qualities. This question becomes an important one when considering the role of sexual difference and its framing in both national and global economies and cultures of consumption.

The testimonial documentary portion of *Night Scene* focuses on interviews with male sex workers who relate their first experiences in exchanging sex for money, their reasons for working in gay nightclubs or entering prostitution, their experiences as gay men in the social world and/or as kept men, their social and economic aspirations, and their life ideals. It immediately becomes apparent that there is no singular history of homosexuality in China, nor any one reason why these young men engage in prostitution. Subsequent and interspersed interviews with social workers, sociologists, and sexologists confer another layer of legitimacy to these sex workers by speaking about them using sexual behavior surveys, Marxist thought, economic labor, pathological and clinical realties, thereby granting the prostitutes a protected visibility as object of study under the cloak of academic scrutiny and taxonomy. The film has the overall feel of a formal documentary that humanizes male sex workers as subjects; however, their lived experiences provide evidence of a social marginalization that academic language cannot describe except within the contained discourses of disease, promiscuity, labor, and family. It is in these documentary moments Cui's film diverges from the practiced unraveling of individual lives caught on tape for the benefit of an audience seeking knowledge about the subjects on exhibition or seeking knowledge of an exoticized, abject other.

Not just in the interviews at the film's opening, but also throughout, fish and other visual impediments expose the inadequacy of the camera's ability to capture experience. Situated between the subject and the camera is initially a large aquarium, wherein the tail or other portions of swimming fish disrupt a complete vision of these young men as they relate their first experiences as sex workers. During some interviews, the camera shifts to other focal points in the frame, such as the bar owner's toddler son playing in the background or the young man sitting passively beside the academic. Other interviews appear to be shot over several takes and at several angles. Even as the academic experts explain these young men's social reality, the camera either refuses to stay still or it keeps a partial figure of a young man, presumably himself a prostitute, just within the frame as if a prop, to remind us of the constructedness of the setting. In this manner, Cui's camera work highlights the containing nature of documentation. That is, in providing only partial views of his subjects, or in the constant shifting of the camera, Cui calls attention to the fact that we privilege vision as a means of knowing. By not letting us see subjects in their so-called totality he keeps us from assembling knowledge about them. He also disarms the viewer's identification with the subject on camera. Instead of making his subjects' experiences visible, he makes evident the act of representation as an incomplete substitute for knowledge. He offer not an "authorized appearance of the 'real'," but a commentary on film's artifice.[23] In this sense, the fish tanks embody containment as well as misshapen reality; they reflect upon the lives therein, and refract the inclusive and exclusiveness of being on the inside/outside of discursive authority.

By not overtly assuming naturalized gender or sexual categories of desire, the film makes evident that there is no uniform experience that brought these young men to prostitution, such as money, love, or community. It does, however, reveal these men's desire to participate in capitalist exchange and heterosexual fantasies. Some men use the camera as if it were for a singles ad, preferring not to talk about their experience but to highlight and promote their best attributes. Prostitution, for many of them, is a means to acquire the necessary capital to recover from previous business deals gone sour, to display one's talents and gain recognition, to make enough money to start a family, to secure a path to bourgeois advancement, or to pay for an education. Some even see it as a means to find a lifelong partner. There are moments when the camera calls attention to a sexual disorientation of its subject, as when it augments an interviewee's assertion that he is "normal" by a quick pan shot of his body to show him bare-chested in a faux fur vest. The camera both certifies and decertifies the body toward and against claimed identification, as if it could essentialize and dessentialize the subject simultaneously. Or when the camera uses the social worker's body as a substitute for the male prostitute who, the social worker tells the camera, would use his earnings to have sex with women after having sex with men so that he could feel like a man again. In this segment the camera shifts from a high angle shot of the social worker's hands and crotch to a close up of his head, and finally a cut to a low angle shot of his crotch and inner thigh. The camera is often drawn to the genital area, which may reflect the desire of the person behind the camera as much as it directs the viewer to read prostitution neither as an expressive form of homosexual nor heterosexual desire per se. That is, attention to genital area suggests that male power is endowed by the penis no matter who one's sexual object choice is.

The film ratifies male prostitution as a legitimate, though ambivalent, means of sexual expression, such as when it captures sociologist Li Yinhe's Marxist interpretation that the only difference between marriage and prostitution is that of wholesale versus retail commodity exchange. In seeing contemporary sexual relations as product of capital formation, Li advocates legalizing prostitution and gay marriages. Another expert, Zhang Beichuan, suggests that recent studies demonstrate male and female sex workers share the same social conditions (young, uneducated, rural, and single), and that their behavior is based on economic factors. As a social progressive, Zhang remarks that a stable and harmonious society accepts all kinds of people, and intolerance creates trouble for it. The real focus of the film, however, appears not to be on the redemption of the filmic subjects but the desiring subject behind the camera, who seeks social inclusion for these marginalized young men.

Heralded by Western media as China's only out homosexual, Cui has spoken openly about homosexuality in China, global culture's effects on social norms within China, and the underrepresentation of gay culture in the media. For the most part, media coverage of homosexuality has been "fanciful and biased" in China.[24] Research indicates that a gay subculture, at least since the 1980s, has operated in the public parks and bathhouses in large- and medium-sized cities.[25] It is only since the 1990s that it has moved into private commercial spaces that offer "protected settings," such as gay bars and nightclubs; thus an emerging entertainment and media market is beginning to court homosexual customers.[26] Cui does not film the male prostitute in action (nor so his clientele) so much as the setting within which sexuality gets commodified: a place and a time where gender and sexual orientation are performed. The place is none other than a nightclub whose main decorative feature is a narrow hallway filled with aquariums.

The reemergence of gender and sexual orientation as operative tools in China's national and global economy has influenced public gender practice and representation. In his study of modern Thailand's same-sex and transgender cultures, Peter Jackson argues that modernity and globalization have radically shifted the "performative norms of masculinity and femininity."[27] His study examines how Thailand's self-civilizing missions incorporated Western critique of Thai society to reorder the public representation of Thai bodies, particularly in a public dress that distinguishes between genders.[28] In its transition to an urban market economy the state worked hard to remold the sense of citizenship to fit generally westernized notions of femininity and masculinity, and to reflect a more "modern," "civilized" society. The effects of such practices have resulted in new connections between national/transnational commerce and cultural production, among which is sex tourism. Ann Anagnost outlines a similar trajectory in contemporary China, where she sees a "corporeal politics of quality (*suzhi*)" defining the value of human bodies.[29] The laboring body of the migrant worker is valued less against the education-invested child of the middle class. Thus, consumption is valued over production. "To know how to consume appropriately is to participate in a highly coded realm of social distinctions where consumption both constructs the body of value and establishes its distance from its other."[30] In conjunction with this new value system, China's sexual culture is increasingly defined by a politics of virtue that is leery of the West's perceived sexual liberalization, yet still attracted to the capital accumulation potential that Westernization presumes to offer.[31] In addition, the belief that the exercise of one's personhood and citizenship reside in capital accumulation and consumption has become part of mainstream cultural ideology.

The effects of globalization on the configuration of modern sexual identities in Asia, especially in the construction of commercial venues for the gay consumer, are equally undeniable. The new commercial bars and clubs for gay men are a part of China's transnational scene, cohabited with foreign men who are living and working in China. Yet Cui's film does not show this foreign element. Perhaps it is because he wants to make visible a Chinese gay presence. Many Chinese are unaware that gay identities exist in China, and the predominant images of homosexuals and lesbians circulating for gays and non-gays alike in China are Western.[32] Such images have a profound effect on self-fashioning and self-identification, tending to minimize national affiliation.

Dennis Altman and Lisa Rofel both discuss the role globalization plays in the configuration of gay Asians in their study of the Phillipines and China, respectively.[33] Both deny claim to a "global gay identity," but are conscious of the fact that transnational formations have altered a culture's articulation of the traditional/modern, masculine/feminine dichotomies. Whereas Altman queries if economic and cultural globalization "can be said to produce a common consciousness and identity based on homosexuality," Rofel offers that Chinese gay identities "materialize in the articulation of transcultural practices with intense desire for cultural belonging, or cultural citizenship, in China."[34] While *Night Scene* does not overtly comment on the effects of global capital on gay male bodies, it does highlight the entrepreneurship that relocates gay culture from the public parks to consumer-driven bars and nightclubs and suggests that economic liberalism democratizes those who can capitalize on China's growing economy.

Capitalizing on Romance

The more overtly fictional strand in *Night Scene* tries to offer a counter-narrative to the documentary by offering a brief feature-film–like story and additional narratives that function more like reenactments. These reenactments relate more to the young men's general experiences than to a particular historical or personal moment. This strand forces the viewer to consider the link between commercial sex work and gay identity. It examines whether gay desire operates outside of economic exchange in a form of "emotional reciprocity,"[35] a position long constituted by the Confucian valuation of the family. Changes promoted by capitalism, transnational gay identification, and the modern interpretation of the Confucian family structure complicate a sense of home or belonging.[36]

Chris Berry has argued that representations of homosexuality have reworked the well-mapped terrain of East-West, past-present binaries, creating the possibility for a "third space" within Chinese society.[37] The presence of homosexuality in Asian cinema has brought it into the mainstream and thwarted "government-centered ideologies of collective identity that attempt to other homosexuality."[38] Elsewhere he suggests that the treatment of gay men in films such as *Happy Together, East Palace West Palace,* and *Vive L'Amour* signifiy individuals without roles in the traditional East Asian family structure. The isolation they face as a result of their sexual orientation make them "sad gay men," whose alienation is symbolic of their contemporary milieu. Yet the sad gay man trope, Berry argues, appears to be the creation of mainstream culture.[39] So while homosexuality has entered mainstream cinema, its position is still marginalized. In other words, could this be the very detrimental "fish" and human "mouth" conflation and ventriloquy that Cui sees happening in Yang Zhenzhong's video installation?

While many artists have sought to define a gay or lesbian Asian identity, others have worked to de-marginalize homosexuality by incorporating it within the heterosexual dominant culture. Zhang Yuan's *East Palace West Palace* (*Donggong xigong*) (1996) may be the first film to directly address gay male culture within China, yet the protagonist, A Lan, speaks of his sexuality along the lines of a pastoral confession that he must reveal to an inquisitive policeman in order to explain his social deviation from the heterosexual norm. Chinese gay culture becomes visible to the audience through interrogation, suggesting that the film's subject matter is secondary to the director's more general concern of representing marginalized people vis-à-vis the state and revealing the numbing effects of state discourse throughout the latter half of the twentieth century.[40] The dialogue between the policeman and the "criminal" reveals the policeman's role as detector and regulator of "socially perverse" behavior. In the words of Lyotard, "'[m]aking someone talk' [is] nothing other than the reestablishment of *jouissance* in the place assigned it by order."[41] The policemen's interpellation that the male homosexual speak his story defers the policeman's having to question his own gender status and denies an alternative language with which to address homosexuality outside the state discourse of criminal behavior.[42]

Hong Kong director Stanley Kwan's *Lan Yu* (2001), conversely, presents homosexuality in mainland China as unremarkable, and thus, an already integrated part of everyday life in the way it shows contemporary cultural acceptance of an openly gay couple. Despite the fact that one of the partners faces jail time for unethical business practices, his sexuality does not emerge as an issue. Commerce and love remain separate entities. The film thus segregates homosexual love from capitalism, suggesting that bourgeois culture, to which the men's partnership belongs, is born of innate desire. The film ignores the economic foundation on which such a partnership is constructed in order to express the time-worn cliché "love conquers all." It incorporates homosexual desire into dominant society and problematically distances the film's fantasy narrative from contemporary life.

Night Scene offers a radically contrasting vision. After the film commences with sex worker interviews, it cuts to the portrayal of a young man, Yang Yang, cruising for what appears to be the first time in one of the public parks, where he meets a man. The film shows shots of the two men moving through public spaces, playing on the citywide outdoor exercise equipment and Yang Yang giving his new partner a tour of his college campus. In a classroom, Yang Yang lectures his partner on what constitutes true love. His partner responds: "It is like you and me." Yang Yang corrects him to say: "True love is you and me. Get it?" In this instance, Yang Yang calls attention to his partner's metaphoric reading of gay desire and corrects him by uniting both the signifier and signified, that is love and its two desiring gay subjects. The film cuts to the two walking the night stalls in Beijing, eating food bought from the vendors. Next, it shows Yang Yang alone spying a gay couple in one of the shopping centers along Wangfujing, a large commercial district. He follows them outside and into what appears to be the following day in another part of town at a fish and bird market. He enters the market and comes across one of the partners selling aquarium fish. Yang Yang has a curt exchange with the fish seller, asking him if he sells his body as well. Later Yang Yang spies the couple in a public park where the other partner expresses his eternal love for the fish seller and desire to have a partner for life. It turns out the other partner is Yang Yang's father, whom Yang Yang accuses the fish seller of seducing. In his frustration over witnessing this scene between his father and his father's lover, Yang Yang encounters another man in the public park on a subsequent day, drags him off near some bushes, and violently forces a kiss on him.

In this dramatized narrative of gay coupling the violent kiss suggests Yang Yang's inability to come to terms with his father's partner, and through it, an alternative kinship formation (or perhaps, more telling, a potential father-son competition for the same partner). Sexual difference, heterosexual love, jealousy, and virile masculinity have become integral to the postsocialist definition of cultural citizenship in China. Desire for cultural belonging predicated on such pressures shapes gay identity as much as it does that of heterosexuals.[43] The conjugal love shared between gay men both supports the conservatism of monogamy in contemporary heterosexual marriage and subverts it through same-sex love. Yang Yang's exchange with the fish seller indicates a rejection of this kind of partnership, but in this rejection he reintroduces the economic and erotic economies of difference. Yang Yang reproduces with his violent kiss the top/bottom hierarchy of the capitalist drive and transnational representations of gay desire that are equally informed by race, gender, and class.[44] He is unable to consider homosexuality apart from commodity exchange and its resultant hierarchies. These scenes evoke China's social stratification within its urban gay communities and the drive for upward mobility that social legitimization and access to capital exemplify. Cui appears critical of both heterosexual norms and homosexual social hierarchies that are derivative of those norms.[45]

The fish symbolism used throughout the film evokes the tension between cultural value and capitalist expansion. Fish have long stood for heterosexual marriage, love, and fertility in the domestic economy of Chinese society. Their use as household adornment reflected the wealth and social status of the owners who could afford and appreciate them. The fish seller's position in contemporary capitalist exchange is limited to antiquated notions of conjugality and luxury consumption. He has a limited customer base among those who have the capital and desire to perpetuate traditional symbols of wealth and happiness. Cui's disruption of the relationship between the fish seller and Yang Yang's father demonstrates that the fish symbolism does not fit with homosexual culture except in the nightclub, where there is a tenuous union of equality and community among gay men. Cui directs our attention away from the economy of domestic consumerism, as in the aquarium fish, to the economy of libidinal exchange, which has greater potential for market expansion. The labyrinthic, fish-laden corridor of the nightclub takes one beyond the quiet contemplation of a family compound and into the chamber of hardcore capitalist exchange in bodies. It is in this "fish market" where masculine exchange reveals its full power.[46]

According to sociologist Li Yinhe, the respondents to her survey of China's male homosexual subculture remark that there are three kinds of men who frequent the "fish market" nightclubs: those who are there for pure sexual release and quickly seek sexual partners, those who frequent the clubs daily, not necessarily for sexual release but because of a sex addiction (*yinpi*), and thirdly, married men who, in their wives' absence, seek temporary sexual release.[47] Also present are foreigners who are visiting or living in China. Not all the male prostitutes or the customers necessarily identify themselves as gay men.

Cui disrupts the narrative of gay male desire (as expressed in the romantic relationship between Yang Yang's father and the fish seller), in order to reveal how the concept of a universal gay identity has become part of the new discourse on human nature. Contemporary sexual desire is informed by bourgeois subjectivity and Cui is critical of social hierarchies instilled among urban gay men who look down upon male prostitutes as abject citizens, and who are deeply concerned about the equation of homosexuality with prostitution.[48] The film offers a critique of the hierarchical structure of contemporary gay culture and the way it devalues prostitution as "undermining the true meaning of homosexuality."[49] According to Cui, the bourgeois gay community's concern about morality risks letting it languish under the same totalizing discourses the state uses to patronize difference.[50] He is thus critical of a gay community that does not question commodity culture and welcomes globalization without questioning the heteronormative strictures latent in capitalism; he, too, concurrently bemoans the fact that Chinese gay men see little reflection of themselves in available media and thus need to rely upon foreign media and information to define their identity. Chinese gay men's class stratification mirrors China's participation in the global economy as both seek strength over historically dominant power structures.

Cui also constantly destabilizes this narrative by switching documentary registers through camera work and mise-en-scene. The split images that the fish create with the interview subjects in the film's documentary strand further reveal the fractured symbolism of China's social veneer, calling our attention to the class issues hidden behind traditional cultural images of love and domesticity, as well as China's rising consumer culture. Not everyone has access to capital, but most everyone can hide behind the cumulative wealth fantasy that the fish symbolism implies and thus refuse to see the social stratification and exclusion. In filming the young men through the fish tanks, Cui effectively demonstrates how these men are cut off from realizing the bourgeois domestic ideal. In some instances, their image is obscured by passing fish. In others, their position behind the tanks look as if they too were inside with the fish, calling our attention to their symbolic, and hence inanimate positions within the economy. By disrupting the romantic image of the fish seller, Cui confronts the value of this symbolic ideal in contemporary China. In equating bourgeois gay male coupledom with traditional symbols of love and domestic harmony, Cui renders such a union valueless against the more profitable network of bars and social spaces that are defining a new gay male community. A bourgeois lifestyle thus becomes part of an antiquated economic and libidinal system; a false heterosexual ideal.

Taken as a whole, *Night Scene* seems to present its subjects as beholden to an economic determinism of transnational capital. His film explores how homosexuality shares "the same [heteronormative] 'phallic economy'" in that the feature film sequences and interviews expose the desire to participate in a masculine-driven modernity.[51] Interstitial shots of the fish in the tank being fed smaller fish draw our attention to the captivity of animals who feed off and who in turn are fed to others, and the hierarchal structure of contemporary society that posits homosexuals and prostitutes as the most base citizens of this food chain.

Cui's critique of this model appears in greater detail in the narrative film *Feeding Boys, Ayaya* (Aiyaya, qu puru 2003), which deals with an urban middle class youth's desire to become a male prostitute. The film centers on two brothers, with the older one trying to convince the younger about the evils of both homosexuality and prostitution with references to the Bible. Meanwhile, the film demonstrates the younger brother having intercourse with a partner in an apartment overcrowded with migrant workers, seeking sexual instruction from a "teacher" in the shower, and interacting with his friends in Beijing's public spaces. At one point in the conflict between the brothers, the younger one exclaims the absurdity of modern progress and bourgeois life by stating that mankind seeks to rise to the heavens while water flows downstream. In other words, he critiques the modern capitalist drive that, according to him, runs counter to human nature. The younger brother wants to be among the prostitutes, beggars, and thieves at the base of society, and not the top, because the rules of nature go downhill, not upward. The film explores Christian and modern interpretations of the purpose of homosexual intercourse, with the younger brother struggling to justify male power in social reproduction. Rejecting the notion that only the woman can nurture society with her breast milk, he asserts that man can also feed through his sperm.

These two films (with *Feeding Boys* shot right after the completion of *Night Scene*) reflect Cui's explorations of male-to-male sexuality's place in contemporary society. Moreover, both posit prostitution as a kind of recovery of masculine strength. As David Halperin suggests, the modern Western construction of sexuality establishes homo- and heterosexuality as constitutively different. Accordingly, "homosexuality introduces a novel element into social organization, into the social articulation of human difference, into the social production of desire, and ultimately into the social construction of the self" by assigning "each individual a sexual orientation and a sexual identity."[52] If contemporary Chinese society is driven by sexual difference, then Cui's films work to position homosexuality within the continuum of upward mobility. Though critical of the bourgeois life that is rapidly establishing itself as the social norm in China, Cui does not detach commodity culture from sexuality. In other words, prostitution becomes the means by which male homosexuals express both a human nature that is predicated on a heteronormativity and a presumed otherness. These male homosexuals' sexual/gender performance improvises constantly within its discursive limits and gain access to capital.

Social Integration and Identification

Social conceptions of family and heterosexual relations have been transformed by capitalist expansion.[53] As wage-labor draws the individual out of family life, it has also released sexuality from biological reproduction and thereby precipitated the reorganization of relationships based upon sexual or emotional desire. Yet capitalism reifies the family as the site of harmony, love, and stability, thereby rendering homosexuals as "scapegoats for the social instability of the [family] system."[54] Family still plays an important role in China, granting men "moral privilege and access to social power."[55] So while capitalism makes room for homosexuals as "consuming subjects" in its economy, it does not necessarily privilege them as "social subjects."[56] The subsequent scenarios that make up *Night Scene,* which I consider more as scripted reenactments than overt fiction, incorporate a community of gay male prostitutes into the larger social structure. Though it is not clear if these moments are the roundtable elements Cui means when speaking about this film, these moments offer contrast to the documentary and fictional elements previously discussed. The subjects speak directly to the camera and offer demonstrations of young men engaged with each other in public spaces. Thus, through the simulation of lived experience, Cui anchors gay male desire and community to China's contemporary context, and cites evidence, not of experience itself, but of gay men's presence in greater capital and social production.

In one scenario, a college student in a public park speaks to the camera, saying he sells his body when he needs money. He doesn't really like it. He receives a phone call and the film cuts to the next scene of a fellow classmate buying his services and the negotiation over the price. A later scenario focuses on three young men sitting outside and speaking directly to the camera, who declare circularly in the rhetoric of state and popular culture discourses that "we have nothing," "so we push forward," "then abandon ourselves to vice," "so we have nothing." Next, the camera shows the three walking through a campus and into a building where two of them head into a bathroom stall. The camera pans the bathroom while we hear sounds of one man instructing the other how to suck his penis. He is educating the other in what he calls "civilized oral intercourse." While this instruction continues the camera contrasts shots of the three men eating hot pot in a restaurant and those of a woman with her son at a nearby table, a scene that suggests a new family model. A final scenario shows social workers dispensing condoms and pamphlets as well as educating a male prostitute about risky sexual behavior and the benefits of HIV testing. All of these scenarios demonstrate gay men's containment in Chinese society as either commodities or consumers. When not selling their bodies, they are learning the rules that allow them social acceptance. In all three scenarios, however, Cui valorizes the homosexual male prostitution community.

The later portion of the film focuses on the gay nightclub where these young men perform on stage, writhing to house music dance rhythms, enacting comedic skits, earnestly crooning a romantic ballad, or parading from the stage through the audience to the back dressing room. Pan shots show men dancing seductively in g-strings and in drag, or a singer belting out the latest pop song. Yet for the most part, the camera limits our view to the fish tanks that line the club's corridor, the stage, and the area backstage where the young men change, wash up, and live. We do not see customers, nor do we witness these young men's interaction with them. Instead, the camera lingers on the crotch and faces of the young men while they are on stage singing or dancing, suggesting both the director's own libidinal interests as caught within the camera and the film's various meta-critiques. As the camera follows the performers off the stage and into the dressing room, it rests on the men changing out of costume into street clothes. While this moment suggests the artifice of the performance we have just witnessed on stage, there is a vulnerability to this liminal space where they traverse the realm of nightclub theater artifice and don the street clothes of the average young laborer. It is also off stage where the young men become indistinguishable from other young men their age and can thus be said to belong to the larger social community. Behind the stage, Cui manages to capture some of the most heartfelt experiences of young men who experienced unrequited love in their hometowns, speak of sex act preferences, and long for the bourgeois dream of a happy family. It is hard not to see these moments of confession as authentic representation of the performers' lives, of bodies at work, even though Cui has already called attention to the fictive element of documentary filmmaking. Though the film sometimes is trapped between wanting to dismantle individual experience as something that can be captured on film and desiring access to the fantasy that these young men create and live for, it too reveals the nightclub as a space where homosexuality participates in China's market economy; and like the prostitute's body, it too is subject to capitalist exchange. While Cui demonstrates these young men as participants, he also presents this economy as teleological, as if it is the only space in which to gain social mobility. In this sense, he works with the dominant paradigm of a neoliberal consumer culture. In so doing, his critique of sex/gender binaries is more sharply articulated than the capital foundation upon which they are formed.

Produced on DVD on a very low budget and shot within a short time, *Night Scene*, reflects Cui's response to those who think that as a gay man in China, he is "like a fish out of water" who will soon "die of thirst."[57] Concerned that contemporary Chinese media has so alienated people from knowing themselves that they know more about Japan and the West, Cui has made his films independently to transmit knowledge across the informal channels of friends and underground film screenings. He has remarked that many emerging Chinese digital video filmmakers have used the subject of homosexuality in their first films, though they do not identify themselves as gay. Arguing that his films are not limited to the concern of gay liberation within or outside of China, he hopes his filmmaking might assist gay liberation through his desire to expand the language of film and its expressive possibilities.[58] This is most evident in the way in which Cui combines the three formal elements of the film with the documentary, feature narrative, and roundtable.

He intersperses these three elements throughout the film in order to disrupt the narrative sequence common in feature and documentary films. While this is not new to the history of film, Cui is consciously working out a way to disrupt both the social realities and representations of Chinese male homosexual culture through refusing a narrative structure. So while Cui's film draws attention to the correlation between sexuality and capitalist enterprise, he is also sympathetic to the fact that many of the male prostitutes in his film are not able to realize the social fantasy of masculine strength and power. Using his own empowered position as director, Cui has commented that he let his actors in *Night Scene* fulfill their fantasy of pursuing true love (untainted by capital) and to seek legitimacy through playing college students and movie stars.[59] In this manner, Cui acts as deconstructionist of the social model of sexual desire yet at the same facilitates its portrayal for those traditionally viewed as powerless. He uses film to create room for multiple sexual identities.

9

Couching Race in the Global Era: Intra-Asian Racism in *Crouching Tiger, Hidden Dragon*

Nick Kaldis

Widely and often wildly praised by international audiences and film critics, *Crouching Tiger, Hidden Dragon* 臥虎藏龍[1] (dir. Ang Lee 李安, 2000; hereafter also referred to as *CTHD*) is one of the most successful Chinese-language films of all time, having earned in excess of $208 million worldwide (as of 2001), and over $128 million in the United States, where it stands as the highest-grossing foreign language film of all time.[2] Much of the academic scholarship on the film explores its global dimensions; the director himself and his long-time collaborator James Schamus have likewise stated in interviews and articles that the film is an authentically transnational[3] co-production, with Chinese, Taiwanese, Japanese, American, and other constituents contributing to its funding, personnel, locations, languages, audiences, profits, and awards.[4] It is also, famously, the first Chinese-language film with record-breaking international box office and video profits. While transnational in its production and reception, *CTHD* is thoroughly "Chinese" in its diegesis, taking place entirely within the (imagined) historical, geographical, and linguistic boundaries of Qing Dynasty China. This combination of localized content with global box office success and international film awards has led many Chinese[5] viewers to praise the film for attracting a worldwide audience with an edifying representation of Chinese people and culture while simultaneously establishing an influential Chinese presence in the global film market. In *CTHD*, cultural globalization and cultural nationalism[6] are wed harmoniously, embodying what Fran Martin has aptly characterized as the film's construction of a new "Pan-Chinese cultural nationalism that constructs a triumphal, post-modern version of 'Chineseness'."[7]

While a variety of critics, journalists, and others have looked at the film from multiple theoretical perspectives, analyzing both its content and production—its ostensible "Chineseness," its relationship to Hollywood film, its (purported) feminist subtext, its Orientalizing characteristics, its funding and profits, its reception in Asia, etc.—what has yet to be discussed is the ubiquitous logic of racial binarism in the film.

Han Chinese in this film are models of social conformity and propriety, displaying obedience to social mores, government authority, and laws, and upholding the quasi-Confucian *jianghu* 江湖 ("knight-errant culture") codes of righteousness, honesty, loyalty, trust, and respect. The Han heroes are represented as spiritually centered and martially supreme upholders of the status quo, thoroughly conservative and hostile toward any type of illicit, uncivil, or antisocial behavior. This holds true for both their public personae and their private—and intimate—relations as well. The lead non-Han characters, on the other hand, are violators of the same social mores, laws, and values dear to the Han characters. Displaying animal-like barbarity, they prioritize the carnal over the mind and spirit, abandoning themselves to lust and impetuously acting on their emotional impulses.

Prior to presenting numerous examples of its racially dichotomized narrative structure, I will first contextualize *Crouching Tiger, Hidden Dragon* with respect to discourses critical of globalization and its attendant cultural trends. I argue that this critical racial component in the structure and content of *CTHD* has not been apprehended in the considerable body of extant scholarship on the film's transnational features and on the globalization of (Chinese) culture in general. I then restate my approach to the film as a response to much of this scholarship.[8] In the subsequent section, I briefly touch upon the film's popular and critical reception, followed by numerous examples of the film's racial binarism. Finally, I conclude with an elaboration of what I believe to be the reasons for (and implications of) the appearance of such a racial[9] logic in a 21st-century transnational Chinese-language film.

Global, Transnational, International: Imaging New Orientalisms

> "Globalization"' has replaced "modernization" as the new center of the Chinese cultural imagination.
>
> —Fan Di'an[10]

> Things and logic that we used to take for granted in the Orient might not be that logical today. It's a good exam—how to tell a story with a global sense. That means more layout of the texture of society, more explanation of rules of the games.
>
> —Ang Lee[11]

> *Crouching Tiger, Hidden Dragon* borrows a mythic sense of the Chinese national to originate a new form of transnational and diasporic identity.
>
> —Chris Berry and Mary Farquhar[12]

Critics of global culture, or "the cultural logic of multinational capitalism," as Žižek has facetiously called it, are frequently confronted with a powerful inertia in global cultural productions and politics.[13] The greater the concretely experienced disruptions, inequalities, and marginalizing processes associated with (Western-originating) globalization, the more global citizens seek refuge in nostalgic and exotic images (often of non-Western cultures), images of the past in general, and nationalistic images. In parasitic fashion, the market created by the demand for such images has in turn become an integral part of the globalization process, sustaining such desires by keeping audiences fixated on images and narratives of everything *but* the socioeconomic realities of their own moment (and their own subjection and contribution to the monopolization of global resources and power in the hands of the few).[14] In her effort to demystify and intervene in the rapid and relentless globalization of (Chinese) culture, Shih Shu-mei has noted how cinematic works, especially commercial films, have frequently catered to this market-driven desire via an Orientalist representational code that manipulates images and narratives of "Third World peoples" as mere "otherness machines" to "produce difference for exoticist consumption or *managed multiculturalism*," as she has so aptly termed it.[15] Media, cinema, and other representations continue to rely on a "consensus between the audience in the West and the Third World writer or director...a contractual relation of mutual benefit and favor that works first to confirm the stereotyped knowledge of the audience and second to bring financial rewards to the makers of those cultural products."[16]

Shih's rigorous critical perspective provides a clear path into the analysis and critique of global culture and transnational (Chinese) cinema in the 21st-century, for it allows us to interrogate the processes through which the production and success of a film like *Crouching Tiger, Hidden Dragon* become possible. Shih's framework first alerts us to the fact that, in the era of globalization of all media and images, to produce a Hollywood-style big-budget costume drama/action film for a transnational audience, set in the distant past (here, "ancient" China), is a supremely ideological move, whether intentional or not. By removing any reference to contemporary—or even modern—historical events and socioeconomic relations, Ang Lee has effectively guaranteed an anxiety-free experience for (Chinese and Western) audiences to reproduce their stereotyped knowledge of China, delighting in the film's combination of dramatic fight scenes and romantic clichés, all set against a pseudo-historical backdrop of traditional Chinese settings and locations.[17] Lee, as cited above, knows that international audiences are necessary to recoup the production costs of an expensive transnational film. Consequently, he understands that such audiences are most easily lured with films that reaffirm the China they already know—(a simulacrum of) a premodern, exotic, mysterious, and ancient China. Lee delivers these orientalist representational tropes in a form that has been likened by Lu to "homogenous, prepackaged cultural fast food to be effortlessly consumed by audiences from all over the world."[18] The formula is indeed quite palatable to both Western and Chinese audiences (across Asia and in the diaspora), who have responded enthusiastically to the film; Berry and Farquhar note, "[t]he film projects a mythic, cultural version of Chineseness for Chinese and non-Chinese audiences."[19] Among the former, much of the praise is couched in the rhetoric of ethnic and nationalistic pride,[20] owing to the combination of the film's "authentic" Chinese content with its success in the international Film Festival market (the film's disputed success in the PRC is treated below), not to mention its garnering best film accolades at both the Hong Kong and Golden Horse Film Awards.

Lee's transnationally-satisfying representational formula is one that includes familiar characters and objects associated with traditional Chinese culture, Confucian social values,[21] architectural splendor, majestic landscapes, thrilling action sequences, and romantic storylines. This cinematic reproduction of "stereotyped knowledge" is, of course, nothing new, displaying an essentialized, whitewashed, stylized, spectacular, glossy version of one's local/national history and culture in the contemporary transnational mall of "unique local cultures" is a reliable strategy for mass marketing any film to an international audience.[22] As Lee himself said, "you have to rediscover the old Chinese feeling in your memory and try to market it to a contemporary audience."[23]

If the critiques of globalization and culture are valid with reference to *CTHD*, what exactly is it that makes this film more than just the latest iteration of Shih's "managed multiculturalism"? What makes *CTHD* unique, to the extent that Fran Martin asks, "If the 'Chineseness' emphatically projected in this film reflects no social or historical reality but a self-conscious fabrication—a form of simulacral Chineseness based on generic citation—then what, precisely, are the effects of the film's wishful fantasy of 'Chinese culture?'"[24] Or, as Kenneth Chan more pointedly poses it: "...if the need to appeal to a Western gaze turns on self-Orientalism (as problematic and questionable as that is), what modes of self-ethnic "writing" does Lee engage in...?"[25]

Expanding on Shih's insights and responding to Martin's and Chan's questions, this essay foregrounds the novel formula of cinematic "Chineseness" and "self-ethnic 'writing'" that is possibly the most egregiously overlooked aspect in the extant scholarship on the film—its racial binarism. For *CTHD*'s familiar orientalist tropes appear within a novel representational scheme—a racialized exaltation of Han ethnicity, its traditions and social mores. This film is arguably the first globally successful Hollywood-style Chinese language film with a ubiquitous local/domestic racist logic as a key element of its narrative structure.[26] All the main characters appear within a structured racial binarism that undergirds its transnational representational aesthetic (its managed multiculturalism). The deployment of race in *CTHD* thus represents a seminal variation on Shih's notions of the global production of difference for exoticist consumption, the otherness machine, and the reproduction of stereotyped knowledge.[27]

Before proceeding to the examples and analysis of the racial binarism structuring the film, I will briefly touch upon the film's popular reception.

Oscar and Cannes: "China" on the Red Carpet

CTHD received a standing ovation at the 2000 Cannes Film Festival, garnered four of the ten Oscar Awards for which it was nominated,[28] and was well-received by audiences around the globe. The producers, cinematographers, actors, musicians, stunt crew, and others involved with the film comprise a veritable who's who of entertainment industry heavy hitters in China, Hong Kong, and Taiwan; Japan, Malaysia, and America are represented in the film's production as well.[29] It is, as Sheldon H. Lu notes, "a quintessential example of global cinema."[30] While there has been some debate over the film's popular and box-office success in the PRC,[31] legal and pirated DVD, VCD, and VHS sales have been strong, especially since Cannes and the Oscars. The film is now the top-grossing foreign-language film of all time (in American and elsewhere), having dethroned Roberto Beningi's *La vita è bella* (*Life is Beautiful*, 1997). In the United States and Canada, the film received the widest release of any subtitled movie in history, and to date has grossed more than 60 million dollars in America.

As this film has grown in popularity and in international critical recognition, audiences, critics, journalists, politicians, presidents, hip-hop artists, film artists, to name a few, have almost universally praised *Crouching Tiger, Hidden Dragon*. Despite disputes over its success among Chinese martial arts film aficionados and mainland audiences, some of the highest praise for the film has come from mainland Chinese and Hong Kong residents,[32] as well as Taiwanese, most of whom tout what the film has done for the Chinese people and the Chinese film industries. After the film's unprecedented success in the West, "centers of the Chinese-speaking world basked in a moment of glory."[33] The *People's Daily* quoted Lee's remarks that the "Chinese people" contributed to the making of the film, that "all ethnic Chinese throughout the world" should share its success, and that *CTHD* Oscar winners include Chinese "from all sides [who] have succeeded in showing Chinese culture and glories to people all over the world."[34] Taiwan-born director Ang Lee was called a "credit to all Chinese people"[35] and lauded for the boost he'd given the Chinese film industry (the film even reportedly inspired Zhang Yimou 張藝謀 to make his first big-budget historical martial arts film, *Ying Xiong* 英雄 [*Hero*, 2002]). As Fran Martin has noted, "*Crouching Tiger* is made to signify 'Chineseness' as the rediscovered cultural identity of the film's director, the generic 'homecoming' of the film paralleling the geographic homecoming of its director."[36] Finally, the film has been credited with giving Chinese movies "a better opportunity to enter the American market" and bringing honor "to Chinese people all over the world."[37] Both the President of Taiwan, Chen Shui-bian 陳水扁, and Taiwan's Premier, Chang Chung-hsiung 張俊雄, personally congratulated Lee for promoting and bringing glory to Taiwan and Chinese culture, as did many Taiwan citizens.[38] While the content, global popularity, and box-office success of *CTHD* inspired an upswell of ethnic pride and cultural nationalist sentiment, it did not give rise to any serious discussions of the unequal and biased representations of Han Chinese versus non-Han minorities in the film.

The Felial and the Feral

> I identify more with Li Mubai [李慕白] and Yu Xiulian [俞秀蓮]. That's the kind of person I am—reasonable and a team player type. (Laughs) A normal person who is a good citizen, becoming a role model, and taking responsibility for his actions.
>
> The promise that *wu xia* makes to the Asian audience…is a fantasy of power, romance, and morality.
>
> —Ang Lee[39]

Though employing a number of exotic and orientalist representational tropes, the "Chineseness" of *CTHD* sheds familiar trappings of a passive, orientalized, feminized, or otherwise subalternized other. In co-writer James Schamus' words "[t]his movie is more about inner strength and centeredness."[40] But Chinese strength and self-assuredness in this film do not manifest themselves in familiar nationalist narratives of resistance to external threats, nor do they imaginatively redress historical injustices or political inequalities. As Sheldon H. Lu has noted, where "nationality and the nation-state are often perceived as a menacing, demonic entity," *Crouching Tiger, Hidden Dragon*, produced in the cultural cuisinart of global commercial film, has detached nationality and ethnicity from "any sense of serious grounding in history and national(ist) politics in an increasingly borderless world."[41] Yet contrary to Lu's concomitant assertion that a film like *CTHD* presents a "deterritorialized" and "harmless, nonthreatening, and benign" version of Chinese "culture/ethnicity" to global spectators, *CTHD* does not "detach" itself from those once-"menacing" ethnic/nationalistic tensions. Instead, it *internalizes and localizes* them in a way that renegotiates China's image in the global popular imagination.[42] Rather than inscribing itself within "serious" national and historical narratives, the image of a powerful and grounded China here takes on a new guise, the patriarchal dominator and subduer of *domestic* chaotic otherness in an *intra-Asian* racializing dynamic. Han Chinese (and Han China, by clear implication) in *CTHD* appear as the masterful and martial upholders of social stability, humanism, and transcendent pacific values. This racializing representational scheme in fact reverses much of the orientalist imagery of an ancient, dynastic, imperial, passive, and feminized China that has for so long been a staple of the global cultural imagination. Far from being a passive *object* of imperial, colonial, or global processes, the Han race in *CTHD* (interchangeable with "China" and "the Chinese" in the greater Chinese and global imaginary) is represented as a stern and noble *subject*, in repeated contrast to their inferior racial others.[43] The racial schematic in this film helps to jettison accumulated orientalist baggage, such as images of China the weak and acquiescing, China the obsequious, China the backward, China the subaltern, or China providing the tea at the table of great nations.[44] Instead, the Han Chinese and China represent the dynamic martial pacifist, peacekeeper, bodyguard, spiritual master, and symbol of all that is civil and law abiding.[45] *CTHD*'s China is possessed of a vigorous Confucian-informed agency that deftly handles all internal disruptions to the status quo, which it is bent on preserving.[46]

Those disruptions are perpetrated by domestic non-Han ethnic minorities, not by stock *wuxia* film antagonists—feuding temple loyalists, scheming imperial advisors, eunuch intriguers, defamers of the nation, abusers of the poor and weak, or those single-mindedly pursuing vengeance.[47] Which exact contemporary ethnic or national other these (historically remote) Manchu and Turkestanish racial others might symbolically or allegorically represent is relatively unimportant; their function is to serve as a dramatic counterpart against whose presence a far more civilized, prudent, non-violent, and munificent Chinese race can display its physical, spiritual, ethical, emotional, familial, and social superiority.[48]

The image of a magnanimous, supremely civilized Han race is manifested in this film not via established *wuxia* film conventions, but through a consistent racial dichotomy at the representational level. Where the racialized/ethnicized villains of Chinese martial arts films in the past have often been Japanese or Western imperialist bullies, the racialized villain in *CTHD* is a barbaric *Asian* other *within* China's borders. Furthermore, what is most unique about the film is its conflation of illegality, incivility, social and sexual impropriety with China's ethnic minorities. Not only does the film consistently associate deviation from conservative mores, social propriety, and sexual chastity with non-Han ethnic minorities,[49] it leads viewers to the conclusion that such violations are synonymous with personal suffering and social unrest. This consistent logic of racial binarism that structures the film, a subtext underlying the film's "decipherable localism,"[50] has been overlooked in all the hype surrounding the international popularity, film festival accolades, and box office success of *CTHD*, and remains essentially unaddressed in the scholarly work on the film, which has been otherwise lucid in dissecting the global/transnational elements and implications of the film's production and reception.[51] To reiterate, the rigid logic of racial binarism I am referring to takes the form of multiple parallel scenes in which ethnic Chinese, the "Han" race, are favorably contrasted to non-Han races, and the non-Hans are negatively portrayed.

Han Chinese are the film's "role models," in Ang Lee's words, models of social conformity, displaying unswerving obedience to the government [Qing-Manchu][52] and its laws, observing social mores, and upholding the patriarchal ethical codes of the *jianghu* brotherhood.[53] Even in private, the Han heroes struggle to adhere to conservative social norms governing gender and sexual relations, and remain chaste in exchange for a higher, mystical, spiritual union that will apparently come in the afterlife. Their sexual propriety and celibacy are implicitly linked to their superior martial arts techniques, development of the mind-spirit complex being morally superior to any pleasures of the flesh and the key to proper training for righteous martial combat. Within the racially superior Han, there is an additional gender hierarchy as well: the Han hero, Li Mubai, is by racial and gender default the most physically, morally, and spiritually adept of all the characters. No woman will ever reach his level.[54]

Non-Han characters, on the other hand, are violators of the social, juridical, and familial codes, laws, mores, and values dear to the Han characters. In contrast to the civilized Han, they frequently display animal-like barbarity and are associated with animals and animal traits. The menagerie includes a Manchu dragon[55] and her evil teacher, the "Jade-eyed Fox," who, having green eyes is not likely Han (she is apparently Manchu, as her feet are clearly not bound and since she refers to Xiulian as "not one of us" ("她是道上的人": literally "she's a member of the [Han] *jianghu* world"). The "tiger" is the film's fantasy conglomeration of "an unspecified and collective non-Han minority,"[56] a Turkistanish-Mongolianish hybrid. In a long flashback sequence, he is associated with the desert and coded as "middle eastern," with curved sword, baggy pants, hirsute mien, jingling earrings, and singing a middle-eastern-sounding song, while in a subsequent scene he is the familiar [leader?] of a group of mountain herders dressed in what appears to be the attire of Mongolian sheep herders, on a cold snow-capped mountain plain, complete with background yurt. In addition to their names, throughout the film the non-Han minorities are associated with animals and animality: riding horses; living and having sex in caves; tearing into desert fowl directly from the skewer; two of the male Han characters refer to Jade-eyed Fox as a "bitch";[57] the tiger sends messages by eagle; and crows appear with the fox.[58] These primitives live by the law of nature: "ni shi wo huo" 你死我活 ("you die, I survive"; spoken by Jade-eyed Fox in a late scene), rather than the principles of true martial artists upheld by the Han characters, such as *dao, xi, yi* 道, 信, and 義 (the Way of proper behavior; honesty and trust; and chivalry, righteousness, philanthropy). In stark opposition to Jade-eyed Fox's cutthroat ethical code, Yu Xiulian posits the latter two as the key to survival in the knight-errant world: "zuo jianghu, kao de shi ren shu, jiang xin, jiang yi" 走江湖，靠的是人熟，講信，講義 ("In the *jianghu* world, one must rely on friends, trust, chivalry").

In direct contrast to their Han counterparts, the non-Han characters are prone to violence, impetuously act on their emotions, cheat in battle, ignore laws, customs, mores, and propriety, and privilege the flesh over the mind and spirit, readily giving in to their animal lust. Jade Fox reveals that she slept with her martial arts mentor then later killed him in order to steal his sect's sacred book of martial arts techniques. The stark contrast between heathen ethnics and Han heroes takes place within a clear narrative arc—the tale's conservative dénouement implies that, having abandoned themselves to the pleasures of the flesh, the non-Hans are destined to forever remain inferior in the martial arts, endowed with a partial physical-technical mastery and relying on malicious and devious subterfuge but lacking the mental means, inner strength, and spiritual quietude that pureblooded, responsible, and chaste Han heroes are able to commix with their superior *gongfu* 功夫, making them martial arts masters and respected champions of the *jianghu* world. Furthermore, the film offers a clear moral lesson from the Han perspective: the minority characters are made to suffer for their transgressions;[59] they endure physical and emotional anguish at the hands of their mentors, parents, and lovers (whom they have often themselves hurt), and they remain unsatisfied in their (sex-based) love relations. Jade-eyed Fox, having slept with then murdered her mentor and several other *jianghu* (Han) heroes and deceived and poisoned her protégée, suffers a horrid death, alone, bitter, and betrayed, spewing emotional venom at her adoptive "daughter" to her last gasp; Lo, an uncivilized brigand and burglar by profession, looses the love of his life and is left forlorn; Jen, having broken sacred familial and nuptial bonds, committed adultery, lied, stolen, vandalized, assaulted others, and betrayed the trust of nearly every other character in the film, chooses suicide over the chance to spend the rest of her life with her lover Lo. "There is a moral here, and nothing is more Confucian than a moral lesson."[60] But even before they meet their tragic fates, the non-Han antagonists are repeatedly and disparagingly contrasted to the Han heroes.

Most telling is the scene in the bandit Turkoman "Tiger" Lo's lair, where the two young minority protagonists make love, explicitly foregrounding the relation between race and feral sexuality. Their coupling occurs during a childish tussle between the two, immediately *after* "Dragon" Jen carefully spells out for Lo and the viewer that she is Manchurian, and not Han Chinese. Following this, she sticks a crossbow arrow into his chest, they struggle and then give in to their aggressive, adulterous (she is engaged), and bestial lust on the floor of a cave.[61] This scene demands to be contrasted to the penultimate scene in the film, which also takes place on the floor of a cave,[62] where the Han heroes display the more proper, civilized, refined version of loving physical intimacy. As a fatally poisoned Li Mubai sits in meditation, he decides to use his final breath to speak his heart to Yu Xiulian. Though she exhorts him not to waste his last breath on her and instead use it to meditate toward a higher level of spiritual enlightenment, with his dying breath he professes his deep love for her, as his body tumbles backward. A weeping Xiulian rushes over to embrace and kiss him, as he vows that his love for her will sustain him in the afterlife, where he'll willingly follow her around as a spirit.[63] The contrast to the language and behavior of the other pair of lovers is even more pronounced if we recall that Li Mubai and Xiulian would have likely been able to "live happily ever after," had it not been for the murderous schemes, foolish impetuousness, and irascibility of the non-Han characters.[64] A final coda is added to this heartrending scene, should the abundant moral fortitude and respect for social propriety of the Han characters not be fully evident: Liu Taibao is shown in a heavy downpour outside the cave, struggling with the corpse of Jade-eyed Fox, giving his ferociously evil non-Han enemy a proper burial in a freshly dug grave.

In a much earlier scene, the first appearance of a non-Han protagonist establishes the hierarchical representational codes in which the racial other invariably appears as a violator of the ethical values and social mores of decent civilized (Han) people. Yu Xiulian and a butler, both dressed in muted tones, are poised to enter the private study (*shuzhai* 書齋) of the master of the (Han architectural) mansion, Sir Te (aka *Beileye*).[65] They are momentarily speechless, shocked to see the Manchu princess Jen (Yu Jiaolong, the "dragon") already inside, in clear, shameless violation of propriety. Against a background of calligraphic scrolls and other literary symbols (mostly gray, black, and white) of the traditional Han male elite, her colorful costume, exquisitely made up hair, jewelry, and haughty deportment all serve to visually emphasize her egregious trespass into what is traditionally the most private cloister of a Han Chinese scholar-official. In a subsequent scene, Jen and Xiulian are having a conversation in which Jen repeatedly reveals her impulsiveness, violent streak, and disregard for propriety, as they discuss *jianghu* life and marriage. In each instance, she is politely countered with a measured, corrective response from Xiulian, invoking *jianghu* ethical codes (see above) and touting marriage as the most important and inevitable event in a woman's life.[66] As Ang Lee intends, Xiulian's "[s]peech, as well as deportment, dress, movement, and attitude are all supposed to be governed by the Confucian ideal of *li*."[67]

Scenes like this proliferate throughout the movie. Without fail, Han characters stand out as more positive or superior when interacting with non-Hans. Other sequences feature one scene in which Han characters interact with one another in a civil and courteous manner while a parallel scene will emphasize non-Han characters' uncivilized, devious, haughty, barbaric nature. In each case, the "binary minority/majority" serves to valorize the "social and political hierarchy."[68] In addition to the cave scenes analyzed above, compare, for example, the following pairs of eating scenes.

In the first scene, we witness the preparation and eating of a meal (stew), in which the Han characters' use of utensils (pots, bowls, chopsticks) and strict observance of propriety by the filial daughter are foregrounded.[69] Viewers are shown that, even in the most dilapidated and dirty hovel, the Han at table are fastidious upholders of manners, familial obligations, and gender hierarchies. Significantly, when their meal is rudely (and almost homicidally) interrupted, it is by a lethally aimed message dart from the non-Han Jade-eyed Fox. Bo runs to the door but the Fox has fled. In the later parallel scene, Jen (Zhang Ziyi) and the bandit Lo are on the floor of Lo's cave, he handing her a crooked stick skewer with the bark still on it, she grabbing it and ravenously tearing into the cooked animal carcass with her teeth, then sloppily slurping down (horse milk)[70] directly from a wooden bowl.

Another eating/drinking sequence begins with Jen at a pastoral outdoor teashop. Even before ordering, her first act is to abruptly clutch the (Han) serving girl's hand and reprimand her for setting down a filthy drinking cup, then smugly grinning at her own behavior. Her actions attract a pair of Han martial artists who appear bothered by her lack of respect toward the serving girl yet civilly introduce themselves and inquire if they may be of assistance to someone like Jen who isn't familiar with the area. She proceeds to insult them and cut their weapons in half with her sword, while lying that she has defeated Li Mubai in combat. This scene is immediately followed by a contrasting parallel scene of Li Mubai and Yu Xiulian sharing a cup of tea at a secluded small pavilion in the forest. Even while discussing their passion and other deep matters, their behavior is thoroughly civil and restrained, in stark contrast to the previous scene.

The following sequence has Jen displaying even more egregiously transgressive epicurean behavior. It takes place inside a large restaurant, where a lone Jen first orders a large and wasteful amount of exotic dishes. When the waiter complains that his humble restaurant doesn't serve such delicacies, she commands him to quickly procure her dishes from a larger restaurant. In addition to her rudeness and arrogance, the scene shows Jen to view the preparation and consumption of food more as amusement than sustenance (just as she has earlier stolen the sword "wo zhi xiang wan wan" 我只想玩玩 ["merely for fun"]). She then insults a group of Han martial artists, provoking a fight in which she defeats them all, wounding many and destroying much of the restaurant, bragging all the while.

To restate, these pairs of scenes and other scenes in the film are structured around a racial binary, contrasting the behavior and disposition of Han characters to that of non-Han characters. The latter are represented as domestic non-Han others who are "less-than-us," and whose brash, lawless, and uncouth behavior and deportment are the perfect foil against which the manifest racial and cultural superiority of Han Chinese can be displayed.

The film's racial othering, as I will elaborate below, is integral to its combination of cultural nationalism and transnational "branding," a marker of Chinese ethnic and nationalist aspirations to the position of subject and agent on the global stage. Furthermore, the premodern era depicted in the film allows for a rearticulation of the well-established anachronistic Hollywood/global image of a passive and exotic China without making any overt claims to ethnic or nationalist superiority in the present; in the words of Yeh and Davis, "*Crouching Tiger*...rehabilitates the reputation of a whole genre and renders it a beacon of cultural China."[71] Nevertheless, in the process of attaining global visibility for a transformed image of China, the ideologies of cultural nationalism and racial supremacy are effectively bolstered, propelled, and enhanced, sans any forthright contemporary jingoistic ramifications.[72]

Couching Race in the Global Era

> [C]ulture is vital to the credibility China wishes to attain as a holistic nation amongst the leading global powers.
>
> —Karen Smith[73]

> To go global, China must perfect its cultural policy and rebuild the image of Chinese culture.[74]

> American audiences will gain a deeper understanding of Chinese culture by watching *Crouching Tiger, Hidden Dragon*.
>
> —Lee Cher-jean[75]

The previously mentioned accolades for this film's glorification of China and the Chinese people, when combined with an awareness of its racial dynamic, mark the point, I believe, where *CTHD* augurs a new development in the "production of difference for exoticist consumption," a development that is both within and beyond critiques of the globalization of (Chinese) culture such as Shih Shu-mei's powerful exposé of "managed multiculturalism."

A new global identity is being formed for China and the Chinese, and the transnational film market is a major venue for making this image visible. No longer satisfied with nor limited to the occasional art-house or international film festival success, many Chinese spectators and film industry personnel see the financial and critical successes of *CTHD* as a bellwether of Chinese cinema's emergent cultural-economic power in transnational commercial cinema, its reception as a mark of their ascendancy and visibility as global subjects, and its content as a thoroughly edifying and appropriate representation of Chinese people and culture.[76]

Martina Köppel-Yang has recently commented on China's increasingly visible desire to promote a new self-image:

> This new China presents itself with a new image and a new identity.... On the one hand, continuity guarantees stability and China therefore appears as a reliable partner in the international community. On the other hand, it assures a specific cultural identity, substantiating the concept of the local within the global. Thus the image of the PR China...as that of a country that at the "wake of the new millennium (*kua shiji* [跨世紀])" has entered into a new stage of its historical development, that of globalization, thus joining the international community on an equal footing without forgetting its cultural roots.[77]

As Köppel-Yang and the *People's Daily* editorial cited above indicate, this new "image of Chinese culture" must incorporate both the local and the global. The creation and circulation of new images of China will need to reconfigure China's traditional symbolic function in the global cultural imaginary from exotic, subaltern other/*object* into a more commanding *subject* with the agency, identity, appearance, behavior, and strength associated with a global power. To forge this new Chinese transnational identity and to occupy the position of a global subject,[78] representations of China and the (Han) Chinese must be dissociated from still-prevalent images of China as a subordinate race, ethnicity, and culture in the global popular imagination.[79] The discrediting of subalternized images of China hinges upon effectively supplanting them in the popular imagination. *CTHD* achieves this by creating transnationally circulating images of China's own internal subaltern and exotic others against which Han China's innately superior race and culture can be favorably portrayed.[80] The status of global subject cannot be achieved, in other words, while one's representation and self-representation—one's identity—is consistently subalternized, defined as the *other* of the very global symbolic order one wishes to enter as an equal and competitive player. To establish and consolidate its niche in the global order, China has to produce cultural products that represent it not as an (exotic) object in/for the global cultural imaginary, but as a vigorous and ascendant national subject.

To reiterate, the Chinese subject projected and imagined in the production and reception of *CTHD* yokes a (renewed) vigorous ethnic and national identity[81] to an emergent image of a powerful, "centered," and assertive global subject, the latter being part of "a larger desire by wealthier Asian nations to take their cultural place in the New World Order."[82] The film's content also implies that there is nothing overtly threatening about this "strong and centered" subject, for it incarnates a model national/global citizen and protector of the status quo whose superiority is established at the expense of *domestic* subalternized others. This film thereby makes a notable cinematic contribution to the transnational forging of a new image of China as a stable, moral, and vigorous authority, dominating over its own internal racialized others and, by implication, less civilized and inferior external others. In the process, the image of the Chinese nation and people visually renounces its longstanding function as passive other to images of more dominant (Western) peoples and nations in the global imaginary.

I believe the clear racial binarism in the film has so easily passed unnoticed or un-remarked upon in part because the film serves a localized (in Chinese communities), counter-hegemonic fantasy of an exalted and unspoiled Chinese essence that resists all that is negative, barbaric, impulsive, acquisitive, violent, and destructive in the (Westernized) process of globalization.[83] Chinese cultural producers and audiences can bask in the reflected glow of the film's success and its representation of "Chineseness," while simultaneously disavowing their assimilation into the Westernizing (American-Euro) norms of the global economy. Furthermore, many educated domestic and diasporic Chinese, well-versed in the discourses and dynamics of Orientalism and globalization, share a strong desire to see a new cinematic image of ethnic China being consumed in the global marketplace, for they understand that "circulating signs of ethnicity is one of the main ways cinema helps to construct national identity."[84] *CTHD* demonstrates that one method for the construction, maintenance, and updating of Chinese national identity in the era of globalization is through the production of cinematic images of its own internalized subaltern and exotic others.[85] For China to be a subject rather than an object in the global imaginary is "an inherent part of a contemporary global problematic of becoming visible," and this essay examines representations of race/ethnicity in *CTHD* as "the less immediately or sensorially detectable elements helping to propel, enhance, [or obstruct] such visibility." The impact of an increasing visibility of racialized cinematic images in the global market should not be underestimated, for as Song Hwee Lim has forcefully argued, "both 'representation' and 'reality' should be understood as social discourses that, by their performativity, not only reify those images, but also codify them as positive or negative."[86]

The process I've described marks a departure from the representational dynamics encapsulated in Shih Shu-mei's description of the "new rainbowlike globe...[where] Culturalization now substitutes for racialization" and "[r]ace becomes culturalized to such an extent that it all but disappears, even though it continues to structure hierarchies of power."[87] In *CTHD*'s creation of a new Chinese image and identity for global consumption, race, I am arguing, does not disappear but *reappears* in a different guise, being manipulated to new ends by a formerly subalternized Third World other against a newly reconstituted vision of its own internalized and subalternized racial others.[88] Race is now the signifier of an inferior domestic other, a sign and necessary byproduct of Chinese aspirations to the position of subject on the global stage.

Conclusion

Even if the nature of their production, content, and reception bears witness to the "gradual deterritorialization of culture" and the eliding of local and historical specificities that are not appealing and marketable to a worldwide audience, as transnational Chinese films begin to compete for larger shares of global box office revenues[89] they will likely continue to construct a variety of new identities, images, and representations of China for domestic and international consumption.[90] The production of China as a "brand state"[91] is fully underway. As this dynamic proceeds apace, the contradictions of globalization that find their way into these films will likewise take on new forms (allegorization, repression, sublimation, sugarcoating, fantasized reconciliation, etc.). A major challenge for the contemporary study of transnational Chinese cinema is to track down and root out, expose, define, and interpret every manifestation of this process. This essay takes up that challenge, attempting to dissect the mechanisms by which *CTHD* reconfigures the representation of "Chinese culture" for a global audience, especially in the way the film "re-imagines and transforms what counts as "Chineseness" in a world film culture today."[92] Probing the underlying structure of this 'Chineseness' reveals a binary racial logic, a narrative fantasy in which race, ethnicity, and culture are successfully deployed to serve both global and local cultural nationalist identities and aspirations at once.[94] In positing reasons for the appearance and uncritical reception of this significantly radicalized twenty-first-century manifestation of "traditional" China[93] in a transnational film like *CTHD*, my analysis has been inspired and informed by Shohat and Stam's argument that exposing the racializing structures in global media is one of the key critical responsibilities of cinema studies today, for "[a]lthough issues of race and ethnicity are culturally omnipresent, they are often submerged in dominant cultural production. Therefore, the analyst...needs to detect those moments of repression—whether through narrative structure...or through generic bifurcations."[95] One important caveat of critiquing this racial dynamic, is, following Cornel West, to avoid presupposing "that a nostalgic undifferentiated unity or homogeneous universality will someday emerge" among the races, but rather "to ensure that such differences are not employed as grounds for buttressing hierarchical social relations and symbolic orders."[96] Following Shohat, Stam, West, and others, by exposing the rigid hierarchical racial relations in *CTHD,* I am not gesturing toward a utopian alternative. Rather, my goal is to intervene in and arrest the process before it advances without resistance or debate.

Finally, I recall the words of Hamid Naficy:

> In the unipolar, postmodern world of today, globalized capital, deterritorialization, fragmentation, and uncertainty are all immanent and imminent. Under such circumstances, nations and communities everywhere seem to be involved in creating an other(s) against whom they can best (re)define themselves...not only (re)creating actual, material borders but also...drawing new discursive boundaries between the self and its others.[96]

10

Filmic Transposition of the Roses: Stanley Kwan's Feminine Response to Eileen Chang's Women

Joyce Chi-hui Liu

> I seemed to have heard every word spoken by Uncle Zhenbao, even the things he did not utter.
>
> —Eileen Chang[1]

The weight and the remains of the past, the past of the culture and the art tradition, the past that was loved but lost, secretly cherished but at the same time denounced, presses the artist to repeatedly invoke and embed in the text the styles of her/his precursors. This invocation and embedment might be a necessary strategy for her/him to confront and relocate the past. The audience, likewise, is bound to experience in the (inter-)textuality and its traces of the borrowings of tradition a tense struggle between the artist and the past, as well as a critique on the current cultural and artistic context.[2] Norman Bryson suggests in his book *Tradition and Desire* that, like ancient Chinese painters who copy and paraphrase works by previous artists so as to present their personal refashioning of the classical images, Western artists, even the Romantic painters such as David, Ingres, and Delacroix, also borrow heavily from their precursors and mix in their works "a multiplicity of styles."[3] Sharing Harold Bloom's theories of revisionism, Bryson proposes that the artist experiences a contest between a "viewer" who enjoys the flood of rich images of the past but who risks the disaster of having his own images drowned, and a "painter" who has to resist the invasion of the past and to remake the images.[4] Bryson views painting as "an art of the sign" and "its representations were self-referring and their meanings to be found not within perception, but within representation."[5] Bryson's semiotic approach to painting is helpful for me to extend the inter-textuality from within one art genre to diverse art genres. In the present case, the inter-art and inter-semiotic dialogue is between film and literature, that is, Stanley Kwan's film *Red Rose/White Rose* and Eileen Chang's novella *Red Rose and White Rose.*

In this paper, I argue that Stanley Kwan's film *Red Rose/White Rose* of 1994 should be read as his "feminine" re-reading of the "feminist" writer Eileen Chang's fiction of 1944, half a century previously. Through Kwan's filmic re-reading and transposition, the power of Eileen Chang's words, and the hidden male-dominated ideology of the madonna/whore dichotomy behind her text, is literally and figuratively challenged and canceled. Furthermore, Kwan presents before the audience a feminine cinema which not only maneuvers the substratum of the filmic space as his commentary on Chang's reticence on the historical context, but also unveils the possibility of the fluidity of female desire and the growth of female subjectivity, which are both denied by Eileen Chang.

The Return of the Past

Eileen Chang,[6] unlike other feminist writers of her time, does not portray the so-called revolutionary and forward-looking New Women;[7] instead, her woman figures are depicted mostly in situations of "entrapment, destruction, and desolation." But, as Rey Chow points out, Chang's elaboration and indulgence in "sensuous, trivial and superfluous textual presences" of the details reveals her unspoken criticism on the "larger vision such as reform and revolution" supposedly shared collectively by the citizens of the new China at the modern era.[8] Also, her women, Chow suggests, presented as negative, incomplete, and cut-off parts and details of the presumed "whole," the idealist notions like "Man," "Self," or "China," figuratively mock the falsehood of the progressiveness of modern society in China.[9] From the description of Qiqiao in *The Golden Cangue,* Chow suggests, the audience can see a typical example of "a detail gone mad":

> Shifang looked over his shoulder and saw a small old lady standing at the doorway with her back to the light so that he could not see her face distinctly. She wore a blue-gray gown of palace brocade embroidered with a round dragon design, and clasped with both hands a scarlet hot-water bag; two tall amahs stood close beside her. Outside the door the setting sun was smoky yellow, and the staircase covered with turquoise plaid linoleum led up step after step to a place where there was no light. Shifang instinctively felt this person was mad.[10]

Thus, Chang's writings, though never treating directly the contemporary historical and social background, form an oppositional force, Chow argues, a disturbing feminine view, which resists against and disrupts the grand narrative of the "nation building" popular in modern Chinese fiction around the 1930s and 1940s.[11]

Chang's high-modernist style, with its lustrous and dense layers of sensuous details and her avoidance of contemporary historical and social reference, I think, by moving a step away from what Chow suggests, shows on the contrary her purposeful borrowing from the tradition of *Honglou Meng,* and by resorting to a previous literary style, her complex attitudes to the past are also revealed. This past is not only the literary style of sensuous details but also the literary world in *Honglou Meng,* that is, the aristocratic tradition which Chang herself descends from.[12] Born in a dysfunctional family, in the modern era, with estranged relations between herself, her father, and her mother,[13] Chang must have felt a sense of alienation and loss for the past which she was too late for, which had deserted her, which she loved but also hated all her life, and which she tried to return to through her language. This displacement of the past through concrete verbal images functions similarly with her habit of constantly masquerading herself in the costume of late Qing style which she designs and makes for herself. Wrapped up in the clothing that represents the past long gone by, Chang herself is a strange mixture of detachment and attachment to the loved but also hated internal cultural Other. This complex embrace of the unwanted traumatic experience explains to some degree her cynical and cold treatment of all her characters, both male and female.

Chang mercilessly discloses through the selfishness and triviality in her characters those who belong to older Chinese society. In weaving the past through detailed verbal images, as the kind the audience sees in Qiqiao and many others, Chang reactivates the uncanny shadows of the past. The traces of the past in Chang's writings though, I think, serve as resistance against the grand vision of the New China, and also reveal Chang's compulsive return and consequently her fundamental emotional bondage with the past. The audience can observe in Chang's writing the deep-rooted conceptual moral distinction between good woman and bad woman, and the contempt for the desire and freedom of woman. Qiqiao, Changan, Liusu, and Yanli are all alike: they are doomed in a society in which women cannot desire.

The intent of Kwan's adaptation of Chang's fiction *Red Rose and White Rose* puzzled his critics. The audience sees now and then the words from Eileen Chang's text projected on the celluloid screen in a very elegant calligraphy, juxtaposed with the English translation, also in an ornate and archaic style, and these two languages are divided on the screen by a decorative bar. The visual presence of the script on the screen gives the audience the impression of opening up a paper-bound book and hence reinforces the pre-existence of Eileen Chang's text. Critics thus often were misguided and complained about the filmmaker's subjection to the original text. Ruite Shih, for example, stated that the "charm" of Eileen Chang's fiction "once again conquered the audience of the celluloid screen," and that Kwan and Yihua Lin, the screen playwright, "did not propose a new or original perspective…nor [did it] subvert the world in Eileen Chang's fiction."[14] Zhensu Duan, on the other hand, criticized Kwan for echoing the woman's position in Eileen Chang's time: "We see wanton women as well as dutiful women deserted in the end. Women are always the losers."[15]

These critics' misinterpretation of Kwan's film is caused by Kwan's strategic borrowing of Eileen Chang's decadent style[16] and his following faithfully the plot in *Red Rose and White Rose.* Through the filmic transposition of the words, I want to point out, Kwan has done just the opposite: he has taken up a postmodern position and playfully changed the story of the roses, politicized the gender issue, and highlighted in his film a feminine writing which is different from what we find in Eileen Chang's text. In the following, I shall show that Kwan's reading of *Red Rose and White Rose* exposes in Chang's text the denied and yet paradoxically re-affirmed patriarchal values passed on through the feudal system of ancient China. Through the inter-semiotic dialogue with Chang's verbal text, Kwan establishes his feminine filmic strategies in *Red Rose/ White Rose* by juxtaposing the surface text along with the marginalized latent text within the same frame, complicating the narrative by inserting heterogeneous off-screen voices, ridiculing while foregrounding the masculine discourse through visual and acoustic icons, and elaborating the feminine writing through the voice of silence.[17] In so doing, Kwan, unlike Eileen Chang, not only charges against the phallogocentric collective morality of traditional Chinese culture, but also proposes the possibility of the autonomy of woman's subjectivity, and hence subverts Chang's prepossessed bias against the freedom and the growth of women's desire. Furthermore, Kwan pieces together the historical background of China during the modernization period in the 1930s and 1940s which was never treated directly in Eileen Chang's fiction, and reveals his remarks on center-margin dialectics.

A Feminine Response in the Marginalized Position

Feminine cinema, suggests Annette Kuhn, gives us a dimension of resistance similar to counter cinema by subverting the mainstream construction of cinematic pleasure, disturbing the identification with the characters, irrupting the narrative flow, and breaking the boundary between fiction and reality.[18] The audience needs to re-locate itself in the heterogenic mode of representation and thus the pleasure in feminine cinema is built upon a kind of active pleasure, that of "working on a puzzle." More significantly, Kuhn argues, feminine cinema reveals a "feminine voice" that stresses the differences of gender.[19]

In his films of the late 1980s and early 1990s, such as *Rouge* and *Ruan Lingyu,* Kwan displayed more and more uneasy traces that question Hong Kong mainstream commercial movies. Kwan himself is aware of the fact that "in the cinematic system of Hong Kong in which the commercial trends prevail and dominate, it is indeed difficult to insist on something different from the mainstream movies."[20] In shooting *Rouge,* however, Kwan began to reconsider the problems of representation through filmic form, and he said, "however moving *Rouge* might be, it is only a film made by Stanley Kwan."[21] The studio "ghost scene" in the final moment of *Rouge* is a parody upon the ghost stories popularized by commercial movies made in Hong Kong.[22] The multilayered intertextuality in *Ruan Lingyu,* shifting from the documentary to the fiction film, from fragments of the past to the reconstructed history, also challenges the audience's film-viewing experience.[23]

In *Red Rose/White Rose,* Kwan further launches his meta-filmic joke on Eileen Chang through the black-and-white play-within-the-play. This segment of a pseudo-classical Chinese cinema of the 1930s and the 1940s, inserted in the middle of the film when Zhenbao has finished his affair with Jiaorui and is about to start a new relationship with Yanli, not only echoes the dialogues between Zhenbao and Jiaorui, but also mirrors Eileen Chang's narrative in a parodic way. In this scene, the woman teasingly says, "Who is using my fan?" This is a playful joke Kwan plays upon Eileen Chang's borrowing the allusion of the fan from Kong Shangren's *Peach Blossom Fan (Tao Hua Shan),* in which Lee Xiangjun defends her chastity by banging her head against the wall, staining the fan with her blood. But Chang changes the allusion of woman's chastity, into an ironic remark on a man's self-claimed chastity:

> At best, the average man's life is like the "peach blossom fan"; he bangs his head and blood flows onto the fan. But painting some little something on it turns it into a branch of peach blossoms. Chen-pao's fan was still empty, but his pen was poised and the ink in readiness; the window was clean and the table cleared. He had only to lower his pen.[24]

Eileen Chang has "used" Kong Shangren's fan and changed the moral connotation; Kwan also wants to "use" Eileen Chang's "rose" and change it into variations of the rose images on the screen. The Red Rose and the White Rose in Eileen Chang's novel have become the roses of different colors in the garden, in the vase, or the rose pattern on the floor carpet, on the sofa cover, as the wall relief, or as the bed frame decoration. Kwan's film is literally "a movie of the roses." Such excessive celluloid images of the roses alter the signifying function of the words and exceed the boundary of the novel, and accordingly the dichotomy which distinguishes the Red Rose and the White Rose disappears.

In telling his version of the story of the roses, Kwan also inserts the contextual information related to the story. Eileen Chang never in her novels dealt with the historical and political contexts. She was even harshly criticized by Tang Wenbiao as totally isolated from her time: "refusing the historical time and escaping from the geographical environment."[25] Kwan adds the contextual information to the film, such as the dates of 1936 and 1943 shown on the *Dagong Newspaper,* the news report on the Sino-Japanese War, the propaganda of wartime nurse services from the radio, the vague off-screen sound of the bombing as well as the occasional pale lighting of the shellfire on the screen. Kwan deliberately marginalizes the information into the substratum of the film narrative, and these background messages never rise up to the surface nor are shared or mentioned by the characters. The entire process of the Sino-Japanese War lies there as a negative narrative, hidden beneath the surface. This substratum filmic space, I find, contains Kwan's comments on the absence of the historical reference in Eileen Chang's text.

The shot of the street scene right before the dinner scene is an epitome of Kwan's undertone shot: the audience sees yellowish flashes of shellfire extended from the left-handed off-screen space, connected with the vague off-screen sound of the bombing. The fire is burning off-screen, but these messages are neither reconfirmed nor followed up by the plot, and the conversation in the dining room continues without acknowledging the activities pertaining to the off-screen space. The postponement, the difference, of the signification of these un-surtured marginal and excessive signs adds layers as well as instability to the narrative voice. Such a neglected and marginalized heterogeneous narrative voice establishes the mode of the feminine writing in Kwan's film.

The peculiar juxtaposition of the Chinese script and the English script on screen, examined with the consciousness of the marginalized messages, functions as a semiotic demarcation which forms a heterogeneous space of a dual language system: one native, the other foreign. The neglected foreign space, the marginalized and suspended dimension of perception, like the neglected off-screen sounding of bombing and the off-screen unconfirmed flash of shell-fire, is a textual space of the Other. The English scripts are even imprinted as if inscribed on the image of Jiaorui, who is addressed by her husband as "they overseas Chinese." This pronoun "they" is a marker, like the decorative bar in the middle of the screen, that separates the social group outside of the Chinese culture, the social Other, from China. The semiotic space of the textual social and cultural Other is the foreign, the feminine, or Jiaorui, which challenges Zhenbao, the Male, the Self, or China.

The Male, the masculine discourse, is represented by Zhenbao through the filmic connections between Zhenbao and both visual icons (such as loudspeaker, microphone, radio, platform, blackboard, newspapers, slogan cloth strips) and the acoustic images of the moral and patriotic lessons amplified through public speeches and radio broadcasting. The dominant key of such discourse is a collective morality which is highlighted by words such as, "The principle of life is to restrain oneself and to help others; the ideal of the nation is obtained through practical improvement," "Movement of constructing new family, new society, new morality, and new thoughts," "Serve the nation and love the family," and so on. These details form the aura of a collective morality, linking the personal with the national, in the modernization period of China, especially during the 1930s and the 1940s, with the Sino-Japanese war in the background.

The feminine response Kwan takes to challenge the Male is to problematize the male authoritative voice of the off-screen third person narrator. This off-screen voice tells the story of Zhenbao, following faithfully Eileen Chang's version, in a detached and neutral tone. Kwan first visualizes the narrator's voice through projecting the scripts on the screen and disrupts the flow of images. The audience experiences a kind of visual frustration when he expects actions and dialogues. Also, the calligraphy on screen appeals to the audience's consciousness of reading. Such devices of visualization and double narrative shatter the illusions of reality and hence create what Pascal Bonitzer calls "the alienation effect."[26] Hence the audience is distanced from the narrative. Kwan further unsettles the power of the off-screen narrator by making Zhao Wenxuan, the actor who plays Zhenbao, the third-person off-screen narrator. This off-screen male voice puts the audience in the position of the girl in Chang's earliest version, in which the girl overhears Zhenbao's story at her aunt's place and laughs at Zhenbao's narrative.[27] Also, the sameness of the voice of the narrator and Zhenbao suggests the split in the representation and makes the audience suspect the authority and sincerity of the narrator.

The discrepancy between the actions on screen and the narrator's texts makes the audience further distanced from the story. One obvious example is seen in the scene in which Zhenbao's wedding talk on "serving his nation and loving his family" is undermined when the sound montage links the wedding cake icon with the off-screen sound of Zhenbao and the prostitute in an obscene bed-scene. The irony and inconsistency behind the collective morality is even intensified in the following scene, when the sound montage links the prostitute's and Zhenbao's business talk with the off-screen radio broadcasting of the advantages of collective wedding ceremony. The collective morality represented by Zhenbao is therefore challenged and criticized. The collective morality, to Kwan, exercises a certain mechanic and even compulsive pressure on people, and Kwan exaggerates this compulsive mode of communication and value judgment through radio broadcasting and loudspeakers. The puritanic and militant propaganda of battlefield nurse service, and the Professor's banal talk at the wedding about serving the nation, are all amplified through the inhuman mechanic loudspeakers. Zhenbao's mechanic moral judgment is further dramatized in the scene in which his suspicion of the affair between his wife Yanli and the tailor Mr. Gu is presented in a soap-opera manner. In Eileen Chang's text, when Zhenbao discovers the ambiguous relation between the two persons, his reaction is to justify himself and complain: "I treated her all right. I didn't love her but I have nothing to apologize for. I didn't treat her badly. The vile thing!"[28]

Kwan replaces Zhenbao's interior thoughts with a segment of the monologue in a radio drama, spoken by a different voice, in a standard radio broadcasting mandarin. This scene is even shot with a yellow filter and soft focus and creates the effect of a dated film;

Zhenbao and Yanli are presented as stage performance postures. The result of this arrangement is hilarious: Zhenbao does not know how to react to Yanli's extra-marital affair; he then mechanically enacts a role dictated and supported by the moral majority, especially the morality presented in the radio drama and shared by the radio drama audience.

Kwan comments on Zhenbao's moral immaturity by twice framing the close-up of Zhenbao's face in juxtaposition with a child's face. Zhenbao's childish mentality is also revealed by the camera movement which links Jiaorui and Yanli respectively with the picture of the Madonna on the wall in the hospital. Zhenbao's moral as well as emotional immaturity reflects the immaturity of the entire patriarchal society of China. Jiaorui's mispronouncing "gui" (to kneel) as "zhu" (the lord) in the train scene is a metonymic illustration of Kwan's comment in this regard. In Eileen Chang's version, it is Mrs. Nash, a British woman who is married to a "bastard," whom Jiaorui and Zhenbao meet in the street. But in Kwan's film the foreigner is changed into a local Shanghai old lady who speaks typical Shanghai dialect. In Kwan's arrangement, Jiaorui's marginal position as an overseas Chinese in Chinese society is foregrounded. Mrs. Shen talks about how she demanded her son to kneel down in front of her and her husband to show his obedience. Jiaorui cannot understand Mrs. Shen's local dialect to the extend that she misreads "kneeling" as "the lord." This innocent misinterpretation reflects an outsider's criticism against the Chinese culture in which the parents are taken as heaven, as the lord, not to be disobeyed, and the man is forever a child.

Along with the gradual process of the collapse of Zhenbao's facade of moral chastity, the narrator in the film also looses control over the facts in the story. Though he is still following Eileen Chang's text and tells her story, the images on the screen have betrayed him. The narrator says, "Still [Yanli] made excuses. Smiling, she loyally covered for him."[29] But the shot cuts to the scene in which Yanli criticizes Zhenbao's misconduct in front of his brother Dubao, and suggests divorce: "Why not a divorce? What's wrong with divorce...? Otherwise I don't know how long I'm going to defend him." This boldness and self-assurance do not exist in Eileen Chang's Yanli in *Red Rose and White Rose,* nor in any other novels by her. Kwan has remolded a different Yanli who, unlike all other women by Eileen Chang, is capable of growth.

Besides upsetting the authority of the off-screen third person narrator's voice and problematizing the Male perspective, Kwan further complicates his woman characters by instilling a certain filmic silence and opaqueness into his women, and hence creating an ambiguity and freedom in the interpretational space. Eileen Chang's narrator enters her character's mind and reveals the trivial and selfish sides in it. With Eileen Chang's ironic distance, none of her characters is allowed to grow, to develop into self-awareness, or to obtain sympathetic identification from her reader. In Kwan's film, however, the audience has no access to the women's mind and cannot determine for them what they think. By remaining an opaque image, Kwan's women keep a larger interpretational space. The toilet scene in Kwan's film in which Yanli sits on the toilet and stares at her own naked belly, for example, is presented with an ambiguous undertone. In Chang's text, the audience reads:

> [Yanli] would lower her head and gaze at her snow-white stomach, sometimes sticking out, sometimes pulled in. Her navel's appearance also changed. Sometimes it was the eye of a calm, expressionless Greek statue; sometimes it was an angry, protruding eyeball; sometimes it was a demonic idol's eye with a malicious smile; but her navel was also cute, its corners curving downward into fan-shaped wrinkles.

Yanli is presented by Chang as a woman suffering constipation, with perverse obsessions and fantasies, which symptomatically reflect the morbidly suppressed conditions of women in Chinese society. In Kwan's film, however, Yanli's toilet scene is presented without any verbal commentary. Also, it is juxtaposed through parallel montage with the male public bath scene and the nude male bodies, connected by the music "Stealing Kiss" in the background. This double-track scene is crowded with unuttered desires. Without Eileen Chang's verbal interpretation, Kwan's Yanli reveals a silent fascination for her naked body, and a vague self-awareness of her erotic desire. The track of the public male bath scene ends with Zhenbao's sexual intercourse with a prostitute, while Yanli's track ends with Yanli's flood of words in her active conversation with Zhenbao's male friend.

In the scene in which Yanli is scolded by Zhenbao as stupid when she is wrapping the silverware up with newspapers for Dubao, the description of her facial expression in Chang's text shows an "anger like a concubine's' (88). But in Kwan's film, the camera's close-up shows the ambivalent expression on Yanli's face. The reader cannot tell whether she is upset or not. In another scene in which Yanli is described in the novel "turned and fled" when Zhenbao sweeps the lamp and the thermos bottle onto the floor and throws the lamp's iron base at her, Zhenbao feels that "she had been completely defeated."[30] But in Kwan's film, the audience sees Yanli stepping down the stairs slowly and starting to play Jiaorui's music "The Fragrance of Roses" on the piano, again with an ambiguous and incomprehensible expression on her face. With this silence, Yanli is in full control of the situation.

Kwan's linking Yanli and Jiaorui through the music "The Fragrance of Roses" indicates his reverting Yanli's position from the laughable weakness to an opaque and ungraspable mysteriousness. This music, which Jiaorui plays again and again, represents the intangibility, the invisibility and the freedom of woman's floating and mutable desire. As the lyric says, desire grows and the roses blossom whenever you are in love. The fluidity and freedom of desire is something Yanli lacks in the beginning, and this lack of desire is symbolically concretized through Kwan's design of her bathroom, clean, neat, bright, and dry, with square ceramic on the walls, as contrasted against Jiaorui's bathroom, misty, messy, dim, with irregular angular patterns on the wall. The tailor reassures Yanli, "if the color of your dress is not right, you can always dye and change it." Yanli gradually grows out of her pale, shapeless personality, as the changes of the color on her dress. In the final shot of the scene in which Yanli shuts herself up in the toilet when her daughter is sent away from her and she goes through a stage of death-like metamorphosis, the audience is surprised to see that, following the camera's close-up, the ceramic pattern on the walls behind Yanli has cracked into the irregular and angular shape as the pattern in Jiaorui's bathroom. Yanli's acquiring the ability to play Jiaorui's music also symbolically indicates that she has grown into a mature and independent woman, like Jiaorui, with her own desire and self-awareness. *Red Rose and White Rose,* the title of Eileen Chang's novel, are no longer two separate beings linked by the conjunction word "and," but two phases of one being sutured with a slash, as suggested by Kwan's title. The moral judgment hinted by the ideology behind red rose and white rose, the dichotomy between bad woman and good woman, between the lustful whore and the chaste Madonna, is dissolved in Kwan's film and changed into the flowing fragrance of the roses, the flowing subjectivity of woman.

A Postmodern Remark

Stanley Kwan thinks and speaks through the materiality of the film. Unlike western avant-garde counter-cinema,[31] which rejects narrative all together, Kwan retains the story-telling tradition but shifts the focus by forcing the marginalized off-screen space upon the viewer's consciousness. The subversive nature of the marginalized messages and the weight of the heterogeneous off-screen voice unsettle the center of the audience's perception. The audience has to piece together the unsutured and unconfirmed signs and allow the signifying process to flow. The foreign, the estranged system, the social and cultural Other, once suppressed and suspended, now gains its visibility and voice in the form of an ambiguous doubleness and opaqueness. *Red Rose/White Rose,* be it a ridicule of the Male, a release of the female desire, a cancellation of the words, a postmodern joke upon the *Peach Blossom Fan,* exposes the power of materiality. Subjectivity flows in the materiality of the text, of the flesh, between the center and the margin, in a dialectic double track. Such is the feminine and postmodern remark Kwan, situated in the Hong Kong of the 1990s, makes to the Chinese discourse exposed in Eileen Chang's women of the early twentieth century.

11

Ethnicity, Nationality, Translocality: A Critical Reflection on the Question of Theory in Chinese Film Studies

Yingjin Zhang

What is the current status of theory in Chinese film studies? This question itself begs questions because the word *theory* habitually refers to Western theory, and, as such, theory actually carries a plural designation to cover theories of semiotics, formalism, psychoanalysis, (post)structuralism, postmodernism, postcolonialism, Marxism, feminism, gender, sexuality, race, class, and so on.[1] The dominance of Western theory has carried two obvious consequences for Chinese film studies in the past three decades. On the one hand, Chinese aesthetic concepts are rarely explored in contemporary film criticism in English.[2] On the other hand, Chinese-language discussions of Chinese aesthetics are often linked to cultural nationalism, according to which cinematic examples of "Chineseness" are enumerated to confirm certain essential elements of an ethnic-national culture.[3] In this context of heightened ethnicity, Chinese national cinema is seen to work for nation-building agendas of cultural self-preservation and self-regeneration. An irony, however, is that as a theory originated from the West, national cinema itself has been increasingly challenged and even theoretically discredited in Western academia,[4] all the while continuing to gain favor among the Chinese political and cultural elite. The pressure of the international film market is such that Chinese filmmakers tend to showcase recognizable features of ethnic-national culture in their films so as to satisfy the expectations—many being Orientalist in nature—of the persistent Western gaze. This creates situations in which Chinese films are frequently criticized—in particular by ethnic Chinese—as selling out to Western audiences.[5]

Intended as a critical reflection on the question of theory in Chinese film studies, this chapter starts with a premise that the term *theory* should be extended to cover not only Western theories but also basic concepts that enable a scholar to engage in different modes of perception, differentiation, articulation, negotiation, and interrogation with regard to cinema's functions and its complex relations to the world. If the national cinema paradigm imagines each national cinema to be somehow "unique," thus inviting comparison with ostensibly "distinct" elements from other national cinemas and cultures, my intervention here is not so much to debunk the myth of homogeneity embodied in the "nationality" of a nation's cinema by showing its heterogeneity and multiplicity,[6] as it is to move beyond a certain usage of transnationalism. Unlike the standard concept of transnationalism, which implies that it is "beyond the national but below the global," in the Chinese context, transnationalism often implies that it is "across national, geopolitical, or linguistic borders," as the term *transnational Chinese cinema* suggests.[7] Given such configuration of the national in Chinese cinema, especially when it involves Hong Kong, Taiwan, and the Chinese diaspora, I want to direct attention away from thinking of transnationalism as always being along the vertical scale. Instead, I emphasize the deployment of horizontal tactics of translocality and polylocality and argue that more often than not, film production, distribution, exhibition, and reception take place at the scale of the local or translocal rather than at the national, particularly in the context of market economy.

As will be elaborated in the following, translocality favors what Arif Dirlik called "place-based imagination," and it reveals dynamic processes of the local/global (or the "glocal" as a synergy) that involve not just the traffic of capital and people but also that of ideas, images, styles, and technologies across places in polylocality.[8] Moreover, translocal traffic is not merely a one-way street, although it could be practiced as such if one would insist on imposing only

Western theory on Chinese cinema and pursuing willful one-sided readings.[9] On the contrary, the polylocality of capital, people, ideas, images, styles, and technologies allows for the reconfiguration of different spaces and patterns of collaboration, competition, contestation, and contradiction. Filmmaking has always been a translocal practice, and Chinese film studies must rethink such translocality in filmmaking, as well as in film scholarship.

Cinema and Ethnicity: Engaging Theory across the East-West Divide

Before tackling the issues of national cinema and translocal practice, I want to examine the question of theory in film studies by delineating two apparently opposite positions—one insistent on the hegemony of critical theory over ethnicity and nationality, and the other grounded on the specificity of the film medium and eager to move to an age of post-theory. The pro-theory position was adopted by Rey Chow, an ethnic Other who conscientiously negotiated her way from the margins to the center by way of theorization in Western academia. The post-theory position, on the other hand, was assumed by David Bordwell and Noël Carroll, who vehemently resisted top-down theoretical imposition and opted instead for empirically verifiable methods of film scholarship.

The predicament of writing about non-Western texts in "the age of theory" is vividly dramatized in Rey Chow's unequivocal declaration in 1991: "'Western theory' is there, beyond my control; yet in order to speak, I must come to terms with it."[10] Her coming to terms with Western theory entailed a specific strategy: "Reading modern Chinese stories *perversely*...[as] a way of challenging the habits of tradition in the field."[11] The tradition she had in mind referred to "specialist methodologies in sinology and China studies," both of which were based in the West but had become the targets of her criticism because both were held responsible for producing "a non-West that is deprived of fantasy, desires, and contradictory emotions."[12] From this initial dichotomy between the "realpolitical" or "factual" non-West and the "imaginative" West, Chow would elaborate other seemingly binary oppositions in her subsequent books, such as oppositions between East and West, between area studies and cultural studies, even between cultural studies and critical theory. For her, the first terms in these pairs are grounded and burdened with culture and history (i.e., particulars), whereas the second terms are transcendent, blessed with imagination and insight (i.e., universals), so she has strategically positioned herself with the second terms.[13]

A grey area—if not quite a blind spot—thus emerged as a result of Chow's self-positioning: her relatively little interest in Chinese-language scholarship on Chinese cultural productions she examines.[14] One reason for her neglect—or even dismissal—of Chinese scholarship is her conviction that behind "the habitual obsession with 'Chineseness'…is a kind of cultural essentialism—in this case, sinocentrism—that draws an imaginary boundary between China and the rest of the world"; namely, "an unabashedly chauvinistic sinocentrism—or what [she] would call, simply, sinochauvinism" that manifests itself in "fascistic arrogance and self-aggrandizement," "in a narcissistic, megalomanic affirmation of China."[15] Provoked in the aftermath of the bloody military crackdown on pro-democracy student demonstration on June Fourth of 1989, Chow issued this instruction:

> Living after catastrophe for Chinese intellectuals is living with the awareness that their "Chinese" identity is an illusion…because "Chinese-ness," to which they intuitively cling, is always an other, which at specific moments also becomes the source of oppression and catastrophe which they will try to survive.[16]

Scrutinized through the lens of Western theory, "Chinese" or "Chineseness" has become suspect in Chow's criticism. To transcend geopolitical—if not ethno-cultural—limitations, Chow pursued her self-proclaimed "perverse" reading in order "to bracket… the term 'Chinese,' and demonstrate the relevance of modern Chinese literature beyond the immediate 'culturally specific' context."[17] Not only did she fancy such conceptual "bracketing" herself, but she was critical of others who had done otherwise. For instance, she found the title of Tani Barlow's article "*Funü, Guojia, Jiating* [Chinese Women, Chinese State, Chinese Family]" objectionable because "ethnic markers such as 'Chinese' easily become a method of differentiation that precisely blocks criticism from its critical task by reinscribing potentially radical notions such as 'the other' in the security of fastidiously documented archival detail."[18]

Chow's peculiar resentment to the archival and the positivist (in her mind associated with sinology and China studies) notwithstanding, her objection to "Chinese" as an marker of ethnicity and/or nationality is extremely ironic because she persistently included the red seals of her Chinese name (Zhou Lei) on the covers of her English books, thereby leaving an undeniably "Chinese" marker on the packaging of her "imaginative" work in English. Would this act of sealing one's creation or possession (as is a millennium-old tradition in Chinese calligraphy and painting) be a subconscious act of "submission to one's ethnicity such as 'Chineseness'"—something she deliberately instructed others to "unlearn" through "writing diaspora"?[19] A further irony emerged when she deployed her "perverse" reading to excavate "primitive passions" from contemporary Chinese cinema. The passions she identified—modernity, reverence of the dead, melancholy, narcissism, defiance, and fidelity—were made "primitive" precisely because they were culturally and historically specific, emerging in her words "at a moment of *cultural crisis*" in post-Mao China, operating as "fantasies of an origin" already lost and necessarily "(re)constructed...after the fact—a fabrication of a *pre* that occurs in the time of the *post*," in an "imaginary space" where "two modes of signification known as 'culture' and 'nature'" are amalgamated as "paradox."[20] These "primitive passions," in other words, were produced as "Chinese" by filmmakers and critics alike and circulated as such in the international film market and in Western film scholarship, including Chow's own. This uncanny return of the "Chinese," which she defined as "an ethnic supplement [that] occurs first and foremost as a struggle for access to representation" and was linked to "the logic of the wound," especially "in the face of a preemptive Western hegemony," has thus continued to haunt Chow's theorization across the East-West divide.[21]

Whereas she might have encountered difficulties in abandoning "Chinese" as an ethnic marker altogether, Chow consistently sided with the imaginative, fantastic, and even phantasmagoric in "the politics of reading between West and East" (note her order of priority in the subtitle of her first book). Her broad strategy, then, was to "grant non-Western authors and texts...the same kind of verbal, psychical, theoretical density and complexity that we have copiously endowed upon Western authors and texts," or, more specifically, to read "the non-West in such a manner as to draw out its unconscious, irrational, and violent nuances, so that, as an 'other,' it can no longer simply be left in a blank, frozen, and mythologized condition known perfunctorily as an 'alternative' to the West."[22]

From the irrational and violent in "primitive passions," Chow recently targeted what she coined as "sentimental fabulations," equating "sentimentalism" to *wenqing zhuyi* (or warm sentimentism) in Chinese and defining it in English as *"an inclination or a disposition toward making compromises and toward making-do with even—and especially—that which is oppressive and unbearable."*[23] As with primitive passions, Chow located the sentimental in situations that bear a visible marker of ethnicity, such as filiality, domesticity, and poverty. She declares that *"at the heart of Chinese sentimentalism lies the idealization of filiality*: as a predominant mode of subjectivization," as *"a mood of endurance,"* or a state of "accommodating and being accommodated."[24] Different from her earlier position, however, this time she was no longer keen on theorizing away "Chineseness," but would rather grant legitimacy to the "concurrent claims to being Chinese" by the populations in Hong Kong, Taiwan, and other diasporic Chinese communities, even while they seek to affirm their autonomies. Chow's change of position was motivated by this geopolitical concern:

> With the uninhibited surge of mainland Chinese nationalism, fueled this time not by conditions of scarcity and deprivation...but by China's imminent ascendance to the status of an economic superpower in the twenty-first century, it is important that the term "Chinese" not be invoked in such ways as to become, automatically and at all times, the equivalent of the People's Republic.[25]

All this sounds enticing, except that in Chow's reading of the non-West, cinema (contemporary Chinese cinema in particular) was made dense and complex almost exclusively in Western theoretical terms, and her critical intervention was carried out in conformity with the "rules of the game" in Western theory. She unraveled these rules of engagement clearly:

> "[C]ritical theory" is, after all, a process of cultivation, a process which, despite its claim to radical alterity and heterogeneity, operates by demanding of its adherents a certain *conformity* with its unspoken rules, rules that have gone without saying until they are revealed for what they are: "deconstruct the best you can—but continue to center on the West!"[26]

Following the imperative of centering on the West, Chow was obliged, in her work on "sentimental fabulations," to start with Lacan and Derrida before analyzing *Happy Together* (*Chunguang zhaxie*, dir. Wong Kar-wai/Wang Jiawei, 1997), with Freud before comparing *Eat a Bow of Tea* (dir. Wayne Wang, 1988) and *The Wedding Banquet* (*Xiyan*, dir. Ang Lee/Li An, 1993), and with Heidegger before discussing *Blind Shaft* (*Mangjing*, dir. Li Yang, 2003).

My discussion of Rey Chow's self-positioning in Western theory is meant to foreground a recent academic tendency to engage theory as a more sophisticated and more prestigious academic exercise than archival, historical, and textual research. Yet theory is not intrinsically antitext, anticulture, or antihistory. Indeed, an explicitly antitheory position itself presupposes a set of theoretical hypotheses, as was illustrated in David Bordwell and Noël Carroll's edited volume, *Post-Theory* (1996). Contrary to Chow's all-too-eager identification with theory, Bordwell and Carroll fervently attacked what they call "Theory" or "Grand Theory," which was divided into two large categories: "subject-position theory" (Althusserian Marxism, Lacanian psychoanalysis, Metzian semiotics) and "culturalism" (Frankfurt School, postmodernism, cultural studies). Specifically, Bordwell interrogated "doctrinal premises" and "reasoning routines" in Grand Theory, which include top-down inquiry, *bricolage* argumentation, and associational reasoning.[27] "Post-Theory" does not mean "the end of film theory," they hastened to clarify; rather, "What is coming after Theory is not another Theory but theor*ies* and the activity of *theorizing*."[28] To distance from the high-level, totalizing theorization in Grand Theory, they promoted "piecemeal" theorizing (Carroll's term) in "middle-level research" (Bordwell's term), which "asks questions that have both empirical and theoretical import."[29] They then cited broad examples of such empirically rich and theoretically informed middle-level research from studies of filmmakers, genres, and national cinemas, various sorts of "new film history" on production, distribution, exhibition, and reception, as well as the stylistic history of cinema.

My juxtaposition of David Bordwell and Noël Carroll, whose attack on Theory was largely ineffective in hindsight, with Rey Chow, who has continued to write as a high-profile theorist of ethnicity,[30] is to drive home this point: just as the "factual" non-West is a discursive construct, so is the "imaginative" West a pure fabrication. What Chow perceived as "fastidiously documented archival detail" does not characterize China studies *alone* (for the field is no longer as monolithic as she sees it) but may describe several established realms of film studies as well. In other words, empirical methodologies—and for that matter, theoretical inquiries—do not necessarily carry a single ethnic supplement like "Chinese" but cut across the entire spectrum of the East-West divide: there are Chinese theories and texts as much as there are Western theories and texts. Interestingly, what Chow envisioned as "the age of theory" is categorically replaced as "the Post-Theory era" by Bordwell, a prolific film scholar who would rather dismiss the temptation of any overarching Theory: "Grand Theories will come and go, but research and scholarship will endure."[31]

Cinema and Nationality: Interrogating National Cinema

To be sure, theories come and go in film studies as much as in other academic disciplines. Just as Bordwell's theory of film style and film narration are grounded in the medium of film, complete with his signature shot-by-shot and scene-by-scene analysis,[32] other theories are grounded in certain culture, history, and geopolitics, as is the case of national cinema. The claims about national cinema emerged in Europe around 1915 through the immediate post-WWI years, when territorial integrity was of paramount importance and the category of the nation-state was taken for granted.[33] Yet, merely a decade before that, cinema was not conceived predominantly in terms specific to the nationality of a state or a culture. "The largest market for [French company] Pathé's products by 1906, however, was not France or even Europe but the United States, particularly with the astonishing growth of the nickelodeon, a storefront theater usually seating no more than several hundred."[34] As Richard Abel reminded us, it had taken years of concerted efforts by American distributors and exhibitors, media critics and educators, as well as producers and directors to construct certain acceptable types of "American" identity (one of them modeled after the tough guy in the then-emerging Western genre) and to drive away the "Red Rooster scare" (Red Rooster being Pathé's trademark icon) by way of the "Americanization of early American cinema." The reluctant recognition that American cinema had also gone through a national cinema phase was clearly illustrated in Stephen Crofts's 1998 addition of the United States cinema to his 1993 typology of seven varieties of national cinema: European art cinema, Third Cinema, Third World and European commercial cinema, self-sufficient commercial markets (Hong Kong and India) that ignore Hollywood, countries (especially Anglophone) that imitate Hollywood, totalitarian cinemas, and regional/ethnic cinemas.[35]

While Crofts's typology elucidated the fact that there is no single model for national cinema across the world, Andrew Higson pointed out two ways in which the imaginary coherence of a national cinema is usually established: first, to move *outward* by comparing and contrasting one national cinema with another or, except in the United States, against Hollywood; second, to move *inward* and examine a nation's cinema in relation to the existing national, political, economic, and cultural identity, and its set of traditions.[36] As an example of the second move, Higson discussed numerous strategies with which British cinema and film culture have gone about the business of constructing nationhood and cultural identity. One strategy is to identify "a select series of relatively self-contained quality film movements to carry forward the banner of national cinema."[37] Another is "to produce a realist national cinema which can 'reflect' the contemporary social and political realities" and "to represent what is imagined to be the national past, its people, its landscape, and its cultural heritage, in a mode that can itself be understood as national, and as traditional."[38] Yet another is to imagine the "community of the nation" by mobilizing "an image of the nation as one large family whose common concerns ride above any sectional interests."[39] Not surprisingly, this family is often projected upon "the symbolic figure of the mother—that is, an ideal version of the feminine—as the centre-point of the family-community-nation," for the mother's suffering unites family members and her female point of view "is admired not because of its femininity, but because of its humanity, in an abstract, generalized, universal sense."[40]

Much of Higson's discussion of film movements, modes, and tropes finds echoes in Chinese film history. The leftist film movement of the 1930s, for instance, was singled out to represent the "progressive" (*jinbu*)—if not always revolutionary—vision and to carry the banner of national cinema forward, while social realism was credited to leftist films whose mobilization of audiences was frequently accomplished through the trope of suffering women and the loss of pastoral landscape. A fundamental problem with the old national cinema paradigm, nonetheless, is that a nation's cinema contains *diverse* practices, genres, and modes, so a wide range of discourses compete in delimiting imagined communities as pertaining to certain kinds of nationhood and identity. With little modification, Higson's reflection on British cinema can be borrowed to illuminate Chinese cinema:

> The ideological function of British cinema as a national cinema is thus to pull together diverse and contradictory discourses, to articulate a contradictory unity, to play a part in the hegemonic process of achieving consensus and containing difference and contradiction.[41]

The relevance of Higson's work on British cinema to Chinese film history demonstrates that national cinemas share similar strategies in their construction of nationhood and identity. Similarities could also be located in the film historiography of national cinemas. Susan Hayward's criticism of the auteurist and movement approaches to French cinema as elitist in their exclusive concentration "on the province of high art rather than popular culture" carries resonance in Chinese film historiography, and her statement that "there is no single cinema that is *the* national cinema, but several" is likewise an apt description of the geopolitical complexity of Chinese or Chinese-language cinema over time.[42] The diversity and heterogeneity of film projects within a nation's cinema have compelled scholars to pay attention to practices that articulate visions of nationhood and identity different from or contradictory to that of the political and cultural establishments, and these visions could be gained from a broad examination of avant-garde and documentary cinema, or even commercial cinema.

Apart from textual representation on and off screen, government policies constitute another area that unites disparate national cinemas in their similar efforts in promoting, protecting, and preserving their national cultures. Ian Jarvie assessed three major arguments in support of national cinema—the protectionist argument (subdivided into the infant industry argument, the anti-dumping argument, and the excess capacity argument), the cultural defense argument, and the nation-building argument—and found all of them theoretically inadequate:

> The cultural defense argument reveals lack of cultural self-confidence in those who use it; this is self-defeating. The nation-building argument is by far the most disreputable [because] proponents are looking to movies to create a particular kind of nation-culture marriage, one which homogenizes differences, and which rejects American models that offer diversity controlled by citizenship and law.[43]

Jarvie further observed an intriguing contrast: whereas calls for national cinema are weak or absent in the immigrant nations of North America, Western European nations, which pretend to have secure and unified national identities, "are singularly prone to such arguments for national cinema."[44] In the case of Western Europe, then, national cinema is utilized as "a project to socialize newly emancipated populations away from radicalism and toward acceptance of the *mores*, outlook, and continuing hegemony of the governing and cultural elites."[45]

Recent critiques of the national cinema paradigm have exposed the myth of consensus in nation building and have foregrounded the diversity and heterogeneity of a nation's cinema. In-depth research into early cinema and late cinema has also highlighted transnational aspects of filmmaking that were previously concealed or ignored. As Geoffrey Nowell-Smith asserted, "cinema has always been international, both culturally and economically,"[46] and this assertion is particularly true if one focuses on the exhibition and reception of foreign films in a nation. Thinking along this line, Hollywood is certainly the most international and least national of all "national" cinemas, since Hollywood's cultural and industrial practices have been consistently transnational since the 1900s and increasingly global since the 1940s.[47]

However, if cinema has always been transnational and international in a global context, why is "national" still preserved as the designated scale of reference in film scholarship? If not for international distribution and exhibition or for government classification, would nationality be a crucial issue to the majority of filmmakers in a nation-state? Do individual filmmakers always intentionally collaborate with their foreign or overseas counterparts at the national scale or as national representatives? What conceptual implications would arise if we go down the geographic scale and reexamine a nation's film not at the national scale but at the local or the translocal? These are some of the questions I would like to explore in the next section.

Cinema and Translocality: Jumping Scales across Polylocality

Historically, cinema did not start at the national level. In the context of early Chinese cinema, neither film production nor film distribution and exhibition started right at the national scale, as state-sponsored nationwide enterprises. On the contrary, local film operations specific to a city were the norm ca. 1900–1920, and translocal and transregional cooperation dominated the industry in the 1920s. "Fengtai Photographic Studio," which reputedly filmed the first Chinese short feature based on a Peking opera performance, *Conquering Jun Mountain* (*Ding Junshan*, 1905), was located inside the walled city of Beijing. "China Cinema Company"

(Yaxiya or Asia) was founded by Benjamin Brodsky, a Jewish-American of Russian descent, in Shanghai in 1909 and produced shorts in both Shanghai and Hong Kong. Li Minwei (Lai Man-wai) first collaborated with Brodsky in Hong Kong and under the company name "Sino-America" (Huamei) produced *Zhuangzi Tests His Wife* (*Zhuangzi shiqi*, dir. Li Beihai, 1913), a short feature based on Cantonese opera and reportedly shown in Los Angeles in 1917. Later, Li Minwei teamed up with his two brothers to launch "China Sun Film Company" (Minxin) in Hong Kong in 1923 and subsequently moved its operations to Shanghai in 1926, where Li's career as film producer would last over a decade. In a similar but larger transregional move, "Great Wall Film Company" (Changcheng) was established in Shanghai in 1924 by a group of patriotic Chinese who had operated a small company of the same name in Brooklyn, New York as early as 1921. Meanwhile, Shao Zuiweng established "Unique Film Production" (Tianyi) in Shanghai in 1925, and in 1926 he was far-sighted enough to send two of his younger brothers, Runme Shaw (Shao Renmei) and Run Run Shaw (Shao Yifu), respectively at age 25 and age 19, to develop their distribution and exhibition network in Southeast Asia.[48]

It is evident that Chinese cinema rarely operated at the national scale before the late 1920s, and Wen-hsin Yeh's suggestion becomes intriguing in this connection: "Chinese cinema in its formative period was...not a national enterprise self-contained within the boundaries of the nation-state but a diasporic venture connecting the Chinese populations in Shanghai, Hong Kong, Singapore, Southeast Asia, Australia, and North America."[49] The transregional connection would be further strengthened in the 1930s, when the exigency of China's war with Japan made it imperative that film companies and filmmakers relocate their operations to places that might or might not match their ideological affiliations, from Shanghai to Hong Kong or Chongqing.[50] Nonetheless, despite this expansive geographic dispersal, Yeh's term "diasporic venture" carries a misleading connotation in that, as mounting evidence suggests, early Chinese filmmaking was not always deliberately decentering or self-marginalizing.

In comparison, Laikwan Pang's deliberation on the potential of the leftist film movement of the 1930s as a "Shanghai cinema" vis-à-vis a "Chinese cinema" is more nuanced. Leftist films, based exclusively in Shanghai, "were specific products of the city rather than of the nation," Pang wrote, but she was quick to confirm that their "self-avowed national profile was obvious."[51] In other words, leftist films were deeply implicated in a multilayered articulation between the city and the nation. As a prominent branch of Shanghai cinema in the 1930s, the leftist film movement departs far from Wen-hsin Yeh's overseas-oriented vision of diasporic Chinese cinema.

Like the leftist film movement, Luo Mingyou's "United Photoplay Service "(Lianhua) was based in Shanghai, but it drew on a larger translocal network he had built for his distribution and exhibition enterprise in central and northeast China during the 1920s, and it would quickly merge several well-known filmmaking enterprises in Shanghai and Hong Kong (e.g., Minxin), thus expanding its transregional networks farther away to places like Singapore and San Francisco in the 1930s. Rather than diasporic, however, Luo's strategy was to assert his film operations as primarily national, and that was why he specifically issued this cultural-nationalist slogan for Lianhua: "rescue national cinema, propagate national essence, promote national industry, and serve national interest" (*wanjiu guopian, xuanyang guocui, tichang guoye, fuwu guojia*).[52] With its unequivocal emphasis on the national, Luo's case demonstrates that national aspirations and local or translocal practices are not mutually exclusive, and the position of cultural nationalism could be adopted to advance one's economic cause, particularly in times of national crisis.

To move from early cinema to contemporary cinema, we are reminded that even what the media nowadays customarily hypes as transnational "blockbusters" (*dapian*) may be more accurately described as *translocal* productions. This is not just because companies involved in joint financing and production are simply not national enterprises but private businesses located in global or cosmopolitan cities like Beijing, Shanghai, Hong Kong, Taipei, Tokyo, and Seoul; this is also because these companies, together with their multinational film crew and cast, do not legitimately represent the nations or national cultures involved. For example, *The Promise* (*Wuji*, dir. Chen Kaige, 2005) was coproduced by mainland China,

Hong Kong, Japan, and South Korea and was billed as the most expensive Chinese blockbuster to make at the time, but it did not necessarily represent these nations. Neither did Korean star Dong-Kun Jang (who plays slave Kunlun) represent Korea nor did Japanese star Hiroyuki Sanada (who plays general Guangming) represent Japan. Similarly, the film's German composer Klaus Badelt did not stand for Germany, nor did his musical score reflect the German tradition. To conceptualize a blockbuster film like *The Promise* as unproblematically "transnational" is to insist on paying lip service to nationality as a necessary geopolitical marker at a time when the frequent cross-border traffic of capital and people has significantly diminished the centrality of the nation-state and has conversely strengthened connections further down on the geographic scale, at multiple localities.

A group of social scientists recently began to theorize translocality with respect to the changing landscape of a globalizing China. Carolyn Cartier recommended that we rethink "scale relations" between global, regional, national, provincial, and local "as a set of 'translocal' processes for the ways in which the translocal are those multiple places of attachment experienced by highly mobile people."[53] In her view, translocality at once connects places (geographic sites), attachments (emotional feelings), and people (human subjects) on the move, and the last category includes globetrotting business elites and migrant rural workers (*mingong*) alike in contemporary China. Tim Oakes and Louisa Schein proceeded from David Goodman's working definition of translocality as "*being identified with more than one location*" and elaborated the concept of translocality in order "to highlight a simultaneous analytic focus on mobilities *and* localities."[54] For them, translocality captures not just the mobility of people but also the circulation of capital, ideas and images, goods and styles, services, diseases, technologies and modes of communication. Thus elaborated, translocality implies multiple sites of identification and the mutability of attachment.

I have investigated the mutual imbrication of cinema and translocality elsewhere,[55] but suffice it to add that Chinese film studies stands to benefit from paying attention to translocality as much as to transnationalism. Rather than transnationalism articulated at a formidable nation-to-nation scale, translocality in cinema operates on a myriad of intriguing ways, from shooting locations to places of financing and post-production to cinematic address and points of identification. As mentioned earlier, except for the apparently "national" scale of distribution and exhibition that involves Chinese and Hollywood blockbusters—a national orientation dictated inside China by the government's monopoly on distribution and maintained overseas by the international distribution business's fundamental reliance on the sale of rights by national territory, the bulk of Chinese film production operates in a predominantly translocal fashion, drawing on piecemeal resources here and there, in ways parallel to the cottage film industry of the silent era.

Indeed, translocal practice best characterizes contemporary Chinese independent film and video production and exhibition, both fiction and documentary, which are situated squarely in multiple localities and are brought into circulation by a variety of translocal agents and agencies (e.g., nonprofit organizations, international film festivals, overseas media channels).[56] What has emerged as a salient feature of Chinese independent films and videos is not its transnational reputation but its translocal practice, which has enabled Chinese artists to jump the vertical scale by simultaneously forming alliances horizontally with other localities and bypassing the nation to connect directly with a global network of translocal personnel and institutions.

Conclusion

We may now revisit the three key terms in the title of this project—ethnicity, nationality, and translocality—in relation to the geopolitical imagination of place, space, and power. Just as the West is habitually taken for granted as the space of the global while the non-West is treated as the place of the local, so is theory honored as the global enhanced by far-reaching abstraction while texts are downplayed as the local burdened with cultural and historical specificities. Like capital, Western theory occupies the space of flows, and it travels with ease across the globe and seems to carry universal application. On the contrary, non-Western texts are grounded in concrete places, and their significance is helplessly restricted.

In recent years, however, scholars in various disciplines have questioned the structurally lopsided view of space and place. Arturo Escobar, for one, interrogated the argument whereby "the global is associated with space, capital, history and agency while the local, conversely, is linked to place, labor, and tradition—as well as with women, minorities, the poor and...local cultures."[57] Similarly, David Harvey problematized the assignment of capital and power to space and, conversely, that of working classes, "racial minorities, colonized peoples, women etc." to place and "placed-bound identity."[58]

Given such pronounced geopolitical unevenness, ethnicity cannot but be place-bound, and the place-based ethnic critic therefore faces two options. The first is to insert oneself in the space of Western theory (construed as the space of power) by renouncing one's ethnicity (a marker of powerlessness) and pursuing a perverse theoretical reading whereby non-Western texts are believed to have secured the same kind of complexity and density that characterizes the West. This is the strategy Rey Chow has chosen and has urged Chinese intellectuals to adopt. The second option is to side with cultural nationalism by strengthening the myth of consensus and helping to build a nation-state symbolically powerful enough to resist the West. This is the strategy preferred by the national cinema paradigm in film studies, which, nevertheless, has been frequently discredited in recent scholarship, as elaborated in the second section above. Both strategies, I contend, are not satisfactory because neither challenges the fundamental hegemony of the West.

As an alternative to two options mentioned above, translocality is a much more promising strategy. The key here is not to renounce place and locality as always already powerless but rather to retheorize them as constituting a network of power as pervasive as global capital. Dirlik's challenging question is worth quoting: "What if the global were local, or placed-based, just as the local or placed-based were global?"[59] Rather than simply endorse the hybridity of the global-local or the glocal, Dirlik encouraged us to move toward "a recognition of the primacy of place, and of its autonomy, and, *on that irreducible basis,* to produce translocal or, better still, transplace alliances and cooperative formations."[60] Translocal or transplace alliances are at the center of what Dirlik called "placed-based imagination." From this place-based imagination, we are inspired—indeed empowered—to envision new scenarios in which localized politics cuts across scales and localities and translocal alliances are formed in polylocality around the world.

Doreen Massey has called for "a global sense of the local, a global sense of place" in her effort to restore a balanced view of place and space in the power geometries of globalization.[61] I conclude this chapter by rephrasing her expression vis-à-vis theory: as far as Chinese film studies is concerned, a global sense of theory means that we include the non-West in our consideration of theory and theorization across the globe, while a local sense of theory means that we engage theory in such a way as to make it locally—or, more often, translocally—relevant and effective. Translocality thus provides a new framework in which we can productively re-envision theory and practice in Chinese film studies.

Notes

Introduction

1. For instance, Rey Chow, ed., *Modern Chinese Literary and Cultural Studies in the Age of Theory: Reimaging a Field* (Durham, NC: Duke University Press, 2000); Gloria Davis, *Worrying about China: The Language of Chinese Critical Inquiry* (Cambridge, MA: Harvard University Press, 2007); Gloria Davis, ed., *Voicing Concerns: Contemporary Chinese Critical Inquiry* (Lanham, MD: Rowman and Littlefield, 2007).
2. Tzvetan Todorov, *Mikhail Bakhtin: The Dialogical Principle*, trans. Wlad Godsich (Minneapolis: University of Minnesota Press, 1984), 24.
3. Trevor Pateman, "Pragmatics in Semiotics: Bakhtin/Volosinov," www.selectedworks.co.uk/pragmatics.html. Lightly revised from the article of the same title appearing in *Journal of Literary Semantics* 18, no. 3 (December 1989): 203–16.
4. For a more detailed discussion, see Yingjin Zhang, *Cinema, Space, and Polylocality in a Globalizing China* (Honolulu: University of Hawai'i Press, 2009).

Chapter 1

1. See, for example, Zhang Xueying, "Thirty Years of Chinese Contemporary Art," *China Today*, April 2008, 4.
2. Wu Hung, *Making History: Wu Hung on Contemporary Art* (Hong Kong: Timezone 8, 2008), 12–16.
3. Wu, *Making History*, 16.
4. Hou Hanru, *On the Mid-Ground* (Hong Kong: Timezone 8, 2002), 75.
5. David Clarke, "Revolutions in Vision: Chinese Art and the Experience of Modernity," in *The Cambridge Companion to Modern Chinese Culture*, ed. Kam Louie (Cambridge: Cambridge University Press, 2008), 287.
6. Martina Köppel-Yang, *Semiotic Warfare: The Chinese Avant-Garde, 1979–1989* (Hong Kong: Timezone 8, 2003), 92–103.
7. Gao Minglu, *The No Name Group* (Guilin: Guanxi Normal University Press, 2006).
8. Köppel-Yang, *Semiotic Warfare*, 20–25 and Hou, *On the Mid-Ground*, 75.

9. Shu Qun, *Image Dialectic: The Art of Shu Qun* (Shenzhen: OCT Contemporary Art Terminal, 2009).
10. Wu, *Making History*, 7.
11. Lynn Pan, *Shanghai Style: Art and Design Between the Wars* (Hong Kong: Joint Publishing Co., 2008), 47–87.
12. Clarke, in ed. Louie, *Cambridge Companion*, 274.
13. Ibid.
14. Shu, *Image Dialectic*.
15. Michael Sullivan, *Modern Chinese Art: The Khoan and Michael Sullivan Collection* (Oxford: Ashmolean Museum, 2001).
16. Köppel-Yang, *Semiotic Warfare*, 188.
17. Gao Minglu, *The Wall: Reshaping Contemporary Chinese Art* (Beijing and Buffalo, New York: Millennium Art Museum and the Albright-Knox Art Gallery, 2005).
18. Smith, Karen, *Nine Lives: The Birth of the Avant-Garde in China* (Zurich: Scalo, 2005).
19. Li Xu, "Chinese Contemporary Art That Has Transcended Its Identity" in *Beyond Boundaries*, ed. Weng Ling (Shanghai: Shanghai Gallery of Art, 2003), 65–73.
20. Kam Louie, "Defining Modern Chinese Culture" in *The Cambridge Companion to Modern Chinese Culture*, ed. Kam Louie (Cambridge: Cambridge University Press, 2008), 16.
21. Ibid., 8.
22. Edward Said, *Orientalism* (London: Routledge and Keegan Paul, 1978).
23. Homi Bhabha, *The Location of Culture* (New York: Routledge, 1994), 53–56.
24. Hou, *On the Mid-Ground*, 64.
25. Ibid., 66.
26. Ibid., 62.
27. Ibid., 73–74.
28. Nadia Choucha, *Surrealism and the Occult* (Oxford: Mandrake, 1991), 39
29. Peter-Cornell Richter, *Georgia O'Keefe and Alfred Stieglitz* (Munich: Prestel, 2001), 40–41.
30. Huang Yongping, "Xiamen Dada—yizhong hou xiandai?" (Xiamen Dada—A Kind of Post-Modernity?) *Zhonguo meishubao* 46 (1986): 1. For a critical commentary on Huang's assertions, also see Paul Gladston, "Chan-Da-da(o)-De-construction or, The Cultural (Il) Logic of Contemporary Chinese 'Avant-Garde' Art," *Yishu: Journal of Contemporary Chinese Art* 7, no. 4 (July 2008): 63–69.
31. Fred Orton, *Figuring Jasper Johns* (London: Reaktion, 1994), 139.
32. See Song Ling, *When We Were Young* (Melbourne: Niagra Publishing, 2008).

33. Philip Vergne and Doryun Chong, eds., *Zhanpu Zhe Zhi Wu: Huang Yongping Huigu Zhan* (House of Oracles: A Huang Yongping Retrospective) (Shanghai, Shanghai Century Publishing, 2008).
34. Paul Gladston, "Song Ling in Conversation with Paul Gladston," *Yishu: Journal of Contemporary Chinese* Art 7, no. 6 (November 2008): 50–60.
35. Jiang Mei, ed., *Deep Breath: 19 Samples of Chinese Contemporary Female Artists* (Shanghai: Creek Art, 2008).
36. Linda Nochlin, "Why Have There Been No Great Women Artists?" *ARTnews* 22, no. 39 (January 1971): 67–71.
37. Cao Cing, "Western Representations of the Other" in *Discourse as Cultural Struggle*, ed. Shi-xu (Hong Kong: Hong Kong University Press, 2007), 106.
38. See Zhang Gan's website at http://blog.artron.net/indexold.php?144950/viewspace-232157 (accessed May 2009).
39. Chang Tsong-sung, Gao Shiming and Sarat Maharaj, eds., *Farewell to Post-Colonialism: The Third Guangzhou Triennial* (Guanzhou: The Guandong Museum of Art, 2008).
40. Paul Gilroy, "Sounds Authentic—Black Music, Ethnicity and the Challenge of a Changing Same," *Journal of Black Music Research* 11, no. 2 (1991).
41. Hou, *On the Mid-Ground*, 174.
42. Ibid., 62.
43. Ibid., 173.
44. Donald Wesling, "Methodological Implications of the Philosophy of Jacques Derrida for Comparative Literature: The Opposition East-West and Several Other Observations" in *Chinese-Western Comparative Literature Theory and Strategy*, ed. John J. Deeney (Hong Kong: Hong Kong University Press, 1980), 79–111.
45. Hou, *On the Mid Ground*, 236.
46. Ibid.
47. Jean Baudrillard, *Simulacra and Simulation*, trans. Sheila Faria Glaser (Ann Arbor: The University of Michigan Press, 1994), 1.

Chapter 2

1. David Barboza, "In China's New Revolution, Arts Greets Capitalism," *New York Times*, Jan 4, 2007.
2. Ibid.
3. The present author witnessed this as part of field research carried out in China during the summers of 2004 and 2005. Research activities included visiting new or old artist villages, art districts, art galleries

in Beijing, Shanghai, and Nanjing and attending a large number of exhibition openings, symposiums, and lectures in Beijing.

4. An example is Sui Jianguo, a sculpture professor from the Central Academy of Fine Arts, according to his students who now continue to use the studio he left behind. Also see Aric Chen, "A New Frontier for Chinese Art," *New York Times*, Apr 1, 2007, Sec. Arts, East Coast Edition.
5. This is based on the author's personal communication with many artists and her observations at the 798 Factory and the Song Zhuang Artist Village.
6. "Socialism with Chinese characteristics" is a phrase coined by the former leader Deng Xiaoping in describing his reform policy. To differentiate the market economy in China from its western capitalist counterpart, Deng applied a prefix "socialist" to "market economy," which then became "market economy with Chinese characteristics," thus legitimizing his introducing of the "market economy" into socialist China. Since then, the term "Chinese characteristics" has been broadly used in Chinese society in almost every field for describing the essential feature of contemporary Chinese national identity and Chinese way of doing things. In short, it is mainly used to differentiate Western-originating free market capitalism in China from its international counterparts.
7. This is a famous phrase Deng coined to legitimize the introduction of a market economy in China. His main idea is that a market economy is not exclusively a property of capitalist societies, and a planned economy is not exclusively a property of a socialist country, and the only criterion to decide which one should be applied in China is its function in the improvement of Chinese economy.
8. Deng Xiaoping's "Southern Tour" in 1992 aimed to observe and evaluate the result of economic development in several "special economic zones" in south China, which were designated as experimental sites for a market economy in the early 1980s. He was reportedly very pleased with the result and after his return back to Beijing, he decided to extend the "special economic zones" to a national level.
9. Joy Annamma and John F. Sherry, Jr., "Framing Considerations in the PRC: Creating Value in the Contemporary Chinese Art Market," *Consumption, Markets and Culture* 7, no. 4 (December 2004): 317.
10. The study of the Chinese art market is still in its nascent stage and there is no systematic research published on the field yet. What are available at the moment are some introductory books on very basic concepts and terminologies of the art market in general or on art market operations outside of China, published no earlier than the late

1990s, for example, Zhang Zhixiong, ed., *Churu Yishu Shichang* [Art market basics] (Shanghai: Shanghai Publishing House on Calligraphy and Painting, 1997), Liu Xiaoqiong & Liu Gang's *Yishu Shichang* [Art market] (Nanchang: Jianxi Fine Arts Publishing House, 1998), and Zhang Liguo's *Yishu Shichang Xue* [Art market studies] (Hangzhou: China Academy of Fine Arts Press, 2003). Other than these books, I have relied on conversations with artists and gallery owners from China, as well as on my own observation.

11. Actually the 1980s' avant-garde movements were also anticommercially motivated. See Gao Minglu et. al., *Zhongguo Dangdai Meishu Shi* [The History of Chinese Contemporary Art 1985–1986] (Shanghai: Shanghai People's Publishing House, 1991).
12. Jiang Zemin, "Zai zhongguo wenlian diqici quanguo daibiao dahui, zhougguo zuoxie diliuci quanguo daibiao dahui shang de Jianghua" [Speech given at the Seventh National Congress of the China Federation of Literary and Art Circles, and at the Sixth National Congress of the Chinese Writers Association], released by Xinhua News Agency on Dec. 18, 2001. http://www.people.com.cn/GB/shizheng/20011218/629941.html (accessed July 18, 2005).
13. Ibid.
14. Earlier publications, in Chinese, on the relationship between culture and national sovereignty and power are Wang Huning, "Zuowei guojia shili de wenhua: ruan quanli" [Culture as a component of national strength: Soft power], *Fudan Xuebao* (1993) no. 3; Wang Huning, "Wenhua Kuozhang yu Wenhua zhuquan: dui zhuquan guannian de tiaozhan" [Cultural expansion and Cultural Sovereignty: Challenges to the Concept of Sovereignty], *Fudan Xuebao* (1994) no. 3; Wang Ning, "Dongfang Zhuyi, hou zhimin zhuyi he wenhua baquan zhuyi pipan" [Orientalism, postcolonialism, and criticism of cultural hegemony], *Beijing Daxue Xuebao* (1995) no. 2; Zhang Yiwu, "Chanshi 'Zhongguo' de Jiaolu" [The anxiety of interpreting "China"], *Ershiyi Shiji* 28 (April 1995); Xia Yinying, "Zhimin wenhua xianxiang yu wenhua zhimin zhuyi" [The Phenomena of colonial culture and cultural colonialism], *Wenyi Lilun yu Piping* (1996) no. 2.
15. Chinese Academy of Social Sciences, *2001–2002 Nian Zhongguo Wenhua Chanye Lanpishu Zongbaogao* [The general blue-book report on the Chinese culture industry, 2001–2002] (Beijing: Social Science Documents Publishing House, 2002), http://www.china.org.cn/chinese/culture/99856.htm (accessed June 8, 2006).
16. Ibid.
17. Jiang Zeming, "Quanmian Jianshe Xiaokang Shehui, Kaichuang Zhongguo Tese Shehuizhuyi Shiye Xinjumian" [To construct a well-

to-do society in full scale, to initiate a new phrase of Chinese characteristic socialist undertaking], released by Xinhua News Agency on Nov. 8, 2002, http://news.xinhuanet.com/newscenter/2002–11/17/content_632239.htm (accessed on July 19, 2005).

18. Xu Gongcheng, "Dang de Shiliuda wei Woguo Wenhua Chanye de Fazhan Zhiming Jiben Fangxiang" [The Sixteenth National Congress of the CCP gives principal directions for the development of our cultural industry], December 11, 2002. http://www.china.org.cn/chinese/zhuanti/244905.htm (accessed June 8, 2006).
19. Han Yongjing, "'Wenhuachanye' *Gainian de Zhengshi Tichu ji qi Beijing"* [The formal application of the concept of "cultural industry" and its background], in Chinese Academy of Social Sciences, *2001–2002 Nian Zhongguo Wenhua Chanye Lanpishu Zongbaogao.*
20. Scholars trace the origin of practicing cultural industry in China back to 1979, when the first music teahouse was opened in Guangzhou Oriental Hotel. Subsequently, other commercial spaces for various cultural activities such as dance and music were opened in big cities.
21. Wu Jing, "Wenming Guguo de 'Jingshen Shengyan'—Zhongguo Wenhua Chanye Rechao Yongdong" [The "spiritual banquet" of the nation of ancient civilization—Chinese cultural industry is surging], October 6, 2002. http://news.xinhuanet.com/newscenter/2002–10/06/content_586247.htm (accessed June 8, 2006).
22. What should be added here is that the launch of the cultural industry is actually part of the Chinese government's efforts in fostering an atmosphere conducive to global trade, through which the Chinese art world greatly benefits economically.
23. Certainly there is no absolute freedom here. Artists are still subject to restrictions placed by the government in terms of what is marketable and what is not.
24. My interviews with artists show that many of them appreciate double identities, holding an official post and practically being an independent artist. So, they can enjoy basic institutional benefits such as housing, wages, publicity programs on the one hand, and on the other move among different cities and be a member of artist groups of several cities at the same time.
25. Charlotte Bydler, *The Global ArtWorld Inc.: On the Globalization of Contemporary Art.* (Uppsala: Uppsala University, 2004). For similar discussions by leading curators and critics, see Tim Griffin, "Global Tendencies: Globalism and the Large-Scale Exhibition," *Artform* 42, no. 3 (November 2003): 152–67.
26. Here I mean large-scale international exhibitions, including biennials, triennales, and transnational touring exhibitions, that have flourished

in the contemporary art world since the 1990s. These types of exhibitions have moved beyond the spaces defined by the concrete museum and have gained their independence as powerful forms of communication and manifestation, and as a primary medium in disseminating contemporary art.

27. The basic assumption behind the enthusiasm of this type of exhibition is that it possesses the unique position of both reflecting globalism and taking up globalism as an idea and thus speaks directly to contemporary issues. Griffin, "Global Tendencies," 152.
28. Ibid.
29. Michael Brenson, "The Curator's Moment," *Art Journal* 57, no. 4 (Winter 1998): 17.
30. Mari Carmen Ramírez, "Brokering Identities: Art Curators and the Politics of Cultural Presentation," in *Thinking about Exhibitions*, ed. Reesa Greenberg, Bruce W. Ferguson, and Sandy Nairne (London and New York: Routledge, 1996), 21–22.
31. Gao Minglu, the renowned critic and curator who now teaches in the U.S.A., was the chief organizer of the exhibition. Many now internationally well-known artists, such as Gu Wenda, Huang Yongping, Wang Guangyi, and Xu Bing, had their works shown. For more detail about the exhibition see Gao Minglu, "The '85 Movement: Avant-Garde Art in the Post-Mao Era" (Ph.D. diss. Harvard University, 2000).
32. The exhibition as a conclusion of the avant-garde art movement was first pointed out by Gao Minglu, Shu Qun, and others in their book, *Zhongguo Dangdai Meishu Shi*, and has generally been accepted by Chinese critics.
33. A strong supporter of avant-garde art, the weekly newspaper *Zhongguo Meishu Bao* (Fine Arts in China), was forced to close down by the authorities at the end of 1989. Those critics, including Gao Minglu and Li Xianting, who were centrally involved in the avant-garde art movement and the China/Avant-Garde exhibition were later asked to leave their official posts.
34. Chinese participation in the 1993 Venice Biennale was made possible through collaborative work by Li Xianting, the ardent advocator of Chinese unofficial art, Francesca dal Lago, then an art history PhD student from New York University, and Achille Bonito Oliva, an Italian curator and the director of that year's Venice Biennale.
35. Tsong-Zung Chang, ed., *China's New Art, Post-1989* (Hong Kong, Hanhart T Z Gallery, 1993).
36. Annamma and Sherry, "Framing Considerations," 328.
37. Gao Minglu, ed., *Inside/Out: New Chinese Art* (San Francisco: San Francisco Museum of Modern Art, 1998).

38. For a detailed discussion on the growing "advertised life" in China since early 1990s see Geremie R. Barmé, "The Velvet Prison of Consumption," in *In the Red: On Contemporary Chinese Culture* (New York: Columbia University Press, 1999), 236–41.
39. "Let China go to the world, let the world go to China" was one of the phrases that Deng Xiaoping often used after he launched the Reform and Open-door Policy. It has been used broadly ever since, almost in every field: sports, films, economics, and culture. It indicates China's determination to be more interactive with the rest of the world and to promote its visibilities in international communities.
40. The Chinese title of "Fuck Off—Uncooperative Stance" was "Bu Hezuo Fangshi," which can be translated simply as "non-cooperation." As Johathan Napack has indicated, differences between the Chinese and English title speak strongly to attitudes within the contemporary Chinese art scene of the late 1990s, where there was "calculated sensationalism for foreigners, self-censorship for local consumption." Jonathan Napack, "Report from Shanghai: It's More Fashionable Underground," *The Art Newspaper*, no. 109, Dec. 2000.
41. Feng Boyi, "'Di Dixia' ji Qita—Guangyu 20 Shiji 90 Niandai Yilai de Zhongguo Qianwei Yishu" ["Underground" and Others: On Chinese Avant-garde Art since the 1990s], *Yishu Tansuo* (2003): no. 4, 23–26.
42. Ibid.
43. Gao, *Inside/Out*, 17.
44. My argument about the relationship between globalization and nationalism in China and the Chinese state's appropriation of both is based on the anthropologist Aihwa Ong's study of the adaptation of new policies by a few Asian states, including the Chinese state, in their mobilization of various transnational resources for nationalistic projects. She problematizes the popular view that globalization has weakened state power and argues instead that governments of relevant states have developed flexible strategies to accumulate capital and power. Borrowing her perspective, I frame Chinese state power as an active force that has responded eagerly and even creatively to the challenges of globalization in my examination of the effect of its newly invented engagements in the art domain. For detail of Aihwa One's ideas, see *Flexible Citizenship: The Cultural Logics of Transnationality* (Durham: Duke University Press, 1999).
45. Gunter Schubert, "Nationalism and National Identity in Contemporary China: Assessing the Debate," *Issues & Studies* 37, no. 5 (September/October 2001): 132.
46. For a comprehensive discussion of Chinese nationalism in the 1990s, see Zheng Yongnian, *Discovering Chinese Nationalism in China: Mod-*

ernization, Identity, and International Relations (New York: Cambridge University Press, 1999); Schubert, "Nationalism," 128–56.

47. Guo Yingjie, *Cultural Nationalism In Contemporary China: The Search for National Identity Under Reform* (London and New York: Routledge, 2004), 2.
48. "'Sange Daibiao' Sixiang" [The thought of "three representatives"], June 13, 2001. http://www.people.com.cn/GB/shizheng/252/5301/5302/20010613/488147.html (accessed December 22, 2005).
49. In Mao Zedong's thought, only workers, peasants, and soldiers were regarded as the people and class struggle was at the core of his politics.
50. Guo, *Cultural Nationalism.*
51. The revived interest in Chinese traditional culture has some earlier roots in Chinese society in the 1980s, when the search for a non-Maoist source of native Chinese culture began with what is known as the "roots seeking" movement, which itself was part of the larger "culture fever" phenomenon of that period. For in-depth studies of the culture fever phenomenon in China, see Wang Jing, *High Culture Fever: Politics, Aesthetics, and Ideology in Deng's China* (Berkeley: University of California Press, 1996) and Zhang Xudong, *Chinese Modernism in the Era of Reforms* (Durham, NC: Duke University Press, 1997).
52. These studies can be generally included under the term Guoxue (national study), which was coined and circulated rapidly in China in the early 20th century, in referring to the studies of Chinese traditional culture. This term has seen renewed popularity in contemporary China. Famous scholars on the field are respected as Guoxue Dashi, meaning national study masters.
53. This point is evident in the large number of publications about Confucianism released in the 1990s.
54. Schubert, "Nationalism."
55. Ibid., 137–44.
56. Xia Yinying, "Zhimin wenhua xianxiang yu wenhua zhimin zhuyi," 137.
57. For a detailed discussion about the origin, development, and major resident artists of Song Zhuang Artist Village, please see Zhao Tielin, *Heibai Songzhuang—Duandai Qingnian de Yishu Zhuiqiu yu Rensheng Ziyou* [Black and white Song village—the art pursuit and new generation youth] (Hainan: Hainan Publishing House, 2003).
58. Shanghai Biennale was established in 1996 and originally was open only to Chinese artists. The 2000 Shanghai Biennale was made open to artists worldwide and became an international biennial.
59. For example, famous critic Jia Fangzhou comments: "This break-

through of the limitation on art forms undoubtedly marks a new chapter in the exhibition history of China." Jia Fangzhou, "Xin de Biaozhi Xin de Kaiduan-Ping 2000 Shanghai Shuangnianzhan" [New Sign and New Beginning—On Shanghai Biennale]. http://www.cn-arts.net/SHANGHAIART/biennale/shb2002/critique_read.asp?id=12 (accessed July 20, 2004). Karen Smith, a close observer of Chinese contemporary art and exhibitions in China, states, "[I]t is the first time for works by contemporary Chinese artists to be given official blessing to enter the hallowed halls of a national art museum." Karen Smith, "The Spirit of Shanghai," http://www.china-avantgarde.com/essays/Karen Smith/shanghai.html (accessed July 20, 2004).

60. A curatorial team of four curators was formed and headed by Hou Hanru, together with Zhang Qing and Li Xu from the Shanghai Art Museum, and Toshio Shimizu from Tokyo.
61. "Zhongguo Dangdai Yishuzhang Berlin Kaimu" [Exhibition of Chinese Contemporary Art Opens at Berlin], *Zhongguo Xinwen She*, September 19, 2001.
62. To know more about this show, please see *The First Guangzhou Triennial: Reinterpretation: A Decade of Experimental Chinese Art (1990–2000)* (exhibition catalog) (Guangzhou: Guangdong Museum of Art, 2002).
63. For detailed discussion of the first national pavilion for the Venice Biennale, see Meiqin Wang, "Officializing the Unofficial: Presenting New Chinese Art," *Modern Chinese Literature and Culture* 21, no. 1 (Spring 2009): 102–40.
64. Pulling back Chinese contemporary art does not necessarily mean just keeping contemporary art within China. The idea is about getting more Chinese people both in and outside China to experience, understand, and interpret Chinese contemporary art.
65. Zhang Shougang, "Zhongguo Meishuguan Jiang Chizi 2.5 yi yuan Zheng Guonei Dashiji Zuopin" [China National Museum of Fine Arts plans to spend 250 million RMB on works by domestic masters], *Beijing Yule Xingbao/Stardaily*, October 21, 2004.
66. Ibid.
67. In 1993, Xu Bing did his "A Case Study" in Beijing, but that piece opened only to a small audience of close friends and alike. It had no open publicity. Theoretically, it was not an exhibition. Xu himself said it was a case study.
68. Personal interview with gallery workers, August 30, 2004; the idea was also stated in the flyer distributed by the gallery in the promotion of these serial exhibitions.
69. Pi Li, "Xiang Ba Zhongguo Dangdai Yishu Chongxin La Huilai" [Thinking of Pulling Back Chinese Contemporary Art], *Jingji Guancha Bao*, December 30, 2002.

70. Personal communication with Yin Kun, September 26, 2006, Song Zhuang Artist Village.
71. Ibid.
72. Hou Hanru, "Towards an 'Un-Unofficial Art': De-Ideologicalisation of China's Contemporary Art in the 1990s," *Third Text* 34 (Spring 1996): 37–52.
73. Annamma and Sherry, "Framing Considerations," 312.
74. Meg Maggio, "Bullish In Beijing," *China Review Magazine* 26, October, 2003. http://www.gbcc.org.uk/iss26art1.htm (accessed May 8, 2005).
75. Hou, "Towards an 'Un-Unofficial Art'."

Chapter 3

1. See John Clark's opening essay in John Clark, ed., *Chinese Art at the End of the Millennium* (Beijing & Hong Kong: New Art Media, 1999).
2. Cited by Li Xianting, "Dangqian zhongguo yishu de wuliaogan-xi wanshi xianshizhuyi shaoliu." *Ershiyi shiji* 9 (Feb. 1992): 2.
3. Ibid.
4. Li Xianting, "Major Trends in the Development of Contemporary Chinese Art," in *China's New Art, Post-1989* (Hong Kong: Hanart TZ Gallery, 1993), xx.
5. Ibid.
6. Ibid., xxi.
7. John Clark, "Pop Goes the Maosell," *Art Monthly Australia* 61 (July 1993), 15–16. The "Maosell" substitutes for the untrustworthy weasel.
8. You You, "Who Play with Who? A Review of Mao Goes Pop," *Yishu Chaoliu*, Oct. 1997, 2–29.
9. Fan Di'an, "Jingyanjiazhi yu houzhimin wenhua zhong de zhongguo jingyan," in Wang Lin, ed., *China: Art of Post 89* (Hong Kong: Yishu chaoliu, 1997), 35.
10. Guy Debord, *Comments on the Society of the Spectacle*, trans. Malcolm Imrie (London: Verso, 1998).
11. Yin Shuangxi, "Kai fang de kongjian," in *Yataidiqu dangdai yishu yaoqingzhan zuopinji* (Fuzhou, 1998).
12. Yi Ying, "Shehuibiange yu zhongguoxiandaiyishu," *Tianya* 5 (1998): 113.
13. See Wang Lin, "Oliva bushi zhongguo yishu de jiuxing," *Dushu*, Oct. 1993, 123–26.
14. Wang Lin, "Yishu zai dangdai de shiming," in idem, ed., *China: Art of Post 89*, 7.
15. Hou Hanru, "Di 45 jie weinisi shuangnianzhan de xianshi yu misi," *Xiongshi meishu* no. 2 (1992): 28–38.

16. Zhu Qingsheng, Wang Lin, and Wang Nanming, "Zhongguo dangdai yishu de guoji chujing," *Dushu* 11 (1998): 107–16
17. Zhu Qingsheng claims in this article that on the occasion he wrote a letter to the organizers to exchange opinions and analyzed their "European culturally colonialist attitude," However, he did not get appropriate response, finally withdrawing his application through the Chinese embassy.
18. Zhu, Wang, and Wang, "Zhonguo dangdai," 107–10.
19. Ibid., 111–14.
20. Ibid., 115–16.
21. "Chinese Art: Egg Roll at an International Banquet?—The Impact of Western Consumer Culture on a Chinese Socialist Stronghold," speech by Li Xianting (at Taipei conference, 1998), in *Yishujia* no. 331 (December 2002): 150–55.
22. Ibid.
23. Francesca Dal Lago, "Inside Out: Chinese Avant-garde Art (A Conversation with Gao Minglu)," *Art AsiaPacific* 20 (1998): 42–49.
24. Huang Du, "Existence of Art and Cultural Identity: The Position and Changes of Chinese Art in 1990s," *Chinese-art.com* 3, no. 2 [online].
25. Ralph Croizier, "Going to the World: Art and Culture on the Cosmopolitan Tide," *China Briefing* (New York: China Council of the Asia Society, 1989).
26. Wang Hui, "Dangdai zhongguo de sixiang zhuangkuang yu xiandaixing wenti," *Tianya* 5 (1997): 133–50.
27. Hou Hanru and Gao Minglu, "Strategies of Survival in the Third Space: A Conversation on the Situation of Overseas Chinese Artists in the 1990s," in *Inside Out: New Chinese Art*, ed. Gao Minglu (Berkeley: University of California Press, 1998), 183.
28. Gao Minglu, "Towards Transactional Modernity: An Overview of the Exhibition," in Gao, *Inside Out*, 16.
29. Hou and Gao, "Strategies of Survival," 183.
30. Ibid.
31. Debord, *Comments*.
32. Huang, "Existence of Art."
33. Huang Du, "Jiushi niandai zhongguo dangdai yishu fazhen yu guojijiandangdai yishu fazhan de jige wenti," in *Shoujiedangdai yishu xueshu yaoqingzhan*, ed. Huang Zhuang et al. (Guangzhou: Lingnan meishu chubanshe, 1996–97).
34. Yi Ying, "Mundane and Profound," *Chinese Contemporary Art Online Bulletin* 4, no. 3 (2001).
35. Gu Chengfeng, "Zhongguo bopu qingxiang," *Jiushi niandai zhongguo meishu:1990–1992*, ed. Zhang Qing (Ürümqi: Xinjiang meishu sheying chubanshe, 1996).

36. Shao Dazhen et al., "90 niandai zhongguo meishu xianzhaung yu qushi yantaohui," *Meishu Yanjiu* no. 1 (1999): 11–12. The conference organized by Zhongyang meishuxueyuan yanjiubu and Zhongyang meishu yanjiu zazhishe was held at Shanxi Wangjiadayuan zhonguo minju yishuguan from Oct. 27 to 30, 1998. Participants included art critics and historians from all over the country: Shao Dazhen, Wang Hongjian, Fan Di'an, Yi Ying, Yin Shuangxi, Zou Yuejin, Pi Daojian, Jia Fangzhou, Huang Zhuan, Lu Long, Huang Du, Feng Boyi, Chen Xiaoxin, Gu Chengfeng, Wang Yigang, Wang Nanming, Gao Ling, Shao Jianwu, Wang Zhaozhong, and Lanping.
37. Shao, "90 niandai zhongguo," 3.
38. Fan Di'an et al, *'98 [Fuzhou] Yatai diqu dangdai yishu yaoqingzhan zuopinji* (Fuzhou: n.p., 1998). The participants included Wang Lin, Yin Shuangxi, Yi Ying, and Gu Chengfeng.
39. Ibid.
40. Ibid.
41. Ibid.
42. Ibid.

Chapter 4

1. "Intellectuals and Power," in Michel Foucault, *Language, Counter-Memory, Practice: Selected Essay and Interviews* (Ithaca: Cornell University Press, 1977), 206.
2. Tzvetan Todorov, *Mikhail Bakhtin: The Dialogical Principle*, trans. Wlad Godsich (Minneapolis: University of Minnesota Press, 1984), 24.
3. Trevor Pateman, "Pragmatics in Semiotics: Bakhtin/Volosinov," www.selectedworks.co.uk/pragmatics.html. Lightly revised from the article of the same title appearing in *Journal of Literary Semantics* 18, no. 3 (December 1989): 203–16.
4. Mikhail Bakhtin, *Problems of Dostoevsky's Poetics*, ed. and trans. Caryl Emerson (Minneapolis: University of Minnesota Press, 1984).
5. Michael Shapiro, *Reading "Adam Smith": Desire, History and Value* (Thousand Oaks, CA: Sage Publications, 1993), 17.
6. Julia F. Andrews, "The Victory of Socialist Realism: Oil Painting and the New Guohua," in *A Century in Crisis: Modernity and Tradition in the Art of Twentieth-Century China*, ed. Julia F. Andrews and Kuiyi Shen (New York: Guggenheim Museum, 1998), 229.
7. George Orwell, *1984* (New York: New American Library, 1961), 248.
8. For an example of his earlier art, see *The Taking of the Presidential Palace*, painted with Wei Jingshan (b. 1943) in 1977, in the Military Museum, Beijing; Andrews and shen, *Century in Crisis*, cat. 165.

9. For a discussion of these issues with respect to artists "coming of age after—but indelibly shaped by—the Holocaust," see James E. Young's *At Memory's Edge: After-Images of the Holocaust in Contemporary Art and Architecture* (New Haven: Yale University Press, 2000).
10. For a fuller discussion, see Ralph Croizier, "The Avant-garde and the Democracy Movement: Reflections on Late Communism in the USSR and China," in *Europa-Asia Studies* 51, no. 3 (1999): 483–513.
11. Luo Zhongli, "Wode fuqin de zhouzhe de laixin" (Letter from the Painter of *My Father*), *Meishu* 158, no. 2 (1981): 4–5. Luo Zhongli, "*Nongmin he wode hua*" ("Peasants and My Paintings"), *Zhongguo Meishu*, February 1981, 28–33.
12. Yuejin Wang, "Anxiety of Portraiture: Quest for/Questioning Ancestral Icons in Post-Mao China," in *Politics, Ideology, and Literary Discourse in Modern China: Theoretical Interventions and Cultural Critique* (Durham: Duke University Press, 1993), 245.
13. Maria Galikowski, *Art and Politics in China: 1949–1984* (Hong Kong: The Chinese University Press, 1998), 204.
14. Ibid.
15. André Fermigier, *Jean-François Millet* (New York: Rizzoli International Publications), 56.
16. We may also bring in for comparison Millet's *The Old Vine-Grower*, executed between 1869 and 1870.
17. Galikowski, *Art and Politics in China*, 203–4.
18. Ibid.
19. Yuejin Wang, "Anxiety of Portraiture," 245.
20. Nina Kolesnikoff, "Defamiliarization," in *Encyclopedia of Contemporary Literary Theory: Approaches, Scholars, Terms*, ed. Irenar R. Makaryk (Toronto: University of Toronto Press, 1993), 529.
21. Lee T. Lemon and Marion J. Reiss, *Russian Formalist Criticism: Four Essays* (Lincoln: University of Nebraska Press, 1965), 4.
22. Caryl Emerson, "Bakhtin, Mikhail Mikhailovich," in Makaryk, *Encyclopedia*, 243.
23. Bakhtin, *Problems of Dostoevsky's Poetics*, xx.
24. Ibid., xxi.
25. Ibid., 93.
26. Ibid., xxiv.
27. Phyllis Margaret Paryas, "Double-voicing/dialogism," in Makaryk, *Encyclopedia*, 537.
28. Ibid., 537–38.
29. Ibid.
30. Mikhail Bakhtin, *Problems of Dostoevsky's Poetics*, 92.
31. Vera Schwarcz, *Bridges Across Broken Time: Chinese and Jewish Cultural Memory* (New Haven: Yale University Press, 1998).

32. *Mahjong: Contemporary Chinese Art from the Sigg Collection*, ed. Bernard Fibicher and Matthias Frehner (Ostfidern-Ruit, Germany: Hatje Cantz Verlag, 2005), 84.
33. Yin Zhaoyun, *Utopia*, exh. cat. Chinablue Gallery (Bejing, 2004), 6, quoted in ibid.
34. Ibid.

Chapter 5

An earlier version of this essay was originally published in the Fall 2009 issue of *Art Journal* (pp. 6–29); reprinted with permission. The epigraphs are from Laurie Anderson, *United States Live*, Warner Brothers 4-CD set, 1984, CD 2. The title of the song "'Language Is a Virus from Outer Space'—William S. Burroughs," also on CD 2, is paraphrased from William S. Burroughs, *Nova Express* (New York: Grove Press, 1964).

1. In a directive that appeared in the December 22, 1968 edition of the *People's Daily*, Mao Zedong called on urban youths to "re-educate" themselves through labor in the countryside, thereby inaugurating what came to be known as the rustication movement, in which millions were relocated—willingly or under coercion—to such peripheral provinces as Yunnan or Guizhou to spend years embedded in remote rural communities. While couched in the ideological language of socialist *Bildung*, the movement was aimed primarily at quelling the chaos of the Cultural Revolution by displacing the youth away from urban centers.
2. François Jullien, *L'encre de chine* (Lausanne: Alfred Eibel, 1978); David E. Apter and Tony Saich, *Revolutionary Discourse in Mao's Republic* (Cambridge, Mass.: Harvard University Press, 1994), 86, 244, 273ff.
3. Rey Chow, "Male Narcissism and National Culture: Subjectivity in Chen Kaige's *King of the Children*," in *Primitive Passions: Visuality, Sexuality, Ethnography, and Contemporary Chinese Cinema* (New York: Columbia University Press, 1995), 127–30.
4. See Christopher L. Connery, *The Empire of the Text: Writing and Authority in Early Imperial China* (Lanham: Rowman & Littlefield, 1998); David N. Keightley, "Art, Ancestors, and the Origins of Writing in China," *Representations* 56 (1996); Jean Levi, "Rite, langue et supériorité culturelle en Chine ancienne," *Le genre humain* 21 (1990); and Mark E. Lewis, *Writing and Authority in Early China* (Albany: State University of New York Press, 1999).
5. On the intersection of writing and polity, see, for example, Harold A. Innis, *Empire and Communications* (Toronto: University of Toronto

Press, 1972); and Jack Goody, *The Logic of Writing and the Organization of Society* (Cambridge: Cambridge University Press, 1986).

6. For a preliminary attempt at such a historicization, see my "The Empire of Fame: Writing and the Voice in Early Medieval China," *positions: east asia cultures critique* 14, no. 3 (2006): 535–66.
7. The locus classicus for the pictographic hypothesis is Fenollosa's famous—notorious in some circles—essay *The Chinese Written Character as a Medium for Poetry* (San Francisco: City Lights, 1936). For linguistic critiques of the notion of Chinese pictography, see for example John DeFrancis, *The Chinese Language: Fact and Fantasy* (Honolulu: University of Hawai'i Press, 1984), 74–130, Viviane Alleton, "Regards actuels sur l'écriture chinoise," in *Paroles à dire, parole à écrire,* ed. Viviane Alleton (Paris: Éditions de l'École des Hautes Études en Sciences Sociales, 1997).
8. On the geomantic associations of Huang Gongwang's landscape painting, see John Hay, "Huang Kung-wang's 'Dwelling in the Fu-ch'un Mountain': Dimensions of a Landscape" (Ph.D., Princeton University, 1978).
9. John Hay has been most eloquent in articulating the inner workings of the post-Song conception of painting. See his "Values and History in Chinese Painting, II: The Hierarchic Evolution of Structure," *Res* 7–8 (1984); "The Body Invisible in Chinese Art?" in *Body, Subject, and Power in China,* ed. Angela Zito and Tani Barlow (Chicago: University of Chicago Press, 1993); and "The Human Body as Microcosmic Source of Macrocosmic Values in Calligraphy," in *Self as Body in Asian Theory and Practice,* ed. Thomas P. Kasulis, Roger T. Ames, and Wimal Dissanayake (Albany: State University of New York Press, 1993).
10. Eugene Y. Wang, "Of Text and Texture: The Cultural Relevance of Xu Bing's Art," in *Xu Bing: Language Lost,* exh. cat. (Boston: Massachusetts College of Art, 1995), 12.
11. On the authority of *wen,* see Haun Saussy, "The Prestige of Writing: *Wen,* Letter, Picture, Image, Ideography," in *Great Wall of Discourse and Other Adventures in Cultural China* (Cambridge, Mass.: Harvard University Asia Center, 2001), 66–71.
12. Wang, "Of Text and Texture," 9.
13. Xu Bing, conversation with author, 1995.
14. On the effect of scale in *A Book from the Sky* and related works, see Robert E. Harrist, Jr., "*Book from the Sky* at Princeton: Reflections on Scale, Sense, and Sound" in *Persistence/Transformation: Text as Image in the Art of Xu Bing,* ed. J. Silbergeld and D. C. Y. Ching (Princeton: Princeton University Press, 2006), 29–32.
15. The fidelity of the books to traditional printing is indeed such that,

according to the artist, the British Museum purchased a set as exemplar of traditional Chinese bookmaking. Xu Bing, conversation with author, 1995.

16. A standard account of the structure of the Chinese script can be found in DeFrancis, *Chinese Language,* 71–88. I owe the notion of the modularity of the Chinese script to Lothar Ledderose, *Ten Thousand Things: Module and Mass Production in Chinese Art* (Princeton: Princeton University Press, 2000), 9–23.
17. Stanley K. Abe, "No Questions, No Answers: China and *A Book from the Sky,*" in *Modern Chinese Literary and Cultural Studies in the Age of Theory: Reimagining a Field,* ed. Rey Chow (Durham: Duke University Press, 2000), 231; Louis Marin, *Utopiques: jeux d'espaces* (Paris: Les Éditions de Minuit, 1973), 20–21.
18. A survey of artists engaging the medium of the book can be found in Wu Hung et al., *Shu: Reinventing Books in Contemporary Chinese Art* (New York: China Institute, 2006).
19. For an in-depth study of this cultural phenomenon, see Jing Wang, *High Culture Fever: Politics, Aesthetics, and Ideology in Deng's China* (Berkeley: University of California Press, 1996).
20. Wu Hung, *Transience: Chinese Experimental Art at the End of the Twentieth Century* (Chicago: The David and Alfred Smart Museum of Art, The University of Chicago, 1999), 40–41. See also Wenda Gu et al., *Wenda Gu: Art from Middle Kingdom to Biological Millennium* (Cambridge, Mass.: MIT Press, 2003).
21. See Norman Bryson's perceptive readings of Qiu Zhijie and Song Dong's works in view of the (post-)ideological condition of contemporary China in "The Post-Ideological Avant-Garde," in *Inside Out: New Chinese Art,* ed. Minglu Gao (Berkeley: University of California Press, 1998).
22. Wang Tiande and Chambers Fine Art (Gallery), *Made by Tiande,* exh. cat. (New York: Chambers Fine Art, 2004).
23. Britta Erickson, *The Art of Xu Bing: Words without Meaning, Meaning without Words* (Seattle: University of Washington Press, 2001), 37.
24. Xu Shen, *Shuowen jiezi zhu* (Shanghai: Shanghai guji chubanshe, 1981), 754 (15A/2a-b).
25. Tetsuji Atsuji, *Kanjigaku: Setsubun kaiji no sekai* (Tokyo Tôkai daigaku shuppankai, 1985), 114.
26. There are some exceptions to this, most of which usually fall in the "indicating things" category (*zhishi* 指事). In Peircian parlance, this category is diagrammatic rather than iconic. On the semiotic diversity of Xu Shen's system, see Saussy, "Prestige of Writing," 66.
27. On the fertility of characters in the *Shuowen* and its cosmological un-

derpinning via the *Classic of Changes*, see Lewis, *Writing and Authority*, 272–74.

28. Takeda Masaya presents an overview of this fascinating history in *Sōketsu tachi no utage: Kanji no shinwa to yūtopia* (Tokyo: Chikuma shobō, 1994).
29. Wu Hung's informed translation of the term *tianshu* as "nonsense writing" (Wu Hung, "A 'Ghost Rebellion': Notes on Xu Bing's 'Nonsense Writing'," *Public Culture* 6, no. 2 [1994]: 411) does not necessarily contradict my reading of the efficacy of the pseudocharacters, for the term's colloquial meaning of gibberish is itself derivative of the more literal meaning of "heavenly script," scriptures (mostly Daoist) believed to have literally appeared in the sky. This entered popular imagination not only through religious activities but also through vernacular fiction, such as in the famous scene in chapter 71 of the 16th-century vernacular novel *Water Margin* (*Shuihuzhaun*), where Song Jiang receives in a dream a three-fascicle "heavenly scripture" from a goddess. On this peculiar tradition, see for example Isabelle Robinet, *Taoist Meditation: The Mao-shan Tradition of the Great Purity*, trans. Julian F. Pas and Norman J. Girardot (Albany: State University of New York Press, 1993), Lü Pengzhi, "Zaoqi lingbaojing de tianshu guan," in *Daojiao jiaoyi yu xiandai shehui*, ed. Guo Wu (Shanghai: Shanghai guji chubanshe, 2003), Gong Pengcheng, *Daojiao xinlun* (Taibei: Xuesheng shuju, 1991), 39–78, Levi, "Rite, langue et supériorité culturelle en Chine ancienne."
30. Martina Köppel-Yang presents a nuanced version of this perspective in her *Semiotic Warfare: A Semiotic Analysis, the Chinese Avant-Garde, 1979–1989* (Hong Kong: Timezone 8, 2003), 169–71.
31. For standard linguistic critiques of the conception of the Chinese script as ideography, see Alleton, "Regards actuels," 187–95; William G. Boltz, *The Origin and Early Development of the Chinese Writing System* (New Haven: American Oriental Society, 1994), 3–24; and DeFrancis, *Chinese Language*, 133–48.
32. I want to underscore the significance of what John Cayley called the "eminent legibility" of Xu's installation, albeit primariy in reference to the print format. See his "Writing (Under-)Sky: On Xu Bing's *Tianshu*," in *A Book of the Book: Some Works and Projections about the Book and Writing*, ed. Jerome Rothenberg and Steven Clay (New York: Granary Books, 2000), 498–500.
33. Jean-François Billeter, *The Chinese Art of Writing*, trans. Jean-Marie Clarke and Michael Taylor (New York: Skira/Rizzoli, 1990), 29.
34. There are a few ways in which the pseudo-graphs can deviate from the morphological norm, which will be discussed later.

35. Billeter, *Chinese Art of Writing,* 33.
36. Xu quoted in the wall text for the exhibition *Word Play: Contemporary Art by Xu Bing* at the Arthur M. Sackler Gallery, Washington, D.C., 2001.
37. Georg Simmel, "The Aesthetic Significance of the Face," in *Georg Simmel,* ed. Kurt Wolff (Columbus: Ohio State University Press, 1959).
38. Jacques Derrida, *De la grammatologie* (Paris: Éditions de Minuit, 1967); Jacques Lacan, "L'instance de la lettre dans l'inconscient ou la raison depuis Freud," in Écrits (Paris: Seuil, 1966); Jean-Luc Nancy and Philippe Lacoue-Labarthe, *The Title of the Letter: A Reading of Lacan,* trans. François Raffoul and David Pettigrew (Albany: State University of New York Press, 1992).
39. See Ernst Robert Curtius's authoritative historical account of the notion of the world as book in his *European Literature and the Latin Middle Ages* (Princeton: Princeton University Press, 1990), 302–47.
40. John Lagerwey, "The Oral and the Written in Chinese and Western Religion," in *Religion und Philosophie in Ostasien,* ed. Gert Naundorf, Karl-Heinz Pohl, and Hans-Hermann Schmidt (Würzburg: Königshausen & Neumann, 1985), 304.
41. One might pursue the analogy between Xu's installation and the Daoist conception of heavenly scriptures further by suggesting a Daoist subtext for the installation's contrast between the unbound unity of the vast scroll hanging from above and the multitude of bound volumes beneath. This forms an interesting parallel to the constitutive opposition inherent in Daoist conception of holy scriptures: the transmitted texts of the scriptures are but degraded versions of the "real writs" that literally materialize in the sky—invisible and illegible to the ordinary eye and certainly not bound. See references in note 29.
42. See Lewis, *Writing and Authority,* 274–75; and Anthony C. Yu, "*Cratylus* and *Xunzi* on Names," in *Early China/Ancient Greece: Thinking through Comparisons,* ed. Steven Shankman and Stephen W. Durrant (Albany: State University of New York Press, 2002), 239.
43. *Bohutong shuzheng,* ed. Chen Li (Beijing: Zhonghua shuju, 1994), 12.567.
44. Dong Zhongshu, *Chunqiu fanlu yizheng* (Beijing: Zhonghua shuju, 1992), 51.346.
45. Lewis, *Writing and Authority,* 271.
46. Thomas Lamarre, *Uncovering Heian Japan: An Archaeology of Sensation and Inscription* (Durham: Duke University Press, 2000), 128–30.
47. Harrist, "*Book from the Sky* at Princeton," 25.
48. Standard English-language accounts of these reform movements are found in John DeFrancis, *Nationalism and Language Reform in China*

(New York: Octagon Books, 1972); and Richard C. Kraus, *Brushes with Power: Modern Politics and the Chinese Art of Calligraphy* (Berkeley: University of California Press, 1991), 75–108.

49. On the persistent primacy of writing in modern Chinese language-reform movements, see Murata Yūjirō, "'Bunpaku' no kanata ni: Kindai chūgoku ni okeru kokugo mondai," *Shisō* 853 (1995).
50. Walter Benjamin, *The Origin of German Tragic Drama* (London: Verso, 1985).

Chapter 6

An earlier version of this essay was presented at the 24th National Comparative Literature Symposium, Taiwan, and published in Chinese in the *Chung-Wai Literature* [*Zhongwai Wenxue*] *Journal* 29, no. 7 (December 2000), 4–40, and in English in *Yishu* 2, no. 1 (March 2003), 27–46 (reprinted with permission). Some passages were included in the author's PhD thesis: "Avant-Garde Art and the Formation of Museums: A Study of the Cultural History of Visuality in Modern Taiwan" (*Jindai Taiwan de qianwei meishu yu bowuguan xinggou: yige shijue wenhuashi de tantao*) (Fu-Jen Catholic University, 2004).

1. A number of exhibitions in Taiwan were curated for museums with specific focuses of study. For instance, "Dis/Continuity: Religion Shamanism Nature" (*Yanxu yu Duanlie: Zongjiao Wushu Ziran*) was created by the critic Hai-Ming Huang for the TFAM in 1992. The first example of a Taiwanese government institute inviting curators to run exhibitions over an extended period was the Art Exhibition of Taipei County, which began in 1994 and was held for four consecutive shows. As the County Art Exhibitions from 1994 to 1996 were not listed as international contemporary art exhibitions, they are not included in the current discussion.
2. The term "curator" originally referred to a museum collection administrator or Catholic Church custodian whose major responsibility was to collect, categorize, and study holdings of artifacts. Today the term is also translated as "exhibition organizer" in Taiwan. Based on the evolution of the role, organizing an exhibition is just one of many jobs a curator performs, and historically it is a relatively new one. As used here, the term refers specifically to "independent curators" who are not associated with any museum and who are responsible for organizing modern art exhibitions. Although its meaning is different in the wider context of museum studies, the use of the term *curator* follows its common usage in today's Taiwanese art community. See

Velson C. Horie, "What Is a Curator?" *The International Journal of Museum Management and Curatorship* 5, no. 3 (September 1986): 267–72; and Gaynor Kavanagh, *History Curatorship* (Leicester: Leicester University Press, 1990), 53–107.

3. These conferences and seminars include "Exhibit Curation—A Seminar on Museum, Practices" (*Cong Zhanlan Cehua Chufa: Bowuguan Shiwu Yantaohui*), sponsored by the National Museum of History (*Guoli Lishi Bowuguan*) in 1997, as well as the "Conference of World Chinese Art Curators" (*Quanqiu Huaren Cezhanren Huiyi*) and "Developing a New Network of Asian Art: An International Conference of Contemporary Asian Art Curatorship" (*Faxian Yazhou Yishu Xin Hangxian Yazhou Meishu Chezhanren Huiyi*), sponsored by the Taiwan Museum of Art (*Guoli Taiwan Meishuguan*) in 1999 and 1999 respectively.
4. For the full text of this oral statement, see an editorial published in the June 1996 issue of the *Hsiung-Shih Art Monthly* as well as articles published on 8 May 1996 in the *China Times* (*Zhongguo shibao*), the *Liberty Times* (*Ziyou shibao*), and the *Min Sheng Daily* (*Minsheng ribao*). No written statement of resignation was released by Chang.
5. A number of Taiwanese critics held a symposium to discuss the event. By reviewing the local artistic environment and exploring the possibilities for a sound and healthy system, participants believed that the event also provided an opportunity to develop a new curatorial system. See articles published on 1 May 1996 in the *United Daily News*, the *China Times*, and the *Min Sheng Daily*.
6. A debate on Taiwanese art localization issues, carried on in the *Hsiung-Shih Art Monthly* after April 1991, was initiated by Tsai-Chin Ni with an essay titled "Western Art, Made in Taiwan: a Criticism of Taiwan Modern Art" (*Xifang Meishu Taiwan Zhizao: Taiwan Xiandai Meishu de Pipan*). The debate ended in February 1993, when Hsing-Yueh Lin published *Art Localization: Explanation and Statements* (*Meishu bentuhua de shiyi yu shenlun*). See Yeh Yu-Ching [Ye Yujing], ed., *Taiwan meishu zhong de Taiwan yishi* (The Taiwan Identity in Taiwan Art) (Taipei: Hsiung Shih Art Books Co. Ltd., 1994).
7. As well as being responsive to discussions involving critics, the active involvement of art museums in the development of Taiwanese art also had an indirect effect on the emerging Taiwanese art auction market. In December 1990, a public art auction run by an independent auction firm took place for the first time in the history of Taiwan. This was the Chuan-Chia Art Company (*Chuanjia Yishu Paimai Gongsi*)'s auction of collections of Taiwanese art. Christie's Hong Kong Ltd. opened its Taipei office the following year and held its first auction in 1993. During that period, there appears to have been a correlation between the items sold by auctioneers and those displayed by art museums.

8. Sponsors of this exhibition include America's Asian Cultural Council, Japan's Interchange Association and Shiseido Co., Ltd., and the Hong Kong Arts Development Council. Among the speakers invited to seminars organized by the curatorial system were Vishakha N. Desal (Deputy Director, Asian Cultural Council), Oscar H. K. Ho (Director, Hong Kong Arts Center), Takashi Senzawa (Director, P3 Art and Environment), Danny Yung (Director, Arts Center, Hong Kong University of Science and Technology), and Hsing-Yueh Lin (Instructor, National Art Institute).
9. Huang Hai-Ming, "Diyijie shuangnianzhan de lianxiang" (Thoughts on the First Biennial), *Xiongshi Meishu* (Hsiung-Shih Art Monthly) 257 (January 1992): 90–93.
10. Michel Foucault, "The Subject and Power," *Critical Inquiry* 8, no. 44 (Summer 1982): 777.
11. The most famous statement in this literature of martyrdom was an announcement published in *Artist Magazine* by eight members of "Beyond the Canvas" (*Huawai Huahui*) over eight consecutive issues from October 1993 through to May 1994. As its title, "Impugning the TFAM'S Taiwan Art (1945–1993) Exhibition as Being Abusive, Arbitrary, Abrupt, Unfair and a Distortion of History" (*Lanquan Zhuanduan, Caoshuai Bugong, Waiqu Shishi*), suggests, the statement, which included text and pictures, expressed a sarcastic stance on the part of its authors. All eight people who authored the statement put their signatures to it.
12. Lu Hsien-Ming [Lu Xianming], "Cong shuangnianzhan kan angyang de zhutixing" (The Biennial and the High Morale), *Yishujia* 256 (September 1996): 347–50; Cheng 1996.
13. Kao Chien-Hui [Gao Qianhui], "Quantou yu zhentou de yishu tequ: Huiying Jiuliunian Taibei shuangnianzhan de shuxing wenti" (Fist and Pillow: a Special Art Zone—a Response to the Nature of the 1998 Taipei Biennial), *Yishujia* 257 (October 1996): 418–21.
14. Huang Hai-Ming, "Taiwan zhutixing shuangnianzhan zhi shi chang 'Wuxin de dabaibai?'" (The Taiwan Identity Biennial: Is It Just a 'Thoughtless Ritual'?), *Yishujia* 259 (October 1996): 416, 411.
15. Ibid. 416–17.
16. See Hubert L. Dreyfus and Paul Rabinow, eds., *Michel Foucault: Beyond Structuralism and Hermeneutics* (Chicago: University of Chicago Press, 1982), 121.
17. Huang, "Taiwan zhutixing," 408.
18. Dreyfus and Rabinow, *Michel Foucault*, 191.
19. Ibid., 211–12.
20. "Contemporary Issues" was comprised of four subsections, among

which "Identity and Memories" was divided into "Historical Statues," "Living Memories," "Cultural Identities," and "From Ancestry to World Identities." "Visual Dialogue" was divided into "Color and Texture," "Form and Diagram," "Spatial Structure," "Time and History," "Geographic Location and Ethnic Groups," and "Information and Media"; "Sexuality and Power" was divided into "Feminism," "Sexuality," "Gender Identity," and "Body Sovereignty." See Li Yu-Ling, ed., *1996 Shuangnianzhan: Taiwan yishu zhutixing* (1996 Taipei Biennial: The Quest for Identity) (Taipei City: Taipei Fine Arts Museum, 1996).

21. Michel Foucault, *Discipline and Punishment: The Birth of the Prison*, trans. Alan Sheridan (New York: Pantheon, 1977), 207.
22. Gilles Deleuze, *Foucault*, trans. and ed. Sean Hand (Minneapolis: University of Minneapolis Press, 1988), 35.
23. Foucault, *Discipline and Punishment*, 73.
24. Nicholas Jose and Wen-I Yang, eds., *Art Taiwan: The Contemporary Art of Taiwan* (Sydney: Gordon and Breach, 1995).
25. Lin Pei-Chun, "Wusheng de Taiwan yishu, wusheng de nüxing yishu" (Voiceless Taiwan Art, Voiceless Taiwan Female Art), *Yishujia* 258 (November 1996): 315.
26. Chang Yuan-Chien [Zhang Yuanqian], "Shijiao de shengyan: Di er jie Yiatai diqu dangdaiyishu shannianzhan" (An Unfocused Gathering: The Second Contemporary Art Triennial in the Asian-Pacific Region), *Yishujia* 258 (November 1996): 320.
27. Shih Jui-Jen (J.J. Shih) [Shi Ruiren], "'Heliu yishuzhan: Yitiao shuixi, sige chongji hekou shang de yishu duihua" (River Exhibition: A Dialogue at Four Alluvial Mouths of One River System), *Yishujia* 269 (October 1997): 366.
28. Ibid., 366–67.
29. Ibid., 367.
30. In addition to *Voyeurism* displayed in the Hsinchuang Cultural Center, Ahn Pil-Yun also performed action art at the exhibiting site.
31. Heather Tomlinson, "Design and Reform: The 'Separate System' in the Nineteen-century English Prison," *Buildings and Society: Essays on the Social Development of the Built Environment*, ed. Anthony D. King (London: Routledge and Kegan Paul, 1980), 94–119.
32. Shih Jui-Jen (J.J. Shih), "Heliu: Xin Yazhou yishu, Taibei duihua" (River: New Asian Art: A Dialogue in Taipei), in *Heliu—Xin Yazhou yishu, Taibei duihua, 1997 Taipeixian meizhan zhuankan* (River: New Asian Art—A Dialogue in Taipei, 1997 Taipei County Art Exhibition) (Taipei County: Taipei County Cultural Center, 1997), 6.
33. Ichi Ikeda, "Shui zhi fangzhou jihua/Taibei zhi hang" (Arching Ark—Voyage to Taipei), in *Heliu—Xin Yazhou yishu*, 122.

34. Shih, "Heliu," 8.
35. Ibid.
36. According to the curatorial statement, seven out of sixteen exhibited works were installation art. One example was Ti-Nan Chi's "Information River," which involved an interaction between a sensor mechanism and blue florescent light that allowed the artist to present two different atmospheric experiences for day/night, with different meanings. See Shih, "Heliu," 13. "Floating Island" (*Piaodao*) by Shih-Yung Ku [Gu Shiyong] was another example: "This work is similarly a space installation in which the participation of the audience is an important element in the development of meaning."
37. Chang Yuan-Chien, "Penbian zhuren zizai ziwei" (Lord of the Rim: In Herself/For Herself), *Yishujia* (Artist Magazine) 272 (January 1998): 338–41.
38. Chang Yuan-Chien, "Penbian zhuren zizaiziwei" (Lord of the Rim: In Herself/For Herself), in *Penbian zhuren zizaiziwei* (Lord of the Rim: In Herself/For Herself) (Taipei County: Xingzhuang Shigongsuo [Xing-zhuang City Office], 1998), 6–8.
39. Ibid., 6.
40. Ibid., 7.
41. Ibid.
42. Ibid.
43. Chien Ying-Ying [Jian Yingying], "Cong 'Xinbie zhengzhi' dao 'Pen-bianzhuren'" (From Sexual Politics to Lord of the Rim), *Lianhe Wenxue* 162 (April 1998): 132.
44. When the curatorial statement was published by *Artist Magazine* in January 1998, this opening paragraph was in bold print to enhance its visibility. But in an exhibition catalogue published in February 1998, the paragraph was replaced by a dialogue with a female worker from Hsinchuang.
45. Chang, "Penbian zhuren zizaiziwei," 8.
46. Chang, "Penbian zhuren zizai ziwei," 341.
47. Lu Jung-Chih [Lu Rongzhi], "Shei de zhuangzhi yishu weishei?" (Installation Art of Whom and For Whom?), *Yishujia* 273 (February 1998): 362.
48. This was a comment made by Ying-Ying Chien on "The Dinner Party." Her original remarks read, "If we re-examine and reconsider 'The Dinner Party' from an Asian/Asian American woman's perspective, the obvious disappointment is not its overemphasis on female symbols (i.e., sex organs and anything related to female functions such as dinnerware and crafts like embroidering, china-painting), but its complete ignorance of Asian women, goddesses, and other

minority females, who are excluded from the creation process and final products. As a Jewish American, Judy's art apparently features white, middle-class, educated women." See Chien Ying-Ying [Jian Yingying], "'Xinbie zhengzhi' zaixian: Judy Chicago de 'Wanyan' yu nüxing zhuyi yishushi" (Sexual Politics Reemerges: Judy Chicago's The Dinner Party and Feminist Art), *Lianhe Wenxue* (United Literature Monthly) 148 (February 1997): 58.

49. Carol Duncan, *Civilizing Rituals: Inside Public Art Museum* (London: Routledge, 1995), 11–20.
50. Lin Mun-Lee [Lin Manli], "1998 Taipei shuangnianzhan tuxiang Yazhou quandian" (Highlighting Asian Perspectives in the 1998 Taipei Biennial), *Yishujia* 278 (July 1998): 306–7.
51. Nanjo Fumio, "Yuwang de shiji: 1998 Taipei shuangnianzhan zong cehuaren zishu" (A Century of Desire—Chief Curator of the 1998 Taipei Biennial: In his Own Words), *Yishujia* 277 (June 1998): 374.
52. Shih Jui-Jen (J.J. Shih), "Yishu changyu zhong de yuwang huizhen" (Diagnosing Desires in Art Fields), *Yishujia* 279 (August 1998): 340; Huang Hai-Ming, "1998 Taibei shuangnianzhan: 'Yuwang changyu' zhi kongjian siwei 1998" (The 1998 Taipei Biennial: Spatial Thinking for the Site of Desire), *Xiandai Meishu* (Modern Art) 79 (August 1998): 3.
53. Nanjo Fumio, "Yangpizhi shi de dushi duochong lun" (Palimpsestus Urbanus), in *1998 Taipei Shuangnianzhan: Yuwang changyu* 1998 (1998 Taipei Biennial—Site of Desire) (Taipei City: Taipei Fine Arts Museum, 1998), 16.
54. Ibid.
55. Lin, "1998 Taipei," 306.
56. Nanjo, "Yangpizhi," 13.
57. Ibid., 15.
58. Ibid., 16.
59. Liu Li, "Yishujia zazhi zhuanfang Nantiao Shisheng: Taibei shuangnianzhan cezhan tiyan" (An Artist Magazine interview with Fumio Nanjo: Experiencing the Taipei Biennial), *Yishujia* 278 (July 1998): 309.
60. See Okakura Kakuzo, *The Ideals of the East* (New York: E. P. Dutton, 1903).
61. Takeshi Hamashita, *Jindai Zhongguo de guoji qiji: Chaogong maoyi tixi yu jindai Yazhou maoyiquan* (International Opportunities for Modern China: A Tributary System of Trading and a Modern Asian Trading Sphere), trans. Zhu Yingui and Ouyang Fei (Beijing: Chinese Social Science Publishing House, 1999), 46.
62. See the TFAM announcement published in *Artist Magazine* 251 (April 1996).
63. Kao Chien-Hui, "Qingcheng zhilian: Hou Jiuling niandai Yazhou

relang xia de quyu yuwang yu cezhan yishi" (Love in a Fallen City—Regional Desire and Curatorial Consciousness under the Asian Heat of the Late 1990s), *Yishujia* 278 (July 1998): 344–51. Critic Chien-Hui Kao's comments implied true distinction and contradiction: "Let us take a realistic view of Taiwan culture from the basic perspective of choosing a curator. It is quite common for museums or institutes in other countries to work with curators from different nations. But if we invite someone from the former colonial power and invading nation to direct an exhibition with a theme about Asian cities searching for a postcolonial identity, we have to admit Taiwan's indifference to national consciousness and self-determination."

64. Lin, "1998 Taipei," 307.
65. Shih, "Yishu changyu zhong de yuwang huizhen," 339; Lu Jung-Chih [Lu Rongzhi], "Yuwang de sheng yu mie: Kan yijiujiuba Taibei shuangnianzhan: Yuwang changyu" (The Birth and Death of Desire: A Perspective on the 1998 Taipei Biennial—Site of Desire), *Yishujia* 278 (July 1998): 331; Huang, "1998 Taibei shuangnianzhan," 16.
66. Shih Ping-Hsi [Shi Bingxi], "Zongrong de fuyu shehui zhi xinyishu fengmao: 1998 Taibei shuangnianzhan guanhougan" (A New Look for Art in an Affluent and Indulgent Society—Impressions from the 1998 Taipei Biennial), *Xiandai Meishu* 79 (August 1998): 25; Kao, "Qingcheng zhilian"; Huang, "1998 Taibei shuangnianzhan," 3–16; Liu Yung-Jen [Liu Yongren], "Wuqing zhi yu, Jiewang zhi cheng: Nantiao banben de Taibei shuangnianzhan" (Desire without Love, Site of Anxiety: Nanjo's Taipei Biennial), *Yishujia* 279 (August 1998): 344–48.
67. Liu Li, "Yishujia zazhi zhuanfang Nantiao Shisheng: Taibei shuangnianzhan cezhan tiyan" (An Artist Magazine interview with Fumio Nanjo: Experiencing the Taipei Biennial), *Yishujia* 278 (July 1998): 310.
68. Pierre Bourdieu, "Social Space and Symbolic Power," *Sociological Theory* 7, no. 1 (1989): 14–25.
69. The present author discovered a very innovative curatorial model when observing a private institute's process of selecting curators. A curator based his curatorial concept on the life experience he shared with participating artists. His curatorial statement was written as a long verse. No fixed roles were assigned the curator and the artists, who constantly alternated their roles as the curatorial apparatus moved ahead.
70. Eilean Hooper-Greenhill, *Museum and the Shaping of Knowledge* (London: Routledge, 1992).
71. Michel Foucault, *The History of Sexuality*, vol. 1, *An Introduction*, trans. Robert Hurley (New York: Vintage/Random House, 1980).
72. Li Wei-Ching [Li Weijing], "Zouping shi wode yizhong ziyan ziyu:

Liu Shifen" (My Works, My Soliloquies—Shih-Fen Liu), *Yishujia* 295 (December 1999): 464.

73. Liu said that she was referring to site-specific installations when stating that she had not "even made one single piece of exhibition or installation art." Prior to the 1998 Taipei Biennial, she had never published a work in the form of a site-specific installation. Most of her works took the form of two-dimensional painting (such as "119 Ways to Read Heart Sounds" [*119 Zhong Yuedu Xinyin de Fangfa*] [1996]), and three-dimensional mixed media (such as "Fable of the Narcissistic Woman Series: Garden of Eden" [*Zilian Nüren de Yuyan Xilie 1: Legu de Huayuan*] [1997] and "Banquet of Daddy" [*Babi de Xiangyan*] [1998]).
74. Foucault, *Discipline and Punishment,* 25.
75. Huang, "1998 Taibei shuangnianzhan," 16).
76. Lu, "Yuwang de sheng yu mie," 328–31.
77. Kao Chien-Hui [Gao Qianhui]. "Qingcheng zhilian: Hou Jiuling niandai Yazhou relang xia de quyu yuwang yu cezhan yishi" (Love in a Fallen City—Regional Desire and Curatorial Consciousness under the Asian Heat of the Late 1990s), *Yishujia* 278 (July 1998): 345.
78. Gao Ming-Lu, *Toward a Transnational Modernity: An Overview of Inside Out: New Chinese Art* (Berkeley: University of California Press, 1998), 15–40.
79. Gao Ming-Lu, "Quanqiuhua quyuxing yu geren ganshou: 'Tuibian tupo: huaren xingyishu' cezhan zishu" (Globalization, Localization and Personal Perceptions—My Own Comments on My Curating of the Exhibition 'Inside Out: New Chinese Art'), *Yishujia* 282 (November 1998): 391.

Chapter 7

An earlier version of this essay was published in *Situations: Project of the Radical Imagination,* vol. 4, no. 1 (2011): 151–64; reprinted with permission. The author would like to thank the journal's special issue editor and the anonymous reviewers for their feedback.

1. See *Zhongguo nongmin gong diaoyan baogao* (A Research Report on Chinese Farmer Migrant Workers), complied by the State Council Research Group (Beijing: Zhongguo yanshi chubanshe, 2006), 2.
2. "The concept of scientific development" is a new political term. It refers to the current official guiding socioeconomic ideology of the Chinese Communist Party (CCP), incorporating sustainable development, social welfare, a person-centered society, increased democracy, and ultimately, the creation of a harmonious society.

3. The Chinese government issued a number of policies regarding Chinese migrant farmer workers in the city in the first decade of the 21st century. Following these policies, a series of books and articles were published either by noted scholars or by government-based writing groups. Among these publications, *Research Report* (n. 1 above), published in 2006, stood out and stunned the reading public in China. The three principles mentioned in my article are my generalization of the points in the book. For more details, see Wei Liqun, "Zhengque renshi he gaodu zhongshi jiejue nongmin gong wenti" (Correct Recognition and High Consideration of Solving the Problems of Farmer Labors), in *Research Report*, 1–11.
4. The details can be found in *Remaking the Chinese City*: *Modernity and National Identity*, 1900–1950, ed. Joseph W. Esherick (Honolulu: University of Hawaii Press, 1999).
5. Mao Zedong, the first leader of the CCP, issued his directive for shifting the Party's focus from the rural to the city at the Second Plenary Session of the Seventh Central Committee of the CCP on March 5, 1949. Mao stated that the CCP focused on the rural during the period from 1927 to 1949, and gathered the CCP's power in the rural, encircling the city with the rural, and finally occupying the city. Mao announced that this phase was over and the new phase should let the city lead the rural. See Mao Zedong, "A Report at the Second Plenary Session of the Seventh Central Committee of the Chinese Communist Party in March 5, 1949," in *Selected Works of Mao Zedong*, Vol. 4 (Beijing: Renmin chubanshe, 1966), 1365.
6. The term *the people's commune* was coined by Chen Boda, one of the Chinese state leaders of New China, and appeared in his article "Completely New Society, Completely New People" (Quanxin de shehui, quanxin de ren), published in the top official magazine, *Red Flag* (*Hongqi*) no. 3 (1958). In his article, Chen Boda stated that the people's commune was an organization, which perfectly combined agricultural and industrial cooperation. This system lasted for about 26 years, from 1958 to 1984. The first people's commune was established in July 1, 1958 in Henan Province in the PRC. The people's commune system transformed a private- and individual-based agricultural ownership into a cooperative-based agricultural ownership. The people's commune was a multipurpose organization for the direction of local government and the management of all economic and social activity. Each commune was organized into progressively larger units: production teams, production brigades, and the commune itself. As a basic unit of China's socialist system, the commune reflected the often-abrupt changes in political and economic policy after 1949.

7. For more information, see Li Duanxiang, "Lun Chengshi renmin gongshehua yundong de lishi biranxing" (On the Historical Inevitability of the Urban People's Commune Movement), in *Dangdai shijie yu shehui zhuyi* (Contemporary World and Socialism) no. 2 (2007): 131–34.
8. See Tang Xiaobing, "Rural Women and Social Change in New China Cinema: From *Li Shuangshuang* to *Ermo*," in *positions: east asia cultures critique* 14, no. 3 (winter, 2003): 647–74, and Chris Berry, "Sexual Difference and the Viewing Subject in *Li Shuangshuang* and *The In-Laws*," in *Perspectives on Chinese Cinema*, ed. Chris Berry (London: BFI Publishing, 1991), 30–39.
9. For more information of Chinese cinema 1949–1978, see Paul Clark, *Chinese Cinema: Culture and Politics since 1949* (New York and Cambridge: Cambridge University Press, 1987).
10. Cai Fang, Du Yang and Wang Meiyan, "Migration and Labor Mobility in China," *Human Development Research Paper 2009/09* (United Nations Development Program, April 2009), 1.
11. Deng Xiaoping appeared on the cover of *Time* magazine eight times during 1976–1997: January 19, 1976; December 25, 1978; January 1st, 1979; February 5, 1979; September 26, 1983; September 23, 1985; January 6 1986; and March 3, 1997.
12. See Jia, Leilei, "Zhongguo nongcun dianying zhong 'chuzou zhuti' de shanbian" (The Changing Themes of 'Runaway' in Chinese Rural Cinema), *Dangdai dianying* 149, no. 8 (2008): 13–17.
13. For more information about these films, see Shell Kraicer, "Rediscovering the Fourth Generation," *Cinema Scope*, no. 33 (winter, 2008); 29–32; Ma Ning, "Signs of Angst and Hope: History and Melodrama in Chinese Fifth-generation Cinema," *Screen* 44, no. 2 (summer, 2003): 183–99; Ma Ning, "New Chinese Cinema: A Critical Account of the Fifth Generation," *Cineaste* 17, no. 3 (1990): 32; Jerome Silbergeld, *China Into Film* (London: Reaktion Books, 1999).
14. Sponsored by the Chinese Writers' Association, the Mao Dun Literature Award is the most prestigious literature prize for writers in China. The award was created by the will of Mao Dun, who was a prominent Chinese writer of the 20th century, with his donation of 250,000RMB (about $42,000) to encourage Chinese novel writing.
15. I interviewed Wu Tianming at the conference of "Chinese Cinema in the U.S. since 1979" at University of South Carolina, October 8–10, 2010. The interview was conducted in Chinese. The English translation of the quoted conversation in this article is mine.
16. For more film critiques of this film, see Ping Fu, "*Ermo*: (Tele) Visualizing Urban/Rural Transformation," In *Chinese Films in Focus II*, ed. Chris Berry (London: British Film Institute Publishing, 2008), 98–105; and Tang Xiaobing, "Rural Women."

17. Chai Xiaofeng, *Zhou Xiaowen ye fengkuang* (Zhou Xiaowen is Also Crazy), (Changsha: Hunan Wenyi Chubanshe, 1996), 313. For more detailed discussions, see Dai Jinhua, "*Ermo* Xiandai Yuyan Kongjian" (*Ermo*: Modern Allegorical Space); Wang Dehou, "*Ermo*: Zhuozhuang yu Mangmu de Jiejing" (*Ermo*: a Crystallization of Sturdiness and Blindness); and Wang Yichuan, "Rushi Biaoyan Quanli Jiaohuan yu Chongfu" (A Realistic Representation of Power Exchange and Repetition), in *Film Art* (*Dianying Yishu*) no. 5 (1994): 39–43, 36–38, and 44–47. In Marshall McLuhan and Bruce Power's *The Global Village* (New York: Oxford University Press, 1989), McLuhan invents this term to refer to globalised telecommunication. According to McLuhan, all Western scientific models of communication are linear, sequential, and logical as a reflection of efficient causality. McLuhan thinks speed-of-light technologies could be used to postulate possible futures (globalization). The "global village" (or "international arena") is controlled by those with the most advanced technology. To a great extent, an advanced telecommunication determines the legitimacy of speech, information flow, and in short, global control in this "global village."
18. Water Benjamin points out the nibbling-yet-inconspicuous function of commodity fetishism in his *Arcades Project*. As Susan Buck-Morss interprets his work, the core of the urban phantasmagoria does not necessarily lie on the commodity-on-display in the market, but on the representational value of the commodity. Every desirable thing could be transformed into commodities as fetishes-on-display, which could stimulate the viewers' desires for the commodity even when possession is beyond their abilities. See Susan Buck-Morss, *The Dialectics of Seeing: Walter Benjamin and the Arcades Project*. (Cambridge, Massachusetts: The MIT Press, 1991).
19. See Fiona Lorrain, "Qiu Ju Goes to Court: Relating Cinematic Art to Juridical Reality." *Asian Cinema* 17, no. 2 (Fall/Winter, 2006): 173–81.
20. This is my translation.

Chapter 8

1. Cui Zi'en, "Women bushi yu, women bushi zui, women bushi qu'er" (We are not fish, we are not mouths, we are not queer, 我们不是鱼，我们不是嘴，我们不是酷儿). *Aibai*, January 7, 2004, http://www.aibai.cn/info/open.php?id=8359 (accessed April 14, 2004).
2. See Taiwan Digital Art and Information Center, http://www.digiarts.org.tw/ShowColumnTW.aspx?lang=zh-tw&CC_NO=80 (accessed February 8, 2009). See also Qiu Zhijie, "Xin mieti yishu de chengshu he zouxiang: 1997–2001" (Maturation and Trends in New Media Art

新媒体艺术的成熟和走向： 1997–2001), Qiuzhijie.com (accessed July 1, 2009).

3. Cui, "Women bushi yu."
4. Cui notes that at least ten underground films have been produced with gay and lesbian themes, yet there is no market or forum in which to discuss these works. The filmmakers create alternative venues through organized screenings and DVD and VCD distribution channels, though the latter presents difficulty because of copyright infringement. Cui's 2003 tour of U.S. colleges and international film screenings exemplifies ways in which he seeks a greater audience for his and other Chinese underground filmmakers' works. Cui Zi'en, "NYU I," audio recording at New York University (October 24, 2003).
5. See Inderpal Grewal and Caren Kaplan, "Global Identities: Theorizing Transnational Studies of Sexuality," *GLQ* 7, no. 4 (2001): 671.
6. Mayfair Mei-hui Yang, "From Gender Erasure to Gender Difference: State Feminism, Consumer Sexuality, and Women's Public Sphere in China," in *Spaces of Their Own: Women's Public Sphere in Transnational China*, ed. Mayfair Mei-hui Yang (Minnesota: University of Minnesota Press, 1999), 41.
7. L. H. M. Ling, "Sex Machine: Global Hypermasculinity and Images of the Asian Woman in Modernity," *positions* 7, no. 2 (1999): 277.
8. Sheldon Lu, "Soap Opera in China: The Transnational Politics of Visuality, Sexuality, and Masculinity," *Cinema Journal* 40, no. 1 (Fall 2000): 28–33.
9. Xueping Zhong takes up the question of contemporary Chinese masculinity in crisis in, *Masculinity Besieged? Issues of Modernity and Male Subjectivity in Chinese Literature of the Late Twentieth Century* (Durham, NC: Duke University Press, 2000).
10. See Lisa Rofel's explanation and critique of the "allegory of postsocialism" and the argument that the end of socialism allows people to recover their "natural humanity" in "Qualities of Desire: Imagining Gay Identities in China," *GLQ* 5, no. 4 (1999): 451–74.
11. Ibid., 458.
12. Lisa Rofel (ibid., 454–56) critiques Dennis Altman's assumptions of gay Asian identity within the global gay context.
13. Chris Berry, "Facing Reality: Chinese Documentary, Chinese Postsocialism," in *The First Guangzhou Triennial. Reinterpretation: A Decade of Experimental Chinese Art (1990–2000),* ed. Wu Hung (Guangzhou: Guandong Museum of Art, 2002), 124.
14. Ibid.
15. Lyotard, *Libidinal Economy*, trans. Iain Hamilton Grant (Bloomington, IN: Indiana University Press, 1993).

16. Pan Suiming, "Three 'Red Light Districts' in China," in *Sexual Cultures in East Asia: The Social Construction of Sexuality and Sexual Risk in a Time of AIDS*, ed. Evelyne Micollier (London and New York: RoutledgeCurzon, 2005), 23–53.
17. Gail Hershatter, *Dangerous Pleasures: Prostitution and Modernity in Twentieth-Century Shanghai* (Berkeley: University of California Press, 1997), 368
18. Ibid., 377.
19. See Tze-Lan Sang, *The Emerging Lesbian* (Chicago: University of Chicago Press, 2003), 170. Leo Bersani ("Is the Rectum a Grave?" in *AIDS: Cultural Analysis, Cultural Activism*, ed. Douglas Crimp [Cambridge: MIT Press, 1988], 211) notes a similarity in nineteenth century European discourse on the prostitute and homosexuals since the AIDS crisis began.
20. Cui speaks to the importance of one's social position or status in order to speak about or on behalf of others in his lectures given at the City University of New York in October, 2003 (Cui, "Filtered Voices: Queer Artistic Production in Today's China," audio recording by the Institute of Tongzhi Studies, presented at the City University of New York (CUNY) [October 23, 2003]).
21. Rofel, "Qualities of Desire," 466.
22. Berry notes that the realist style documentaries have sought to grant ordinary people agency. The spontaneous and unscripted styles offer them a direct voice in their representation ("Facing Reality," 124). He quickly points out, however, that the ability to produce such films results from the filmmakers' direct involvement with a mainstream media that concerns itself less with their subjects' agency. See also Paola Vioci's discussion on documentaries in the 1990s and the roles authenticity (*zhenshi*) and reality play, "From the Center to the Periphery: Chinese Documentary's Visual Conjectures," *Modern Chinese Literature and Culture*, 16, no. 1 (Spring 2004), 73, 75.
23. Joan W. Scott, "The Evidence of Experience," in *The Lesbian and Gay Studies Reader*, ed. Henry Abelove, Michele Aina Borale, and David M. Halperin (New York: Routledge, 1993), 399.
24. Sang, *Emerging Lesbian*, 170.
25. Li Yinhe, *Tongxinglian yawenhua* (Homosexual subculture 同性恋亞文化) (Beijing: Zhongguo youyi chubanshe, 2002).
26. This is not unlike Richard Parker's observations on emerging commercial spaces for gay communities in Brazil. See his "Changing Sexualities: Masculinity and Male Homosexuality in Brazil," in *Changing Men and Masculinities in Latin America*, ed. Matthew C. Gutmann (Durham, NC: Duke University Press, 2003), 314.

27. Peter Jackson, "Performative Genders, Perverse Desires: A Bio-History of Thailand's Same-Sex and Transgender Cultures," *Intersections: Gender, History and Culture in the Asian Context* 9 (August 2003), http://intersections.anu.edu.au/issue9/jackson.html (accessed March 8, 2004), paragraph 9.
28. Ibid., paragraphs 39, 49.
29. Ann Anagnost, "The Corporeal Politics of Quality (*Suzhi*)," *Public Culture* 16, no. 2 (2004): 189–208.
30. Ibid., 200.
31. Gary Sigley, "Sex, Politics and the Policing of Virtue in the People's Republic of China," in *Sex and Sexuality in China,* ed. Elaine Jeffreys (New York: Routledge, 2006).
32. Cui, "Filtered Voices."
33. Dennis Altman, "Rupture or Continuity? The Internationalisation of Gay Identities," in *Social Text,* 48, 14, no. 3 (1996): 77–94.
34. Ibid., 79; Rofel, "Qualities of Desire," 453.
35. Altman, "Rupture or Continuity," 83.
36. Chris Berry examines Asian film narratives of sad young gay men and their alienation from the blood family context in "Happy Alone? Sad Young Men in East Asian Gay Cinema," in *Queer Asian Cinema: Shadows in the Shade,* ed. Andrew Grossman (New York: Harrington Park Press, 2000), 192–93.
37. Chris Berry, "Sexual DisOrientations: Homosexual Rights, East Asian Films, and Postmodern Nationalism," in *Pursuit of Contemporary East Asian Culture,* ed. Xiaobing Tang and Stephen Snyder (Boulder, CO: Westview Press, 1996); Sang Tze-lan, *Emerging Lesbian.*
38. Berry, "Sexual DisOrientations," 167.
39. Berry, "Happy Alone?" 198.
40. Ibid., 192–93.
41. Lyotard, *Libidinal Economy,* 83.
42. Homosexuality was declassified as a mental illness by the Chinese Psychiatrists' Association in 2000. While not a crime, it is still equated with hooliganism and other socially undesirable behaviors.
43. See Rofel's extended discussion in "Qualities of Desire."
44. It is beyond the subject of this paper to discuss the racial hierarchization involved in the concept of a transnational gay identity. Rofel critiques Altman in her essay for his implicit valorization of Western society. In a separate, yet parallel critique, the Asian Canadian experimental and documentary filmmaker Richard Fung critiques the racial hierarchies in Asian representations in Western gay pornography videos that position gay Asians as "bottoms" (Fung, "Looking for my Penis: The Eroticized Asian in Gay Video Porn," in *Q & A: Queer*

in Asian America, ed. David L. Eng and Alice Y. Hom. [Philadelphia: Temple University Press, 1998]). See also Nguyen Tan Hoang's "The Resurrection of Brandon Lee: The Making of a Gay Asian American Porn Star," in *Porn Studies,* ed. Linda Williams (Durham, NC: Duke University Press, 2004).

45. Li Yinhe observes that some cohabitating gay couples refer to their living arrangement as a "real marriage," hence perpetuating the notion of husband and wife and its constitutive realities (286). Rofel remarks that the gay community in China considers "money boys" (male prostitutes) to be problematic to gay urban life (466).
46. Gay bars and nightclubs have been called "sex markets" and also "fish markets" in Chinese. Li Yinhe attributes the latter term's genesis to Hong Kong. The nightclub owner must have been conversant with the term when designing and naming it. When talking about public toilets, parks, and other public spaces, Li Yinhe also uses the term "fish market."
47. Li, *Tongxinglian yawenhua,* 273.
48. Cui, "Filtered Voices."
49. Quoted in Li, *Tongxinglian yawenhua,* 283.
50. Cui remarks that many homosexuals often speak of their minority status along the lines of China's official discourse on its ethnic minorities. He points out how this discourse puts the minority group in a position of weakness and in need of the majority's recognition (hence legitimacy) and care ("Filtered Voices").
51. Scott, "Evidence of Experience," 400.
52. David M. Halperin, "How to Do the History of Male Homosexuality," *GLQ* 6, no. 1 (2000), 112–13.
53. See John D'Emilio's discussion in "Capitalism and Gay Identity," in Abelove, Aina Barale, and Halperin, *Lesbian and Gay Studies Reader,* 469.
54. Ibid., 473.
55. Rofel, "Qualities of Desire," 463.
56. Danae Clark, "Commodity Lesbianism," in Abelove, Aina Barale, and Halperin, *Lesbian and Gay Studies Reader,* 195.
57. Cui, "Filtered Voices."
58. Cui Zi'en, "NYU I."
59. Cui, "Filtered Voices."

Chapter 9

An earlier version of this essay appeared as "Couching Race in the Global Era: Intra-Asian Racism in *Crouching Tiger, Hidden Dragon,*" *Journal of*

Modern Literature in Chinese [現代中文文學學報], special issue, "Center and Periphery in Modern Chinese Literature and Culture" [專號: 中心與邊緣], vol. 10, no. 1 (Summer 2010): 16–44; reprinted with permission.

1. Ang Lee's deliberate orientalizing of old China begins with the title itself. "Crouching Tiger Hidden Dragon" 臥虎藏龍 at first glance appears to be an ancient aphorism. However, this particular arrangement of these four characters is apparently a modern construction, borrowed for the movie from the book title (the fourth entry in Wang Dulu's 王度廬 "Crane-Iron Pentalogy" 鶴鐵五部曲, an acronym for "Crane Precious Sword Crouching Iron Pentalogy" 《鶴驚崑崙》、《寶劍金釵》、《劍氣珠光》、《臥虎藏龍》、《鐵騎銀瓶》). "Crouching tiger" 臥虎 is traditionally used to describe an awe-inspiring government official, often used pejoratively, referring to an administrator who is an extremely severe enforcer of the law, a cruel, excessively violent person, or a fierce warrior. The oldest combination of any two of the four characters in the title is "crouching *dragon*" 臥龍. It refers to a sleeping dragon and, by extension, to a person of exceptional abilities (namely, a benevolent martial/intellectual genius) who remains in hermitage, undiscovered. The earliest applications of this combination are in references to Zhuge Liang 諸葛亮, 184–234 A.D., a.k.a. Kongming 孔明 and "Mr. Crouching Dragon" 臥龍先生, famous general of the early Three Kingdoms era (220–265 C.E.). There is also a Northern Zhou Dynasty (6 Dynasties era) poem by Yu Xin 庾信 (513–581 C.E.) in which "藏虎" and "臥龍" are used to describe rocks and tree roots in the surrounding landscape. When glossed in reference works at all, the combination of the four characters comprising the title is described in dictionaries and compendiums of aphorisms as referring to "a person of rare talents," "undiscovered person[s] of exceptional abilities," "a collection of men of remarkable talents," or "person[s] of outstanding talent, hero[es]." Many dictionaries do not list the aphorism, and in none of them is a primary ancient textual source for the aphorism given, indicating its historically recent origins.
2. See Su Tuo-Yu, Jang Hyun Kim, and Junhao Hong, "A Socio-Cultural Study of the Growing Popularity of Pan-Chinese Movies in the U.S.: Trends, Contributing Factors, and Implications," *Asian Cinema* 18, no. 1 (Spring–Summer 2007): 66, 86–87. Despite its financial success and numerous awards, there has been some nitpicking concerning the popularity of the film in Asia, largely owing to its poor showing at the PRC box office. See Henry Chu, "'Crouching Tiger' Can't Hide from Bad Reviews in China," *Los Angeles Times* (January 29, 2001): A1; James Schamus, "Letter to the Editor: 'Tiger' scribe Schamus responds

to article," *Variety* (Feb. 11, 2001), http://www.variety.com/article/VR1117793505.html?categoryid=9&cs=1 (accessed July 2, 2007); Derek Elley, "Asia to 'Tiger': Kung-fooey: 'Hidden' draggin' at the Orient B.O. Despite Breaking Records in U.K," *Variety* (Feb. 7, 2001), http://www.variety.com/article/VR1117793505.html?categoryid=9&cs=1 (accessed July 2, 2007); Mark Landler, "Lee's 'Tiger,' Celebrated Everywhere But in China," *New York Times* (Feb. 27, 2001): E1; Jessica Tan, "Gongfu Not Good Enough?" *Straits Times* (Singapore) (Feb. 12, 2001): L10; and others address the issue from many different perspectives.

3. Sheldon H. Lu defines *transnational cinema* "as an emergent mode of filmmaking [that] implies the trespassing of national borders in the processes of investment, production, circulation, and consumption." See Sheldon H. Lu, "Crouching Tiger, Hidden Dragon, Bouncing Angels: Hollywood, Taiwan, Hong Kong, and Transnational Cinema," in *Chinese-Language Film: Historiography, Poetics, Politics,* ed. Sheldon H. Lu and Emilie Yueh-Yu Yeh (Honolulu: University of Hawai'i Press, 2005), 221.
4. See Schamus for a concise discussion of creating this "global film" and a history of the film's multinational financing and production in his "The Polyglot Task of Writing the Global Film," *New York Times,* Arts and Leisure (Nov. 5, 2000): 25; see also Lee, Ang, et. al., eds., *Crouching Tiger, Hidden Dragon: A Portrait of the Ang Lee Film* (New York: Newmarket Press, 2000); "The Guardian/NFT Interview: Ang Lee and James Schamus," *Guardian Unlimited* (Nov. 7, 2000), http://film.guardian.co.uk/interview/interviewpages/0,6737,394676,00.html#early (accessed July 5, 2007); and, Oriental Films, "'Crouching Tiger Hidden Dragon: An Interview with Ang Lee and James Schamus," (2001), http://www.orientalfilms.co.uk/newfilms/crouchingtiger/cthdconversation. htm (accessed Jul. 17, 2007) for detailed production notes, including short biographies of many cast and crew. While acknowledging Ang Lee's Taiwanese roots and New York residency of several decades, this essay will treat *CTHD* as both a transnational production and a Chinese-language film. Although Lee is a diasporic (New York based) Chinese filmmaker from Taiwan, he identifies himself as a "Chinese filmmaker" (Michael Berry, "Ang Lee: Freedom in Film," in *Speaking in Images: Interviews with Contemporary Chinese Filmmakers,* ed. Michael Berry [New York: Columbia University Press, 2005], 352), and has clearly stated that *CTHD* is an attempt to provide a worldwide audience with a vision of his own "dream of China, a China that never existed, except in my boyhood fantasies" (Linda Sunshine, ed., *Crouching Tiger, Hidden Dragon: Portrait of the Ang Lee Film* [New York: Newmarket Press, 2000], 7). Yeh and Davis aver "as far as its capital

was concerned, this is indeed a Chinese project.... All the financial risk on this film was borne by Ang Lee, Xu Ligong...and Bill Kong" (Emilie Yueh-Yu Yeh and Darrel William Davis, *Taiwan Film Directors: A Treasure Island* [Columbia University Press, 2005], 189). For a detailed treatment of Lee's diasporic status as a key element of his filmmaking, see Christina Klein, "*Crouching Tiger, Hidden Dragon*: A Diasporic Reading," *Cinema Journal* 43, no. 4 (2004): 18.

5. Expanding on the definitions of Kenneth Chan and others (see Kenneth Chan, "The Global Return of the *Wu Xia Pian* (Chinese Sword-Fighting Movie): Ang Lee's *Crouching Tiger, Hidden Dragon*," *Cinema Journal* 43, no. 4 [2004]: 14, n4), and echoing elements of Tu Wei-ming's notion of "cultural China," when I refer to the "Chinese" involved in both the production and reception of the film, I am using the term quite generally to include Chinese in the PRC, Taiwan, Hong Kong, Singapore, and in the diaspora. In doing so, I also draw on the arguments of Rey Chow, who states that "the term 'Chinese'" be inclusive of people from the PRC as well as "the populations of Hong Kong, Taiwan, and other diasporic Chinese communities...[whose] claims to being Chinese—in numerous historical and linguistic connections...must also...be granted their legitimacy." See Rey Chow, *Sentimental Fabulations, Contemporary Chinese Films: Attachment in the Age of Global Visibility* (New York: Columbia University Press, 2007), 24.
6. For some of the historical antecedents of these terms and phenomena, see Prasenjit Duara's discussion of (Levenson's analysis of) "culturalism," nationalism, and "culture protected by the state (politicization of culture)." See Prasenjit Duara, *Rescuing History from the Nation: Questioning Narratives of Modern China* (Chicago: University of Chicago Press, 1995), 56.
7. Ibid., 149.
8. My essay is a contribution and reply to the extant scholarship on the film, not a rejoinder. Among many scholarly treatments cited throughout, I am responding to Hsiao-hung Chang's compelling argument that *CTHD*'s "transnational reception itself poses new challenging questions to the current discourse on globalization and asks for a radically new theorization of body imagination and power deployment." See Chang Hsiao-hung, "The Unbearable Lightness of Globalization: On the Transnational Flight of *Wuxia* Film," in *Cinema Taiwan: Politics, Popularity and the State of the Arts,* ed. Darrel William Davis and Ru-shou Robert Chen (London: Routledge, 2007), 105. I draw upon many other insightful analyses of the film below, where pertinent to stages and terms in my argument.

9. I shall be using "race" and "ethnicity" somewhat interchangeably throughout this essay, to refer to "perceived" physical, biological, or "attendant sociocultural differences" (Duara, *Rescuing History from the Nation*, 21, n2). See also Duara's discussion of the notion, established by Sun Yat-sen and others, that the "Han nation…was the world's most perfectly formed nation because the people were bound together by all five of the criteria that it took to form a nation: blood/race, language, custom, religion, and livelihood" (32).
10. Fan Di'an, "Synthi-scapes," exhibition catalogue for the 50th Venice Biennale 2003, http://www.gdmoa.org/english/exhibitions/50venice/fandian.htm (accessed Aug. 2004).
11. "The Guardian/NFT Interview: Ang Lee and James Schamus," *Guardian Unlimited* (Nov. 7, 2000).
12. Chris Berry and Mary Farquhar, *China on Screen: Cinema and Nation* (New York: Columbia University Press, 2006), 11.
13. I will use the terms "global," "transnational," "global/transnational capitalism," etc. interchangeably throughout, in reference to the general underlying conditions of life on the planet, which are now by and large determined and driven by the imperative of capitalism to gain hegemony over every social formation and interaction, seducing or coercing all peoples and places to ascribe to the laws and demands of the profit motive and ceaseless acquisitiveness, unimpeded by geographical, national, local, or personal boundaries. This holds true in greater China, Asia, and America, regardless of recent upsurges in nationalism or cultural nationalism (in places like America and the PRC, for example). For more on globalization and (Chinese) culture, see Liu's book-length study: *Globalization and Cultural Trends in China* (Honolulu: University of Hawai'i Press, 2004); Emily Davis for a concise, nuanced definition of globalization in her "The Intimacies of Globalization: Bodies and Borders On-Screen," *Camera Obscura* 21, no. 2 62 (2006): 34–37; and Eqbal Ahmad for an analysis of the ways that globalization creates barriers and inequalities rather than smooth flows and broader distributions of people and wealth: "Knowledge, Place, and Power: A Critique of Globalization," in *Localizing Knowledge in a Globalizing World: Recasting the Area Studies Debate*, ed. Ali Mirsepassi, Amrita Basu, and Frederic Weaver (Syracuse, New York: Syracuse University Press, 2003), 216–29.
14. Arif Dirlik notes the ways that global culture can buttress cultural nationalism: "The culture industry…contributes in the name of globalization to the reification of national traditions, which are commodified and relayed back to the people who claim them, further sharpening boundaries between such traditions." See Arif Dirlik,

"Culture against History? The Politics of East Asian Identity," in Mirsepassi, Basu, and Weaver, *Localizing Knowledge*, 199.

15. Shih Shu-mei, "Global Literature and the Technologies of Recognition," *Publications of the Modern Language Association of America* 119, no. 1 (2004): 21, 29, 28; emphasis added.
16. Ibid., 21. Shih unabashedly uses the term "Third World" in her recent work, where it stands for Chinese and other global "minorities" in this era of [unequal] globalization. I would qualify Shih's formulation with Shiao-ying Shen's argument that, where transnational film production, marketing, and spectatorship are concerned, "there is actually not much difference between the East and the West today… Hollywood has already successfully interpellated the global film-viewing subject—shaping the film-viewing habit of audiences around the world" (cited in Lim Song Hwee, *Celluloid Comrades: Representations of Male Homosexuality in Contemporary Chinese Cinemas* [Honolulu: University of Hawai'i Press, 2006], 22). Indeed, the global audience for Chinese films now includes significant numbers of both Western and Chinese viewers, as evidenced in films such as *CTHD*, *Ying Xiong* 英雄 [*Hero*] (dir. Zhang Yimou 張藝謀, 2002), *Shi mian mai fu* 十面埋伏 [*House of the Flying Daggers*] (dir. Zhang Yimou, 2004), *Huo Yuan Jia* 霍元甲 [*Fearless*] (dir. Ronny Yu, 2006), and *Kungfu* 功夫 [*Kungfu Hustle*] (dir. Stephen Chow, 2004).
17. Sheldon H. Lu witheringly remarks, "Paradoxically, the nonexistent imaginary old China as admittedly invented by [Ang] Lee is a dehistoricized, disembedded entity in the global commercial film market… China in Lee's film has become a shallow fantasy world, a wishful thinking, a stage for global entertainment. The seeming return to history and resort to national culture is a décor, a show, a contemporary spectacle." See Lu, "Crouching Tiger, Hidden Dragon, Bouncing Angels," 231.
18. Ibid.
19. Berry and Farquhar, *China on Screen*, 69.
20. Lo Kwai-cheung similarly argues that some Chinese ("mainly Hong Kong") popular films help to "constitut[e] an ethnic identity for diasporic Chinese communities and a distinct otherness for the western gaze." See Lo Kwai-Cheung, "There is No Such Thing as Asia: Racial Particularities in the 'Asian' Films of Hong Kong and Japan," *Modern Chinese Literature and Culture* 17, no. 1 (Spring 2005): 136. Ang Lee himself was concerned that he might be doing a disservice to the Chinese martial arts genre if "lao wei" 老外 (foreigners) were to perceive *CTHD* as a "B Movie." See Hsieh Tsai-miao, *Xunzhao qingmingjian: Cong "Wohu canglong" tan huayu diangying guojihua* 尋

找青冥劍：從《臥虎藏龍》談華語電影國際化 [*Searching for the Green Destiny: Crouching Tiger, Hidden Dragon and the Internationalization of Chinese-language Cinema*] (Taipei: Yatai Tushu, 2004). Also see Kenneth Chan for a thoughtful discussion of some Chinese viewers' negative reactions to the film, and "what it means to be Chinese in the context of the Asian 'invasion' of Hollywood" ("Global Return of the *Wu Xia Pian*," 4). Chan observes that some Chinese viewers critical of the film react to it from a "nationalist/anti-Orientalist" mindset, revealing a "cultural anxiety about identity and Chineseness in a globalized, postcolonial, and postmodern world order" (3–4).

21. See Shih Shu-Mei, "Globalisation and Minoritisation: Ang Lee and the Politics of Flexibility," *New Formations* 40 (2000): 86–101 for her insightful analysis of Ang Lee's consistent cinematic conservatism and its relationship to Chinese audience needs. Kenneth Chan also foregrounds some of Lee's patriarchal predilections in *CTHD* (Chan, "Global Return of the *Wu Xia Pian*," 10–14).
22. On spectatorship, see Lim for a discussion of Hollywood's successful interpellation of "the global film-viewing subject" (*Celluloid Comrades*, 22).
23. See Yu Sen-lun, "A Director's Dream," *Taipei Times* (Jul. 2, 2000), http://www.taipeitimes.com/News/feat/archives/2000/07/02/42294, 17 (accessed Jul. 18, 2007). Where only ten years ago, Hamid Naficy examined the (then-dominant) trend in which exilic "Third World" transnational filmmakers worked predominantly "outside the studio systems and the mainstream film industries of the host countries," and produced largely dystopic visions of their home cultures in confrontation with the forces of globalization, with Ang Lee's *CTHD* we confront the appropriation of emigré filmmakers by Hollywood, transnational marketing and production systems, and even cooptation of the filmmaker in producing "authentic" "national" film for the global market. See Hamid Naficy, "Phobic Spaces and Liminal Panics: Independent Transnational Film Genre," in *Multiculturalism, Postcoloniality, and Transnational Media,* ed. Ella Shohat and Robert Stam (Rutgers: Rutgers University Press, 2003), 204–5; 202–26. Sheldon H. Lu, citing another essay by Naficy, makes an argument similar to the current one, noting that "*Crouching Tiger, Hidden Dragon* allows us to reexamine the nature of a new type of film culture from the Third World," one which lacks "the pathos of displacement, alienation, homelessness, and quest" ("Crouching Tiger, Hidden Dragon, Bouncing Angels," 222–23).
24. Fran Martin, "The China Simulacrum: Genre, Feminism, and Pan-Chinese Cultural Politics in *Crouching Tiger, Hidden Dragon*," in *Island*

on the Edge: Taiwan New Cinema and After, ed. Chris Berry and Lu Feii (Hong Kong: Hong Kong University Press, 2005), 158.

25. Chan, "Global Return of the *Wu Xia Pian*," 6.
26. Although my effort here is to bring to light a rather unfortunate—and, I gather, unintentional—aspect of this film, I nonetheless must nod my head in agreement with Fran Martin's argument about the multicoded meanings of *CTHD* and other films, where she states, "in the era of cultural globalization, films that aim to be accessible and appealing to multiple, distinct audiences may more or less intentionally encode multiple possible interpretations at the moment of production; interpretations that can then be picked up selectively by differently positioned audiences." See Fran Martin, "Taiwan (Trans)national Cinema: The Far-flung Adventures of a Taiwanese Tomboy," in Davis and Chen, *Cinema Taiwan*, 141. I also feel redeemed in pursuing this angle by James Schamus's generous, erudite, and remarkably candid response to two academic interpretations of the film. Schamus not only challenges all interpretations of the film to ask: "[I]f the idea of Chineseness [in *CTHD*] is centralizing, what is its own center? Is it 'official' Han nationality, proprietary Manchu power, or a multiethnic gathering of the Chinese *minzu*, the 'people'?" He even goes so far as to pronounce it a "more than dubious" "fantasy" for anyone to aver that *CTHD* "is so politically correct that it has somehow miraculously escaped any deep trafficking with the powers that be," and avoided "hidden complicities with hegemonic social orders" (James Schamus, "Aesthetic Identities: A Response to Kenneth Chan and Christina Klein," *Cinema Journal* 43, no. 4 [Summer 2004]: 45, 47).
27. Todd McGowan argues that all films "internally posit their own spectators," the main "task of interpretation" being to locate the response that this positing demands. See Todd McGowan, *The Impossible David Lynch* (New York: Columbia University Press, 2007), 23. The spectator posited by *Crouching Tiger, Hidden Dragon* is one who will subliminally consume the film's validation of an essentialistic Han ethnicity and debasement of non-Han minorities, and the response demanded is this essay's exposure of the film's racialized subtext.
28. For Best Foreign Film, Best Cinematography, Best Original Score, and Best Art Direction; the film also garnered 6 other nominations that it did not win, including Best Film and Best Director. It is the first Asian film ever nominated for best picture.
29. For a cornucopia of facts and statistics on the film, in addition to Lu, "Crouching Tiger, Hidden Dragon, Bouncing Angels," see Martin, "China Simulacrum," 149–59; Jennifer W. Jay, "'Crouching Tiger Hidden Dragon': (Re)packaging Chinas and Selling the Hybridized

Culture and Identity in an Age of Globalization," in *Reading Chinese Transnationalisms: Society, Literature, Film,* ed. Maria N. Ng and Philip Holden (Hong Kong: Hong Kong University Press, 2006), 131–42; Felicia Chan, "*Crouching Tiger, Hidden Dragon*: Cultural Migrancy and Translatability," in *Chinese Films in Focus: 25 New Takes,* ed. Chris Berry (London: British Film Institute, 2003), 56–64; Sunshine, ed., *Crouching Tiger, Hidden Dragon: Portrait of the Ang Lee Film.*

30. Lu, "Crouching Tiger, Hidden Dragon, Bouncing Angels," 231. Lu notes "the politics of labeling, naming, and categorizing [this film] becomes messy and murky," owing to the unprecedented nature of this film as "a classic example of *global cinema* in the age of globalization." (221–22).
31. See Lu for a brief discussion and survey of the literature surrounding the contested degree of success the film had (or didn't) with Chinese-speaking audiences in Asia ("Crouching Tiger, Hidden Dragon, Bouncing Angels," 227, 232n9, and passim). See also Emilie Yueh-yu Yeh's response to the negative reception of the film, where she foregrounds its overlooked *wenyi* elements, including "the interior, feminine, and the Confucian." See Emilie Yueh-yu Yeh, "The Road Home: Stylistic Renovations of Chinese Mandarin Classics," in Davis and Chen, *Cinema Taiwan,* 204. Berry and Farquhar discuss *Wen* 文 together with *Wu* 武, drawing on the work of Kam Louie (*China on Screen,* 140–43; 200).
32. The film was nominated for 16 and won eight awards at the 20th Hong Kong Film awards in 2001.
33. Lu, "Crouching Tiger, Hidden Dragon, Bouncing Angels," 220.
34. See Du Minghua, "Glory of 'Crouching Tiger' Belongs to All Chinese: Ang Lee," *People's Daily* English online version (Mar. 28, 2001), http://english.peopledaily.com.cn/English/200103/28/eng20010328_66220.html (accessed Jul. 17, 2007). Cinematographer Peter Pau, in his Oscar speech, also declared the honor that the film brought to himself, "the people of Hong Kong and to Chinese people all over the world." See "'Crouching Tiger' Wins Third Award," *People's Daily* English online version (Mar. 26, 2001), http://english.peopledaily.com.cn/english/200103/26/eng20010326_65997.html (accessed Jul. 17, 2007). For more glowing praise of the film in a journal marketed to a global Chinese readership, see Wu Qixing, "Zhonghua minzhu de yishu jiejing" 中華民族的藝術結晶 ["Chinese People's Art Produces a Gem"], *Asiaweek* 亞洲週刊 (Apr. 2–8, 2001): 34; Wu Qixing, and Wang Yunyi, "Wohu zanglong zhan qi lai le" 臥虎藏龍站起來了 ["Crouching Tiger Hidden Dragon Stands Up"], *Asiaweek* 亞洲週刊 (Apr. 2–8, 2001): 30–33.
35. Cited in Chan, "*Crouching Tiger, Hidden Dragon*: Cultural Migrancy

and Translatability," 58. These and other instances of cultural pride in the film confirm its substantial contribution to pan-Chinese cultural nationalism and Jameson's notion of "neo-ethnicity." See Frederic Jameson, *The Geopolitical Aesthetic: Cinema and Space in the World System* (Bloomington: Indiana University Press, 1992), 117.

36. Martin, "China Simulacrum," 151.
37. Chan, "*Crouching Tiger, Hidden Dragon*: Cultural Migrancy and Translatability," 58.
38. For numerous quotations and a contextualization of these and other accolades heaped upon *CTHD*, see ibid.
39. Cited in Berry (*Speaking in Images,* 343) and Chute ("Year of the Dragon," *Premier* [December 2000]: 77).
40. Sunshine, ed., *Crouching Tiger, Hidden Dragon: Portrait of the Ang Lee Film,* 42.
41. Lu, "Crouching Tiger, Hidden Dragon, Bouncing Angels," 230–31.
42. See Lim for a more sanguine view of Ang Lee's cinematic corpus and cinema as a "socially discursive act in itself," and the ways that "minority groups and mainstream culture" interact and mutually affect one another in cross-cultural and inter-cultural cinematic representations (*Celluloid Comrades,* 66–68). Significantly, *CTHD* is absent from the list of Ang Lee films that Lim cites over the course of his argument.
43. There is arguably also the implication that the Han in this film are the repository of all the physical vigor, "inner strength," ethics, morality, spirituality, and civility the West has left behind in its crass rush into the industrial age, modernity, now post-industrialism, and now neo-imperialism.
44. Emerson famously wrote, "But China, reverend dullness! hoary ideot!, all she can say at the convocation of nations must be—'I made the tea'" (1824). See Ralph Waldo Emerson, *Journal & Miscellaneous Notebooks,* entry dated 1824, cited in Paul Cohen, *China Unbound: Evolving Perspectives on the Chinese Past* (London: RoutledgeCurzon, 2003), 49.
45. At the risk of complicating my own argument, I would here add that, in the global orientalist imaginary, Tibet (since at least 1937, when *Lost Horizon* [dir. Frank Capra] was released) holds the status of noblest Other to the modern West. Perhaps this is one of the subtle but insidious allegorical associations that transnational viewers of *CTHD* are encouraged to make, to see the Han in the film as the new image of Asian spiritual authority and magnanimity, thereby undermining Tibet's exclusive claim to the same. As stated earlier (see note 26), I do not believe that this is the result of a *conscious* or deliberate representational strategy on the part of the director or

scriptwriters. Rather, it is indicative of the kind of multicoding of films with numerous potential interpretations that occurs "in the era of cultural globalization." (Martin, "Taiwan (Trans)national Cinema," 141). See also Ulf Hedetoft's teasing out of the factors at work in "the push-and-pull dialectic between national identities and cultural globalization…forms of tension between its [contemporary cinema's] transnational forms of production, dissemination, and (sometimes) contents, and its routinely national modes of reception, decoding and interpretation, based on national identities, cultural history, and aesthetic traditions." See Hedetoft, "Contemporary Cinema: Between Cultural Globalization and National Interpretation," in *Cinema and Nation*, ed. Mette Hjort and Scott MacKenzie (London: Routledge, 2000), 278–79.

46. This dynamic partakes only partially of some common paradigms in Qing chivalric fiction, where the "co-optation of roving knights by the political establishment is a common occurrence…. Especially in the hybrid genre, chivalric-tales-cum-detective-stories (*xiayi gongan xiaoshuo* 俠義公案小說), [where] fearless heroes cooperate with an upright official to eliminate criminals and uphold the status quo, instead of defying imperial rule" (Tze-Lan Deborah Sang, unpublished manuscript).
47. Or some version of indigenous Chinese spirituality and martial ethics gone awry, e.g., the evil Daoist, Lamaist, and Buddhist individuals/sects who have betrayed their culture and turned ancient Chinese physical, mental, and spiritual training to evil ends.
48. Viewer's association with the racially superior Han heroes might be the true "*choice* of identificatory points of view," "cross-identi[fication]," and "*allo-identification*…with an image of an 'other'" offered by the film, as interpreted by Martin in "China Simulacrum," 153–54, and passim.
49. Around 55 ethnic minorities are officially recognized by the PRC government. The Han, at around 91% of the total population, are the vast majority. Two of these minorities are prominently featured in the film: the Manchu and the minorities of Turkestan 新疆. The latter are a mostly Islamic population residing atop China's largest reservoirs of fossil fuel reserves, and who arguably represent the greatest contemporary racial threat to domestic socioeconomic stability. For analyses of discourse and politics of race, ethnicity, and identity in China, see Wu David Yen-ho, "The Construction of Chinese and Non-Chinese Identities," in *China Off Center: Mapping the Margins of the Middle Kingdom*, ed. Susan D. Blum and Lionel M. Jensen (Honolulu: University of Hawai'i Press, 2002), 167–82; Frank Dikötter, *The*

Discourse of Race in Modern China (Stanford: Stanford University Press, 1992); Anne Csete, "China's Ethnicities: State Ideology and Policy in Historical Perspective," in *Global Multiculturalism: Comparative Perspectives on Ethnicity, Race and Nation,* ed. Grant Cornwell and Eve Stoddard (Lanham: Rowman and Littlefield, 2000), 287–307; Dru C. Gladney, *Dislocating China: Muslims, Minorities, and Other Subaltern Subjects* (Chicago: University of Chicago Press, 2004); Pamela Kyle Crossley, *A Translucent Mirror: History and Identity in Qing Imperial Ideology* (Berkeley: University of California Press, 2000); Pamela Kyle Crossley et. al., eds., *Empire at the Margins: Culture Ethnicity, and Frontier in Early Modern China* (Berkeley: University of California Press, 2006); Gang Zhao, "Reinventing *China*: Imperial Qing Ideology and the Rise of Modern Chinese National Identity in the Early Twentieth Century," *Modern China* 32, no. 1 (2006): 3–30. See also essays in Eric P. Kaufmann, *Rethinking Ethnicity: Majority Groups and Dominant Minorities* (London: Routledge, 2004). For analyses of the largely exoticizing representation of ethnic minorities in Chinese films, see Paul Clark, "Ethnic Minorities in Chinese Films: Cinema and the Exotic," *East-West Film Journal* 1, no. 2 (Jun. 1987): 15–31; Chris Berry, "'Race' ([min] [zu]): Chinese Film and the Politics of Nationalism." *Cinema Journal* 31, no. 2 (Winter 1992): 45–58; and Zhang Yingjin, "From 'Minority Film' to 'Minority Discourse': Questions of Nationhood and Ethnicity in Chinese Cinema," *Cinema Journal* 31, no. 2 (Winter 1992): 73–90.

50. Shih coins this term to refer to the ways that the "minoritised" must package "the presentation of local national culture" in order for it to be readily understood and consumed by a "non-local audience." See Shih, "Globalisation and Minoritisation," 100. Jay views this process from an opposite perspective, arguing that a "transnational" film like *CTHD* "despite being Westernized and hybridized, retains its Chinese identity and culture in the eyes of the global film audience." See Jay, "'Crouching Tiger Hidden Dragon': (Re)packaging Chinas," 142.
51. Kenneth Chan is one author who has paid significant attention to the representations of race in the film, which he condenses under "the binary logic of [the] social responsibility [Han characters] versus personal freedom [non-Han characters]" (Chan, "Global Return of the *Wu Xia Pian*," 9). Contra the current reading, Chan perceptively finds political implications in this binarism, linking the representation of non-Han minorities in the film to Ang Lee's perceived and salutary attempt to "unpack[s] Han hegemony in his formulation of a Chinese national imaginary," which also "provides a political metaphor for the Chinese government's role in the marginalization and oppression

of recalcitrant ethnic minorities and territorial enclaves" as well as "a trope for the conflict the Taiwanese people face in confronting the larger national issue of Taiwan's political reunification with mainland China." Ibid., 10. Emilie Yueh-yu Yeh has likewise perceived a binarism in the representation of the two couples, which she interprets not racially, but as Ang Lee's effort to "contain these problems by juxtaposing *wenyi* [文藝] and *wuxia* [武俠] and creating a tight synergy of these two styles" ("Road Home," 204). Yeh and Davis discuss the organization of characters along "binaries" and the consequent "binarization and structural simplicity" of the film, but do not list race/ethnicity among the "themes" these simple binaries are designed to convey to a "world audience" (Yeh and Davis, *Taiwan Film Directors: A Treasure Island,* 197). Jay finds the film to represent an "inclusionist China of blurred ethnicities." See Jay, "'Crouching Tiger Hidden Dragon': (Re)packaging Chinas," 136.

52. Ironically, a notable feature in *CTHD* and numerous other martial arts films is, for lack of a better term, the "Ah-Q postcolonialism" that is manifested in the representation of the Manchu colonization as a triumphal era of Han ethnicity and culture (and in related phenomena, such as cinematic treatments of the Opium War or the 2006 PRC celebrations of Genghis Khan as a Chinese hero).

53. See Oriental Films, "'Crouching Tiger Hidden Dragon: An Interview with Ang Lee and James Schamus." "*Jianghu* 江湖 encompasses an abstract community within the Chinese literary tradition that is ruled not by state legislation but by moral principle and decorum.... Its members are not above the state laws, but are accorded the moral authority to reject the implementation of those law should they serve corrupt ends. *Crouching Tiger* is sustained by the tension between the various characters and their varying abilities to adhere to *jianghu* principles." See Chan, "*Crouching Tiger, Hidden Dragon*: Cultural Migrancy and Translatability," 59. In the diegetic, the emphasis on Confucian "moral principle and decorum" across civil society and the *jianghu* world is in no way counterbalanced by a Buddhist ethic or "Taoist sensibility" (Lu, "Crouching Tiger, Hidden Dragon, Bouncing Angels," 225) associated with the Wudan or other martial arts schools (Jay, "'Crouching Tiger Hidden Dragon': (Re)packaging Chinas," 137). In fact, it is implied that the non-Han female characters' (Jade-eyed Fox and Yu Jialong玉嬌龍) ignorance and impulsive and selfish violations of (patriarchal) Confucian mores and civil laws and the Han ethical codes of the *jianghu* are precisely what keeps them from mastering the Wudan style. See Chow Kenny Ka-nin, "Hong Kong Animation: The Uncanny Brush in *Wuxia* film," *Asian Cinema* 18, no.

1 (Spring-Summer 2007): 138–49 for a recent concise history of the term *wuxia*. From a more syncretic perspective, one might say that Li Mubai's combination of Confucian/Jianghu ethics and Chinese Taoist "stillness" and mysticism further elevates him above both the non-Han characters and Xiulian.

54. Chan avers, "Each character has a social role to play within this world, and the gender relations depicted in the film are but part of this larger framework. There is no direct evidence of male oppression in the film other than the one we are primed to expect from the period setting of ancient China" ("*Crouching Tiger, Hidden Dragon*: Cultural Migrancy and Translatability," 61). While I find the film quite conservative where gender is concerned, I do not have space in the present essay to address this issue in detail.
55. Zhang Ziyi's 章子怡 character is named Yu Jiaolong, but in the film's subtitles and in the Chinese text of the published script (with a foreword by Ang Lee), the English transcription of her name is given as "Jen"; likewise, Michelle Yeoh's 楊紫瓊 character is named Yu Xiulian while the English transcription of her name is given as "Yu Shu Lien." Following Martin in "China Simulacrum" and others, one may use these English transcriptions from the script when referring to the characters. A further possible linguistic coding in the names of these characters: a very selective—and therefore tenuous—lexicographic comparison reveals that Jen's surname is homophonous with the word *yù* 慾 "desire, passion; lust; greed" while Xiulian's surname is homophonous with (and written quite similarly to) yǘ 瑜 "fine and flawless jade or gemstone; virtues; excellences." Furthermore, Jiaolong is literally "spoiled/pampered dragon."
56. Jay, "'Crouching Tiger Hidden Dragon': (Re)packaging Chinas," 135.
57. Liu Taibao 劉泰保, aka "Bo" in the subtitles, played by Gao Xi'an 高西安, has just asked police inspector Tsai Jiu 蔡九 played by Wang Deming王德明 if Jade-eyed-Fox is a "male or female animal/bitch" ("這碧眼狐狸是公的還是母的？").
58. Granted, some of the ragtag bunch of Han martial artists who confront Jen in the teahouse have animal names as well, but they are still shown to follow—or at least profess to follow—the *jianghu* codes of chivalry and propriety, and it is Jen (Yu Jiaolong) who insults, boasts, threatens, then attacks them.
59. The conservative treatment of the youthful and impetuous minority characters is not present in Wang Dulu's original series of novels, according to Tze-Lan Deborah Sang. Sang's study of gender and ethnic identities in Wang Dulu's series reveals "no flagrant biases against the Manchus or the Mongols" (personal correspondence).

Ang Lee acknowledges "completely changing portions of the novel" for the screenplay, of which he wrote half (Berry, "Ang Lee: Freedom in Film," 340). Interestingly, a 2000 revision of the novel, also titled *Crouching Tiger Hidden Dragon*, which combines plot elements from two of Wang Dulu's novels in the series (寶劍金釵 and 臥虎藏龍), is quite straightforward about its conservative message, stating in the author's preface: "Li Mubai, who avoids love for the sake of righteousness, is nonetheless able to be united with Yu Xiulian. Why does Yu Jiaolong, who renounces family for the sake of love, choose to have a fateful one night stand yet not remain together with Luo Xiaohu?" (Bi Xingguo, *Wohu canglong: Chongchu jianghu ban* 臥虎藏龍：重出江湖版 *Crouching Tiger, Hidden Dragon: Reemerging from the Underworld* [Taipei: Lianjing chuban shiye gongsi, 2000]: 1; my translation).

60. See Yeh and Davis, *Taiwan Film Directors*, 195. Impulsiveness, rebellion, sexual passion, challenging social mores—any behavior or attitude fundamental to resistance and opposition—is cast in a negative light and associated with characters who ultimately find no lasting pleasure or happiness in life. In the film's most romantic subplot, the two impetuous adolescent young non-Han lovers are associated with animality, violence, and criminality. Further aspersions are implicitly cast on Jen, through her numerous associations with her governess. When critics fail to contextualize Zhang Ziyi's character Jen within the value-coded racializing framework of the film, it leads to differing interpretations of this "young upstart" who "achieves freedom from emotional, familial, and social inhibitions" in Lu, "Crouching Tiger, Hidden Dragon, Bouncing Angels," 225; but manifests a "failure to comprehend *jianghu* etiquette and values" in Chan, "*Crouching Tiger, Hidden Dragon*: Cultural Migrancy and Translatability," 60; and is a character whose representation is so "multicoded" she can for some audiences be "descendant of the legion celluloid *nüxia* 女俠 dating back to the 1920s," for others "a far-flung sister to Buffy, Max, Lara, and Xena" in Martin (in an otherwise masterful survey of the film's reception), "China Simulacrum," 156. See Yeh and Davis for a nuanced reading of Jen's character, taking into account Confucian-moralist and other perspectives See Emilie Yueh-Yu Yeh (*Taiwan Film Directors: A Treasure Island,* 198). Cai Rong's analysis of "gender images in martial arts discourse" in *CTHD* notes the film's "conventional binarism." See Cai, "Gender Imaginations in *Crouching Tiger, Hidden Dragon* and the *Wuxia* World," *positions: east asia cultures critique* 13, no. 2 (Fall 2005): 443, 461.

61. Robert Stam reminds us of Fanon's argument, in language that resonates powerfully with the dynamics of this film, that "the

colonizer 'cannot speak of the colonized without having recourse to the bestiary'…[and] the…'animalizing trope,' the discursive figure by which the colonizing imaginary rendered the colonized as beastlike and animalic." See Shohat and Stam, *Multiculturalism, Postcoloniality, and Transnational Media,* 19. To paraphrase Shohat and Stam, "[t]he ideological production of Han Chinese rationality and civility goes hand in hand with the production of non-Han irrationality and immorality" (ibid. 13).

62. In the script, the setting for this scene is described as "廢棄作坊," an abandoned workshop or abandoned mill, but the mise-en-scène, lighting, and camera angles convey a thoroughly cave-like appearance and atmosphere.

63. Yu Xiulian and Li Mubai's final conversation does not appear in the published script. That version is arguably even more conservative, as Li Mubai says, "Xiulian, agree to marry me [this moment]…I—won't wait until I'm a ghost to be able to love you!" A sobbing Xiulian cries out "I long ago consented!" See Wang Huiling, James Schamus, and Cai Guorong, *Wohu Canglong* 臥虎藏龍 [*Crouching Tiger, Hidden Dragon,* based on the original novel by Wang Dulu; Chinese Filmscript, cast list, and photos, with preface by Ang Lee] (Xindian: Tianxing Guoji wenhua, 2000), 135; my translation.

64. We must also note that only the seductive lure of the primitive other is shown to sexually arouse and distract the otherwise reserved and spiritually centered Li Mubai (with fatal results), as he pursues Jen in the previous bamboo grove sequence and the earlier part of this cave scene.

65. The appellation "*Beile*" 貝勒 refers to "a Manchu prince." See Immanuel C.Y. Hsü, *The Rise of Modern China,* 6th Edition (New York: Oxford University Press, 2000), 23. Nonetheless, the casting choice of Lung Sihung 郎雄, the patriarchal character actor from Lee's popular "father knows best" trilogy (*Pushing Hands* 推手, 1992; *The Wedding Banquet* 囍宴, 1993; and *Eat Drink Man Woman* 飲食男女, 1994), combined with his sympathetic portrayal as the fatherly mentor and family friend of Xiulian (and Li Mubai), as well as his words and actions (and home) in the film, all serve to mark him as a thoroughly Sinicized, Han-assimilated character in the film.

66. As Martin notes, "Jen sees the *jianghu* underworld as one of unfettered freedom and fails to understand the chivalric code of honor by which its warriors must treat one another…she offends people left and right by failing to observe the chivalric code, instead cutting a swathe of indiscriminate destruction" ("China Simulacrum," 152). Berry and Farquhar see Jen's rejection of "both the Confucian and underworld [*jian-*

ghu] codes of conduct" as part of her "quest for individual freedom," making her "not a villain but a very modern heroine" (*China on Screen*, 72). Martin, Berry and Farquhar, Yeh and Davis, and others are not mistaken in stressing Jen's adolescent quest for freedom from authority, but the overarching racial binarism structuring the representation of characters and themes in the film overrides the sympathetic cinematic codes of romantic youthful rebellion, casting a negative light on Jen (and Xiaohu/[little]Tiger).

67. Yeh and Davis, *Taiwan Film Directors*
68. See Gladney, *Dislocating China*, 91. Gladney's enlightening account of minority representation in Chinese cinema (74–98) considers, among many issues, the contribution that such films make to constructing "an 'imagined' national identity" (91). *CTHD* contributes to both an imagined Chinese national *and global* identity.
69. Police inspector Tsai's daughter uses her chopsticks to prevent Bo from taking the first bite of stew, before her father.
70. According to the script (Wang et al., *Wohu Canglong*, 86).
71. Yeh and Davis, *Taiwan Film Directors*, 182.
72. For a more accepting interpretation, see Yeh and Davis's view that "[t]he aesthetic of defiance and assertive cultural nationalism is gone, but a vague wistfulness and longing for cultural China remains." Ibid., 182.
73. Karen Smith, "The Future: in Whose Hands?" *Yishu: Journal of Contemporary Chinese Art* (June 2004): 56.
74. *People's Daily* Editorial, cited in Antoaneta Bezlova, "From Cultural Revolution to Culture Exports," *Inter Press Service* (Jul. 28, 2006), reprinted in *Global Policy Forum*, http://www.globalpolicy.org/globaliz/cultural/2006/0728china.htm.
75. Cited in Martin, "China Simulacrum," 158. Lee is Deputy Director-General of the R.O.C. Government Information Office.
76. I would also note that the appearance of sophisticated special effects and state-of-the-art CGI technology contributes to the globalized cultural nationalist identity I've been discussing, for it feeds into the transnational Chinese spectator's pride in and association with new signs of China's cultural advancement, part of what Wu Hung, has termed the "obsessive pursuit of *dangdaixing* 當代性 or 'contemporaneity'." See Wu Hung "About *between Past and Future: New Photography and Video from China*," *Yishu: Journal of Contemporary Chinese Art* (Jun. 2004): 7. See Shih Shu-mei, "Globalisation and Minoritisation" for a similar discussion of spectator reception of Ang Lee's *The Wedding Banquet*.
77. See Martina Köppel-Yang, "The Ping-Pong Policy of Contemporary

Chinese Art," *Yishu: Journal of Contemporary Chinese Art* (Jun. 2004): 60–66. For a contrasting view that perceives a zero-sum antagonistic tension between "national specificity" and a "more transnationally powerful, assertive, and successful...universality," see Hedetoft, "Contemporary Cinema, 280. See also Jing Wang for an analysis of the relationship between a "resurgent nativism," growing Chinese affluence, "cultural capital," "international cosmopolitanism," and China's "bid for global citizenship" in Wang, "Culture as Leisure and Culture as Capital," *positions: east asia cultures critique* 9, no. 1 (Spring 2001): 97–98, and passim.

78. My working definition of the terms "subject" and "subjectivity" in this specific argument is akin to the Lacanian imaginary and Freudian ego (defense ego in some later formulations), both of which refer to the collective conscious identifications subjects construct for themselves and their national identities. "Subjectivity" in this usage is analogous to the notion of "identity," which necessitates and cannot exist without its real and imagined objects/others, the two (subject/self and object/other) normally being separated and distinguished via conscious and unconscious processes of selection, disavowal, projection, repression, etc. Spivak has referred to this as the "colloquial language" version of subjectivity, distinguishing it from a "subject-formation producing the reflexive basis for self-conscious social agency." See Gatyatari Spivak, "Not Really a Properly Intellectual Response: An Interview with Gayatari Spivak," *positions: east asia cultures critique* 12, no. 1 (Spring 2004): 153. For a thorough, lucid, and rigorous definition of subjectivity, see Walter A. Davis, *Inwardness and Existence: Subjectivity in/and Hegel, Heidegger, Marx, and Freud* (Madison: University of Wisconsin Press, 1989).

79. These include orientalizing, self-orientalizing, feminizing, exoticizing, and other subalternizing representational schema. See Kaldis for a discussion of the criticism of Chinese films (many by Zhang Yimou and other fifth-generation filmmakers), which deplores the selling of false, exoticized images of China to Western viewers presumably eager for simple, unthreatening, frequently sexualized representations of "China." See Nick Kaldis, "Compulsory Orientalism: Hou Hsiao-hsien's *Flowers of Shanghai*," in *Island on the Edge: Taiwan New Cinema and After*, ed. Chris Berry and Fei-i Lu (Hong Kong: Hong Kong University Press, 2005), 127–36. Sheldon Lu asks, somewhat rhetorically, whether or not Ang Lee is "susceptible to the accusation of orientalist self-fantasy" for making *CTHD* ("Crouching Tiger, Hidden Dragon, Bouncing Angels," 227).

80. For recent rigorous psychoanalytic interpretations of the dynamics

of racism and nationalism in the twenty-first century, see the work of Slavoj Žižek and numerous articles in the journal *Psychoanalysis, Culture & Society* (formerly *Journal for the Psychoanalysis of Culture & Society*), especially vol. 9, no. 2 (August 2004). For a psychoanalytic interpretation of superego development and functioning in Chinese culture, see Yao Ping, "Some Observations on the Superego in China and in the United States," *Journal for the Psychoanalysis of Culture & Society* 7, no. 2 (Fall 2002): 190–95.

81. See essays in Colin Mackerras, ed., *Ethnicity in Asia* (London: RoutledgeCurzon, 2003) for numerous elaborations of the historically-contingent nature of Han Chinese and other types of (discourses of) Asian identity.
82. See C. J. W.-L. Wee, "Staging the Asian Modern: Cultural Fragments, the Singaporean Eunuch, and the Asian Lear," *Critical Inquiry* 30, no. 4 (Summer 2004): 773. In a similar vein, Rey Chow addresses the desire for global visibility embodied in Chinese films, with an in-depth analysis of how "sentimentality" in Chinese films functions as one of several "forms of attachment [that] are likely to persist—and evolve—in the age of global visibility" (*Sentimental Fabulations, Contemporary Chinese Films*, 200; see also 17–23). Borrowing from both Wee and Chow, I argue that the "Chinese" desires and aspirations that I speak of as being embodied in the film are one such form of attachment, and are not necessarily in this case the (conscious) product of auteur/authorial intention, nor can they be exclusively located in a single person, locale, or document; they are instead captured in phenomena such as the transnational production and reception of this film.
83. I can agree with Dirlik that the knee-jerk reactions of some "U.S. scholars" against any manifestation of cultural nationalism can empower westernization and globalization by impeding "those who inhabit Asia or East Asia" from asserting "autonomous identities against a hegemonic globalization" ("Culture against History?" 202). However, in the present essay, I am exposing what I believe to be an insidious intra-Asian racist dynamic that empowers this film's particular instantiation of a nascent Chinese global identity. Furthermore, this identity is celebrated not as a local resistance to globalization, but rather as proof that Chinese people have ascended to a place of power and visibility on the global stage. For other perspectives, see Liu on China's "spectacular" failure "to reconstruct a new cultural and ideological counterhegemony" (Liu Kang, *Globalization and Cultural Trends in China* [Honolulu: University of Hawai'i Press, 2004]), 12, and passim; Lu on the potential for liberation of "the local from domination by the party-state" that

globalization offers. See Sheldon H. Lu, *China, Transnational Visuality, Global Postmodernity* (Stanford: Stanford University Press, 2001), 73 and passim, Wee for an optimistic view of the way globalization facilitates "a potentially emerging Asian metropole in relation to the modern capitalist West inextricably in its midst" ("Staging the Asian Modern," 774), and Haugerud for a nuanced reading of the problematics of construing the local in opposition to the global. See Angelique Haugerud, "The Disappearing Local: Rethinking Global-Local Connections," in Mirsepassi, Basu, and Weaver, *Localizing Knowledge*, 60–81.

84. See Berry and Farquhar, *China on Screen*, 171. From a psychoanalytic perspective, a national identity grounded in ethnic difference is attained by the projection of one's own abject qualities onto a racial other *within* the nation's cultural and geographic borders. One's anxieties and weaknesses vis-à-vis the global order are thereby translated into local relationships with one's domestic others.
85. Spivak and others have demonstrated that "the colonizing *Other* is established at the same time as its colonized *others* are produced as subjects." See Bill Ashcroft, Gareth Griffiths, and Helen Tiffin, "othering," in *Post-Colonial Studies: The Key Concepts* (London: Routledge, 2000), 171.
86. *Celluloid Comrades*, 44.
87. See Shih, "Global Literature and the Technologies of Recognition," 23. Shih's larger argument concerns the repression/loss of difference and antagonisms that enables the logic of "global multiculturalism," antagonisms upon which the possibilities for socioeconomic and cultural alternatives to globalization rest.
88. This marks a generic movement away from Chinese self-representation in commercial martial arts films in which cycles of humiliating defeats at the hands of an external, non-Chinese racial/ethnic other are punctuated by climactic moments of triumphant righteous vengeance, via native fists of fury.
89. Stanley Rosen, citing a plethora of skeptical statistics, is not optimistic about the potential future global box-office successes of Chinese films. See Rosen, "Chinese Cinemas in the Era of Globalization: Prospects for Chinese Films on the International Market, with Special Reference to the United States," Proceedings of the Conference *From Past to Future: 100 Years of Chinese Cinema*: College of Staten Island, CUNY, 2005 (unpublished conference proceedings): 80–121.
90. June Yip, *Envisioning Taiwan: Fiction, Cinema, and the Nation in the Cultural Imaginary* (Durham: Duke University Press, 2004), 243.
91. The term was apparently coined by Peter van Ham in "The Rise of

the Brand State: The Postmodern Politics of Image and Reputation," *Foreign Affairs* 80, no. 5 (Sept.-Oct. 2001): 2–6. See also John Fraim, *Battle of Symbols: Global Dynamics of Advertising, Entertainment and Media* (Einsiedeln: Daimon Verlag, 2003), and passim. The related term "China Inc." has also begun to circulate in western media over the last few years.

92. Martin, "China Simulacrum," 158.
93. See Lim on the "global film viewing subject" (*Celluloid Comrades*, 22), and Higson for a very different take on this issue, based on analyses of the overlooked "international" aspects of European, English, and American cinema(s). See Andrew Higson, "National Cinema(s), International Markets and Cross-cultural Identities," in *Moving Images, Culture and the Mind,* ed. Ib Bondebjerg (Luton: University of Luton Press, 2000), 205–14, and passim.
94. Berry and Farquhar note that, in the twentieth century, "Confucian codes provided an ethnic symbol of a past order" and that these codes "provide a fictional and historical anchor in China's twentieth-century transition from empire to modern nation-state." (*China on Screen,* 139; see also 170–72). As *CTHD* demonstrates, in the early twenty-first century, these same codes can be put in the service of imagining and screening an ethnic polarization that helps anchor [Han] China's rearticulation of its emergent transnational image.
95. Ella Shohat and Robert Stam, "Introduction," in Shohat and Stam, *Multiculturalism, Postcoloniality, and Transnational Media,* 12.
96. Cornel West, "Marxist Theory and the Specificity of Afro-American Oppression," in *Marxism and the Interpretation of Culture,* ed. Cary Nelson and Lawrence Grossberg (Urbana and Chicago: University of Illinois Press, 1988), 26, n1. See also Paul Gilroy's scathing analyses of the larger forces underlying racist representations, where he repeatedly warns against "utopian racial allegiances that make a spectacle of identity" and the "'cheap pseudo-solidarities offered by ethnic loyalty'." Cited in Derek Conrad Murray, "Hip-Hop vs. High Art: Notes on Race as Spectacle," *Art Journal* 63, no. 2 (Summer 2004): 11. For more psychoanalytic analyses of race, see the essays collected in *Psychoanalysis, Culture, and Society* 9, no. 2 (August 2004); see individual articles in other issues as well.
97. Naficy, "Phobic Spaces and Liminal Panics," 222–23.

Chapter 10

An earlier version of this essay was published in Peng-hsiang Chen and Whitney Crothers Dilley, eds., *Feminism/Femininity in Chinese Literature*

(Amsterdam and New York: Rodopi, 2002), 145–58; reprinted with permission.

1. "Red Rose and White Rose," *Zazhi Yuekan [Magazine Monthly]* (May 1944): 125.
2. I deliberately echo Norman Bryson's opening sentences of the chapter on Ingre in his book *Tradition and Desire: From David to Delacroix* (Cambridge: Cambridge University Press, 1987). I'm indebted to Norman Bryson's insightful interpretation of the traces of borrowing and remaking of the visual past in Western art history. But, instead of analyzing the semiotic change within one art genre, as what Bryson has done with the painting, I extend my discussion to cross-genre semiotics. My emphasis is on the boundary crossing among different art genres. I shall also indicate that the semiotic shift in the textuality reveals the artist's comment on the culture of the past as well as of the present.
3. Bryson, *Tradition and Desire,* 1, 24.
4. Ibid., 5.
5. Ibid., xviii–xix.
6. Eileen Chang (1920–95) has been praised as one of the most influential and most important writers in modern Chinese literature. C. T. Hsia (*A History of Modern Chinese Fiction,* 2nd ed. [New Haven: Yale University Press, 1971]) ranked her as important as Lu Xun and concluded that Chang's *Golden Cangue* is the greatest novella in Chinese literary history. David Der-wei Wang points out the significance of Chang's position in modern Chinese literature: a transition from language to images, from male voice to female utterance, from the vision of grand history to that of the fragmented history ("The Wheat Grain Which Falls on the Ground Does Not Die," *China Times Literary Supplementary* [September 14, 1995]).
7. To name just a few examples: Feng Yuanjun, Bing Xin, Ding Ling, Xiao Hong, Su Qing.
8. Rey Chow, *Woman and Chinese Modernity: The Politics of Reading between West and East* (Minnesota and Oxford: University of Minnesota Press, 1991), 85.
9. Ibid., 114, 120.
10. Quoted in ibid., 118.
11. Ibid., 87.
12. Eileen Chang's grandfather, Zhang Peilun, used to serve at the Qing imperial court, and her grandmother was the daughter of the famous Qing imperial official Li Hongzhang.
13. Eileen Chang was never very close with her father and mother. Her

father Zhang Tingzhong is an embodiment of the vices of older culture, such as smoking opium, drinking liquor, prostitution, gambling, etc. Once Zhang Tingzhong beat up Eileen severely and locked her up only because she had visited secretly her divorced mother. Her mother, Huang Yifan, who went to France after she separated from Zhang Tingzhong, is the incarnation of the West and the modern for the young Eileen.

14. Ruite Shih, "The Vile Thing—*Red Rose and White Rose,*" *Yingxiang Film Magazine* 57 (January 1995): 190.
15. Zhensu Duan. "*Red Rose and White Rose*—the Joy of Man and the Sorrow of Woman." *Yingxiang Film Magazine* 57 (January 1995): 70.
16. Wang teasingly addresses Chang as "grandma" and lists up to fourteen important male and female writers in Taiwan, Hong Kong and mainland China as under Chang's direct influence (David Derwei Wang, "The Gospel of the fin de siècle," *China Times, Literary Supplementary* [September 13, 1995]). Meili Cai also has pointed out the rise of the decadent pseudo-Chang style in Taiwan and Hong Kong during the 1970s and 1980s (Meili Cai, "Mundane vs. Contemporary: Thoughts on Eileen Chang."*Contemporary* 14 [June 1987]: 112).We can see this style in Kwan's early film *Rouge* till his recent film *Rum Lingyu.* Kwan himself admitted that Eileen Chang is one of his most loved novelists (Law Wai Ming, "Stanley Kwan: Carrying the Past Lightly," *Cinemaya* 19 [1993]: 12).
17. Masculine discourse here means the phallogocentric discursive practices in the West which dominate the formation and construction of all kinds of communal language and ideologies, such as law, politics, nation, society, morality, religion, gender differences, and so on. Feminine writing, according to French feminist theorists, such as Julia Kristeva's "poetic revolution" ("The System and the Speaking Subject" in *The Kristeva Reader,* ed. Toril Moi [Oxford: Blackwell, 1987], 24–33), Luce Irigaray's "feminine language" ("Women's Exile," *Ideology and Consciousness* 1 [1977]: 64), or Hélène Cixous's "feminine text" ("The Laugh of the Medusa" in *New French Feminism,* ed. Elaine Marks and Isabelle de Courtivron [New York: Schocken Books, 1981], 258), is the alternative writing which resists the monolistic symbolic system and opens up the signifying process. Kristeva, for example, suggests that through poetic revolution, the speaking subject transgresses the boundaries and renews the rules of the language games. Irigaray, similarly, believes that "feminine language" challenges the Aristotelian logocentric masculine discourse and breaks the fixed system. Cixous, furthermore, states that "feminine text" can "shatter the framework of institutions, to blow up the law, and break up the truth with laughter."

18. Annette Kuhn, *Women's Pictures: Feminism and Cinema* (London and New York: Verso, 1994), 11–13, 155–57.
19. Ibid., 163.
20. Liwen Xu, "Go Through with His Thought on Femininity: An Interview," *Elle* (Taipei Edition) 17 (1993): 76.
21. Renjun Gao, "The Self-reflection and Growth of a Director: Stanley Kwan and *Ruan Lingyu*," *Yingxiang Film Magazine* 23 (December 1991): 65.
22. Before *Rouge* was finalized, Kwan was requested by the film company to cut and add scenes and make *Rouge* a "real" ghost commercial (Yi Chu, "Stanley Kwan's Remorseless Job," *Film Bi-Weekly* 230 [1988]: 17–18). Other ghost stories, such as *Ah Ying, Ghost Bride,* prevail in the commercial market.
23. Robert Ruxiu Chen pointed out the "multiple narrative" and "metanarrative" in *Ruan Lingyu* (Ruxiu Chen, "A Belated Critique—Deconstructing *Ruan Lingyu*," *Yingxiang Film Magazine* 28 [May 1992]: 170), and Qijiang Zhang discussed the "de-framing" meta-filmic strategies in *Ruan Lingyu* (Qijiang Zhang, "The Deframing Skill and the Color Aesthetics in *Ruan Lingyu* and Good Man Good Woman," *Lianhe Literary Magazine* 130 (August 1995): 82–83).
24. Page 3.
25. Wenbiao Tang, ed., *The Complete Sources of Eileen Chang* (Taipei: Shibao Wenhua Publisher, 1984), 65.
26. Pascal Bonitzer, "The Silences of the Voice," in *Narrative, Apparatus,Ideology: A Film Theory Reader,* ed. Philip Rosen (New York and Oxford: Columbia University Press, 1986), 331.
27. This narrative strategy echoes the manuscript version of Eileen Chang's *Red Rose and White Rose,* which was first published in the May, June, and July issues of *Zazhi Monthly* in 1944. It was later compiled in *The Complete Sources of Eileen Chang,* ed. Wenbiao Tang (Taipei: Shibao Wenhua Publisher, 1984) and translated into English by Carolyn Thompson Brown (University Microfilms International, 1992). In the earliest edition, Eileen Chang makes Zhenbao's niece the first-person narrator who retells the story her uncle Zhenbao told which she overheard at her aunt's place. She says, "I seemed to have heard every word spoken by Uncle Zhenbao, even the things he did not utter." This narrator reveals her sophisticated and even sarcastic distance from Zhenbao's story; she even "laughs out loud" when she hears Zhenbao said, "I loved only two women in my life: one is my white rose, the other is my red rose." This narrative frame is later omitted by Chang in the version published the next year, compiled in the *Supplementary Edition of Chuanqi* in 1945, but the third-person

omniscient narrator, with no sex or age identity, takes the same sophisticated and sarcastic distance shown by the girl narrator. Following the narrator's observation of Zhenbao's internal thoughts, the reader has free access to the self-centered world in Zhenbao's mind.

28. Page 70.
29. Ibid., 74.
30. Ibid., 77.
31. Jean-Luc Godard's film belongs to the typical counter-cinema type. See Peter Wollen's "Godard and Counter-Cinema: *Vent d'Est*," in *Narrative, Apparatus, Ideology: A Film Theory Reader*, ed. Philip Rosen (New York and Oxford: Columbia University Press, 1986), 120–29.

Chapter 11

1. For treatments of these categories of film theory, see John Hill and Pamela Church, eds., *The Oxford Guide to Film Studies* (New York: Oxford University Press, 1998), 51–175.
2. An exception is Linda Erhlich and David Desser, eds., *Cinematic Landscapes: Observations on the Visual Arts and Cinema of China and Japan* (Austin: University of Texas Press, 1994), which includes a section—mostly translations of Chinese scholarship—on Chinese aesthetics.
3. This is particularly true in recent studies of the martial arts genre. See Chen Mo, *Zhongguo wuxia dianying shi* [A history of Chinese martial arts films] (Beijing: Zhongguo dianying chubanshe, 2005); Jia Leilei, *Zhongguo wuxia dianying shi* [A history of Chinese martial arts films] (Beijing: Wenhua yishu chubanshe, 2005).
4. See Mette Hjort and Scott MacKenzie, eds., *Cinema and Nation* (London: Routledge, 2000); Alan Williams, ed., *Film and Nationalism* (Brunswick, NJ: Rutgers University Press, 2002).
5. See, for example, this denunciation of *Raise the Red Lantern* (*Da hong denglong gaogao gua*, dir. Zhang Yimou, 1991) as a film that was "really shot for the casual pleasures of foreigners ... [who] can go on and muddleheadedly satisfy their oriental fetishism"; see Dai Qing, "Raised Eyebrows for *Raise the Red Lantern*," *Public Culture* 5 (1993): 336. Years later, Jia Zhangke found it painful when his *Xiao Wu* (*Xiao Wu*, 1997) was criticized in exactly the same terms, as "pleasing foreigners" (*quyue waiguoren*); see his interview in Wu Wenguang, ed., *Xianchang (di yi juan)* [Document, volume 1] (Tianjin: Tianjin shehui kexue yuan chubanshe, 2000), 206.
6. For the myth of homogeneity, see Yingjin Zhang, *Chinese National Cinema* (London: Routledge, 2004), 1–10. For the problematic of the

national cinema paradigm, see Yingjin Zhang, "Chinese Cinema and Transnational Film Studies," in *World Cinemas, Transnational Perspectives*, ed. Natasa Dorovicová and Kathleen Newman (London: Routledge, 2009), 123–36.

7. For transnationalism in film studies, see Dorovicová and Newman, *World Cinemas, Transnational Perspectives*, ix–xv. For Chinese cinema, see Sheldon Hsiao-peng Lu, ed., *Transnational Chinese Cinemas: Identity, Nationhood, Gender* (Honolulu: University of Hawai'i Press, 1997), 1–3; Chris Berry and Mary Farquhar, *China on Screen: Cinema and Nation* (New York: Columbia University Press, 2005), 1–16.
8. See Arif Dirlik, "Placed-Based Imagination: Globalism and the Politics of Place," in *Places and Politics in an Age of Globalization*, ed. Roxann Frazniak and Arif Dirlik (Lanham, MD: Rowman & Littlefield, 2001), 15–51. For translocal traffic in China, see Tim Oakes and Louisa Schein, eds., *Translocal China: Linkages, Identities, and the Reimagining of Space* (London: Routledge, 2006).
9. For a critique of such one-way imposition of Western theory on Chinese cinema, see Yingjin Zhang, *Screening China: Critical Interventions, Cinematic Reconfigurations, and the Transnational Imaginary in Contemporary Chinese Cinema* (Ann Arbor: Center for Chinese Studies, University of Michigan, 2002), 115–47.
10. Rey Chow, *Woman and Chinese Modernity: The Politics of Reading between West and East* (Minneapolis: University of Minnesota Press, 1991), xvi. The term "the age of theory" is taken from Rey Chow, ed., *Modern Chinese Literary and Cultural Studies in the Age of Theory: Reimagining a Field* (Durham, NC: Duke University Press, 2000).
11. Chow, *Woman and Chinese Modernity*, xii; original emphasis.
12. Ibid., xii–xiii.
13. Ibid., xiii; Rey Chow, *Writing Diaspora: Tactics of Intervention in Contemporary Cultural Studies* (Bloomington: Indiana University Press, 1993), xv, xxi.
14. This is exemplified in her concentration on a dozen or so Chinese films and a few references to Chinese scholarship; see Rey Chow, *Primitive Passions: Visuality, Sexuality, Ethnography, and Contemporary Chinese Cinema* (New York: Columbia University Press, 1995). For further discussion, see Y. Zhang, *Screening China*, 72–73.
15. Chow, ed., *Modern Chinese*, 5.
16. Chow, *Writing Diaspora*, 98.
17. Chow, *Woman and Chinese Modernity*, xvi.
18. Chow, *Writing Diaspora*, 6. See also Tani Barlow, "*Funü, Guojia, Jiating* [Chinese Women, Chinese State, Chinese Family]," *Genders* 10 (1991): 132–60. Chow rationalizes her objection this way: "Had the title been

'la femme, l'état, la famille,' would it be conceivable to append a phrase like 'French woman, French state, French family'?" (*Writing Diaspora,* 6). Although Chow's rhetorical question implies a negative answer, a French scholar may conceivably specify whether these terms refer to universal concepts or to some particular French cases, as does Barlow in the Chinese case.

19. Chow, *Writing Diaspora,* 25.
20. Chow, *Primitive Passions,* 10, 22–23; original emphases.
21. Chow, ed., *Modern Chinese,* 3–4.
22. Rey Chow, *Ethics after Idealism: Theory-Culture-Ethnicity-Reading* (Bloomington: Indiana University Press, 1998), xxi.
23. Rey Chow, *Sentimental Fabulations, Contemporary Chinese Films: Attachment in the Age of Global Visibility* (New York: Columbia University Press, 2007), 17–18; original emphasis.
24. Chow, *Sentimental Fabulations,* 18–22; original emphases.
25. Ibid., 24.
26. Chow, *Ethics after Idealism,* xviii; original emphasis.
27. David Bordwell, "Contemporary Film Studies and the Vicissitudes of Grand Theory," in *Post-Theory: Reconstructing Film Studies,* ed. David Bordwell and Noël Carroll (Madison: University of Wisconsin Press, 1996), 3–36.
28. Bordwell and Carroll, *Post-Theory,* xiii–xiv; original emphases.
29. Bordwell, "Contemporary Film Studies," 27.
30. Rey Chow has succeeded in situating herself at the center of Western theory, as evidenced by this endorsement from Fredric Jameson: "In this wide-ranging, theoretically rich, and provocative book, Rey Chow completely restructures the problem of ethnicity; all future discussions and debates will have to come to terms with it." See the back cover of Rey Chow, *The Protestant Ethnic and the Spirit of Capitalism* (New York: Columbia University Press, 2002).
31. Bordwell, "Contemporary Film Studies," 29–30.
32. See David Bordwell, *On the History of Film Style* (Cambridge, MA: Harvard University Press, 1997); David Bordwell, *The Way Hollywood Tells It: Story and Style in Modern Movies* (Berkeley: University of California Press, 2006).
33. Kristin Thompson, "Nation, National Identity and the International Cinema," *Film History* 8 (1996): 259.
34. Richard Abel, "The Perils of Pathé, or the Americanization of Early American Cinema," in *Cinema and the Invention of Modern Life,* ed. Leo Charney and Vanessa R. Schwartz (Berkeley: University of California Press, 1995), 184.
35. Stephen Crofts, "Concepts of National Cinema," in Hill and Gibson,

Oxford Guide to Film Studies, 389–90. An earlier typology that does not include the United States is found in Stephen Crofts, "Reconceptualizing National Cinema/s," *Quarterly Review of Film and Video* 14, no. 3 (1993): 52–57.

36. Andrew Higson, "The Concept of National Cinema," *Screen* 30, no. 4 (1989): 42.
37. Andrew Higson, *Waving the Flag: Constructing a National Cinema in Britain* (New York: Oxford University Press, 1995), 22.
38. Ibid., 16–17.
39. Ibid., 274.
40. Ibid., 264.
41. Ibid., 275.
42. Susan Hayward, *French National Cinema* (London: Routledge, 1993), 7, 14; original emphasis. Crofts similarly criticizes the movement approach as "not only nationalist but also elitist in its search for the 'best' films"; see Crofts, "Reconceptualizing National Cinema/s," 62.
43. Ian Jarvie, "National Cinema," in Hjort and MacKenzie, *Cinema and Nation*, 86.
44. Ibid., 81.
45. Ibid.
46. Quoted in Tom O'Regan, *Australian National Cinema* (London: Routledge, 1996), 48.
47. See Toby Miller, Nitin Govil, John McMurria, and Richard Maxwell, *Global Hollywood* (London: BFI Publishing, 2001).
48. See Y. Zhang, *Chinese National Cinema*, 19, 31–32, 47. See also relevant sections in these three books: Michael Curtin, *Playing to the World's Biggest Audience: The Globalization of Chinese Film and TV* (Berkeley: University of California Press, 2007); Law Kar and Frank Bren, *Hong Kong Cinema: A Cross-Cultural View* (Lanham, MD: Scarecrow, 2004); and Zhang Zhen, *An Amorous History of the Silver Screen: Shanghai Cinema, 1896–1937* (Chicago: University of Chicago Press, 2005).
49. Wen-hsin Yeh, "Between Shanghai and Hong Kong," *American Historical Review* 110, no. 5 (Dec. 2005): 1501.
50. For wartime situations, see Yingjin Zhang, "Beyond Binary Imagination: Progress and Problems in Chinese Film Historiography," *Chinese Historical Review* 15, no. 1 (2008): 65–87.
51. Laikwan Pang, *Building a New China in Cinema: The Chinese Left-Wing Cinema Movement, 1932–1937* (Lanham, MD: Rowman & Littlefield, 2002), 166.
52. See Y. Zhang, *Chinese National Cinema*, 60–62. See also Jubin Hu, *Projecting a Nation: Chinese National Cinema before 1949* (Hong Kong: Hong Kong University Press, 2003).

53. Carolyn Cartier, *Globalizing South China* (Oxford: Blackwell, 2001), 26.
54. Oakes and Schein, *Translocal China*, xii, 1; original emphases.
55. See Yingjin Zhang, *Cinema, Space, and Polylocality in a Globalizing China* (Honolulu: University of Hawai'i Press, 2009), 1–12.
56. See Yingjin Zhang, "Thinking outside the Box: Mediation of Imaging and Information in Contemporary Chinese Independent Documentary," *Screen* 48, no. 2 (2007): 179–92. See also relevant chapters in these two volumes: Paul G. Pickowicz and Yingjin Zhang, eds., *From Underground to Independent: Alternative Film Culture in Contemporary China* (Lanham, MD: Rowman & Littlefield, 2006); Zhang Zhen, ed., *The Urban Generation: Chinese Cinema and Society at the Turn of the Twenty-first Century* (Durham, NC: Duke University Press, 2007).
57. Arturo Escobar, "Culture Sits in Places: Reflections on Globalism and Subaltern Strategies of Localization," *Political Geography* 20 (2001): 155–156.
58. David Harvey, *The Postmodern Condition* (Oxford: Blackwell, 1989), 302–303.
59. Dirlik, "Placed-Based Imagination," 24.
60. Ibid., 41; original emphasis.
61. Doreen Massey, "A Global Sense of Place," *Marxism Today* (June 1991): 29.

About the Editor

Jason C. Kuo is Professor of Art History and Archaeology and a member of the Graduate Field Committee in Film Studies at the University of Maryland and has taught at the National Taiwan University, Williams College, and Yale University. He is the author of *Wang Yuanqi de shanshuihua yishu* [*Wang Yuanqi's Art of Landscape Painting*] (Taipei: National Palace Museum, 1981); *Long tiandi yu xingnei* [*Trapping Heaven and Earth in the Cage of Form*] (Taipei: Shibao wenhua, 1986); *The Austere Landscape: The Paintings of Hung-jen* (Taiwan and New York: SMC Publishing in cooperation with University of Washington Press, Seattle and London, 1992); *Zhuang Zhe, 1991–92* (Taipei: Longmen hualang, 1992); *Cuo wanwu yu biduan* [*Embodying Myriad of Things as the Tip of Brush*] (Taipei: Dongda tushu, 1994); *Word as Image: The Art of Chinese Seal Engraving* (New York: China House Gallery, China Institute in America; distributed by University of Washington Press, Seattle and London, 1992); *Chen Qikuan* (Taipei: Jinxiu chuban shiye, 1995); *Yishushi yu yishu piping de tansuo* [*Rethinking Art History and Art Criticism*] (Taipei: National Museum of History, 1996); *Yishushi yu yishu piping de shijian* [*Practicing Art History and Art Criticism*] (Taipei: National Museum of History, 2002); *Transforming Traditions in Modern Chinese Painting: Huang Pin-hung's Late Work* (Berlin and New York: Peter Lang Publishing, 2004); and *Chinese Ink Painting Now* (New York: Distributed Art Publishers, 2010).

He is the editor of several books and exhibition catalogs, including *Heirs to a Great Tradition: Modern Chinese Painting from the Tsien-hsiang-chai Collection* (College Park, MD: Department of Art History and Archaeology; distributed by University of Washington Press, Seattle and London, 1993); *Discovering Chinese Painting: Dialogues with American Art Historians* (Dubuque: Kendall/Hunt Publishing, 2000); *Understanding Asian Art* (Dubuque: Kendall/

Hunt Publishing, 2001); *Discovering Chinese Painting: Dialogues with Art Historians* (Dubuque: Kendall/Hunt Publishing, 2006); *Visual Culture in Shanghai, 1850s–1930s* (Washington, DC: New Academia Publishing, 2007); *Perspectives on Connoisseurship of Chinese Painting* (Washington, DC: New Academia Publishing, 2008); and *Stones from Other Mountains: Chinese Painting Studies in Postwar America* (Washington, DC: New Academia Publishing, 2009).

His writings have appeared in a broad spectrum of publications, including *Art Journal, Asian Culture Quarterly, Chinese Culture Quarterly, Chinese Studies, National Palace Museum Bulletin, National Palace Museum Research Quarterly, Orientations, China Quarterly, China Review International, Journal of Asian Studies, Journal of Asian and African Studies,* and *Ars Orientalis*. He is a contributor to *The Dictionary of Art,* ed. Jane Turner (New York: Grove, 1996) as well as *Oxford Art Online* published by Oxford University Press and *Allgemeines Künstlerlexikon: Die bildenden Künstler aller Zeiten und Völker,* ed. Günter Meissner (München and Leipzig: K. G. Saur, 1992–).

He has received an Andrew W. Mellon Foundation Fellowship, a grant from the National Endowment for the Humanities, two Stoddard Fellowships in Asian Art at the Detroit Institute of Arts, two fellowships from the J. D. Rockefeller III Fund, and many other scholastic honors. In 1991–92, he received the Lilly Fellowship for teaching excellence at the University of Maryland. In 1992–93 he organized and directed a National Endowment for the Humanities Summer Institute for College Teachers on "The Art of Imperial China." From 1993 to 1998, he undertook the study of the nineteenth- and twentieth-century art of Shanghai, a research project funded by the Henry Luce Foundation that combined the work of six scholars from China and six from the United States. He directed the Summer Institute of Connoisseurship in Chinese Calligraphy and Painting from 2001 to 2003, also funded by the Luce Foundation. He was a Fulbright Scholar in Taipei in 2001–2.

In 2011, he delivered a lecture, "Beauty and Happiness: Chinese Perspective," at Darwin College, Cambridge University; the lecture will be published by Cambridge University Press.

About the Contributors

Po-shin Chiang is Assistant Professor of the Graduate Institute of Art History and Art Criticism at Tainan National University of the Arts, where he teaches Taiwanese art history, visual culture, and art criticism. He received his Ph.D. degree in Comparative Literature from Fu Jen Catholic University, Taipei. He is currently the chief editor of *Art Critique of Taiwan, ACT*. His research interests include the history of vision in colonial Taiwan, curatorship in contemporary Chinese and Taiwanese Art, crosscultural comparative art between China and Taiwan, and issues of visuality and subjectivity in art practice. He has published widely on modern Chinese art history, visual culture in the 1920s, and contemporary Taiwanese art in recent years, including a book *Taiwanese Art Criticism: Liu Guo-sung* (1999) and *Curatorial Apparatus and Bio-politics* (2010). He is currently working on a project entitled "Contemporary Visual Art and Activism in East Asia."

Megan Ferry is Associate Professor of Chinese and East Asian Studies at Union College, Schenectady, New York. She received her Ph.D. in Comparative Literature at Washington University in St. Louis in 1998, and graduated with a major in Asian Studies and German from Mt. Holyoke College in 1989. The results of her studies have yielded a diverse body of research and courses. She has written on women writers and the literary field in 1920s and 1930s; China advertising, consumerism, and sexuality in contemporary China; and on Chinese-Latin American and Chinese-African relations.

Ping Fu received her Ph.D. in Comparative Literature and Film Studies from the University of Colorado and her M.A. from the University of Oregon. Now Assistant Professor of Chinese and Asian Studies and Director of the Chinese Program at Towson

University, she has received many academic awards and grants. Her teaching and research focus on film theory/criticism, world and Asian cinemas, and contemporary Chinese theatre, literature, and media. She has published in journals and anthologies on Chinese cinema, theatre, and popular culture, including *Chinese Films in Focus II*, edited by Chris Berry (New York and London: Palgrave Macmillan with British Film Institute, 2008). She is completing a book on Chinese farmers on screen.

Paul Gladston is Associate Professor of Culture, Film and Media and Director of the Centre for Contemporary East-Asian Cultural Studies (CEACS) at the University of Nottingham. Between 2005 and 2010 he was the inaugural Head of the Department of International Communications and Director of the Institute of Comparative Cultural Studies at the University of Nottingham Ningbo, China. He has written extensively on contemporary Chinese art with particular reference to the concerns of critical theory. His book-length publications include *Art History after Deconstruction* (Magnolia, 2005), *China and Other Spaces* (Critical, Cultural and Communications Press, 2009) and *Contemporary Art in Shanghai: Conversations with Seven Chinese Artists* (Timezone 8–Blue Kingfisher, 2011). He is currently preparing monographs on Chinese "avant-garde" art groups and associations of the late 1970s and 1980s as well as the theory and practice of contemporary Chinese art.

Stephen J. Goldberg is Associate Professor of Asian Art History, in the Art History Department at Hamilton College, Clinton, New York. He received his Ph.D. in Art History from the University of Michigan in 1980. He was a visiting professor at Stanford University and Colgate University, and has taught at the University of Hawai'i and the University of Denver. He has served as a member of the Board of Directors of ASIANetwork from 2001 to 2004. His research interests include the history and aesthetics of Chinese calligraphy; cross-cultural comparative aesthetics; issues of identity, subjectivity, and voice in traditional Chinese painting; history, memory, and the search for national identity in contemporary Chinese art. He recently worked on two exhibitions held concurrently in the

Emerson Gallery at Hamilton College: "Dislocating the Center: Contemporary Chinese art Beyond National Borders: Arnold Chang, Michael Cherney, and André Knéib" and "Cherishing the Past: Chinese Painting and Calligraphy from the Herbert F. Johnson Museum of Art, Cornell University." These were held in conjunction with Ai Weiwei's *Fairytale* (a video installation), from August 25, 2008 to January 4, 2009. Currently, he is working on two projects. The first is a text to be published by the Association of Asian Studies titled *Art, Culture, and Society in Pre-Modern and Modern China* in the series Key Issues in Asian Studies. It is designed for use in the curriculum and by undergraduates and advanced high school students and their teachers.

Nick Kaldis is Associate Professor of Chinese Studies in the Department of Asian & Asian-American Studies at Binghamton University (S.U.N.Y.). He received his Ph.D. in East Asian Languages and Literatures from The Ohio State University. He serves on the Editorial Board of *Journal of Chinese Cinemas* and he is Literature Book Review Editor for the journal *Modern Chinese Literature & Culture*. His teaching and scholarship focus on Chinese cinema, literature, and language. He has published essays on modern Chinese literature and contemporary Chinese film, and has produced numerous translations. His manuscript on Lu Xun's *Yecao* is currently under submission, and he is co-editing a collection of nature writing essays by Taiwanese author and naturalist Liu Kexiang.

Joyce Chi-hui Liu is Professor of Cultural Studies, Critical Theory and Comparative Literature in the Graduate Institute for Social Research and Cultural Studies, Chiao Tung University, Taiwan. She received her Ph.D. in Comparative Literature from the University of Illinois at Urbana-Champaign in 1984. She taught and chaired the English Department and the Graduate Program of Comparative Literature at Fu Jen University. She is currently the chair of the Graduate Institute for Social Research and Cultural Studies, Chiao Tung University, which she founded in 2002. She was also the former chair of the Association of Cultural Studies in Taiwan. Her research covers contemporary French critical and psychoanalytic thoughts on the one hand and questions of discursive and visual modernity in the context of Taiwan, China, and Japan on the other. Her theoretical interests focus on the interrelations between the political, the aesthetic, and ethics.

Hajime Nakatani is Associate Professor, School of Intercultural Communication, Rikkyo University, Tokyo. He received a joint-degree Ph.D. in Art History and Social Anthropology in 2004 from the University of Chicago, and a master's degree in Social Anthropology from the School of Oriental and African Studies, University of London, in 1992. He received, among others, a Junior Scholar Grant from the Chiang Ching-kuo Foundation in 2007–8, an "Établissement de nouveaux professeurs-chercheurs" Grant from the Fonds québécois de la recherche sur la société et la culture (FQRSC) in 2008–2011, and a Andrew W. Mellon Predoctoral Fellowship from the Center for Advanced Study of the Visual Arts (CASVA), National Gallery of Art, in 2000–2002. Since 2005, he has served as senior board member for *Mechademia: An Academic Journal for Anime, Manga, and the Fan Arts* (University of Minnesota Press). His publications include articles on the cultural history of the Chinese script, late imperial painting, and comparative semiotics. He is currently writing a book about the cultural history of writing and calligraphy in early medieval China.

Yiyang Shao is Associate Professor of Art History and Theory and head of the World Art Studies Program at the Central Academy of Fine Art, Beijing. She received her Ph.D. in 2003 in Art History and Theory from the University of Sydney, and her master's degree at the University of Western Sydney. She is currently the leader of the major research project on visual culture studies from the Culture Ministry of China. Her teaching and research focus on world and Chinese modern/contemporary art. She has published widely on contemporary art and theory in Chinese in recent years, including the book *Hou xian dai zhi hou* (Art after Postmodern). Her writing on Chinese modern art was presented at the 32nd International Congress of the History of Art, CIHA Melbourne, 2008, and the 29th Art History Conference organized by Verband deutscher Kunsthistoriker (Association of German Art Historians) in Regensburg, 2007.

Meiqin Wang is Associate Professor of Art History at California State University, Northridge, with a specialization in modern and contemporary Chinese art. She received her Ph.D. in Contemporary Chinese Art History from the State University of New York at Binghamton and master's degree in Art History from the Chinese Academy of Arts in Beijing. She received her B.F.A. in Art Education and Painting from the Fujian Teacher's University in Fuzhou. Her dissertation and published materials focus on the recent developments of contemporary art from China and their social, political, economic, and institutional implications in the context of globalization. Her research interests also include contemporary art of the Asian world and international exhibitions. Her teaching covers historical and contemporary arts from Asia and her courses emphasize the cultural and political context of artistic production.

Yingjin Zhang is Professor at the University of California, San Diego (UCSD), where he teaches courses in Modern Chinese Literature, Chinese Literature, Comparative Literature, Cinema and Media Studies, Visual Culture, Literary and Cultural History, Urban Studies, and Transnational Cultural Politics. He is also Director of the Center for Chinese Studies at UCSD. He received his M.A. from the University of Iowa in 1988 and Ph.D. in Comparative Literature from Stanford University in 1992. Before joining the UCSD faculty in 2001, he taught at Indiana University in Bloomington, where he was honored with an Outstanding Junior Faculty Award in 1996. He served as President of the American Association of Chinese Comparative Literature in 1993–94 and received, among others, a Postdoctoral Fellowship from the University of Michigan in 1995–96, a Summer Faculty Fellowship from the National Endowment for the Humanities in 1999, a Pacific Cultural Foundation Research Grant (Taipei) in 2000, a Fulbright China Research Fellowship in 2003–4, and a University of California (Irvine) Humanities Research Institute Fellowship in 2005. He taught at the University of Chicago as a visiting professor in 2006. He serves on the advisory or editorial boards of *Film Art* (Beijing), *Journal of Chinese Cinema* (England), and *Scope: An Online Journal of Film Studies* (England).

www.ingramcontent.com/pod-product-compliance
Lightning Source LLC
LaVergne TN
LVHW050930080826
845145LV00001B/277

* 9 7 8 0 9 8 6 0 2 1 6 6 4 *